PROPERTY
and
FREEDOM

SOCIAL
PHILOSOPHY
& POLICY CENTER

PROPERTY
and
FREEDOM

THE CONSTITUTION, THE COURTS, and LAND-USE REGULATION

Bernard H. Siegan

transaction

Transaction Publishers
New Brunswick (USA) and London (UK)

Published by the Social Philosophy and Policy Center and by Transaction
Publishers 1997

Library of Congress Cataloging-in-Publication Data

Siegan, Bernard H.
    Property and freedom : the constitution, the courts, and land-use regula-
tion / by Bernard H. Siegan.
       p.   cm.—(Studies in social philosophy & policy ; no. 19)
    Includes bibliographical references and index.
    ISBN 1-56000-323-5 (hc).—ISBN 1-56000-974-8 (pbk.)
    1. Land use—Law and legislation—United States. 2. Right of property—
United States. 3. Zoning law—United States. 4. Eminent domain—United
States. I. Title. II. Series.
KF5698.S55   1997
346.7304'5—DC21   97-19241
                                              CIP

Cover Design: Kathy Horn

To Shelley

Series Editor: Ellen Frankel Paul
Series Managing Editor: Harry Dolan

The Social Philosophy and Policy Center, founded in 1981, is an interdisciplinary research institution whose principal mission is the examination of public policy issues from a philosophical perspective. In pursuit of this objective, the Center supports the work of scholars in the fields of political science, philosophy, law, and economics. In addition to this book series, the Center hosts scholarly conferences and edits an interdisciplinary professional journal, *Social Philosophy & Policy*. For further information on the Center, write to: Social Philosophy and Policy Center, Bowling Green State University, Bowling Green, OH 43403.

Contents

Introduction

The late 1980s was a most eventful period in the history of property rights. In 1987, the United States Supreme Court decided three cases that substantially raised the level of constitutional protection accorded to private ownership. Two years later, the world witnessed an occurrence of even greater importance to property rights. Communism, the philosophy that rejected and condemned private ownership, collapsed in all the Eastern European countries, crushing the idea that government could, through public ownership and planning, successfully control a nation's economy.

This book is primarily concerned with analyzing and evaluating the 1987 Supreme Court decisions and subsequent ones that are similarly protective of private property. I will show that the current position of the Court on property matters is consistent with constitutional intention and meaning, and additionally merits support for philosophical and pragmatic reasons. The rise and fall of communism provides powerful support for the Court's position by demonstrating that government ownership and control of property is devastating to public welfare.

For about a half-century prior to 1987, during a period in which the Supreme Court extended substantial constitutional guarantees to many activities, property rights were in the basement of protected liberties. As an example of this neglect, consider the deference accorded to local government in zoning cases. Zoning is the nation's most pervasive property-use control, yet the courts relied on a precedent for determining the constitutionality of a zoning ordinance that had been established in a landmark case in 1926, *Euclid v. Ambler Realty Co.*[1] In that case, the Court ruled that "before [a zoning] ordinance can be declared unconstitutional [it must be shown to be] clearly arbitrary and unreasonable, having no substantial relation to the public health, safety, morals, or general welfare."[2] Moreover, property owners attacking a zoning ordinance had the burden of proving that the municipality had not met this test, a burden that often proved insurmountable. The Court excepted from this broad standard only instances in which "the general public interest would so far outweigh the interests of the municipality that the municipality would not be allowed to stand in the way."[3]

Despite this largely overlooked exception, the years that followed *Euclid* were marked by a near abdication of any meaningful judicial review of zoning regulations. Victories for property owners were rare. By the 1980s, after a decade of regulatory zeal by federal, state, and local governments, housing prices were frequently escalating beyond the reach of the middle class. When Ronald Reagan took office, the "housing crisis" was a prime national issue, and his administration wondered whether there was a connection between judicial passivity and housing-price inflation. Early in his administration, the president appointed a commission to consider ways to increase the production of housing and lower its cost. In 1982, after one year of study, the Commission on Housing submitted a report to the president containing its findings and recommendations.[4] The report expressed dissatisfaction with the *Euclid* standard. Under it, the Commission noted, the rights of property owners to use their property were not adequately protected, disadvantaging owners as well as discouraging new investment in housing construction. By changing course and ensuring the rights of owners, the judiciary could curb overregulation by government and encourage more housing production. The Commission's report concluded that the public interest lies in securing property rights, not in undermining them. I served on the Commission, and I fully concurred with its findings. Happily, the Supreme Court would take important steps in this direction in cases decided in 1987.

The Court's new course in interpreting the Constitution's property protections is consistent with the objective of eliminating unnecessary and unreasonable government regulation. According to the new property rights jurisprudence, a regulation of property is not valid unless it substantially advances a legitimate state interest, and does not deny an owner economically viable use of his land. This is a much tougher standard than *Euclid*'s for governments to satisfy. Thus, the *Euclid* precedent has been seriously eroded. In Sections I–V of Chapter 5 and Section I of Chapter 6, I shall discuss and analyze the six pivotal property rights decisions handed down by the Supreme Court from 1987 to 1994. These cases imposed stringent limitations on the powers of government to regulate the use of land, and they changed the legal landscape in ways not fully appreciated by many legal commentators, or, indeed, many sitting federal and state judges. Chapter 4 will set the stage for our understanding of the post-1987 changes by sketching a picture of the fate of property rights in the preceding one hundred years. The earlier and later chapters will examine what property rights mean, why they are so important, how the Framers of the U.S. Constitution protected them, and the impact of their protection (or lack of it) on the quality of life of the American people.

1

Why Property Rights Are Important

I often wonder why the fall of communism has had so little impact on our consciousness. Even the most obvious result—that the peril of imminent destruction that had haunted our lives since the Second World War suddenly vanished—has hardly received much notice. Before we entirely forget this great scourge, I would like to mention some lessons for the protection of property rights that we ought to learn from this failed experiment in state ownership and control of all land and productive assets. These are lessons that the Framers of the Constitution, thankfully, understood. The closing section of this chapter will discuss the Framers' insights, for they have not always been well understood or practiced in our country in the twentieth century.

I. The Death of Communism

The communist experience of Eastern Europe provides an extraordinary testimonial for property rights. After the collapse of communism, the Soviet Union separated into fifteen nations, and they, along with the other East European communist nations, began demolishing their collectivist systems and turning to private ownership and enterprise. They and many socialist-oriented nations in other parts of the world sought economic salvation in capitalism. As of this writing, leaders of most nations of the world agree that economic viability demands recognition and protection of property rights.

In the long period of their reign, communist leaders continually expressed their intention to provide a better life for their constituents. They imposed every conceivable law toward that end and were ever ready to adopt new regulations

5

"in the public interest." As a result, the communist nations had an abundance of law, but as it turned out, never an abundance of food, clothing, and shelter. The problem was that communism identified the public good with ever greater governmental authority.

By contrast, the market-oriented countries have obtained many more goods and services for their citizens by following the opposite principle: equating the public interest with individual freedom. Capitalist countries such as the United States rely on individual ingenuity, creativity, and productivity to improve and advance human society. Even if communist leaders had sincerely acted on their professed desire to improve the lot of the people, creating wealth by government just did not work.

Changing from a communist to a market system can make an enormous difference, as the experience of China has shown. Initiated in 1978, the progressive decollectivization of Chinese agricultural land, Zbigniew Brzezinski writes, "had prompted a dramatic surge in productivity. . . . China was transformed from a net importer of food to an actual exporter." This agricultural rebirth "stimulated growth in the output of the Chinese rural industry, which increased by a staggering 400% between 1981 and 1986 and which grew by a further 36% in 1987 alone."[1]

The road from communism to capitalism is long and difficult, and individual nations have traveled it at different speeds. All the nations that turned away from communism abolished central planning, restored private ownership, made efforts to privatize the firms they owned, and reduced economic regulation. Most officials and members of the public in these nations appear to be generally in support of these reforms. Experience reveals that economic well-being depends on these reforms; the greater their extent, the more prosperous the economy.

Under communism, government owned all or almost all of the firms engaged in the production and distribution of goods and services, and national planners and other officials controlled the operations of every firm. These officials had little personal incentive to find ways to produce new, better, or less costly products. The result was that these nations had stagnant and regressive economies. The contrast with capitalist society is immense. To meet competition, private entrepreneurs must continually cater to consumer demand and improve their products. The quality and quantity of food, clothing, and shelter—in fact, of all material things—is consequently much superior under capitalism.

In a competitive world economy, privatization of the means for producing and distributing goods and services—that is, transferring ownership from government to private enterprise—is essential for economic survival. However, by itself it is insufficient to maintain a nation's economic viability. It must be accompanied by a general deregulation of the economy. Privatization in the former communist nations inevitably causes unemployment, since these regimes kept people on the payroll even if they did little to earn compensation. More workers were employed than were needed to produce or distribute a firm's output. Reducing unemployment that results from privatization requires the existence of a free market that, by encouraging ownership and investment, will "soak up" the unemployed people.

The Czech Republic provides a dramatic example of this outcome. The rate of unemployment there in 1996 was below 3 percent—which means virtually full employment—because that nation's free-market policies caused a high degree of labor-market flexibility. As much as one-third of the Republic's work force changed jobs during the first three years of transition from communism, and vigorous growth in employment opportunities and services alleviated the impact of contraction in manufacturing and agriculture.[2] The growth occurred because the government removed most restraints on private investment and ownership. The estimated inflation rate for 1996 was 7 percent.

Bulgaria provides an example of a nation that has (as of January 1997) rejected the Czech perspective with disastrous consequences. I was a member of the Bulgarian Economic Growth and Transition Project, which was appointed by the U.S. Chamber of Commerce in 1990 at the request of the Bulgarian government to advise it on transforming the economy to capitalism. In our report of December 1990, we urged swift privatization of Bulgaria's more than 2,200 state enterprises, its farms, and its thousands of small trade and service enterprises. Economist Ronald Utt wrote in our report: "The chief cause of Bulgaria's low standard of living is the inefficiency of its government-owned and managed enterprises which misuse Bulgaria's skilled workforce, scarce capital and raw materials." We recommended that the privatization process be coupled with adoption of a program to protect private property, severely limit economic regulation, and minimize taxes, all essential to attracting local and foreign investment.

By January 1997, less than 10 percent of the Bulgarian economy had been privatized. The problems Dr. Utt referred to had greatly intensified, and early in the month riots broke out in the capital city of Sofia, with large crowds protesting the economic policies of the existing government, which, along with prior ones, had done little to convert the economy to capitalism. Inflation reached 300 percent, and although the government through its employment of the bulk of the workforce maintained a low-double-digit unemployment rate, wages were at an all-time low. The currency, the lev, fell during 1996 from a high of 70 to the American dollar to a low of 550. Monthly pensions for the elderly poor were worth less than $10.[3]

The experiences of the Czech Republic and Bulgaria demonstrate that the extent of the transition from a command economy to a free one will determine a country's economic success. As of early 1997, the Czech Republic, Poland, Hungary, and Estonia have led in the establishment of free economies, and they are the most successful, in terms of employment and inflation, of the nations emerging from communism. The nations that have lagged behind in establishing free markets have done less well economically.[4]

Studies show the vast differences between economic systems. For example, Professor Gerald Scully measured the success of open and closed societies, and concluded that nations that have chosen to suppress economic, political, and civil liberties have greatly reduced the standard of living of their citizens. By contrast, material progress is greatest if individuals have the right to pursue their affairs unmolested by the state. According to Scully's studies, politically open societies, which bind themselves to the rule of law, to private property, and to the private allocation of resources, grew at three times the rate (2.73 to 0.91 percent annually) and were two and a half times more efficient than societies where those freedoms were circumscribed or proscribed.[5]

In "Economic Freedom of the World: 1975–1995," economists James Gwartney, Robert Lawson, and Walter Block show a close connection between economic freedom and economic well-being.[6] Using seventeen measures grouped into four categories, they rated economic freedom in 103 countries. These economists write that the core ingredients of economic freedom are personal choice, protection of private property, and freedom of exchange. Individuals have economic freedom when (a) property they acquire without the use of force, fraud, or theft is protected from physical invasions by others, and (b) they are free to use, exchange, or give their property to another as long as their actions do not violate the identical rights of others.

According to this study, the nations with the largest increases in economic freedom during the period from 1975 to 1990 registered an average annual growth in per-capita gross national product (GNP) of 2.7 percent from 1980 to 1994. Average real per-capita GNP declined at an annual rate of 0.6 percent from 1980 to 1994 in countries for which this index of economic freedom fell the most. The authors contend that with a one-point increase in economic freedom, on a scale of 0 to 10, a country can raise its growth rate by one percentage point.

In *1996 Index of Economic Freedom,* Bryan T. Johnson and Thomas P. Sheehy, economic analysts at the Heritage Foundation, examined ten measures of national economic health to determine why some countries prosper and others suffer economically. The ten factors examined were trade policy, taxation policy, government consumption of economic output, monetary policy, capital flows and foreign investment, banking policy, wage and price controls, property rights, regulation, and the size and scope of a nation's underground economy. The authors conclude that countries with the highest level of economic freedom also have the highest living standards. Likewise, countries that have the least amount of economic freedom have the lowest living standards.[7]

According to the Cato Institute's report *The Ten Freest Economies in 1995,* the fourteen nations with the highest measure of economic freedom had an average per-capita gross domestic product (GDP) of $14,280 in 1994, while the twenty-seven lowest had an average GDP of only $1,650. Published by Cato and ten overseas think tanks, the report measured economic freedom on a scale of 1 to 10 (with 1 being the least free and 10 the most free) in 102 countries. Its criteria for the existence of economic freedom included inflation stability, low marginal tax rates, government spending as a small percentage of national output, legal fairness, and the right to open a foreign bank account. The top fourteen countries scored 6.7 to 9.1, while the bottom twenty-seven scored 4.2 or less.[8]

While these measurements may differ, the foregoing studies show that the protection of private ownership is essential for a nation to obtain a successful and prosperous society.

Many "experts" argue that culture and not the economic system accounts for the economic success of nations. The experience of the formerly communist countries undermines this argument and indicates that while culture may be a factor in a country's economic success, it is far less so than economic incentive. Support for my position that the economic system is decisive for economic success is provided by the records of nations that have adopted both free and command economies. The existence of market incentives explains the economic well-being of Taiwan, West Germany, and South Korea. The lack of such incentives under communism accounted for the economic failures of pre-market-reform China, East Germany, and North Korea.

II. Property Rights and Freedom

The previous discussion reveals one of the major purposes for securing property rights. Human experience demonstrates that this protection is essential to maintain a viable economy upon which general welfare depends. Equally important, the protection of property rights secures and augments personal freedom.

Freedom is enormously beneficial to human existence. In whatever activity or endeavor it is exercised, freedom enables most people to obtain much greater personal development and satisfaction with life than they would under a regime of government coercion. However, freedom's unlimited exercise may be harmful to an individual and society. John Locke's state of nature, described in his *Second Treatise of Government,* is uncomfortable and unsafe. Accordingly, a line must be drawn beyond which the exercise of freedom is subject to limitation by the state. Americans have confronted the question of where to draw this line and agonized over it since the formation of the nation. In determining the limits of property rights, it is important to know the position of the nation's founders. Both the Declaration of Independence and the United States Constitution provide information vital to this understanding.

Thomas Jefferson's immortal language in the Declaration of Independence of 1776—"that all men are created equal, that they are endowed by their Creator with certain unalienable Rights, that among these are Life, Liberty and the pursuit of Happiness"—was predicated on both moral and pragmatic grounds. Liberty, the Declaration asserted, was the highest state of human beings, and its exercise both fulfilled the needs of the person and the aspirations of the state:

"That to secure these rights, Governments are instituted among Men, deriving their just powers from the consent of the governed." In his reference to rights, Jefferson did not use the common trilogy of the time that denoted the elements of freedom: life, liberty, and property. His choice of language has been the subject of much discussion over the years, and some have suggested that the protection of property was not, in his view, a matter of highest priority. Jefferson never explained why he omitted a reference to property in his trilogy. However, the language speaks for itself. The acquisition, use, and disposal of private property is necessarily comprehended in the pursuit of happiness.

At a minimum, happiness comprehends ownership of material possessions in two situations: First, to secure the right of survival, the most fundamental of all rights. A human being cannot survive without food, clothing, and shelter. Second, to secure, as a matter of fairness, ownership of property that people derive from their own labor. But for early Americans the pursuit of happiness had a broader meaning. As writer Catherine Drinker Bowen puts it, if nobody knew exactly what the Declaration's words meant, they did not need to know. "They felt it, breathed it in the Revolutionary air. To pursue happiness signified that a man could rise in the world according to his abilities and his industry."[9]

For most people, freedom means that they will be able to retain the fruits of their labor, knowledge, ingenuity, and industry. It makes meaningful that portion of life devoted to physical or mental endeavors. What does it mean to labor, innovate, or create if the material rewards of those efforts can be arbitrarily taken away by the state? The existence of such governmental powers would destroy the incentive to work, save, invest, and plan for the future.

People whose property is not secure from government are extremely limited in their freedom, for, as Supreme Court justice Felix Frankfurter noted, "the free range of the human spirit becomes shriveled and constrained under economic dependence."[10] The right to property therefore preserves other personal rights and maintains a separation between the state and the individual.

In understanding the meaning of happiness as the word is used in the Declaration, the most important question is the role of government in advancing it. The Declaration condemns both the commissions and omissions of the British government, leaving some doubt in this regard. For me, the most persuasive interpretation of the Declaration's meaning is provided by the United States Constitution framed eleven years later in 1787, by a convention whose fifty-five members included eight who had signed the Declaration. Both documents express the thinking and beliefs that existed in an important period in American history. The Framers of the Constitution confronted the task of implementing the ideas of the Framers of the Declaration. The result was the establishment of a government of limited and enumerated powers with less authority than probably any other government presently has or ever has had. The Framers of the Constitution sought to protect liberty by eliminating the oppressive powers of government and not by mandating the government to provide people with benefits and entitlements. As with other liberties, they resolved the issue of property rights by limiting government powers over them.

Accordingly, the government was structured to prevent any person or group of persons from being able to impose its unchecked will over the people. The Constitution separates the three branches of government, confines each to specific powers, and grants each checks and balances over the others. According to James Madison, who is generally considered the most important of the Constitution's Framers, "[t]he powers delegated by the proposed Constitution to the federal government are few and defined [to be] exercised principally on external objects, as war, peace, negotiation and foreign commerce."[11] The executive and judicial branches have the power to monitor the legislature to make certain that it stays within its limits. Even the Congress is divided into two bodies for additional dispersal of power.

However, the structural restraints on constitutional power were insufficient by themselves to prevent the government from treating people unequally and not impartially. Madison expressed these apprehensions in *Federalist No. 44:*

> The sober people of America are weary of the fluctuating policy which has directed the public councils. They have seen with regret and indignation that sudden changes and legislative interferences, in cases affecting personal rights, become jobs in the hands of enterprising and influential speculators, and snares to the more industrious and less informed parts of the community. They have seen, too, that one legislative interference is but the first link of a long chain of repetitions, every subsequent interference being naturally produced by the effects of the preceding. They very rightly infer, therefore, that some thorough reform is wanting, which will banish speculations on public measures, inspire a general prudence and industry, and give a regular course to the business of society.[12]

To prohibit such abuses, the Framers inserted protections against the arbitrary dispensing of favors or preferences and imposing of penalties. The federal government was limited in power to suspend the writ of habeas corpus, to give preferences to ports, to pass bills of attainder and ex post facto laws, or to grant titles of nobility; moreover, jury trials were required in all criminal matters, usually to be held in the state where the crime was committed, treason was narrowly defined, and no religious test was ever to be required as a qualification for any office or public trust. Congress could lay and collect taxes, duties, imposts, and excises only for the purpose of paying the debts and providing for the common defense and general welfare of the United States. In *Federalist No. 41,* Madison explained that the term "general welfare" was confined to specific powers listed in Article I, Section 8. All duties, imposts, and excises were required to be uniform throughout the nation. Direct taxes were required to be laid in proportion to the population of the state. No tax or duty could be imposed on exports from a state.

With reference to property rights, these provisions limit the power of the

Congress or other officials of government to either harm or help owners and entrepreneurs. Legislatures which have the power to pass the kinds of laws forbidden under the U.S. Constitution, and executives who have authority to veto or approve them, have enormous discretion over the lives, liberties, and property of their constituents. Economic markets cannot function when government has arbitrary powers over participants in those markets.

Most of the Framers thought that the structural protections and prohibitions against arbitrariness were sufficient protections for individual liberty. There was no need for a Bill of Rights, asserted Alexander Hamilton during the heated debate that raged throughout the states over the ratification of the new Constitution. "For why declare that things shall not be done which there is no power to do?"[13] Indeed, said James Wilson, another Framer, itemizing all the people's rights would have been futile. "[I]n no one of those books [by the great political writers], nor in the aggregate of them all, can you find a complete enumeration of rights appertaining to the people as men and as citizens."[14] Despite these arguments, state ratification conventions called for specific guarantees in a Bill of Rights. The nation subsequently adopted a Bill of Rights protecting the people's liberties from abridgment by the federal government. After the Civil War, the nation ratified the Fourteenth Amendment to apply constitutional protections of individual rights against the powers of the states. In particular, property rights are protected from the federal government in numerous provisions in the original Constitution, in seven provisions of the Bill of Rights, and in Section 1 of the Fourteenth Amendment.

As interpreted by our Constitution, the Declaration of Independence's "pursuit of Happiness" meant freedom to seek and obtain what the Constitution's preamble refers to as the "Blessings of Liberty." Thus, the pursuit of happiness necessitates limiting the coercive powers of the state in order to enable human beings to do what comes naturally. In other words, people should be free to pursue their own interests as they deem best, confident that the government will not interfere with those efforts.

In brief, the Framers of the Constitution accomplished what Thomas Jefferson in his first inaugural address in 1801 described as "necessary to make us a happy and prosperous people": they established "a wise and frugal government, which shall restrain men from injuring one another, which shall leave them otherwise free to regulate their own pursuits of industry and improvement. . . ."[15]

As Jefferson wisely indicated, in an organized state, no liberties can be absolute; for if they were, government would not have the power to "restrain men from injuring one another." With respect to property rights, the limitations on the pursuit of happiness are obvious: first, this right, like all others, must terminate when its exercise invades the rights of others; second, an owner must compensate the state or another person with money or property for costs that are actually imposed by the exercise of the right.[16] In recent years, the United States Supreme Court has sought to apply these principles in its property jurisprudence and, as subsequent pages will explain, has done so quite effectively.

2

The Constitution Secures Property Rights

In this chapter, I shall discuss the guarantees for private ownership provided in the United States Constitution. Protection is provided by many provisions in the original Constitution framed in 1787 and ratified in 1788, and the Bill of Rights framed in 1789 and ratified in 1791. Property is also secured in Section 1 of the Fourteenth Amendment, which was framed in 1866 and ratified in 1868.

Little doubt should exist as to the constitutional importance of property rights. The Constitutional Convention of 1787 was convened because of the widespread dissatisfaction with the failure of the Articles of Confederation to protect free trade among the states. The states had imposed trade and tax barriers and economic regulations preventing the existence of a free and common market. The United States Constitution was framed in large measure to overcome these problems by providing substantial protection for the material liberties, including property, economic, and contractual rights.

The Framers sought to create a commercial republic based on ownership, investment, and entrepreneurship.[1] This republic could not survive unless these liberties were secured from abridgment by legislative or executive bodies. In part to shield commercial activities from the might of government, the Framers established a system of separation and limitation of powers.[2]

They rejected majority rule in favor of divided rule because the former, as James Madison observed, "is only re-establishing, under another name and more specious form, force as a matter of right."[3] Madison also warned about the power of the legislature: "[I]t is against the enterprising ambition of this department that the people ought to indulge all their jealousy and exhaust all their precautions."[4]

Consistent with the prevailing ideas of their times, the Framers supported protection of property rights as essential both to the fulfillment of the human condition and to the advancement of the society. During the Constitutional Convention of 1787, Madison asserted that in civilized society the preservation of property, as well as other personal rights, was an essential object of the law.[5] Later he wrote:

> Government is instituted to protect property of every sort; as well that which lies in the various rights of individuals, as that which the term particularly expresses. This being the end of government, that alone is a *just* government, which *impartially* secures to every man, whatever is his *own*. . . .[6]

A government "which [even] indirectly violates [individuals'] property in their actual possessions," concluded Madison, "is not a pattern for the United States."[7] For him, protection of property was of critical importance because the acquisition of property "was a necessary by-product of the freedom of action he deemed an essential part of liberty."[8] As a member of the First Congress, Madison proposed that the Constitution be amended to contain a declaratory statement "[t]hat government is instituted and ought to be exercised for the benefit of the people; which consists [among other things of] the right of acquiring and using property. . . ."[9]

Gouverneur Morris, another prominent and influential Framer, expressed similar views at the Convention about ownership:

> Life and liberty are generally said to be of more value, than property. An accurate view of the matter would nevertheless prove that property was the main object of society. The savage state was more favorable to liberty than the civilized; and sufficiently so to life. It was preferred by men who had not acquired a taste for property; it was only renounced for the sake of property which could be secured by the restraints of regular government.[10]

William Paterson was a delegate to the Constitutional Convention from New Jersey, and he subsequently became a justice of the U.S. Supreme Court. In *Vanhorne's Lessee v. Dorrance* (1795), a Supreme Court case that interpreted the Pennsylvania Constitution, which had no "just compensation clause" to protect owners from government seizure of their property, Paterson declared:

> [T]he right of acquiring and possessing property and having it protected, is one of the natural, inherent, and unalienable rights of man. . . . The preservation of property then is the primary object of the social compact. . . . The legislature, therefore, had no authority to make an act divesting one citizen of his freehold and vesting it in another, without a just compensation. It is inconsistent with the principles of reason, justice and moral rectitude; it is incompatible with the com-

fort, peace and happiness of mankind; it is contrary to the principles of social alliance in every free government. . . .[11]

Other delegates to the Constitutional Convention emphasized property rights as well. Rufus King of Massachusetts and John Rutledge of South Carolina agreed that the protection of property was the primary or principal object of society. Pierce Butler of South Carolina contended that "property was the only just measure of representation. This was the great object of government: the great cause of war, the great means of carrying it on." William R. Davie of North Carolina, Abraham Baldwin of Georgia, and Charles Pinkney of South Carolina thought the Senate should represent property or wealth. George Mason of Virginia stated that an important objective in constituting a senate was to secure the right of property. John Dickinson of Delaware considered freeholders as the best guarantors of society.[12] Inequality of property ownership should not cause the society to abridge liberty, said Alexander Hamilton:

> Differences in wealth are already great among us, nothing like equality of property exists. Inequality will exist as long as liberty exists, and it unavoidably results from that liberty itself.[13]

The records of the Convention reveal that only one delegate disputed the primacy of property rights. For James Wilson "the cultivation and enforcement of the human mind was the most noble object" of government and society.[14] However, he did believe that ownership of property was a natural right that must be protected against legislative encroachment.

The expressions of the Framers favorable to private ownership were not unusual, since the right to property was an unquestioned assumption of that period.[15] As the founders of a free society, the Framers must have understood that such a society could not exist unless government was prohibited from confiscating or eroding private property. If government can seize something owned by a private citizen, it can exert enormous power over that person. As Hamilton stated, a power over a man's subsistence amounts to power over his will.[16]

It is probable that most Framers, like many of their contemporaries, agreed with the libertarian positions expressed by the foremost commentators of their time—the Englishmen William Blackstone (1723–1780), Edward Coke (1552–1634), and John Locke (1632–1704), each of whom extolled the rights of life, liberty, and property as essential to human fulfillment and societal justice. Members of the revolutionary and constitutional generation were steeped in Locke's political philosophy and learned their law from Coke and Blackstone.

During the revolutionary and constitutional periods, members of the legal community in North America looked to Blackstone as the leading philosophical interpreter of English law. Among these was the famous Chancellor James

Kent of New York, who acknowledged that "he owed his reputation to the fact that when studying law . . . he had but one book, Blackstone's *Commentaries* [1765–69], but that one book he mastered."[17] A biographer of Blackstone states that most members of the Constitutional Convention of 1787 "were familiar with, and they were no doubt greatly influenced by, Blackstone's analysis of the English governmental system."[18]

Coke's four-volume *Institutes of the Laws of England* (1628–44) was also a major source for colonial lawyers. Throughout the eighteenth century, Coke was one of the most frequently cited legal and political thinkers.[19] His judicial rulings on legislative limitations were used in the colonies to justify resistance to the British Parliament. Coke's interpretation of Chapter 29 of a subsequent issue of the Magna Carta (Chapter 39 in the original issue) was widely quoted and cited by judges and legal commentators in the United States. Coke and Blackstone did have their differences. Coke, for example, espoused judicial review and consequently did not accept Blackstone's argument for the sovereignty of Parliament. But on the essential issues of individual freedom they were in agreement. Some commentators have criticized Coke's writings; however, Coke's influence, "as the embodiment of the common law, was so strong, that it is useless to contend that he was either misled by his sources or consciously misinterpreted them, for Coke's mistakes, it is said, *are* the common law."[20]

Widely read and quoted in the last half of the eighteenth century, John Locke's theories on the limited role of government (set forth in his *Two Treatises of Government,* first published in 1690) were very persuasive to a colonial populace apprehensive about governmental powers. Locke's idea of a social contract entered into by individuals in a state of nature preparatory to the formation of government became increasingly meaningful in the years after 1776.[21]

Locke wrote that people sought the sanctuary of political society because of the uncertain conditions existing in the state of nature, in which everyone who lacked the physical power to defend himself might be victimized by the unscrupulous and evil. In forming society, men entered into a social contract, defining the authority and purposes of government and relinquishing many of their individual powers to the state, which then became responsible for protecting life, personal liberties, and possessions, all of which were included in the term "property." "The great and *chief end,* therefore, of Mens uniting into Commonwealths, and putting themselves under Government, *is the Preservation of their Property.* To which in the state of Nature there are many things wanting."[22]

The legislature, as the supreme body of the organized state, must have the power to rectify the defects existing in the state of nature; but that power must necessarily be limited, at least to the extent that lawmakers could not impose conditions worse than those existing in the state of nature. The legislature may not deprive the individual of fundamental rights—first, because the social compact does not provide government with this power, and second, because government's purpose is to play a fiduciary role in safeguarding and enhancing these rights. Limitations on governmental power are central to Locke's theory:

> It cannot be supposed that they [individuals] should intend, had they a power so to do, to give to any one, or more, an *absolute Arbitrary Power* over their Persons and Estates, and put a force into the Magistrates hand to execute his unlimited Will arbitrarily upon them: This were to put themselves into a worse condition than the state of Nature, wherein they had a Liberty to defend their Right against the Injuries of others, and were upon equal terms of force to maintain it, whether invaded by a single Man or many in Combination.[23]

> The *Supream power cannot take* from any Man any part of his *Property* without his own consent. For the preservation of Property being the end of Government, and that for which Men enter into Society, it necessarily supposes and requires, that the People should *have Property,* without which they must be suppos'd to lose that by entring into Society, which was the end for which they entered into it, too gross an absurdity for any Man to own.[24]

The public perceived Locke as standing for the proposition that government powers must be confined to securing natural rights. "[W]henever the *Legislators,*" Locke professed, "*endeavour to take away, and destroy the Property of the People* . . . they put themselves into a state of War with the People, who are thereupon absolved from any farther Obedience. . . ."[25]

Coke offered a much less drastic remedy for the tyranny of the legislature. He asserted that the courts are empowered to apply the common law and annul legislation contrary to it. Notwithstanding the great authority of a legislature under a parliamentary system, Coke believed in the power of the judiciary to protect an owner from governmental abridgment of his property and other fundamental rights.[26]

Blackstone accepted parliamentary sovereignty but spoke in absolute terms about the rights of life, liberty, and property. This is his interpretation of the property right:

> The third absolute right, inherent in every Englishman, is that of property: which consists in a free use, enjoyment, and disposal of all his acquisitions, without any control or diminution, save only by the laws of the land.[27]

Parliament, Blackstone wrote, must exercise great restraint in limiting the property right: "So great moreover is the regard of the law for private property, that it will not authorize the least violation of it; no, not even for the general good of the whole community."[28] An owner could only forfeit his property right by doing wrong. A variety of ancient statutes, Blackstone wrote, enacted into law the principle "that no man shall be disinherited, nor put out of his franchises or freehold, unless he be duly brought to answer, and be forejudged by course of law; and if any thing be done to the contrary, it shall be redressed, and holden for none."[29]

But how does the government acquire private property? Blackstone replied: "Not by absolutely stripping the subject of his property in an arbitrary manner; but by giving him a full indemnification and equivalent for the injury thereby sustained."[30] This is but one instance "in which the law of the land has postponed even public necessity to the sacred and inviolable rights of private property."[31] Blackstone echoed the views of earlier Continental natural law theorists Hugo Grotius, Samuel Pufendorf, and Cornelius von Bynkershoek — influential European thinkers of this period, who were generally in accord with him on the requirement for indemnification. Blackstone and the natural law theorists set the stage for the takings clause of the U.S. Constitution's Fifth Amendment, which requires "just compensation" when government takes private property for a "public use."

Protection of property, Blackstone professed, did not include protection of offensive and obnoxious uses. Accordingly, statute and common law could regulate and penalize the maintenance of both public and private nuisances. Property owners could not engage in uses that actually harmed the property of others.[32] To vindicate their absolute rights when violated, people were entitled, first, to seek judicial relief; second, to petition the king and Parliament; and lastly, to use armed force.[33]

Unlike Coke, Blackstone believed in the complete supremacy of the Parliament, and consequently one might conclude that Blackstone's observations on protecting human rights were merely philosophic exercises. But this would be a hasty judgment. Blackstone accepted the idea that Parliament had the power to suppress the exercise of liberties. However, Blackstone's *Commentaries* was more than a philosophic exercise; it was a record of English law, setting forth the existing rules that society observed. This was important information for lawyers, judges, and legislators. Members of English society expected that their leaders would abide by these rules even if they were not codified in a constitution. Blackstone apparently believed that Parliament would never violate what he referred to as the "absolute" rights of the people. The U.S. Constitution replaced legislative supremacy with a government of separated powers, yet Blackstone's *Commentaries* served as very persuasive support for the protection of individual rights, even though he had discussed rights within the English context of parliamentary supremacy. This is evident from two leading treatises authored in the early years of our nation, both of which were influenced by Blackstone's writings: Joseph Story's *Commentaries on the Constitution of the United States* (1833) and James Kent's *Commentaries on American Law* (1826). Story was a justice of the United States Supreme Court, and Kent was chief judge of the New York Supreme Court and Chancellor of the court of equity. Both rejected the idea of legislative sovereignty under the U.S. Constitution, yet often cited Blackstone when discussing individual rights. Similarly, Blackstone's observations on natural rights were widely cited by both federal and state court judges in the early years of this nation.

I. The Original Constitution

In the original Constitution, the Framers did not specifically protect the general right of property ownership. There are two explanations for this omission. First, the Constitution contained two ex post facto clauses, prohibiting the federal government and the states from enacting legislation that retroactively makes some activity illegal that was legal at the time it occurred. The evidence is persuasive that the clauses were also intended to secure the right of property from retroactive impositions. However, the 1798 case of *Calder v. Bull*[34] held that the ex post facto clauses related only to criminal and not civil matters, a decision which has never been overruled. Many constitutional scholars have disagreed with this interpretation over the years, contending that the clauses were intended to be broadly construed to include civil matters.[35] I will have much more to say on this subject in Chapter 5.

Other major protections for property are the two clauses prohibiting passage of bills of attainder by the federal and state governments. A bill of attainder is a legislative act that inflicts punishment without a judicial trial. Originally the term was limited to capital punishment, but in time it was applied to legislative confiscation of property. The attainder provisions were interpreted by Chief Justice John Marshall as having both criminal and civil meaning: "A bill of attainder may affect the life of an individual, or may confiscate his property, or may do both."[36] A number of other protections for property ownership are contained in the original Constitution, as previously set forth in Section II of Chapter 1.

The second explanation for the lack of specific protection of the general right of property ownership in the original Constitution is the fact that, in order to avoid confining freedom to stated rights which could never comprehend the whole of liberties, the Framers left most rights to be protected by limiting government to those powers that the Constitution enumerated.[37] The proposed national government was one of limited and enumerated powers; it possessed only those powers vested in it. According to Madison, the Constitution would never have been ratified if the people believed that all unstated liberties were totally under the control of the national government.[38] In *Federalist No. 84*, Alexander Hamilton contended that the absence of a bill of rights in the Constitution was not harmful to the people, because the new government had no power to deprive them of their liberties: "[T]he people surrender nothing; and as they retain everything they have no need of particular reservations." Therefore, a bill of rights was superfluous. "For why declare that things shall not be done which there is no power to do?"[39]

In the absence of enumerated constitutional authority, the federal government's powers in relation to private ownership were defined by the common law—the law made by English and American judges—which was generally held to embody the principles of natural law, the unwritten law that secured human rights. As Hamilton, a prominent lawyer, and many jurists of his time stated, the colonists brought with them to America the liberties they possessed in England, which included the right of property. In the United States, according to these authorities, these rights could not be limited without an express constitutional provision to that effect.

In the ratification debates of 1787–88, supporters of the Constitution argued that the Constitution did not give Congress the power to infringe on any natural right.[40] Opponents of the Constitution sought specific guarantees and demanded the inclusion of a Bill of Rights which was subsequently framed and ratified. The Bill guarantees rights of ownership in seven provisions, evidencing a strong commitment to their preservation and protection.[41] Although the Bill of Rights originally applied only to the federal government, after the adoption of the Fourteenth Amendment in the aftermath of the Civil War, and subsequent Supreme Court decisions, most of the Bill's provisions, including those protecting property rights, were extended to the states.[42]

II. The Bill of Rights

"[T]he Constitution," Hamilton asserted, "is itself, in every rational sense, and to every useful purpose, A BILL OF RIGHTS."[43] Thus, he thought, there was no need for framing one. However, the demand for insertion of personal protections in the Constitution led to the framing of the Bill of Rights by the First Congress in 1789. James Madison, as a representative from Virginia, introduced legislation for this purpose. Many of the Bill's provisions are directed to the protection of property and economic rights.

In addition to the takings provision of the Fifth Amendment—"nor shall private property be taken for public use, without just compensation"—the Bill of Rights contains six other material guarantees: the prohibition on infringing the people's right to keep and bear arms (Amendment II); the prohibition on quartering soldiers on private property (III); the prohibition on unreasonable searches and seizures of property (IV); the prohibition on depriving any person of life, liberty, or property without due process of law (V); the right to trial by jury for controversies exceeding twenty dollars (VII); and the prohibition of excessive bails and fines (VIII). These guarantees shielded from federal intrusion those property interests of most concern in that period: one's home, land, office, firearms, and financial resources.

The ordinary acquisition, use, and transfer of private property are secured by the due process and takings clauses. The records of the First Congress reveal little about the meaning of either. Congress accepted Madison's draft of the due process clause; but it changed his wording of the takings clause, which required payment of just compensation only to a person "obligated to relinquish his property where it may be necessary for public use,"[44] to language that permits the taking "for public use." Madison's original language offered a relatively small exception to the otherwise unqualified language of the due process clause which precedes the takings clause. (As will be explained later, under the due process clause, life, liberty, or property can be taken only pursuant to a judgment in a fair trial, which can be held only when some wrongdoing is alleged to have occurred.) The change in language of the takings clause provided a somewhat broader exception than did Madison's to the scope of the due process clause. Over time, through judicial interpretation, the takings clause as adopted would cover taking by overregulation, something that Madison's original "relinquish" language would not have allowed. Madison's proposed takings clause is set forth and discussed in Section IV of this chapter.

III. The Due Process Concept and the Due Process Clause

A. The History

The due process concept originated in Chapter 39 of the Magna Carta, which was obtained by the English barons from King John at Runnymede in 1215, after they had captured the city of London. Chapter 39 provides that no freeman shall be arrested, or detained in prison, or deprived of his freehold, or outlawed, or banished, or in any way molested unless by the lawful judgment of his peers and by the law of the land.[45] "A King had been brought to order . . . by the community of the land under baronial leadership; a tyrant had been subjected to laws which hitherto it had been his private privilege to administer and modify at will."[46] The nobles sought to eliminate the king's arbitrary powers and impose on him the rule of law. Under Chapter 39, he could no longer deprive freemen of life, liberty, or property except as a penalty for wrongdoing as determined by fair and proper processes and proceedings. The king's legislative powers were necessarily limited, for "if by 'law of the land' was meant any law which the king might enact, the provision was a nullity."[47]

The Magna Carta was corroborated by thirty-two statutes, and its principles were confirmed by many others. It achieved an exalted status in English law. Parliament adopted it and made it part of the common law. All statutes contrary to the Magna Carta were declared void, and its liberties were proclaimed to be the birthright of the people of England. In a 1354 statute interpreting Chapter 39, the words "due process" were substituted for both "judgment of his peers" and "law of the land": "That no man of what state or condition that he be, shall be put out of his lands or tenements, nor taken, nor imprisoned, nor disinherited, nor put to death, without he be brought to answer by due process of law."[48] In time, "due process of law" became synonymous with "the law of the land," and the two terms have been used interchangeably in state constitutions in the United States.

One cannot be certain as to the precise meaning of a document written generations ago and at a time of limited communications. For purposes of interpreting the United States Constitution, the most important meaning of a particular term is that given to it by its Framers and ratifiers. The evidence is persuasive that these people accepted the position of Blackstone and Coke that Chapter 39 (and Chapter 29 of a subsequent revision of the charter) had more than procedural meaning; it was meant to prevent the king from depriving his subjects of their rights.

Both commentators interpreted Chapter 39 and its successors as protective of human rights. Blackstone stated that this chapter "alone would have merited the title that [the Magna Carta] bears, of the *great* charter."[49] He construed the chapter as protecting "every individual of the nation in the free enjoyment of his life, his liberty and his property, unless declared to be forfeited by the judgment of his peers or the law of the land."[50] Blackstone considered the rights of life, liberty, and property to be comprehended in the common law's "absolute rights of personal security, personal liberty, and private property."[51]

> So long as these [rights] remain inviolate, the subject is perfectly free; for every species of compulsive tyranny and oppression must act in opposition to one or other of these rights, having no other object upon which it can possibly be employed. To preserve these from violation, it is necessary that the constitution of parliaments be supported in it's full vigor; and limits certainly known, be set to the royal prerogative. . . . And all these rights and liberties it is our birthright to enjoy entire; unless where the laws of our country have laid them under necessary restraints.[52]

Blackstone condemned, as "destructive of liberty," laws "without any good end in view" and those that were "wanton and causeless" restraints, "whether practiced by a monarch, a nobility, or a popular assembly."[53] "[T]hat system of laws, is alone calculated to maintain civil liberty, which leaves the subject entire master of his own conduct, except in those points wherein the public good requires some direction or restraint."[54] These restraints should be so gentle and moderate "that no man of sense or probity would wish to see them slackened."[55] That Blackstone regarded Chapter 39 as securing substantive rights (in addition to procedural ones) is evident from his discussion of the power of eminent domain—government could not rightfully deprive owners of their property unless it compensated them. This is a substantive restraint on government. Although he considered the power of Parliament to be absolute, it was still required to respect the fundamental rights of the people.

Coke similarly construed Chapter 29 of a subsequent issue of the Magna Carta as substantively protecting the fundamental guarantees of Englishmen, which included property and economic rights.[56] He wrote that the prohibition against being disseised—that is, unjustly deprived of one's property—provided Englishmen with extensive protection:

> No man shall be disseised, that is, put out of seisin, or dispossessed of his freehold (that is) lands, or livelihood, or of his liberties or free-customs . . . as belong to him by his free birth right, unless it be by the lawful judgment, that is, verdict of his equals (that is, men of his own condition) or by the law of the land (that is, so to speak it once and for all) by the due course and process of law.[57]

Coke based his conclusions on statutes and prior judicial interpretations. In explaining disseisin of property, Coke referred to two civil cases in which denials of property interests without any resort to judicial process were adjudged "against the law of the land."

One case concerned a "custome" of a town that allowed the lord to enter and occupy the freehold of a tenant who was two years in arrears in rent, and to possess the freehold until the debt was satisfied. It was held to be against the law of the land to enter into a man's freehold without judicial proceedings. In the other case, the king granted the cloth dyers of London power to search for and seize cloth illegally dyed with logwood. In finding this grant in violation of the law of the land, it was adjudged that no forfeiture can be based upon the king's grant of an exclusive right to one group to make and sell a particular product.[58]

Discussing protection for "liberties," Coke asserted that "[g]enerally all monopolies are against this great charter, because they are against the liberty and freedom of the subject, and against the law of the land." "Liberties" included other economic activities. An ordinance by a company of merchant tailors "having power by their charter to make ordinances" required members to buy their clothes only from certain sellers. This ordinance was adjudged to violate the law "because it was against the liberty of the subject, for every subject [has] freedom to put his clothes to be dressed by whom he will."[59]

Forfeiture of a property or economic right can occur only when its possessor is "brought in to answer . . . by due process of the common law." As Coke explains it, "process of the law" means "by indictment or presentment of good and lawful men where such deeds be done in due manner, or by writ original of the common law."[60] Hence the denial by the king or other governmental authorities of life, liberty, or property without the person being "brought in to answer" violated the required process of law.

In his famous *Dr. Bonham's Case* opinion, Coke stated that the judiciary had the power to monitor the legislature, declaring that "when an Act of Parliament is against common right and reason, or repugnant, or impossible to be performed, the common law will controul it, and adjudge such Act to be void."[61]

The commentaries on Chapter 39 by Coke and Blackstone rejected the position that the due process guarantee (as distinguished from the concept) related only to procedure. Both regarded it as the fundamental provision protecting individual liberties. The American legal community, which played a critical role in the framing and ratifying of the Constitution and Bill of Rights, considered both men to be leading authorities on English law and was greatly influenced by them. This common understanding is vital to interpreting the due process clauses in American federal and state constitutions.

Despite this strong evidence, the scope of due process protection has long been a major source of controversy in the legal community. Some contend that the clauses relate only to maintaining fair and proper judicial processes and procedures, while others consider them, as Coke and Blackstone did, to be safeguards against government oppression, whether such oppression emanates from the judiciary or the other branches. Over the years, American courts have found merit in both positions.

Based on its English heritage, which encompasses Chapter 39 of the Magna Carta and the commentaries of Locke, Coke, and Blackstone, the due process guarantee is at the root of a society founded on individual autonomy and dignity. Persons who abide by the law and do not inflict harm should be safe in their persons and possessions from deprivation by government. Those accused or convicted of violating the law are entitled to fair and proper judicial proceedings. Thus, interpreting the Fifth Amendment's due process clause requires distinguishing between the due process *concept* and the due process *clause* guaranteeing it. The *concept* relates only to requiring fair and proper judicial processes and proceedings based on criminal wrongdoing. The *clause* is a restraint on government, prohibiting any branch of it from depriving people of life, liberty, or property without such fair and proper judicial processes and proceedings.

As with most other protections in the Constitution, the due process guarantee is set forth in absolute language and, similar to others such as the First Amendment's guarantee of freedom of speech, it should not be limited by the government in the absence of very strong justification. However, not all governmental restraints are constitutional violations. Since no individual has a right to use his property to create a nuisance or otherwise harm others, the government does not deprive a person of anything when it enjoins a nuisance or near-nuisance. Nor is there any constitutional deprivation when government prohibits obscene or highly provocative language[62] or untruthful advertising. Contemporary rights jurisprudence has interpreted deprivation of a protected right in Blackstonian terms. As I have noted, Blackstone referred to laws "without any good end in view" or those that are a "wanton and causeless restraint of the will of the subject" as "destructive of liberty." In modern constitutional adjudication, deprivation of a right generally does not occur when the legislative purpose is legitimate and the statute achieves the legislative purpose. This subject will be discussed extensively in Chapter 5.

B. Due Process in the Bill of Rights

On June 8, 1789, Congressman James Madison introduced in the First Congress a series of amendments to the United States Constitution that would later, with changes, become the Bill of Rights. These proposed amendments contained a due process clause identical to the one that is now in the Constitution. The history of the clause, therefore, begins with Madison's preparation of his amendments.

In ratifying the federal Constitution, seven states (Massachusetts, South Carolina, New Hampshire, Virginia, New York, North Carolina, and Rhode Island) recommended a series of amendments to the Constitution, and of these the Declaration of Rights proposed by Virginia evidently had the most important influence on the draft amendments that Madison submitted to the House.[63] Virginia and three other states, New York, North Carolina, and Rhode Island, urged the Congress to include provisions specifically guaranteeing life, liberty, and property. Virginia's recommendations contained two such provisions:

> First, that there are certain natural rights of which men, when they form a social compact cannot deprive or divest their posterity, among which are the enjoyment of life and liberty, with the means of acquiring, possessing and protecting property, and pursuing and obtaining happiness and safety. . . . Ninth, that no freeman ought to be taken, imprisoned, or disseised of his freehold, liberties, privileges, or franchises, or outlawed or exiled, or in any manner destroyed or deprived of his life, liberty or property but by the law of the land.[64]

The first recommendation is declaratory in nature while the ninth is substantive, and together they correspond to the text and spirit of Chapter 39. North Carolina's ratification of the Constitution contained identical language. Rhode Island's ratification, which occurred after the Bill of Rights had been framed, differed only in the addition of the words, "by the trial by jury or" preceding "the law of the land" at the end of Virginia's ninth proposal.[65] The wording of New York's recommendation was as follows:

> That no person ought to be taken, imprisoned or disseised of his freehold, or be exiled or deprived of his Privileges, Franchises, Life, Liberty or Property but by due process of law.[66]

Virginia, North Carolina, and Rhode Island offered language categorically securing life, liberty, and property. Such a strong affirmation of these rights might well be responsible for the unqualified character of the federal due process clause. New York's use of the words "due process" in its proposal does not change the character of its proposed protection, which was similarly broad and unqualified. Support for this conclusion is provided by Alexander Hamilton's now famous definition of due process contained in a speech he made to the New York legislature on February 6, 1787. The New York Constitution, Hamilton asserted, declares that

> no man shall be disfranchised or deprived of any right, but by *due process of law,* or the judgment of his peers. The words *"due process"* have a precise technical import, and are only applicable to the process and proceedings of the courts of justice; they can never be referred to an act of legislature.[67]

Hamilton was arguing against passage of a bill by the legislature that would disqualify former privateers from holding public office.[68] He insisted that the due process clause prohibited the legislature from depriving persons who had been privateers of their right to hold office and that only the judiciary had this power. He noted that an article of the state's constitution stated that

> no man shall be disfranchised or deprived of any right he enjoys under the con-stitution, but by the *law of the land,* or the judgment of his peers. Some gentle-men hold that the law of the land will include an act of the legislature. But Lord Coke, that great luminary of the law, in his comment upon a similar clause, in Magna Charta, interprets the law of the land to mean presentment and indictment, and process of outlawry, as contradistinguished from trial by jury. But if there were any doubt upon the constitution, the bill of rights enacted in this very ses-sion removes it. It is there declared that, no man shall be disfranchised or deprived of any right, but by *due process of law,* or the judgment of his peers.[69]

According to Hamilton, due process means the same as law of the land, and New York's due process clause consequently removed the power of the legisla-ture to deprive a person of his rights. "Are we willing to endure the inconsistency of passing a bill of rights, and committing a direct violation of it in the same ses-sion?" Hamilton asked. Understandably, he is reported to have stated in 1787 that "I hold it to be a maxim which ought to be sacred in our form of government, that no man ought to be deprived of any right or privilege which he enjoys under the Constitution, but for some offense provided in due course of law."[70] Hence, Hamilton's interpretation of New York's due process clause supports the position that, pursuant to this clause, only the judiciary and not the legislature has the power to deprive persons of their rights, and then only for wrongdoing which has been fairly and properly determined. Legislatures do not possess adjudicative powers.

In drafting his due process clause, Madison chose language similar to that contained in the due process clause recommended by New York as an amend-ment to the Constitution. New York's constitution contained a due process clause which Hamilton interpreted as strongly protective of individual rights. Since Madison and Hamilton were friends and constitutional collaborators at the time, it is likely not a coincidence that Madison chose the New York lan-guage. One might well conclude that Madison's due process clause was in-tended to guarantee protections similar to those of New York's clause.

IV. Relationship of the Due Process and Takings Clauses

The takings clause of the Fifth Amendment does, however, permit government to deprive people of their property, but only under the conditions therein set forth. Framed together by the First Congress, the takings and due process clauses adjoin each other in the Fifth Amendment and must naturally be considered to be consistent with each other. Together, the provisions state as follows:

> No person shall . . . be deprived of life, liberty, or property without due process of law; nor shall private property be taken for public use, without just compensation.

To deprive ordinarily means to remove or withhold something from the possession or enjoyment of a person. Because of the unqualified protection against deprivation of property contained in the due process guarantee, the takings clause seems necessary to preserve the power of eminent domain (an unenumerated power in our Constitution, but one traditionally exercised by governments) under which government can acquire property from a person unwilling to part with it. In the absence of the takings clause, the due process clause might have been interpreted to deny government the power of eminent domain, as Justice James Iredell (in *Calder v. Bull*) wrote might occur if the ex post facto provisions were interpreted as applying to retroactive laws affecting the ownership of property.[71] A retroactive property law is one that eliminates a property right an owner had previously acquired. Iredell feared that if the ex post facto clause applied to property laws, government would not be able to invoke eminent domain powers. An owner could resist eminent domain by claiming that he had no notice of it at the time of purchase. Partly on this basis, Iredell justified his construction of the Constitution's ex post facto ban as not relating to property ownership and other civil matters. Together, the due process and takings clauses bar the federal government from depriving a person of life, liberty, or property except as punishment for wrongdoing, or, with respect only to property, for public use upon payment of just compensation. This protection would not extend to persons engaged in harmful activities (such as fraud, defamation, or nuisance) that are not criminal. As an exception to the due process guarantee, the takings clause confirms the eminent domain power and enables the public to acquire, by payment of just compensation, all or partial interests in property when needed for public use.

Some commentators contend that the takings clause applies only to actual acquisitions of private property by the government for public purposes. They reject the idea that the clause relates to the regulation of property. However, this is not a matter of concern if the due process and takings clauses are interpreted together as securing private property. Regulation requires deprivation of one or more prerogatives of ownership, and even if it is not subject to the takings clause, it would come under the prohibition of the due process clause.

Support for the foregoing interpretation of the due process and takings clauses comes from the language contained in one of Madison's proposed constitutional amendments which, with several changes, became the Fifth Amendment:

> No person shall be subject, except in cases of impeachment, to more than one punishment or one trial for the same offense; nor shall be compelled to be a witness against himself; nor be deprived of life, liberty, or property without due process of law; nor be obliged to relinquish his property, where it may be necessary for public use, without a just compensation.[72]

The last clause is an exception to the categorical language of the clause preceding it. Both Madison's proposal and the final version of the Fifth Amendment provide protection from governmental oppression, and that would include payment for property needed by the government for public use.

In the above paragraph authored by Madison, the just compensation provision is the only clause that relates exclusively to civil matters, and the due process clause is the only one applicable to both criminal and civil matters. The same pattern is evident in the final version of the Constitution. The Fifth and Sixth Amendments consist largely of criminal-law protections intended to safeguard the rights of persons accused or convicted of wrongdoing. The only provision in either of the amendments that concerns solely civil matters is the takings clause, and it follows the due process clause because it is applicable to it.

Additional evidence for the suggested relationship between the due process and takings clauses is provided by the text of the important Northwest Ordinance adopted by the United States Congress on July 13, 1787, while the Constitution was being framed and the Articles of Confederation were in force. This was an ordinance for the government of the territory northwest of the Ohio River. Article II guarantees private property rights as follows:

> No man shall be deprived of his liberty or property, but by judgment of his peers, or law of the land, and should the public exigencies make it necessary, for the common preservation, to take any person's property, or to demand his particular services, full compensation shall be made for the same.[73]

Again, the protection accorded to law-abiding persons was unqualified, except when the acquisition of property or services was necessary for "the common preservation," and then the payment of compensation was mandated.

In addition to the paragraph previously quoted, Madison also referred to protecting life, liberty, and property in another of his proposed constitutional amendments. He suggested that the following language be prefixed to the Constitution, a recommendation which the Congress did not accept.

> That government is instituted and ought to be exercised for the benefit of the people; which consists in the enjoyment of life and liberty, with the right of acquiring and using property, and generally of pursuing and obtaining happiness and safety.[74]

The only clause of Madison's proposed amendments that guarantees the right of acquiring and using property is the due process clause, suggesting that the clause was intended to implement the proposed prefix and served substantive as well as procedural purposes. If it were not implemented by language elsewhere in the Constitution, the security of the property rights referred to in the proposed prefix would have been only an aspiration in the Constitution, and it is not likely that Madison would have been satisfied with this kind of outcome. Substantive language is supposed to make declaratory language enforceable, a purpose which only Madison's due process provision served with respect to the right of acquiring and using property.

The thinking of the late-eighteenth-century American leaders becomes understandable when viewed from the perspective of the Magna Carta, and the positions of Locke, Coke, and Blackstone on the protection of the individual in a free and viable society. With respect to property, the Constitution imposes on government the universal command that "Thou shalt not steal." Theft is wrong whether committed by one person or a majority of persons. Some people alone must not bear public burdens which, in all fairness and justice, should be borne by the public as a whole.[75] As Justice Samuel Chase wrote in 1798, "[i]t is against all reason and justice, for a people to entrust a legislature with the power to take property from A and give it to B."[76]

V. Early Federal and State Decisions

Several decisions of the early Marshall Supreme Court strongly secured property ownership. In *Fletcher v. Peck* (1810),[77] the Supreme Court applied natural law and the Constitution's obligation of contracts clause to annul a Georgia law canceling the purchasers' title to millions of acres of land in what is now most of Alabama and Mississippi. This land had been bought in good faith from grantors who had acquired it through legislative corruption. Justice John Marshall combined alternate grounds for decision making by holding that the law in question was oppressive as well as a violation of the obligation of contracts provision (Article I, Section 10, which bars states from passing any "Law impairing the Obligation of Contracts"):

> It is, then, the unanimous opinion of the Court, that, in this case, the estate having passed into the hands of a purchaser for a valuable consideration, without notice, the State of Georgia was restrained, either by general principles which are common to our free institutions, or by the particular provisions of the Constitution of the United States, from passing a law whereby the estate of the plaintiff in the premises so purchased could be constitutionally and legally impaired and rendered null and void.[78]
>
> It may well be doubted whether the nature of society and of government does

not prescribe some limits to the legislative power; and, if any be prescribed, where are they to be found, if the property of an individual, fairly and honestly acquired, may be seized without compensation.

To the legislature all legislative power is granted; but the question whether the act of transferring the property of an individual to the public, be in the nature of a legislative power is well worthy of serious reflection.[79]

In ruling on the contracts issue, Marshall interpreted the obligation of contracts clause by examining its language and meaning, concluding that it prohibited the passage of the challenged statute.

Justice William Johnson (a Jeffersonian and, therefore, presumably not disposed to accept Marshall's Federalist outlook) concurred, despite his inability to find a provision in the Constitution denying a state power to revoke its own land grants. "But I do it," he wrote, "on a general principle, on the reason and nature of things: a principle which will impose laws even on the Deity."[80]

In *Terrett v. Taylor* (1815),[81] Justice Joseph Story, writing for the Supreme Court, invoked the spirit of the Constitution, principles of natural justice, and the fundamental laws of all free governments to strike down a Virginia statute that would have deprived the Episcopal Church of its property. Story did not base his opinion on any specific provision of the Constitution. Infringing the church's rights would be "utterly inconsistent with a great and fundamental principle of republican government, the right of the citizens to the free enjoyment of their property legally acquired."[82]

Subsequently, in *Wilkinson v. Leland* (1829),[83] the Supreme Court, again per Justice Story, asserted that the legislature was limited in its power to restrict the rights of ownership: "We know of no case in which a legislative act to transfer the property of A to B without his consent has ever been held a constitutional exercise of legislative power in any State of the Union. On the contrary, it has been consistently resisted as inconsistent with just principles by every judicial tribunal in which it has been attempted to be enforced." The Court expressed strong support for the natural right of property:

That government can scarcely be deemed free, where the rights of property are left solely dependent upon the will of the legislative body, without any restraint. The fundamental maxims of a free government seem to require, that the rights of personal liberty and private property should be held sacred. At least no court of justice in this country would be warranted in assuming, that the power to violate and disregard them — a power so repugnant to the common principles of justice and civil liberty — lurked under any general grant of legislative authority, or ought to be implied from any general expressions of the will of the people. The people ought not to be presumed to part with rights so vital to their security and well being, without very strong and direct expressions of such an intention.[84]

The judiciary also construed due process and law of the land provisions as providing substantive protections. The first time the United States Supreme Court considered the meaning of "law of the land" was in 1819, when Justice Johnson interpreted the law of the land clause of the Maryland Constitution as "intended to secure the individual from the arbitrary exercise of the powers of government, unrestrained by the established principles of private rights and distributive justice."[85] Thus, law of the land provided substantive protection.

The Fifth Amendment's due process clause was first interpreted by the Supreme Court in *Murray's Lessee v. Hoboken Land and Improvement Company* in 1855.[86] The Court was asked to declare unconstitutional a federal statute which provided for the imposition of a summary judgment by the Secretary of the Treasury without the exercise of judicial power against a collector of customs for a balance due on his account. Citing Coke's *Institutes,* the Court interpreted the words "due process of law" as having the same meaning as the words "by the law of the land" in the Magna Carta. Rejecting the position that the due process clause placed no restrictions on the legislative power, the Court interpreted it as a restraint on every branch of government:

> It is manifest that it was not left to the legislative power to enact any process which might be devised. The article is a restraint on the legislative as well as on the executive and judicial powers of the government and cannot be so construed as to leave Congress free to make any process "due process of law," by its mere will.[87]

The Court went on to ascertain whether the process at issue was due process:

> To what principles, then, are we to resort to ascertain whether this process, enacted by Congress, is due process? To this the answer must be twofold. We must examine the Constitution itself to see whether this process be in conflict with any of its provisions. If not found to be so, we must look to those settled usages and modes of proceeding existing in the common and statute law of England, before the emigration of our ancestors, and which are shown not to have been unsuited to their civil and political conditions by having been acted on by them after the settlement of this country.[88]

The Court concluded that the sort of summary proceeding provided for by the federal statute was in accordance with such "settled usages and modes of proceeding" and was exercised subsequent to settlement. By the common law of England and the laws of many of the colonies before the revolution, and of states before the formation of the federal constitution, a summary process existed for the recovery of debts due to the government.

> For, though "due process of law" generally implies and includes *actor, reus, judex,* regular allegations, opportunity to answer, and a trial according to some settled course of judicial proceedings, [citations omitted] yet, this is not univer-

sally true: There may be, and we have seen that there are cases, under the law of England after *Magna Charta,* and as it was brought to this country and acted on here, in which process, in its nature final, issues against the body, lands, and goods of certain public debtors without any such trial. . . .[89]

The Court's citations in support of its view on the general meaning of due process consisted of Lord Coke's *Institutes of the Laws of England,* a U.S. Circuit Court decision, and five state court decisions, including *Hoke v. Henderson* (1833), a North Carolina case, and *Taylor v. Porter* (1843), a New York case, both of which are discussed later in this section, as well as *Vanzant v. Waddel* (1829), a Tennessee case referred to below in Section VII. These decisions accord "law of the land" and "due process of law" the same meaning Alexander Hamilton gave them in his speech to the New York legislature on February 6, 1787. Likewise citing Lord Coke in support of his position, Hamilton stated that by reason of either due process or law of the land, legislators have no authority to deprive people of their rights. Only the judiciary has this authority, and then solely when it adheres to principles of due process or law of the land.[90] In *Murray's Lessee* (1855), the Supreme Court agreed with Hamilton with respect to the usual and ordinary legislative actions. However, as I have noted, the Court stated that "there are cases . . . in which process . . . issues against . . . certain public debtors without any such trial,"[91] but these are exceptions based on particular historical practices. These exceptions to Hamilton's position on due process still leave his interpretation largely intact.

Justice Benjamin Curtis was the author of the Supreme Court's opinion in *Murray's Lessee* and earlier wrote (in his capacity as a circuit justice) the opinion in the circuit court case he cited, which was *Greene v. Briggs* (1852).[92] In *Greene,* he stated the following:

> [Law of the land] does not mean any act which the assembly may choose to pass. If it did, the legislative will could inflict a forfeiture of life, liberty, or property, without a trial. The exposition of these words, as they stand in Magna Charta, as well as in the American constitutions, has been, that they require "due process of law"; and in this is necessarily implied and included the right to answer to and contest the charge, and the consequent right to be discharged from it, unless it is proved. Lord Coke, giving the interpretation of these words in Magna Charta (2 Inst. 50, 51), says, they mean due process of law, in which is included presentment or indictment, and being brought in to answer thereto. And the jurists of our country have not relaxed this interpretation.[93]

A number of state decisions provide support for Hamilton's position. In 1792, South Carolina's high court in *Bowman v. Middleton*[94] adjudicated a challenge to a state law that transferred a freehold from one person to another without provision for a trial by jury or other judicial process. Declaring the statute invalid, the Court held that "it was against common right, as well as against *Magna Charta,* to take away the freehold of one man and vest it in another, and that, too, to the prejudice of third persons, without any compensation or even a trial by the jury of the country, to determine the right in question."[95] In two subsequent South Carolina cases, a concurring judge, without objection from his colleagues, interpreted the "law of the land" provision of a Magna Carta–type article of the state constitution (Article IX) as limiting the powers of the state legislature to terminate a person's property rights.[96]

In *Turpin v. Locket* (1804),[97] the Virginia high court unanimously agreed that section 1 of the Virginia Bill of Rights protected an individual from the legislature's deprivation of ownership. This section declared that all men have inherent rights: "namely, the enjoyment of life and liberty, with the means of acquiring and possessing property."

The North Carolina Supreme Court, in *University of North Carolina v. Foy and Bishop* (1805),[98] viewed that state constitution's "law of the land" clause as unqualified, holding that it secured the right of property and prohibited the legislature from repealing a prior grant of lands to a university:

> The property vested in the trustee must remain for uses intended for the University, until the Judiciary of the country in the usual and common form, pronounce them guilty of such acts, as will, in law, amount to a forfeiture of their rights or a dissolution of their body.[99]

The celebrated jurist and legal scholar James Kent applied this perspective in a case involving a partial deprivation of property. Taking a position similar to that of the *Foy* court, Kent held that government could not deprive an owner who was innocent of wrongdoing of a portion of his property. At issue was a stream of water that flowed over the owner's land. In the often-cited case of *Gardner v. Trustees of the Village of Newburgh* (1816),[100] Chancellor Kent found that a right to a stream of water "is as sacred as a right to the soil over which it flows."[101] It was, therefore, "part of the freehold of which no man can be disseised 'but by lawful judgment of his peers, or by due process of law.' "[102] The New York Constitution contained a due process provision but no takings clause. Kent held that due process would be violated if the owner of the land through which the stream flowed was not compensated for the loss he suffered if the flow over his land was diverted by the city.

In the North Carolina decision of *Hoke v. Henderson* (1833),[103] another much-cited case, Chief Justice Ruffin of North Carolina's high court asserted that once there had been a legitimate vesting of property rights, only the owner's wrongdoing could be cause for forfeiture. According to him, the term "law of the land" requires that before anyone shall be deprived of property, he shall have a judicial trial according to the common law.[104] This case challenged a statute which, in providing for the future election of court clerks, caused some appointed clerks to lose their employment. The property rights in question were those of the incumbent clerks to their positions.

In *Taylor v. Porter* (1843), citing the Magna Carta and Coke's *Institutes*, New York's Chief Justice Bronson explained that the state's law of the land provision meant

> that no member of the state shall be disfranchised or deprived of any of his rights and privileges, unless the matter be adjudged against him upon trial had according to the course of the common law. It must be ascertained judicially that he has forfeited his privileges, or that some one else has a superior title to the property he possesses, before either of them can be taken from him. It cannot be done by mere legislation.[105]

A number of New York decisions went along the same lines, culminating in the famous case of *Wynehamer v. People*,[106] an 1856 case involving a New York State penal statute that forbade the sale of intoxicating liquors owned at the time of enactment (except those for medicinal and religious purposes), and required the destruction of those intended for sale. The decision in *Wynehamer* held that the statute violated the state constitution's due process clause. The clause protected the prerogatives of ownership; that is, while some regulation is possible, said one of the justices,

> where [property] rights are acquired by the citizen under the existing law, there is no power in any branch of the government to take them away; but where they are held contrary to the existing law, or are forfeited by its violation, then they may be taken from him—not by an act of the legislature, but in the due administration of the law itself, before the judicial tribunals of the State. The cause or occasion for depriving the citizen of his supposed rights must be found in the law as it is, or, at least it cannot be *created* by a legislative act which aims at their destruction. Where rights of property are admitted to exist, the legislature cannot say they shall exist no longer; nor will it make any difference, although a process and a tribunal are appointed to execute the sentence. If this is the "law of the land," and "due process of law," within the meaning of the Constitution, then the legislature is omnipotent. It may, under the same interpretation, pass a law to take away liberty or life without a preexisting cause, appointing judicial and executive agencies to execute its will. Property is placed in the Constitution in the same category with liberty and life.[107]

As a decision of the highly respected New York high court, these words proved to be highly influential in forming the nation's jurisprudence. The basic principle of the decision was merely an affirmation of the principle that a person who abides by the law and commits no wrong shall not be penalized. Insofar as it restricted legislative power to control liquor traffic, the *Wynehamer* precedent was generally not followed. The alcohol control statutes were generally upheld under the police power of the state, as explained in Chapter 4, Section II. However, as is evident from the prior discussion in this chapter, at the time *Wynehamer* was decided there was a considerable body of law that provided a similar interpretation for the due process guarantee. According to Professor Edward Corwin, a leading commentator on that period, in less "than twenty years from the time of its rendition, the crucial ruling in *Wynehamer v. People* was far on the way to being assimilated into the accepted constitutional law of the country."[108] As will be discussed in later sections of this chapter, the Framers of the Fourteenth Amendment likely agreed with the meaning that *Wynehamer* gave to due process clauses.

VI. Section 1 of the Fourteenth Amendment

One result of the Civil War was the adoption of three amendments to the Constitution—the Thirteenth, Fourteenth, and Fifteenth—intended to limit the power of the states to restrict the liberty of their residents. The second sentence of Section 1 of the Fourteenth Amendment declares: "No State shall make or enforce any law which shall abridge the privileges or immunities of citizens of the United States; nor shall any State deprive any person of life, liberty, or property, without due process of law; nor deny to any person within its jurisdiction the equal protection of the laws."

This sentence is a limitation on the power of states to pass laws abridging, depriving or denying people their liberties. Section 1 was drafted to accord substantive protection for liberty at the state level. Each clause of its second sentence (quoted above) was directed toward this end; and collectively they constitute a formidable barrier against state excesses and oppressions. Although this general commitment is quite plain, it does not reveal which specific activities are safeguarded and to what extent. This issue may not be resolved for many areas, but it can be satisfactorily resolved for the liberties relating to property and economics. In the civil area, these were liberties of highest concern to the Thirty-ninth Congress, which framed the Fourteenth Amendment in 1866.

Virtually all commentators agree that Section 1 of the amendment was intended to incorporate the principles of the Civil Rights Act of 1866 into the Constitution, so that they could not be repealed by a subsequent Congress. This act, the legal decisions, and the legal commentators on which the Thirty-ninth Congress most relied in framing Section 1 all emphasized the importance in a free society of ownership and enterprise and the liberties required to make them meaningful. The act protected the rights of United States citizens "to make and enforce contracts . . . [and] to inherit, purchase, lease, sell, hold and convey real and personal property." Although not confined to the newly freed slaves, a major purpose of the act was to enable them to exercise property rights and economic freedoms without being subject to restraints special to them. After the Civil War ended, the defeated Southern states quickly enacted onerous restrictions upon the freemen, limiting their freedom of labor, their right to own property, and their mobility. It was to foil these Black Codes, which tried to emulate the conditions of slavery, that the Reconstruction Congress passed the 1866 Civil Rights Act and then framed the Fourteenth Amendment.

The debates of the Thirty-ninth Congress reveal that Sir William Blackstone and Chancellor James Kent were the most authoritative legal commentators for this Congress on the powers and purposes of government. I have already discussed Blackstone's influence on the Framers of the Constitution and the nation's early jurists. Nearly eighty years later, his shadow was just as compelling. Consistent with Blackstone's views, Chancellor Kent wrote, in his influential *Commentaries on American Law* (1826), that "the right to acquire and enjoy property [is] natural, inherent, and unalienable."[109] According to Kent, "property leads to cultivation of the earth, the institution of government, the acquisition of the comforts of life, the growth of the useful arts, the spirit of commerce, the productions of taste, the erections of charity, and the display of the benevolent affections."[110]

Consistent with Alexander Hamilton's position, expressed to the New York legislature in 1787, Kent considered due process to guarantee the rights of life, liberty, and property:

> The words, "law of the land," as used originally in Magna Charta, in reference to this subject, are understood to mean, due process of law, that is, by indictment or presentment of good and lawful men: "and this," says Lord Coke, "is the true sense and exposition of those words." The better and larger definition of due process of law is, that it means law in its *regular course of administration through courts of justice*.[111]

As mentioned in Section V, in the case of *Gardner v. Trustees of the Village of Newburgh* (1816), Kent ruled that compensation was due not only for property directly taken by government, but also under due process for loss due to government actions—what we now refer to as inverse condemnation. He ruled that the fundamental right to due process of law would be violated if the owner of the land through which a stream flowed was not compensated for the loss he suffered when the flow was diverted by the city.[112] Kent wrote that government may, by general regulations, forbid such use of property as would create nuisances, and become dangerous to the "lives, or health, or peace, or comfort of the citizens." The burden rested on the legislature to prove that the uses in question would actually and substantially injure other owners.[113] Regulation was to be the exception and not the rule.

VII. The Fourteenth Amendment's Due Process Clause

The author of the second sentence of Section 1 of the Fourteenth Amendment was John Bingham, a Republican representative from Ohio. In a speech he delivered some years before he drafted the sentence, Bingham stated that the due process guarantee of the Fifth Amendment secures natural rights for all persons, requires equal treatment by the law, and comprehends the highest priority for ownership.[114] He believed that acquisition of private property by government required the owner's consent,[115] a stronger affirmation of property rights than that set forth in the Fifth Amendment's takings clause, which contains no such qualification.

Justice Hugo Black, in a 1947 dissent, dubbed Bingham "the Madison of the first section of the Fourteenth Amendment."[116] Regarded as an expert on the subject by his colleagues, Bingham spoke a great deal in Congress about the Constitution and its protection of liberty. He was a moderate in his party, and unlike most of his Radical Republican colleagues—the architects of Reconstruction—he opposed the Civil Rights Act of 1866 because he could find no authorization for it in the Constitution. He saw the proposed Fourteenth Amendment as the remedy for this constitutional problem. Though Bingham was not known for the orderliness of his thinking—an affliction hardly unique among politicians—his interpretations of such key terms as "privileges and immunities," "due process," and "equal protection" were generally consistent with those of most members of the Republican Party. It was these Republicans who had comprised the political wing of the abolitionist cause. They were impassioned believers in freedom, human dignity, and the equality of all men, irrespective of race. Abolitionist philosophy was generally libertarian, particularly in its antagonism toward state economic powers, as the following remarks by Bingham on the concept of due process reflect:

> Who . . . will be bold enough to deny that all persons are equally entitled to the enjoyment of the rights of life and liberty and property; and that no one should be deprived of life or liberty, but as punishment for crime; nor of his property, against his consent and without due compensation?

> It must be apparent that the absolute equality of all, and the equal protection of each, are principles of our Constitution, which ought to be observed and enforced in the organization and admission of new States. The Constitution provides, as we have seen, that *no person* shall be deprived of life, liberty, or property, without due process of law. It makes no distinction either on account of complexion or birth—it secures these rights to all persons within its exclusive jurisdiction. This is equality. It protects not only life and liberty, but also property, the product of labor. It contemplates that no man shall be wrongfully deprived of the fruit of his toil any more than of his life. . . .[117]

> Representatives, to you I appeal, that hereafter, by your act and the approval of the loyal people of this country, every man in every State of the Union, in accordance with the written words of your Constitution, may, by the national law, be secured in the equal protection of his personal rights. Your Constitution provides that no man, no matter what his color, no matter beneath what sky he may have been born, no matter in what disastrous conflict or by what tyrannical hand his liberty may have been cloven down, no matter how poor, no matter how friendless, no matter how ignorant, shall be deprived of life, or liberty or property with-

out due process of law—law in its highest sense, that law which is the perfection of human reason, and which is impartial, equal, exact justice; that justice which requires that every man shall have his right; that justice which is the highest duty of nations as it is the imperishable attribute of the God of nations.[118]

Thus, asserts Bingham, no one can be deprived of life, liberty, or property without a fair, just, and proper judicial proceeding to determine if an accused person has violated the law and is deserving of penalty. Hence, Bingham's views on the meaning of due process were the same as those expressed by Hamilton in his 1787 speech before the New York legislature.[119]

For Bingham, the concept of due process and the due process clause were strong weapons against all forms of state oppression, regardless of its source—a view which went unchallenged in the debates of the Thirty-ninth Congress.[120] In these debates, there were relatively few references to due process, far fewer than there were to privileges and immunities.[121] All of the references assumed that due process provided substantive protections. Representative James Wilson, chairman of the House Judiciary Committee, and floor chairman for the proposed Civil Rights Act of 1866, went so far as to assert that the act applied the substantive protections of the Fifth Amendment's due process clause to the states.[122] He believed that the federal government had the power under that clause to secure persons from deprivations of their "priceless" liberties by the states. Representative M. Russell Thayer argued that the Fifth Amendment's due process clause gave, by implication at least, sufficient power to Congress to pass the Civil Rights Act.[123] For Representative John Baker of Illinois, the proposed due process clause was "a wholesome and needed check upon the great abuse of liberty which several of the states have practiced, and which they manifest too much purpose to continue."[124] Senator Luke P. Poland and Representative George F. Miller asserted that the due process and equal protection clauses implemented the Declaration of Independence.[125] Representative Thomas Williams opined that if suffrage were regarded as a property right, its deprivation would violate the due process clause.[126]

"Due process" was a term in frequent use before, during, and after the Civil War. Both sides of the slavery controversy employed it to further their own causes. Proslavery forces contended that slaves were property, and therefore, that owners were protected against loss of their slaves without due process. In contrast, beginning in the mid-1830s, antislavery activists thought of the due process guarantee as "constitutionalizing" their natural-rights beliefs in the sanctity of life, liberty, and property. They repudiated any notion that a person could be someone else's property; people possessed property in their own selves, and the due process clause obligated the national government to secure their property right in the territories of the U.S.[127] Slavery was not a natural condition, antislavery activists said, and legislatures had no power to deprive people of their liberty and place them in this condition.

The due process concept was a major verbal weapon for the abolitionists.

The respected Fourteenth Amendment scholar Howard Jay Graham observed in his 1968 book that due process

> was snatched up, bandied about, "corrupted and corroded," if you please, for more than thirty years prior to 1866. For every black letter usage in court, there were perhaps hundreds or thousands in the press, red schoolhouse, and on the stump. Zealots, reformers and politicians—not jurists—blazed the paths of substantive due process.[128]

From 1834, "due process as a substantive conception, became part of the constitutional stock in trade of abolitionism."[129] Thus, the political parties committed to eradicating slavery used the term "due process" to advance this position. In 1843, the Liberty Party platform declared that the Fifth Amendment's due process clause legally secured the inalienable rights referred to in the Declaration of Independence.[130] The 1848 and 1852 platforms of the Free Soil Party contended that the clause served both as a restraint on the federal government and as an obligation on the government to enforce the inalienable rights set forth in the Declaration.[131] More significantly, according to the 1856 and 1860 platforms of the Republican Party, the clause denied Congress the power to allow slavery to exist in any territory in the Union: "[I]t becomes our duty to maintain [the due process provision] by legislation against all attempts to violate it."[132] In the 1856 political campaign, "due process of law" was a leading catch phrase of Republican orators.[133] Some of those who were involved in the drafting or consideration of the Republican platforms would probably later, as members of Congress or in other political roles, be responsible for framing or ratifying the Fourteenth Amendment.

People who viewed slavery favorably argued that the due process clause supported their position. They found support in Chief Justice Roger Taney's decision in the famous *Dred Scott* case, decided in 1857.[134] Dred Scott was a slave who traveled to and lived with his master for five years in free territory (the state of Illinois and the Minnesota territory) and subsequently moved to Missouri, a slave state. Alleging that he was a citizen of Missouri, Scott filed suit in a federal court in St. Louis against John Sandford of New York, his master, for assault and sought damages in the amount of $9,000. Pursuant to Article III, Section 2 of the Constitution, Congress authorized the federal courts to adjudicate cases between citizens of different states. The case reached the United States Supreme Court on the question of whether the federal court had jurisdiction to decide the case, and the decision rested on Scott's citizenship status. He claimed freedom because he had traveled and lived in territory declared free by the United States Congress.

Taney wrote that blacks could not be considered citizens because they were not "people of the United States." As part of his opinion, he held that Congress had no power to prohibit slavery in specified areas because the "powers over person and property . . . are not granted to Congress, but are in express terms denied, and they are forbidden to exercise them." Taney explained this "express" limitation as follows:

> [A]n act of Congress which deprives a citizen of the United States of his liberty or property, merely because he came himself or brought his property into a particular Territory of the United States, and who has committed no offense against the laws, could hardly be dignified with the name of due process of law.[135]

Although a majority concurred with Taney's decision, only two justices went along with this reasoning.

Justice Curtis, author of the 1855 *Murray's Lessee* decision, disagreed with Taney. He asserted that the due process clause was not violated because no deprivation had occurred. According to Curtis, a property right in a slave existed only pursuant to the laws of the state in which the slave was held, and that condition terminated when the owner voluntarily placed his slave permanently within another jurisdiction where no municipal law on the subject of slavery existed.

Taney had previously interpreted the Fifth Amendment's due process clause as banning Congress from depriving an owner of a property right. In writing for the Court in *Bloomer v. McQuewan* (1853), he had observed that a special act depriving licensees of their right to use property protected by patent "certainly could not be regarded as due process of law"; however, the case was resolved on other grounds.[136]

During the time that the Fourteenth Amendment was framed (1866) and ratified (1868), the position that due process prevented legislative deprivations continued to receive support from most justices of the U.S. Supreme Court. In a federal circuit court case in 1865, Supreme Court Justice Robert Grier, sitting as a circuit court judge, held that a Pennsylvania statute repealing a railroad corporation charter violated the "due course of law" provision of the state constitution.[137] The first Supreme Court ruling on due process after ratification of the Fourteenth Amendment was *Hepburn v. Griswold,*[138] delivered February 7, 1870, by a Court then consisting of seven members. For the majority of four, Chief Justice Salmon Chase held (among other matters) that holders of promissory contracts entered into prior to the effective date of the Legal Tender Act of 1862 were deprived by that act of the right to receive payment in gold or silver coin, in violation of the Fifth Amendment's due process guarantee. At the time the contracts were entered into, only gold and silver were legal tender; that is, all payments of debts had to be made in gold or silver. Desperate to finance the armies of the North, Congress passed the Legal Tender Act, which allowed the federal government to issue paper money—the soon-to-be-infamous "greenbacks"—which were not redeemable in gold or silver. The law declared that this paper money had to be accepted in all forms of commerce, including payments of debts.

The majority in *Hepburn* assumed that the Fifth Amendment's due process clause secures owners of real estate, and concluded that it protects holders of contracts to the same extent. According to Chief Justice Chase, the clause (as well as other provisions of the Fifth Amendment) operates "directly in limitation and restraint of the legislative powers conferred by the Constitution."[139] Justice Samuel Miller, for the minority of three, did not deny that the clause was a substantive limitation on the legislature. He objected that the effect on holders of contracts was incidental to the purpose of the Congress to further the war effort. President Ulysses Grant subsequently appointed two justices to the vacant seats, and on May 1, 1871, in *Knox v. Lee*,[140] these justices joined with the three dissenters in *Hepburn* to reverse it. Writing for the majority in *Knox,* Justice William Strong applied the same analysis to the due process issue as Miller had, and Chase, now in the minority, followed his prior interpretation. According to Strong, the due process "provision had always been understood as referring only to direct appropriations, and not to consequent injuries resulting from the exercise of lawful powers."[141]

One of the dissenting justices in *Hepburn* was Noah Swayne, and he and newly appointed Justice Joseph Bradley voted with the majority in *Knox*. Neither should be considered antagonistic to the idea of applying the due process guarantee to legislative deprivations. On the contrary, both would contend in their dissents in the famous *Slaughter-House Cases*,[142] decided the following year, that the Fourteenth Amendment's due process clause secured property and economic interests. On the issue of protecting vested property interests, these two justices would probably have agreed with the four who had made up the majority in *Hepburn*.

John Bingham, the author of the second sentence of the Fourteenth Amendment's first section, believed that existing law supported his interpretation of the due process clause of the Fifth Amendment: that it was a guarantee against deprivation without a fair and proper judicial proceeding. During the debates of the Thirty-ninth Congress he was asked about the meaning of "due process of law." Bingham replied that "[t]he courts have settled that long ago, and the gentlemen can go and read their decisions."[143] The most important decision on the due process clause prior to the framing of the Fourteenth Amendment in 1866 was *Murray's Lessee* (1855) which interpreted the Fifth Amendment's due process clause as essentially similar to Bingham's position except for a relatively minor historical precedent. (See discussion in Section V above.) The Court's interpretation of the due process guarantee was based on Lord Coke's *Institutes of the Laws of England,* a federal Circuit Court of Appeals decision, and five state high court decisions. The *Murray's Lessee* position is generally consistent with the position in *Wynehamer* (1856), the constitutional commentaries of Justice Joseph Story and Chancellor James Kent, and Alexander Hamilton's interpretation of New York's due process clause. Justice Taney's

opinions in *Dred Scott* and *Bloomer* also support the *Murray's Lessee* interpretation of due process.

The judiciary also provided meaning as to what constitutes due process of
law. Justice Comstock in *Wynehamer* rejected a retroactive law as inconsistent
with due process. The Tennessee Supreme Court issued important opinions on
the fairness required by the law of the land provision of its state constitution.
Two of these opinions were authored by Judge John Catron, who later served
as a justice of the United States Supreme Court from 1837 to 1865. In *Vanzant
v. Waddel* (1829), Catron wrote in a concurring opinion that the words "law of
the land" meant a general public law, equally binding upon every member of
the community.

> [The rights of every individual] must stand or fall by the same rule or law which
> governs every other member of the body politic, or "Land," under similar cir-
> cumstances; and every partial or private law which directly proposes to destroy
> or affect individual rights or does the same thing by affording remedies leading
> to similar consequences, is unconstitutional and void.[144]

In this case, Catron concluded that no constitutional violation occurred.

Two years later, in *Wally v. Kennedy,* he ruled for a unanimous court that a
statute directing the dismissal of certain suits relating to the reservation of land
to heads of Indian families under treaties between the United States and the
Cherokee Nation of Indians was a partial law and therefore unconstitutional.[145]

VIII. The Fourteenth Amendment's Privileges and Immunities Clause

The case that the due process clause of the Fourteenth Amendment secured the
right of property is a strong one, and an equally compelling case can be made that
the privileges and immunities clause also served this purpose. A considerable
amount of the debate over the Civil Rights Act of 1866 and the proposed Fourteenth Amendment revolved around the meaning and application of the privileges
and immunities concept. I have read the relevant portions of the various debates,
and in my opinion, one cannot help but conclude that this concept comprehended,
among other things, protection for property and economic rights. These were
rights of highest priority to the Thirty-ninth Congress, and I am convinced that
most of the Congress sought to give them the highest protection, and probably
believed that they had done so in Section 1 of the Fourteenth Amendment. Yet
the U.S. Supreme Court has never applied the privileges and immunities clause
for this purpose. The reason is that in the *Slaughter-House Cases* decided in
1872,[146] about four years after the amendment's ratification, the U.S. Supreme
Court by a 5-to-4 vote interpreted this clause as having very limited scope, and
specifically as not applicable to any of the material rights. The majority justices

in that case made little effort to ascertain the meaning accorded to this clause by the Framers of the Fourteenth Amendment.

The *Slaughter-House Cases* concerned economic liberties. In 1869, Louisiana's legislature granted a twenty-five-year exclusive privilege to a private corporation it had created to operate a regulated livestock and slaughterhouse business within a specified area of about 1,150 square miles, comprising New Orleans and two other parishes. The privilege required that all cattle brought into this area for commercial purposes be slaughtered by the corporation in its facilities. An association of butchers adversely affected brought suit on the basis that the monopoly grant violated the Thirteenth Amendment (abolishing slavery) and the Fourteenth Amendment—it violated the former, they said, by creating an involuntary servitude and the latter by depriving plaintiffs of their privileges and immunities as United States citizens. The butchers maintained that privileges and immunities included the right not to be deprived of liberty and property without due process of law, and the right to the equal protection of the law. The arguments presented to the Court revolved principally around the privileges and immunities clause. The Supreme Court upheld the monopoly grant by a 5-to-4 vote. But the dissenting justices contended—despite the seeming remoteness of the claimed right to freely operate slaughterhouses from the Fourteenth Amendment's purpose to protect the freedmen from racial discrimination—that the Louisiana statute violated Section 1. One or more of the last three clauses of that section seemed breached: privileges and immunities, due process, and/or the equal protection clause.

As their counsel, the butchers had hired John Campbell, a former member of the Supreme Court, who had resigned when his home state of Alabama seceded from the Union. He argued that the privileges and immunities clause extended federal safeguards to all citizens for a variety of civil rights, including the protection of the plaintiffs' interests in pursuing their business. According to Campbell, the Fourteenth Amendment's Framers intended to convert the privileges and immunities of state citizenship under Article IV, Section 2 of the Constitution into privileges and immunities of national citizenship. "The States . . . have been placed under the oversight and restraining and enforcing hand of Congress."[147] Supporting Campbell's position was the definition Justice Bushrod Washington had given, in *Corfield v. Coryell* (1823),[148] to the privileges and immunities clause contained in Article IV. Washington's decision contains a passage which was often quoted in Congress in its debates on the Civil Rights Act of 1866 and the Fourteenth Amendment. The passage would be cited, but not considered applicable, by the *Slaughter-House* majority. Washington wrote:

> We feel no hesitation in confining [the constitutional provision] to those privileges and immunities which are, in their nature, fundamental. . . . They may, however, be all comprehended under the following general heads: Protection by the government; the enjoyment of life and liberty, with the right to acquire and pos-

sess property of every kind, and to pursue and obtain happiness and safety. . . .
The right of a citizen of one state to pass through, or to reside in any other state,
for purposes of trade, agriculture, professional pursuits, or otherwise, to claim the
benefit of the writ of habeas corpus; to institute and maintain actions of any kind
in the courts of the state; to take, hold and dispose of property, either real or personal; and an exemption from higher taxes or impositions than are paid by the
other citizens of the state; may be mentioned as some of the particular privileges
and immunities of citizens, which are clearly embraced by the general description of privileges deemed to be fundamental: to which may be added, the elective
franchise, as regulated and established by the laws or constitution of the state in
which it is to be exercised. These, and many others which might be mentioned,
are, strictly speaking, privileges and immunities, and the enjoyment of them by
the citizens of each state, in every other state, was manifestly calculated (to use
the expressions of the preamble of the corresponding provision in the old articles
of confederation) "the better to secure and perpetuate mutual friendship and in-
tercourse among the people of the different states of the Union."[149]

Justice Samuel F. Miller, writing for the majority in the *Slaughter-House Cases,*
rejected the argument of the butchers' lawyer, John Campbell, that the Fourteenth
Amendment provides federal protection for the rights specified by Justice Washington in the passage just quoted. In the process, the Court virtually struck the privileges and immunities clause from the Fourteenth Amendment. Miller said that
this clause was not intended as protection for the citizens of a state against the legislative power of their own state. Instead, the clause places the privileges and immunities of United States citizens under federal protection. These privileges and
immunities, Miller contended, are different and more circumscribed than those
spelled out by Justice Washington, and include the right to come to the seat of government, to assert claims against it, to seek its protection from foreign governments, to transact business with it, to have free access to the nation's seaports and
courts, to assemble and petition for redress of grievances, and to be protected by
the writ of habeas corpus. As some of the dissenting justices observed, preservation of these rights hardly required an extensive constitutional amendment. However, Miller insisted that the construction that was sought by the butchers would
jeopardize the existing federal structure of government and

constitute this court a perpetual censor upon all legislation of the States, on the
civil rights of their own citizens, with authority to nullify such as it did not approve as consistent with those rights, as they existed at the time of the adoption
of this amendment. . . .[150]

Miller was even less impressed with the plaintiffs' arguments on due process
and equal protection. He did not address at all their contention concerning deprivation of liberty, and he demolished their economic liberties arguments almost in passing. He stated that inquiring into the meaning of the due process
clause was unnecessary, for

it is sufficient to say that under no construction of that provision that we have ever seen, or any that we deem admissible, can the restraint imposed by the State of Louisiana upon the exercise of their trade by the butchers of New Orleans be held to be a deprivation of property within the meaning of that provision.[151]

Miller claimed that the equal protection clause was intended to remove discrimination against Negroes and doubted very much whether any state action not directed to such discrimination would ever be held to come within the purview of this provision.[152]

Each dissenting *Slaughter-House* opinion viewed property and liberty in the more expansive terms that would, pace Justice Miller, in time become judicially acceptable. Justices Stephen Field, Joseph Bradley, and Noah Swayne filed separate dissents; in addition, Bradley and Swayne concurred with Field's dissent, as did Chief Justice Salmon Chase. (Justice Swayne also concurred in Bradley's dissent.) The dissenters acknowledged that the well-being of Negroes may have been the Fourteenth Amendment's primary concern, but they nevertheless maintained that its language was purposefully made general in order to embrace all citizens. They accepted lawyer Campbell's argument that the amendment provided federal safeguards for all people in the United States against deprivation of their fundamental rights by state legislatures.

The dissents contain many memorable passages on the proper relationship between the government and the governed. For the most part, Field limited his remarks to privileges and immunities, but in later opinions he applied this same reasoning to due process. Bradley and Swayne argued that all three of the key clauses of Section 1 had been violated. Field castigated the legislative grant of a monopoly as encroaching "upon the liberty of citizens to acquire property and pursue happiness"[153] and violating the privileges and immunities clause. Bradley declared that "a law which prohibits a large class of citizens from adopting a lawful employment, or from following a lawful employment previously adopted, does deprive them of liberty as well as property, without due process of law."[154] For Justice Swayne, the language of all three clauses is unqualified in its relation to ownership and enterprise: "There is no exception in its terms, and there can be properly none in their application."[155] Field, who also asserted that the Fourteenth Amendment was intended to give practical effect to the Declaration of Independence, interpreted the privileges and immunities clause to mean that all pursuits were open to citizens, subject to some regulations imposed equally upon everyone similarly situated.

The minority justices saw no problem in considering the butchers' loss to be a loss of both liberty and property. Thus, as Bradley stated, "[t]his right to choose one's calling is an essential part of that liberty which it is the object of government to protect; and a calling, when chosen, is a man's property and right. . . . Their [i.e., citizens'] right of choice is a portion of their liberty; their occupation is their property."[156]

The *Slaughter-House* dissenters echoed the views on these issues of the leaders of the Thirty-ninth Congress, which framed the Fourteenth Amendment. These views are set forth below in Chapter 3, Section III.

IX. Summarizing the Historical Basis for Property Rights

The United States Constitution established a government of limited and enumerated powers that was not accorded any authority to deny or deprive its constituents of the right to acquire, use, and enjoy property. In the absence of such powers, the rights of owners were based on the common law, the judge-made law that originated in England and was much influenced by the Magna Carta and the commentaries of Locke, Coke, and Blackstone. The common law in the late eighteenth century provided strong protections for life, liberty, and property.

To ensure against constitutional violations and government oppression, the Framers divided and separated government into three branches, enabling each to exercise checks and balances over each of the others. While the Framers did not by explicit proclamation declare the sanctity of property rights, they inserted specific guarantees that would protect owners and entrepreneurs from deprivations of their property and that would forbid oppressive and preferential economic practices by government. These guarantees include prohibitions against passage of ex post facto laws and bills of attainder, both of which were, in my considered judgment, specific protections for property rights. To prevent government from arbitrarily imposing preferences and inflicting penalties, the Framers limited the government's powers over taxation, commercial practices, the writ of habeas corpus, the act of treason, and hiring based on religious preference, and they required jury trials in criminal matters. As James Madison said, these provisions were required to "banish speculations on public measures" and "give a regular course to the business of society."[157]

The Bill of Rights adds to the Constitution's property rights guarantees, containing seven provisions protecting private ownership, the principal ones being the due process and takings clauses of the Fifth Amendment. These two clauses secured the common-law protections of life, liberty, and property for all people who abided by the law and did not inflict harm on others.

The Framers of the Fourteenth Amendment (the Thirty-ninth Congress) protected property rights and economic liberties against state action in the privileges and immunities and due process clauses contained in Section 1. Their purpose was similar to that of both the Framers of the original Constitution and the Bill of Rights: to secure the rights of life, liberty, and property for law-abiding persons. Unfortunately, the *Slaughter-House Cases* emasculated the privileges and immunities clause, leaving the due process clause as the Fourteenth Amendment's guarantor for property rights and economic liberties.

3

The Judicial Obligation to Protect Liberty

A considerable portion of the legal community favors largely or entirely eliminating judicial review of property regulation. Even if it results in serious losses in property value, writes Stanford University professor Robert Girard, the courts "should leave legislative bodies broad flexibility to do what legislators determine can be done politically and ethically to meet social and environmental needs."[1] Although people take this position for a variety of reasons, the predominant one is their belief that legislatures are more competent to determine the use of land than either the judiciary or the private market. This group includes a wide range of individuals, from United States Supreme Court justices to law school professors and practicing attorneys.

Many in this group do not repose the same confidence in legislators when political and intellectual liberties are at stake. The question naturally arises: Why not entrust legislators with power over all liberties? Legions of experts have written compelling books describing the limitations and failings of the legislative process. But most of these tomes concern the political and intellectual liberties, and the opinions expressed in them have been decisive in our society. Hardly anyone in contemporary society dares to contend that legislators should have "broad flexibility" to regulate speech, press, religious exercise, or personal mobility. Of course, those who defend political and intellectual liberties are right, but, unfortunately, they are also terribly myopic.

Why is government regulation so reprehensible when it limits speech, press, or religion, and so desirable when it controls property? Why is government so tyrannical and stupid in the one case and so benevolent and wise in the other?

Apparently, many believe that a leopard can change its spots, depending on its intended victim. Our society treats political (or "personal") rights and property rights in different ways. There is relatively little control of one and much of the other. Government needs only modest excuse to restrict the use of property, as the experience of zoning demonstrates. But when it comes to political and intellectual rights, as Justice Hugo Black once wrote about free speech, "only the gravest abuses endangering paramount interests give occasion for permissible limitation."[2]

Few have a better understanding of government abuses than the leaders of many organizations in the country dedicated to protecting civil and political rights. However, they never seem to extrapolate from this knowledge, and prefer to look the other way when governmental agencies effectively deprive people of property—the fruit of their labor, savings, energy, and knowledge. They strenuously fight against the imposition of regulation when political liberties are involved, and stand absolutely mute when the most arbitrary zoning and environmental restrictions reduce by hundreds or thousands of dollars the value of property owned by people of average means.

Yet, as economics professor Ronald Coase of the University of Chicago Law School has observed: "For most people in most countries (and perhaps in all countries) the provision of food, clothing and shelter is a good deal more important than the provision of the 'right ideas,' even assuming we know which they are."[3] Professor Coase was discussing the sharp distinction made in the treatment between the ordinary market for goods and services and what he referred to as the "market for ideas" (in which he included the exercise of religious beliefs, speech, and writing). But for some activists and legal commentators, apparently, the government's motivation, judgment, competency, or efficiency is good or bad, depending on which market is involved.

Consider the outcry that occurred when the U.S. Supreme Court decided that South Carolina may have unconstitutionally deprived David Lucas of the right to build homes on his coastal lots.[4] Lucas purchased the lots for about $1 million in order to build two houses, which the law of the state permitted at the time of purchase. The state subsequently reclassified the land for supposedly environmental reasons and prohibited erection of habitable structures. No provision was made for compensating Lucas for the huge financial loss that he sustained as a result of the state's action. Lucas filed suit to recoup his loss and after many years of litigation obtained a favorable decision from the U.S. Supreme Court. That the state's claim to have reclassified the land to prevent environmental damage was without merit is shown by its subsequent actions. In settlement of Lucas's claims, it purchased the land from him, and instead of restricting it for parkland or open space, sold the land to a developer who will use it to erect two homes.

As attorney R. S. Radford reports,[5] the Supreme Court's *Lucas* decision "brought forth a deluge of criticism" in the academic journals, such as the following:

Any economic harm suffered by Mr. Lucas is clearly offset by the public need for the Beachfront Management Act.[6]

Lucas and his colleagues . . . are asking the public to sacrifice the safety of an entire littoral in order to permit million-dollar playhouses for the rich.[7]

The [Supreme] Court displayed no appreciation of the factors that led South Carolina to conclude that the physical characteristics of Lucas' land made it the wrong place for the construction of a house.[8]

We have become so taken with the pursuit of individual rights and personal economic gain that we have lost sight of the community and the social fabric of mutuality and reciprocity without which our economic and political systems cannot operate.[9]

Radford observes that there has been no similar outpouring of hostile rhetoric condemning South Carolina's decision to sell the property for development of two homes after having sought to keep Lucas from doing the same thing. It is doubtful that the critics would have acted similarly had government interfered so drastically with the pursuit of one of the preferred liberties. Indeed, numerous journal articles would have blasted the government for being stupid and evil.

In terms of individual liberty and the public interest, however, property rights are just as important as free speech or freedom of the press. Considerable similarity exists between the marketplace for ideas and that for goods and services. Maximum competition in the economic marketplace allows for maximum satisfaction of consumer needs and desires, and provides consumers with new and better products at lower cost. A regulated market, in contrast, gives the power of government to bureaucrats who decide what and how much will be produced or created and for whom. That awesome power must necessarily disadvantage some, possibly most, and benefit others. The same sorts of distortion and favoritism would occur in the "marketplace of ideas" if certain ideas were censored.

I. Separation of Powers Is a Fundamental Principle

The position that the judiciary should not review property regulation is contrary to a fundamental principle of American constitutional government. In our nation, the powers of government are supposed to be limited and separated. This is true not only for the federal government but also for each of the states. The checks and balances of our separation-of-powers system are intended to limit the power of government to oppress the people. Since their early years, American courts, including the Supreme Court, have struck down measures they deemed oppressive, notwithstanding that they sometimes had little basis for such action in the textual language of the Constitution. The Supreme Court's record in protecting free expression is a spectacular example. It is very difficult to demonstrate that the Court's current broad interpretation of this liberty is based on original understanding—that is, the meaning of this liberty in 1789 when the First Congress framed the Bill of Rights. Yet this broad reading is essential to preserving freedom, and it is our system of separation of powers and checks and balances that enabled the Court to perform this vital function.

The Framers greatly feared legislative bodies and sought to limit their powers. Thus, in his discussion of the separation doctrine, James Madison observed "that the people ought to indulge all their jealousy and exhaust all their precautions" against the enterprising ambition of the legislature. "The legislative department," warned Madison, "is everywhere extending the sphere of its activity and drawing all power into its impetuous vortex."[10] Many other Framers were of similar opinion.[11] The separation of powers and the institution of checks and balances, Alexander Hamilton asserted, "are means, and powerful means, by which the excellencies of republican government may be retained and its imperfections lessened or avoided."[12]

Historian Gordon S. Wood has observed: "Perhaps no principle of American constitutionalism has attracted more attention than that of separation of powers. It has in fact come to define the very character of the American political system."[13] Separation of powers requires the judiciary to engage in serious inquiry regarding whether the legislature or executive has infringed or denied liberty. Under the separation system, no branch has power to oppress the people, and each branch has some authority over the other branches to prevent this from occurring. Government was intended to function within these restraints. Indeed, Chief Justice John Marshall asserted that his Court "never sought to enlarge the judicial power beyond its proper bounds, nor feared to carry it to the fullest extent that duty required."[14]

A major objective both of England's unwritten constitution and America's written one is to preserve liberty by denying government the power to enact oppressive legislation. English-speaking people trace their liberties to the Magna Carta, which deprived the king and his agents of all *arbitrary* power over life, liberty, and property.[15] This understanding was secured over the years by many acts of Parliament and by the judiciary in the common law. With the advent of parliamentary supremacy, the people believed that English custom and tradition would protect their liberties. As Supreme Court Justice Bradley once dramatically explained: "England has no written constitution, it is true; but it has an unwritten one, resting on the acknowledged, and frequently declared, privileges of parliament and the people, to violate which in any material respect would produce a revolution in an hour."[16]

The English solution was not acceptable in the New World. When they became independent, individual states rejected the English system of parliamentary supremacy in favor of a separation-of-powers system, making the creation, implementation, and enforcement of laws a shared responsibility for the legislative, executive, and judicial branches. By the time the Constitutional Convention of 1787 was convened, the principle of separating governmental powers had long been established in North America.

Framers of state constitutions objected to parliamentary government primarily in the belief that it was not consistent with human liberty. They harbored serious apprehensions and misgivings about governmental power and insisted on dispersing and confining it.

Recent historical analysis of the Revolutionary period confirms that the colonists greatly feared and distrusted government. In *Ideological Origins of the American Revolution,* historian Bernard Bailyn discusses the philosophy of those who inspired the Revolution.[17] He is convinced that fear of a comprehensive conspiracy against liberty lay at the heart of American Revolutionary thought. For protection against this conspiracy, many looked for guidance to the advocates of a new liberty that espoused natural rights and sought elimination of institutions and practices that harbored despotism. The key concepts were natural rights, the contractual basis of government, the uniqueness of English liberty, and the framing of constitutions founded on dispersed authority. Government was thought to be by its nature hostile to human liberty and happiness, and especially susceptible to corruption and despotism. Therefore, it should be confined to serving those needs of the people that could not otherwise be satisfied.

The means for restricting governmental powers was through a constitution, which would define authority and create a separation and mixture of functions that would prevent any one group from gaining ascendancy. Creating this balance of forces was essential to preserve the capacity to exercise natural rights—those God-given, inalienable, and indefeasible rights founded on immutable maxims of reason and justice and inherent in all people by virtue of their humanity. Those rights were expressed—not created—in the English common law, in the statutory enactments of Parliament, and in the charters and privileges promulgated by the Crown. However, because not even these sources could exhaust the great treasure of human rights, they delineated the minimum, not the maximum, boundary of liberty. Government had to be so constituted that it could not infringe these rights, for the legitimacy of positive law (government-made law) rests on the degree to which it preserves natural rights.

While the passions may have subsided after the Revolutionary War was won and the explanations become more pragmatic, these libertarian ideas were prominent and influential during the time when the United States Constitution was drafted and ratified. It is evident from the ratification debates that the protection of the individual from government oppression was still the predominant political concern. Opponents of the proposed Constitution displayed great apprehension and antagonism toward centralized government, while the Constitution's supporters responded that the federal government would have no more power than necessary to secure the people from foreign and domestic perils.[18]

The leading theoretician among the Framers on the subject of separation of powers was James Madison. In replying to the concerns of the Constitution's opponents about excessive government powers in the proposed Constitution, Madison devoted five *Federalist Papers* to discussing and explaining the Constitution's separationist elements.[19] The separation of powers consisted of two parts: first, the division of functions; and second, checks and balances held by each branch with respect to the others. Responding to attacks on the proposed Constitution, Madison asserted: "Were the federal Constitution, therefore, really chargeable with this accumulation of power, or with a mixture of powers, having a dangerous tendency to such an accumulation, no further arguments would be necessary to inspire a universal reprobation of the system."[20] An opponent of majority rule, Madison extolled the separation principle: "No political truth is certainly of greater intrinsic value, or is stamped with the authority of more enlightened patrons of liberty. . . ."[21]

> The accumulation of all powers, legislative, executive, and judiciary, in the same hands, whether of one, a few, or many, and whether hereditary, self appointed, or elective, may justly be pronounced the very definition of tyranny.[22]

Protection of the separation principle would not only be accomplished by the legal text but also "by so contriving the interior structure of the government as that its several constituent parts may, by their mutual relations, be the means of keeping each other in their proper places."[23]

> But the great security against a gradual concentration of the several powers in the same department consists in giving to those who administer each department the necessary constitutional means and personal motives to resist encroachments of the others. The provision for defense must in this, as in all other cases, be made commensurate to the danger of attack. Ambition must be made to counteract ambition. The interest of the man must be connected with the constitutional rights of the place. . . . In framing a government which is to be administered by men over men, the great difficulty lies in this: you must first enable the government to control the governed; and in the next place oblige it to control itself. A dependence on the people is, no doubt, the primary control on the government; but experience has taught mankind the necessity of auxiliary precautions.[24]

Under separation, government power would be used to control government power. As previously noted, Madison was particularly concerned about legislative excesses[25] because "[i]n republican government, the legislative authority necessarily predominates."[26] And the experience in this regard had been very poor. The legislature "was the real source of danger to the American Constitution [necessitating] giving every defensive authority to the other departments that was consistent with republican principles."[27] Madison rejected majority rule as a matter of principle. "In fact, it is only re-establishing, under another name and more specious form, force as a matter of right."[28] In a letter to Jefferson, he asserted that the invasion of private rights is chiefly to be apprehended "from acts in which the Government is the mere instrument of the major number of the constituents."[29]

According the legislature unlimited power, Madison wrote, violated a fundamental principle of a free society:

> No man is allowed to be a judge in his own cause, because his interest would certainly bias his judgment, and, not improbably, corrupt his integrity. With equal, nay with greater reason, a body of men are unfit to be both judges and parties at the same time; yet what are many of the most important acts of legislation but so many judicial determinations, not indeed concerning the rights of single persons, but concerning the rights of large bodies of citizens? And what are the different classes of legislators but advocates and parties to the causes which they determine?[30]

In his farewell address, President George Washington lauded the separation of powers and urged the country to reject consolidation of powers since it would create "a real despotism":

> But let there be no change [by] usurpation; for though this, in one instance, may be the instrument of good, it is the customary weapon by which free governments are destroyed. The precedent must always greatly overbalance in permanent evil any partial or transient benefit which the use can at any time yield.[31]

There are numerous provisions in the U.S. Constitution that are intended to be used by the branches to confine the exercise of government power. The objective is to secure what the Preamble refers to as "the Blessings of Liberty." This, after all, is the basis for the rejection of parliamentary government, as Chief Justice Warren Burger explained nearly two hundred years after the framing of the Constitution:

> The choices we discern as having been made in the Constitutional Convention impose burdens on governmental processes that often seem clumsy, inefficient, even unworkable, but those hard choices were consciously made by men who had lived under a form of government that permitted arbitrary governmental acts to go unchecked. . . . With all the obvious flaws of delay, untidiness, and potential for abuse, we have not yet found a better way to preserve freedom than by mak-

ing the exercise of power subject to the carefully crafted restraints spelled out in the Constitution.[32]

Measures that are oppressive are outside of the government's authority, since, to borrow from John Locke, "[b]y this breach of Trust they *forfeit the Power,* the People had put in their hands, for quite contrary ends. . . ."[33] In addition, reducing government power is pragmatically rewarding, for it enables and encourages the people, as the primary source of creativity, innovation, and productivity, to advance the society.[34]

Madison supported the separation of powers in part because of his serious doubts about the wisdom and competence of government to advance human welfare. He was not very disturbed that the separation of powers would at times impede governmental finality and cause deadlock among the branches. He was a great proponent of individual liberty both for philosophical and pragmatic reasons, as the following quotations concerning the commercial area illustrate:

> [D]emocracies have ever been spectacles of turbulence and contention; have ever been incompatible with personal security or the rights of property; and have in general been as short in their lives as they have been violent in their deaths.[35]

> Government is instituted to protect property of every sort; as well that which lies in the various rights of individuals, as that which the term particularly expresses. This being the end of government, that alone is a *just* government, which *impartially* secures to every man, whatever is his *own.* . . .[36]

> That is not a just government, nor is property secure under it, where arbitrary restrictions, exemptions, and monopolies deny to part of its citizens that free use of their faculties, and free choice of their occupations, which not only constitute their property in the general sense of the word; but are the means of acquiring property strictly so called. . . .[37]

> I own myself the friend to a very free system of commerce, and hold it as a truth, that commercial shackles are generally unjust, oppressive, and unpolitic; it is also a truth, that if industry and labor are left to take their own course, they will generally be directed to those objects which are the most productive, and this in a more certain and direct manner than the wisdom of the most enlightened Legislature could point out.[38]

Madison was far from alone in fearing majoritarian power.[39] James Wilson, an influential Framer, expressed a common belief that after the destruction of royal supremacy in England, "a more pure and unmixed tyranny sprang up in the parliament than had been exercised by the monarch."[40]

Alexander Hamilton was concerned about the dangers an unlimited legislature posed for a society:

Are not popular assemblies subject to the impulses of rage, resentment, jealousy, avarice, and of other irregular and violent propensities? Is it not well known that their determinations are often governed by a few individuals in whom they place confidence, and are, of course, liable to be tinctured by the passions and views of those individuals?[41]

Only the judiciary was in a position to secure the constitution.

The complete independence of the courts of justice is peculiarly essential in a limited Constitution. By a limited Constitution, I understand one which contains certain specified exceptions to the legislative authority; such, for instance, as that it shall pass no bills of attainder, no *ex post facto* laws, and the like. Limitations of this kind can be preserved in practice no other way than through the medium of the courts of justice, whose duty it must be to declare all acts contrary to the manifest tenor of the Constitution void. Without this, all the reservations of particular rights or privileges would amount to nothing.[42]

Limiting the legislature could hardly have been a difficult proposition for Framers who, in keeping with the general consensus of the time, were strongly supportive of property rights; the viability of the national government which the Framers contemplated required that the legislature's powers over property be substantially limited. This distrust of government obviously was not confined to the right to property. According to Charles Grove Haines, in his authoritative work on judicial review, a commonly held belief in 1787 was that the greatest peril to liberty in all of its forms comes from the expanding powers of legislative bodies:

[T]here was more concern as to the restrictions under which governments should operate than as to the functions to be performed. Governments were to be prohibited from interfering with freedom of person, security of property, freedom of speech and of religion. The guaranty of liberty was, therefore, to give the rulers as little as possible and then to surround them with numerous restrictions — to balance power against power.[43]

II. The Judiciary's Duty to Protect Liberty

In practice, the major restraint on government authority in a separation-of-powers system is the judiciary. Over the last two centuries, the question has often arisen of how much power the Framers of the Constitution envisioned the Supreme Court would possess in the cause of protecting liberty. Was the Court's power confined to construing the text of the Constitution, or could the Court go beyond the text when it thought liberty imperiled? In *Federalist No.*

78, Hamilton spelled out an answer. Not only was the judiciary the guardian of the stated liberties—which were few at the time, inasmuch as the Bill of Rights had not been adopted—but it was also the guardian of others not stated. Hamilton asserted that the judiciary had an obligation to preserve liberty, including those aspects of it that were not specified in the Constitution:

> This independence of the judges is equally requisite to guard the Constitution and the rights of individuals from the effects of those ill humors which the arts of designing men, or the influence of particular conjunctures, sometimes disseminate among the people themselves, and which, though they speedily give place to better information, and more deliberate reflection, have a tendency, in the meantime, to occasion dangerous innovations in the government, and serious oppressions of the minor party in the community. . . .
>
> But it is not with a view to infractions of the Constitution only that the independence of the judges may be an essential safeguard against the effects of occasional ill humors in the society. These sometimes extend no farther than to the injury of the private rights of particular classes of citizens, by unjust and partial laws. Here also the firmness of the judicial magistracy is of vast importance in mitigating the severity and confining the operation of such laws.[44]

Thus, under Hamilton's analysis, the Supreme Court is empowered to "mitigat[e] the severity and confin[e] the operation" of "unjust and partial laws," as well as to protect against "dangerous innovations in the government, and serious oppressions of the minor party in the community." Final judgment over unjust and oppressive measures rests with the judiciary and not the legislature. By this measure, the Court could invalidate those legislative measures condemned by Blackstone ("wanton and causeless" restraints) and Coke ("against common right and reason").[45] Hamilton asserted that in

> the form of this government, and in the mode of legislation, you find all the checks which the greatest politicians and the best writers have ever conceived. . . . This organization is so complex, so skillfully contrived, that it is next to impossible that an impolitic or wicked measure should pass the scrutiny with success. . . .[46]

Other of Hamilton's writings reveal that he accepted the idea that the Constitution protected unenumerated rights. He believed in natural rights, and his strong endorsement of the proposed Constitution suggests that it was satisfactory in this respect. He wrote in 1774:

> The sacred rights of mankind are not to be rummaged for, among old parchments, or musty records. They are written, as with a sunbeam, in the whole volume of human nature, by the hand of the divinity itself; and can never be erased or obscured.[47]

Subsequently, in 1796, Hamilton in his capacity as a private attorney wrote that natural law was a decisive consideration in determining whether purchasers of land in good faith were protected under the Constitution from the Georgia legislature's attempted revocation of their title:

> Without pretending to judge of the original merits or demerits of the purchasers, it may be safely said to be a contravention of the first principles of natural justice and social policy, without any judicial decision of facts, by a positive act of the legislature, to revoke a grant of property regularly made for valuable consideration under legislative authority, to the prejudice even of third persons on every supposition innocent of the alleged fraud or corruption. . . .[48]

In his writings in *The Federalist Papers,* Madison did not discuss specifically the judiciary as the protector of individual rights. He condemned the failings of legislatures and considered the executive and judiciary departments as restraints on legislative usurpations: "[T]he success of the [legislative] usurpation will depend on the executive and judiciary departments, which are to expound and give effect to the legislative acts."[49] He did not define usurpation. It surely meant violation of constitutional terms and provisions. It probably also included violation of natural rights. In *Federalist No. 44,* Madison displayed his belief in natural rights doctrine in the following passage:

> Bills of Attainder, *ex post facto* laws, and laws impairing the obligation of contracts, are contrary to the first principles of the social compact and to every principle of sound legislation. The two former are expressly prohibited by the declarations prefixed to some of the State constitutions, and all of them are prohibited by the spirit and scope of these fundamental charters.[50]

As would be expected from the discussion in Chapter 2, the natural law perspective pervaded the thinking of the Framers at the Constitutional Convention. When the prohibitions on bills of attainder and ex post facto laws were introduced, Oliver Ellsworth, a Connecticut delegate who later became Chief Justice of the U.S. Supreme Court, argued that these protections were superfluous, stating "there were no lawyer, no civilian who would not say that ex post facto laws were void of themselves."[51] James Wilson, who also later served on the Supreme Court, likewise opposed inserting the prohibitions, explaining that "[i]t will bring reflections on the Constitution—and proclaim that we are ignorant of the first principles of Legislation, or are constituting a Government which will be so."[52]

As a member of the First Congress, Framer Roger Sherman drafted a proposed bill of rights, a document that has just recently been discovered. It contained a "natural rights" provision: "The people have certain natural rights which are retained by them when they enter into Society." He then went on to name them (religion, property, expression, assembly, and others), and concluded: "Of these rights therefore they shall not be deprived by the Government of the United States."[53]

Madison, in presenting amendments to the Constitution in the First Congress—amendments that would be adopted with changes as the Bill of Rights—explained the role of the judiciary in guaranteeing them:

> If [these amendments] are incorporated into the Constitution, independent tribunals of justice will consider themselves in a peculiar manner the guardians of those rights; they will be an impenetrable bulwark against every assumption of power in the Legislative or Executive; they will be naturally led to resist every encroachment upon rights expressly stipulated for in the Constitution by the declaration of rights.[54]

Congressman Madison sought extensive protections for liberty, beyond those rights enumerated. He expressed concern that a bill of rights might not encompass protections for all the liberties of the people:

> It has been objected also against a bill of rights, that, by enumerating particular exceptions to the grant of power, it would disparage those rights which were not placed in that enumeration; and it might follow by implication, that those rights which were not singled out, were intended to be assigned into the hands of the General Government, and were consequently insecure. This is one of the most plausible arguments I have ever heard against the admission of a bill of rights into this system; but, I conceive, that it may be guarded against. I have attempted it, as gentlemen may see by turning to the last clause of the fourth resolution.[55]

The clause Madison refers to became, in time, the Ninth Amendment, and read initially in Madison's draft as follows:

> The exceptions here or elsewhere in the Constitution, made in favor of particular rights, shall not be so construed as to diminish the just importance of other rights retained by the people, or as to enlarge the powers delegated by the Constitution; but either as actual limitations of such powers, or as inserted merely for greater caution.[56]

The final form of the Ninth Amendment is essentially a shorter version of this provision: "The enumeration in the Constitution, of certain rights, shall not be construed to deny or disparage others retained by the people."[57]

Madison's language that the judiciary "will be an impenetrable bulwark against every assumption of power in the Legislative or Executive," together with his view that the Constitution provides very broad protection for freedom, reveal that his position on the judicial power was not essentially different from

Hamilton's. Neither position was tied to specific constitutional language, but both gave the Court considerable discretion to eliminate oppressive laws and regulations.

Perhaps more than any other provision, the Ninth Amendment reveals the intended constitutional relationship between the government and the citizen under the original Constitution. The federal government was not granted authority to abridge the people's liberties, whether identified or not, except when so provided in the Constitution. The rights specifically protected in the original Constitution must have been those of greatest concern to the Framers. They expected that the judiciary would secure these few specified rights, as well as the greater number they did not specify. The Framers of the Bill of Rights followed the same approach. Under the pressures generated in the ratification proceedings and subsequently, they specified the rights they considered of greatest concern. Similarly, they anticipated that the judiciary would safeguard these, as well as those not named. The Ninth Amendment was the means they used for the latter purpose. Without this amendment, unenumerated rights might not have been protected, and freedom would have been less secure than under the original Constitution, which by limiting government powers safeguarded liberties whether specified or not.

III. The Legitimacy of Judicial Review

Over the years, some scholars have contended that judicial review is not legitimate because it is nowhere authorized in the Constitution. My response is that judicial review is inherent in a separation-of-powers government and does not require enumeration. Indeed, as previously set forth, it was the fear of legislative excesses and finality that largely led to the separation of powers. Political economist Friedrich Hayek wrote that "it must indeed seem curious that the need for courts which should declare laws unconstitutional should ever have been questioned."[58] As Chief Justice Marshall asserted, to allow Congress to be the judge of the constitutionality of its own acts "would be giving to the legislature a practical and real omnipotence, with the same breath which professes to restrict [its] powers within narrow limits. It is prescribing limits, and declaring that those limits may be passed at pleasure."[59]

Whatever remained of it, the argument that judicial review is not constitutionally authorized was demolished with the ratification of the Fourteenth Amendment. The first sentence of Section 1 of this amendment was adopted specifically to overcome the *Dred Scott* decision of the U.S. Supreme Court.[60] This decision declared that persons of African descent were not eligible to obtain state or federal citizenship. While some members of the Thirty-ninth Congress, which framed the Fourteenth Amendment in 1866, sought to curtail judicial review, no such action was taken, notwithstanding the strong feelings in Congress and the nation that the Supreme Court had seriously erred in the *Dred Scott* case.

Members of Congress who participated in the debates on the Fourteenth Amendment generally assumed that the meaning of the amendment would be interpreted by the courts, exercising the same power of judicial review as already existed. Thus, Senator Jacob Howard, who introduced the amendment in the U.S. Senate, stated that a prior judicial interpretation of the meaning of privileges and immunities gives "some intimation of what probably will be the opinion of the judiciary."[61]

The second sentence of Section 1 contains the privileges and immunities clause, the due process clause, and the equal protection clause, all of which are prohibitions on state actions and greatly increased the Constitution's guarantee of liberties, effectively according the Supreme Court much greater powers to monitor and invalidate state legislation than it possessed prior to the ratification of the amendment. The fact that the Thirty-ninth Congress considered the review power and did nothing to limit it, and then actually enlarged it by adopting the proposed Fourteenth Amendment, is persuasive evidence that the power was approved constructively by the Congress sitting as a constitution-writing body. Likewise, the ratification conventions in the states might have rejected the amendment for this reason, but none did. A case could be made that the Framers and the state conventions that ratified the original Constitution did not envision the review power for the Supreme Court. Clearly, that argument could not be made for those who framed and ratified the Fourteenth Amendment. They knowingly accepted the review powers of the Supreme Court, in the belief that the Court would do more good than evil.

Strictly construed, separation of powers in the Constitution prior to the adoption of the Fourteenth Amendment relates only to the three branches of the federal government and has no application to the states. Assuming that the separation-of-powers principle mandates judicial review over federal legislation, what permitted federal courts to exercise such power with respect to state legislation? In *Fletcher v. Peck* (1810), *Terrett v. Taylor* (1815), and *Wilkinson v. Leland* (1829) (all property cases discussed in Chapter 2), the early Supreme Court either by rule or dicta[62] asserted supremacy of the U.S. Supreme Court over oppressive state legislation. Doubts about the propriety of such judicial practices were resolved with the ratification of the Fourteenth Amendment in 1868. Section 1 was intended to provide citizens with the protections against the states that they possessed against the federal government.

My conclusion about the objectives of Section 1 is based on the debates on the Fourteenth Amendment in the Thirty-ninth Congress. With regard to interpreting the meaning of this section, the most important participants in these debates were Congressman John Bingham of Ohio, the principal author of the second sentence of Section 1; Senator Jacob Howard, who introduced the proposed amendment in the Senate; and Representative Thaddeus Stevens, who presented it to the House of Representatives.

Bingham explained Section 1 as follows:

> There was a want hitherto, and there remains a want now, in the Constitution of our country, which the proposed amendment will supply. What is that? It is the power in the people, the whole people of the United States, by express authority of the Constitution to do that by congressional enactment which hitherto they have not had the power to do, and have never even attempted to do; that is, to protect by national law the privileges and immunities of the citizens of the Republic and the inborn rights of every person within its jurisdiction whenever the same shall be abridged or denied by the unconstitutional acts of any State.[63]

In his speeches, Bingham used the term "inborn rights" to mean natural rights, and included all other guaranteed rights within the term "privileges and immunities."[64] Senator Howard, after quoting Justice Bushrod Washington's broad definition of the privileges and immunities provision in Article IV of the Constitution,[65] interpreted the privileges and immunities clause of the proposed Fourteenth Amendment as follows:

> To these privileges and immunities [as set forth by Justice Washington], whatever they may be — for they are not and cannot be fully defined in their entire extent and precise nature — to these should be added the personal rights guarantied and secured by the first eight amendments of the Constitution; such as the freedom of speech and of the press; the right of the people peaceably to assemble and petition the Government for a redress of grievances, a right appertaining to each and all the people; the right to keep and to bear arms; the right to be exempted from the quartering of soldiers in a house without the consent of the owner; the right to be exempt from unreasonable searches and seizures, and from any search or seizure except by virtue of a warrant issued upon a formal oath or affidavit; the right of an accused person to be informed of the nature of the accusation against him, and his right to be tried by an impartial jury of the vicinage; and also the right to be secure against excessive bail and against cruel and unusual punishments.
>
> Now, sir, here is a mass of privileges, immunities, and rights, some of them secured by the second section of the fourth article of the Constitution, which I have recited, some by the first eight amendments of the Constitution. . . . The great object of the first section of this amendment is, therefore, to restrain the power of the States and compel them at all times to respect these great fundamental guarantees.[66]

Representative Stevens asserted that Section 1 applied protections identified in the Declaration of Independence and contained in the Constitution to the states:

The first section prohibits the States from abridging the privileges and immunities of citizens of the United States, or unlawfully depriving them of life, liberty, or property, or of denying to any person within their jurisdiction the "equal" protection of the laws.

I can hardly believe that any person can be found who will not admit that every one of these provisions is just. They are all asserted, in some form or other, in our declaration or organic law. But the Constitution limits only the action of Congress and is not a limitation on the States. This amendment supplies that defect and allows Congress to correct the unjust legislation of the States. . . .[67]

Inasmuch as there was no serious disagreement in the debates of the Thirty-ninth Congress among the Fourteenth Amendment's proponents about the meanings given by Bingham, Howard, and Stevens to Section 1, the foregoing excerpts can be regarded as reasonably accurate interpretations. The conclusion is warranted that the purpose of Section 1 was to accord citizens of and other persons legally within the United States the same protections from the state governments that they enjoyed from the federal government.[68]

IV. Protecting Enumerated and Unenumerated Liberties

If, in its initial years, the federal judiciary were confined to protecting enumerated liberties, its members would have enjoyed considerable leisure. Only a small number of liberties are protected in the original Constitution. However, the absence of personal protections was not regarded as a decisive factor in determining the authority of the proposed government. Madison believed that the Constitution would never have been ratified if the people had believed that all unstated liberties were totally under the control of the federal government.[69]

According to the Federalists (supporters of the Constitution), the proposed national government was one of limited and enumerated powers; it possessed only those powers specifically vested in it. Theophilus Parsons of Massachusetts, a leading Federalist, who was later to become Chief Justice of Massachusetts, asserted that the Antifederalist fears of a powerful national government were groundless, since "[n]o power . . . was given to Congress to infringe on any one of the natural rights of the people by this Constitution; and, should they attempt it without constitutional authority, the act would be a nullity and could not be enforced."[70] Madison agreed: "[E]very power not granted thereby [i.e., by the Constitution] remains with the people, and at their will."[71]

The Federalists contended that the national government was so limited in power that a bill of rights was unnecessary; moreover, an enumeration of specific rights might be harmful because, first, it would imply the existence of power where there was none, and second, it might not list all rights that were protected, to the detriment of those omitted. In *Federalist No. 84,* Alexander

Hamilton argued against any need for including a bill of rights in the Constitution. He asserted that the proposed Constitution was intended to regulate not personal and private concerns, but rather, the nation's general political interests. Unlike the situation in England, under the U.S. Constitution, "the people surrender nothing; and as they retain everything they have no need of particular reservations." Therefore, a bill of rights was superfluous. Such a bill might even be dangerous, Hamilton thought, because it "would contain various exceptions to powers which [were] not granted," and to this extent would furnish a "colorable pretext" for claiming more than was granted—possibly by those disposed to usurpation.[72] Indeed, for Hamilton the Constitution is a bill of rights:[73] Congress has no authority to oppress the people, and the judiciary is obligated to annul measures that do this.

The ratification arguments over the protection of press freedom provide an illustration of the function the judiciary would exercise in securing liberties. Hamilton wrote in *Federalist No. 84* that there was no need to be concerned about securing freedom of the press, inasmuch as the Constitution does not grant the government any power to restrain it.[74] Does this mean, then, that as far as the national government is concerned, freedom of the press is absolute, and not subject to any restraint? James Wilson, a member of the Constitutional Convention, explained during the ratification debates that freedom of the press was subject to the powers of government under the common law, which were then considerable.[75] In other words, the national government had no power to diminish freedom of the press as the term was defined under the common law.

From this example, it is apparent that the judiciary would have a large role in defining and protecting freedom, not an unusual role for judges at the time of the framing of the Constitution. In that period, common-law tradition espoused the progressive enlargement of the people's liberties. In applying the common law, judges changed it continually pursuant to new understandings and conditions. From the earliest years of the English state, judges and Parliament created and steadily expanded common-law protections; while at one time only the meager rudiments of criminal procedure were required, by Blackstone's day "absolute rights" to life, liberty, and property were acknowledged.

When the Constitution was framed, the judiciary was highly regarded as a guardian of individual rights. Hamilton praised the American judiciary: "The benefits of the integrity and moderation of the judiciary have already been felt in more States than one; and though they may have displeased those whose sinister expectations they have disappointed, they must have commanded the esteem and applause of all the virtuous and disinterested."[76] For many Americans, the unwritten English constitution, which consisted principally of common-law rights, provided a great measure of human freedom. As historian Gordon S. Wood has put it, "what made their Revolution seem so unusual [was that] they revolted not against the English constitution but on behalf of it."[77]

Judicial review arrived at the federal level with Chief Justice John Marshall's unanimous opinion in *Marbury v. Madison* (1803), in which he ruled that the Supreme Court had the power to invalidate a congressional statute that violated the terms of the Constitution. Marshall applied customary rules of statutory construction to the Constitution, similar to what he would have done if a legislative act were involved. Once he resolved the issue of judicial review, there was nothing extraordinary about the process he employed in interpreting the constitutional provision in question.

However, another approach to constitutional construction already existed. Some state courts reviewed the validity of legislation on the basis of natural and common-law principles.[78] At the federal level, Justice William Paterson in *Vanhorne's Lessee v. Dorrance* (1795), previously discussed in Chapter 2, invoked natural law to protect property rights on the basis that the preservation of property is the primary object of the social compact. In the 1798 case of *Calder v. Bull*, Justice Samuel Chase presented the theory of constitutional government—consistent with the Federalists' position in the ratification debates on the limitations of the federal government—under which legislatures were devoid of authority to deprive people of their natural rights:

> I cannot subscribe to the omnipotence of a state legislature, or that it is absolute and without control; although its authority should not be expressly restrained by the constitution, or fundamental law, of the state. The people of the United States erected their constitutions or forms of government, to establish justice, to promote the general welfare, to secure the blessings of liberty, and to protect their persons and property from violence. The purposes for which men enter into society will determine the nature and terms of the social compact; and as they are the foundation of the legislative power, they will decide what are the proper objects of it. The nature, and ends of legislative power will limit the exercise of it. . . . There are acts which the federal, or state legislature cannot do, without exceeding their authority. There are certain vital principles in our free republican governments, which will determine and overrule an apparent and flagrant abuse of legislative power. . . . An act of the legislature (for I cannot call it a law), contrary to the great first principles of the social compact, cannot be considered a rightful exercise of legislative authority.[79]

> A law that punished a citizen for an innocent action . . . ; a law that destroys or impairs the lawful private contracts of citizens; a law that makes a man a judge in his own cause; or a law that takes property from A. and gives it to B.: it is against all reason and justice, for a people to intrust a legislature with such powers; and therefore, it cannot be presumed that they have done it. The genius, the nature, and the spirit of our state governments, amount to a prohibition of such acts of legislation; and the general principles of law and reason forbid them.[80]

In the same case, Justice James Iredell wrote an opinion rejecting Chase's position that a legislative act against natural justice is void. According to

Iredell, only an act of the legislature that exceeds its "marked and settled boundaries" is void. However, Chase tied constitutional protections to the specific purposes for which legislatures were created in the United States, seemingly a smaller limitation on the legislature than natural rights would be, although some might argue the two are the same, since both theories would not protect oppressive laws.[81] This debate between Chase and Iredell has continued among other justices and commentators throughout the existence of the Constitution.[82] The United States today is one of the freest countries in the world due in large part to the fact that it has protected individual rights far beyond the limitations that Iredell sought to place on legislatures. To this extent, the Framers' objective of confining government power has been achieved.

Thus, with the decision in *Marbury,* two theories of interpretation existed in cases where legislation was challenged as being unconstitutional. First, the judiciary was supposed to annul laws contrary to the meaning of constitutional provisions; and second, the judiciary could strike down oppressive legislation without reference to constitutional text. *Marbury v. Madison* is an example of the first power. Marshall ruled that Congress could not supplement the original jurisdiction accorded to the Supreme Court in Article III of the Constitution, and that therefore the statutory provision authorizing the Court to entertain mandamus suits (i.e., suits requesting the Court to issue an order to another government agency) as an original matter was invalid. The Court thereby refused to enforce Marbury's right to serve as a justice of the peace—a position, Marshall acknowledged, to which Marbury had been properly appointed. *Calder* and *Vanhorne's Lessee* are examples of the second power.

The Supreme Court applied both theories in *Fletcher v. Peck* (1810) per Justice Marshall, and applied the *Calder* perspective in Justice Joseph Story's opinions in *Terrett v. Taylor* (1815) and *Wilkinson v. Leland* (1829). (These opinions were discussed in Chapter 2.) In 1823, Justice Bushrod Washington attempted to import the natural rights doctrine into the Constitution by way of the privileges and immunities clause of Article IV, Section 2. In *Corfield v. Coryell,*[83] the first federal interpretation of the clause, Washington held that it protects those privileges "which are, in their nature, fundamental; which belong, of right, to the citizens of all free governments. . . ."[84] He declared that the federal Constitution guarantees nonresidents' fundamental rights against encroachment by a state.[85]

Chancellor James Kent supported Justice Chase's position on constitutional government, stating in an opinion he wrote in 1811 as Chancellor of New York that judges were not to be confined by the rights enumerated in constitutions:

> Our Constitutions do not admit the power assumed by the Roman Prince and the principle we are considering [no retroactive laws] is now to be regarded as sacred. It is not pretended that we have any express constitutional provisions on

the subject; nor have we any for numerous other rights dear alike to freedom and justice.[86]

In his *Commentaries on American Law* (1826), Kent wrote that a statute "affecting and changing vested rights is very generally considered in this as founded on unconstitutional principles, and consequently inoperative and void." By "unconstitutional," Kent did not mean contrary to the provisions of the document, but rather, contrary to what he considered to be general limitations implicit in all free governments—limitations based on natural rights and the nature of the social compact.[87]

In these observations, Kent was expressing views prominent among jurists. According to Edward Corwin, during the initial period of federal constitutional history, which closed about 1830, leading judges and lawyers accepted the ideas of natural rights and the social compact as bases for constitutional decisions.[88] Professor J. A. C. Grant reports that between 1816 and 1860, state high courts or federal courts in New York, New Jersey, New Hampshire, Georgia, Maryland, Arkansas, and Iowa held or expressed the belief that natural justice required payment of compensation when private property was taken for public use.[89]

V. Contemporary Decisions Expanding Freedom

An examination of contemporary U.S. Supreme Court decisions protecting liberties reveals that, like its predecessors, the twentieth-century Court has engaged in two kinds of inquiry: first, whether the law in question violates the language or meaning of provisions of the Constitution, and second, whether the law is oppressive.[90] Chief Justice Marshall applied the first inquiry to determine constitutionality in *Marbury,* and Justice Chase relied on the second in *Calder.* "It is, emphatically, the province and duty of the judicial department, to say what the law is," asserted Marshall, which in *Marbury* meant interpreting constitutional text and meaning.[91] By contrast, Justice Chase did not feel bound by the language of the Constitution; he said that the purposes for which men enter into society will determine the limits of the legislative power, even if not expressed. To maintain that the legislature has the power to oppress the people, if not expressly restrained, would be contrary to reason, "a political heresy altogether inadmissible in our free republican government."[92]

These early views of the judicial responsibility have prevailed throughout the Supreme Court's existence. By its rulings and dicta, the U.S. Supreme Court has acknowledged that its obligation to preserve liberty requires it to strike down laws that are oppressive regardless of whether the Constitution's text requires such action. Accordingly, the Court presently guarantees liberties which are not enumerated and has expanded the meaning of enumerated liberties far beyond original understanding.

Consider the history of free expression in the United States. Although noted for his support of free expression, Justice Oliver Wendell Holmes held in a 1907 opinion that the constitutional guarantees of speech and press were quite limited:

> [T]he main purpose of such constitutional protections is "to prevent all such previous restraints upon publications as had been practiced by other governments," and they do not prevent the subsequent punishment of such as may be contrary to the public welfare [citations omitted]. The preliminary freedom extends as well to the false as to the true; the subsequent punishment may extend as well to the true as to the false. This was the law of criminal libel apart from statute in most cases, if not in all [citations omitted].[93]

Holmes cited Blackstone in support of his ruling. Blackstone modestly construed freedom of the press:

> The liberty of the press is indeed essential to the nature of a free state; but this consists in laying no *previous* restraints upon publications, and in freedom from censure from criminal matter when published. Every freeman has an undoubted right to lay what sentiments he pleases before the public; to forbid this is to destroy the freedom of the press; but if he publishes what is improper, mischievous or illegal he must take the consequences of his own temerity.[94]

Holmes interpreted the First Amendment on the basis of the common-law definition of free press at the time the amendment was ratified. He was following an accepted form of inquiry for determining the meaning of a law. Subsequently, he turned sharply from this approach and interpreted the First Amendment by reasoning based on the importance of the "marketplace of ideas" both to the individual and to society. This interpretation resulted in the celebrated "clear and present danger" test. There is little connection between the First Amendment's textual meaning and the "clear and present danger" test:

> The question in every case is whether the words used are used in such circumstances and are of such a nature as to create a clear and present danger that they will bring about the substantive evils that Congress has a right to prevent. It is a question of proximity and degree.[95]

Holmes believed it was oppressive for government to punish expression unless it produced great harm. Once the Court adopted the "clear and present danger" test, it rarely looked back to original meaning, and continued instead to broaden the Constitution's protection of expression. In 1964, the Court threw out the common law of libel and slander as it had existed when the Constitution was ratified and for a long time after. The Court substituted instead a modified interpretation of defamation intended to encourage public debate that is "uninhibited, robust, and wide-open," even if it meant at times the publication of sharp attacks on government and public officials without penalty for untruths.[96] The Court has also enlarged the scope of the expression guarantee. Although the language of the First Amendment applies only to Congress, in expression cases the Court has effectively substituted the word "government" in place of "Congress" and applies the protection as against all the branches of state and federal government.[97]

Under the *Brandenberg* test, the successor to the "clear and present danger" test, even the advocacy of force and violence is not necessarily wrongful under the First Amendment:

> [T]he constitutional guarantees of free speech and free press do not permit a State to forbid or proscribe advocacy of the use of force or of law violation except where such advocacy is directed to inciting or producing imminent lawless action and is likely to incite or produce such action.[98]

Thus, the advocacy is not punishable unless it is likely to incite or produce imminent lawless action. A controversial flag-burning case decided in 1989 illustrates the interpretation of these rules. The Supreme Court found that burning of the American flag to express condemnation of American society was not likely to incite or produce "imminent lawless action" and therefore constituted protected expression.[99]

There is little relationship between original understanding and contemporary interpretation of the expression guarantees of the First Amendment. But, of course, according to Justice Chase, among others, constitutional language was not decisive in determining the protection society should accord to critical liberties.

The U.S. Supreme Court has subscribed to and continues to subscribe to this position and routinely secures liberties nowhere mentioned in the Constitution. Consider another example in the area of expression. For those who insist on smoking-gun evidence to determine constitutional meaning, it is difficult to conclude that the Constitution secures speech intended to generate profits, which is referred to as commercial speech. That it did not secure such speech was the position of the United States Supreme Court until 1976, when it decided *Virginia State Board of Pharmacy v. Virginia Citizens Consumer Council, Inc.*[100] In this case, a Virginia statute provided that a pharmacist licensed in the state was guilty of unprofessional conduct if he or she advertised the price for any drugs dispensed only by prescription. The legal attack against the statute was brought by a number of prescription-drug consumers who claimed that they would greatly benefit if the prohibition were lifted and advertising freely allowed. The three plaintiffs included a Virginia resident who suffered from a disease that required her to take prescription drugs daily, a Virginia consumer organization, and the state's AFL-CIO.

Reversing its prior rulings, the Supreme Court held that the advertising ban violated freedom of expression, stating that the First Amendment's "protection . . . is to the communication, to its source and to its recipients both."[101] Explaining why this advertising warranted First Amendment protection, Justice Harry Blackmun wrote for the Court that Virginia's ban prevented consumers from learning about differences in the prices of prescription drugs, principally to the very serious disadvantage of older people, who are the biggest users of such drugs and who frequently subsist on modest fixed incomes. Because elderly and poor people are less mobile than the rest of the population, they cannot shop around for bargain prices. In the absence of advertising, pharmacists can charge relatively high prices, secure in the knowledge that many of their customers will not be able to learn that the cost is less elsewhere.[102]

Blackmun's opinion presented several arguments explaining that the ban on advertising prescription drugs operated oppressively:

> So long as we preserve a predominantly free enterprise economy, the allocation of our resources in large measure will be made through numerous private economic decisions. It is a matter of public interest that those decisions, in the aggregate, be intelligent and well informed. To this end, the free flow of commercial information is indispensable. . . . And if it is indispensable to the proper allocation of resources in a free enterprise system, it is also indispensable to the formation of intelligent opinions as to how that system ought to be regulated or altered. . . .
>
> . . . As to the particular consumer's interest in the free flow of commercial information, that interest may be as keen, if not keener by far, than his interest in the day's most urgent political debate. . . .[103]

With some exceptions, the Court has, over the years, followed this Virginia case. In *44 Liquormart, Inc. v. Rhode Island,* a 1996 case, the justices unanimously struck down Rhode Island's statute banning, except at the place of sale, advertising of the retail price of alcoholic beverages either by vendors or the communications media.[104] The purpose of the ban was to significantly reduce alcohol consumption. The Court held that Rhode Island had not produced evidentiary support to justify the prohibition on advertising. In his opinion, Justice John Paul Stevens, following Blackmun's lead, also rejected paternalistic governmental policies that prevent people from hearing truthful information that might not be good for them.[105] Instead, he championed freedom of the commercial marketplace:

> The First Amendment directs us to be especially skeptical of regulations that seek to keep people in the dark for what the government perceives to be their own

good. That teaching applies equally to state attempts to deprive consumers of accurate information about their chosen products.[106]

Consider some of the other unenumerated liberties the Court protects. Without basis in original meaning, and notwithstanding the furor raised in many quarters, the Court secured a pregnant woman's right to an abortion as part of the right of privacy, on the general theory that government's prohibition of this operation is oppressive. The Constitution does not enumerate either the right of privacy or the right of abortion. The Court found that severe mental detriment might occur to a pregnant woman who was not permitted to abort her fetus.[107]

In providing protection for freedom of mobility, which the Court has referred to as the right to travel, the Court asserted: "We have no occasion to ascribe the source of this right to travel interstate to a particular constitutional provision." The basis for protecting the right was that it "occupies a position fundamental to the concept of our Federal Union."[108] In the absence of strong justification, it is oppressive to deny a person freedom of mobility between the states of the Union.

The position that the Court's review powers are not confined to constitutional text is operative in gender-classification cases as well. When the Fourteenth Amendment was ratified in 1868, women enjoyed far fewer civil rights than men. Despite agitation by early feminists, the equal protection clause of that amendment was not intended to apply to gender. In 1971, in *Reed v. Reed,* the Supreme Court provided women substantial protection against preferential treatment for men.[109] To withstand constitutional challenge, classifications by gender must serve important governmental objectives and must be substantially related to the achievement of those objectives.[110] This test is without basis in the original meaning of the Fourteenth Amendment, yet it controls current interpretations.

The Supreme Court has also protected numerous other liberties—such as the right of association, the right to be presumed innocent, the right to be judged by a standard of proof beyond a reasonable doubt in a criminal trial, and the right to attend criminal trials—none of which are mentioned in the Constitution. The Court has created a very high standard of review, referred to as *strict scrutiny,* which is applicable to certain rights and legal classifications—a standard that is very difficult for legislatures to satisfy.

Clearly the U.S. Supreme Court has frequently provided protection for liberty without regard to constitutional language and original meaning. This practice is consistent with the objective of judicial review under the separation of powers—that is, with the objective of voiding measures of the legislature or executive that are oppressive to the people. Were the judiciary to be confined to textual meaning, the libertarian objectives of the Framers in creating a government based upon separation of powers would be only partially achieved.

The quintessential case on modern rights jurisprudence is *Griswold v. Connecticut* (1965), in which the Supreme Court found a right of privacy in the Constitution although it is nowhere listed.[111] This was a test case in which Griswold and others intentionally violated a Connecticut statute prohibiting any person from assisting another in the use of any drug or instrument for the purpose of preventing conception. According to the state, the purpose of the law was to discourage extramarital relations. Justice William Douglas wrote an opinion for the majority that he sought to confine to constitutional text and meaning. He began by condemning the Court's earlier activism on behalf of economic liberties as a violation of constitutional restraints on the judiciary. The Court had operated as a super-legislature, determining the wisdom, need, and propriety of economic and social laws. Douglas's ire was directed at the Supreme Court of the first four decades of the twentieth century, when it protected economic liberties under a broad interpretation of the two due process clauses of the Fifth and Fourteenth Amendments. He had long been a critic of these decisions.

The Connecticut law involved the intimate relationship between husband and wife, and there was no constitutional protection directly applicable to it. Douglas observed that a number of rights are judicially protected even though they are not mentioned in the Constitution. In each of these instances, the Court secured the rights as implicitly protected under an enumerated liberty. These decisions suggest, Douglas asserted, that specific guarantees in the Bill of Rights have penumbras "formed by emanations from those guarantees that give them life and substance."[112] Thus, while each guarantee provides particular protections, the First, Third, Fourth, and Fifth Amendments also create zones of privacy that would implicitly include marital privacy:

> The right of association [is] contained in the penumbra of the First Amendment. . . . The Third Amendment in its prohibition against the quartering of soldiers "in any house" in time of peace without the consent of the owner is another facet of that privacy. The Fourth Amendment explicitly affirms the "right of the people to be secure in their persons, houses, papers, and effects, against unreasonable searches and seizures." The Fifth Amendment in its Self-Incrimination Clause enables the citizen to create a zone of privacy which government may not force him to surrender to his detriment. . . .[113]

The Framers did not list a right of sexual privacy, but it "concerns a relationship lying within the zone of privacy created by several fundamental constitutional guarantees,"[114] and was consistent with their constitutional aspirations. Douglas cited the Ninth Amendment as providing the Court with discretion to protect unenumerated rights: "The enumeration in the Constitution, of certain rights, shall not be construed to deny or disparage others retained by the people."

Justice Douglas found that Connecticut had excessively invaded this liberty. The application of the law to married people was not likely to significantly achieve the legislative purpose of discouraging sexually promiscuous activity. This purpose could be served with less destructive impact on the marriage relationship by a law regulating the sale or manufacture of contraceptives.

Douglas's opinion can be divided into two parts. First, he reasoned that the Constitution protected the privacy of the marriage relationship. This was largely a subjective exercise which reached a conclusion about which there is room for debate and for a sincere difference of opinion. Second, he found that the law made little sense. The statute was a serious invasion of marital privacy that swept unnecessarily broadly, "reaching far beyond the evil sought to be dealt with and intruding upon the privacy of all married couples."[115] A cannon had been used to destroy a fly. All married people should not be deprived of their liberty in order to prevent promiscuity, mostly by unmarried people. Those who have done no wrong should not be penalized. (Moreover, Connecticut already had statutes prohibiting adultery and fornication.) This cause-and-effect reasoning is less debatable than the "emanations" and "penumbras" part of the opinion. Determining whether or not a close relationship exists between a law and its purpose—what is referred to as a means-ends inquiry—is a fairly objective endeavor, much more so than ascertaining unenumerated rights. This means-ends inquiry can be used to analyze laws limiting almost any kind of human activity, and need not be coupled with special constitutional protection for the activity in question. Means-ends analysis is common in constitutional rights jurisprudence and will be extensively considered in the discussion of the *Nollan* and *Dolan* land-use cases in Chapter 5.

A law that does not narrowly achieve the objective for the sake of which the legislature passed it imposes illegitimate restraints on people's liberties. Blackstone condemned acts of Parliament that were contrary to reason,[116] and wrote that civil liberty "is no other than natural liberty so far restrained by human laws (and no farther) as is necessary and expedient for the general advantage of the publick. . . . [E]very wanton and causeless restraint of the will of the subject . . . is a degree of tyranny."[117]

In *Griswold v. Connecticut,* concurring justices applied the Ninth Amendment and the due process clause of the Fourteenth Amendment to find the law in question unconstitutional. But Justice Hugo Black dissented, accusing Douglas and his colleagues who formed the majority of undermining constitutional law by invoking natural law concepts extraneous to the Constitution: "I like my privacy as well as the next one, but I am nevertheless compelled to admit that government has a right to invade it unless prohibited by some specific constitutional provision." He cited and quoted favorably Justice Iredell's 1798 opinion in *Calder v. Bull* in support of his position.[118] Black's mistake, as I see it, is that he did not understand that as an overinclusive law, the Connecticut statute was not a legitimate restraint on liberty.[119] History reveals that the U.S. Supreme Court has been more favorable to the broad position on constitutional interpretation expressed by Justice Chase in *Calder* than the narrow one supported by Iredell.

As we have just seen, constitutional interpretation by the Court of First Amendment and other liberties of the person has been expansionist, and with good reason. The Framers intended it that way. Until very recently, however, that broad reading has not been accorded to property rights. This "double standard," as some critics have called it, is both perplexing and unjustified, as I shall argue. For, measured by the number of provisions protecting it, no liberty is more prominent in the United States Constitution than the right of private ownership. Experience throughout the world reveals that this liberty is of extraordinary importance to both the individual and society. In terms of constitutional interpretation, therefore, the Supreme Court clearly has the authority to protect property rights, just as it has exercised that power so vigilantly in defense of the other fundamental rights of life and liberty.

VI. Powers and Limitations

Under the separation of powers as supplemented by Section 1 of the Fourteenth Amendment, the judiciary has the duty to secure the liberties of citizens and persons legally residing in the country from abridgment by government. Inasmuch as the Constitution only enumerates liberties and does not define them, the Supreme Court has considerable discretion in ascertaining the activities they encompass. In addition, the broad language of the two due process clauses and the Ninth Amendment empowers the Court to protect liberties that are not enumerated in the Constitution.

It is apparent that the Constitution accords the judiciary vast powers to protect liberties. However, there are definite limitations on these powers as well:

1. The Supreme Court has no legislative or executive authority and must confine itself to monitoring the branches that have these powers. It must not interfere with the political processes of government, including spending and taxation policies and practices. All of these matters are reserved to the legislative and executive branches.

2. The Constitution must not be interpreted by the Court in a way that would protect harmful activities, such as criminal conduct, fraud, nuisances, defamation, obscenity, and highly provocative language.

3. Regulatory legislation should be upheld when its objective is legitimate, its restraints substantially achieve its objective, and its limitations do not compromise any specially protected constitutional guarantees.

In the subsequent portions of this book, particularly in Chapter 5, I will show that the Supreme Court has taken steps in recent years toward according property rights the kind of protection that falls clearly within these constitutional objectives and constraints. In other words, the Court has, at long last, made great strides toward overcoming its "double standard" of granting a lower level of protection to property rights than it grants to intellectual and political liberties.

My position is controversial, also, from the opposite perspective. I recognize that some distinguished commentators, Robert Bork among them, view the Supreme Court's expansionist rulings in defense of liberties quite differently. They believe that in going beyond constitutional text the Supreme Court has usurped the democratic rights of the majority. Not only should the Court refrain from protecting unenumerated liberties, they argue, but the Court should never have expanded the listed liberties to begin with. Indeed, Judge Bork favors a constitutional amendment making any federal or state court decision rescindable by a majority vote of each House of Congress.[120] However, I do not regard the constitutional role of the Supreme Court and other courts as subordinate to that of the legislature or executive, nor did the Framers. Each branch has its own functions and duties in the cause of preserving liberty. The system works best when all three are performing their proper functions.

Each of the branches has, over the years, exceeded its "rightful" powers under the Constitution on numerous occasions, and surely the Supreme Court is no exception. In my book *The Supreme Court's Constitution,* I criticized decisions of the Court that I considered wrongful interpretations of the Constitution. Here, too, I am critical of many other decisions. In Chapter 5, I will also describe serious abuses of rights by other governmental agencies, including the California Coastal Commission, the legislature of South Carolina, and the city council of Tigard, Oregon. I fear that property rights, among other rights, would be in grave danger in the absence of a vigorous Supreme Court exercising its power of judicial review. Like the various framers of our most important political documents—the original Constitution, the Bill of Rights, and Section 1 of the Fourteenth Amendment—I too fear the unchecked power of the majority.

4

Major Takings Cases Prior to 1987

The Supreme Court's takings jurisprudence prior to 1987, I shall argue, did not fulfill the Court's constitutional duty to secure property rights.[1] On issues relating to the regulation of property, the Court continued to apply case law that accorded great deference to government authority at the expense of liberty. In zoning cases, in particular, the holding of *Euclid v. Ambler,* decided in 1926,[2] made it very difficult for an owner to successfully challenge arbitrary and even capricious regulation.

The *Euclid* holding found support in *Mugler v. Kansas* (1887),[3] which spawned a line of cases that gave to the legislature the power to prevent or abate a use of property it considered offensive. In their early years, both English and American courts accorded an owner strong protection in the use of property except in the instance of a common-law nuisance. The theory was that no person has a right to use his property so as to create a nuisance, and consequently, that the government does not deprive an owner of anything when it enjoins a nuisance. Property rights advocates supported this rule on the basis that it guaranteed the ordinary and normal use of property. In the *Mugler* case, however, the Supreme Court enlarged the concept of harm, stating that "all property in this country is held under an implied obligation that the owner's use of it shall not be injurious to the community."[4] Subsequently, in *Miller v. Schoene* (1928), the Court asserted that where the public interest is involved, it should be preferred over a private property interest "to the extent even of [the private interest's] destruction."[5] The *Euclid, Mugler,* and *Schoene* decisions allowed the government to forbid or extinguish uses that it considered harmful or undesirable. In a memorable phrase from *Euclid*, a municipality had the power to prevent "a right thing in the wrong place, like a pig in the parlor instead of the barnyard."[6]

The ordinary and normal use of property was rendered insecure after these decisions. Many federal and state courts, taking their cue from the Supreme Court, concluded that almost any regulation of property that a state or munici-pality adopted was constitutionally valid. Then, in a 1980 zoning case, *Agins v. City of Tiburon,*[7] the Supreme Court seemed to want to curtail this passive ac-quiescence, setting forth rules on land-use regulation similar to those applica-ble to other protected rights. These rules appeared to have appreciably elevated the standard of scrutiny in land-use controversies, but the Court in *Agins* inter-preted the new rules at a level of scrutiny consistent with the old rules in *Eu-clid*. Understandably, the lower courts paid little attention and continued to up-hold land-use regulation under minimal scrutiny, as before.

For more than sixty years after the *Euclid* decision in 1926—during which time the Supreme Court expanded constitutional protections for the other lib-erties—the Court heard practically no property rights cases, and did little to bol-ster liberty when it deigned to hear such a case. But there were two exceptions worthy of mention. In *United States v. Causby* (1946),[8] the Court found that the United States government had imposed an easement on private property when its military aircraft repeatedly flew over the property at a height of eighty-three feet emitting bright lights and loud noises. It held that a taking of an interest in the property had occurred, rejecting the government's contention that the re-duction in value was consequential and therefore noncompensable.[9] According to this decision, a government action short of physical invasion can constitute a taking when it results in "as complete [a loss] as if the [government] had en-tered upon the surface of the land and taken exclusive possession of it."[10]

The other exception was *Loretto v. Teleprompter Manhattan CATV Corp.* (1982),[11] in which the Court found that a taking had occurred under a New York law requiring a landlord to allow a television cable company to install cable fa-cilities in a small space on the roof of his apartment building. The Court stated that a taking exists "when the 'character of the governmental action' . . . is a permanent physical occupation of property . . . without regard to whether the action achieves an important public benefit or has only minimal economic im-pact on the owner."[12] It makes no difference whether the state or, instead, a party authorized by the state, is the occupier.

Another noteworthy opinion supporting property rights, but this time in dis-sent, was that of Justice William Brennan, joined by three colleagues, in *San Diego Gas & Electric Co. v. San Diego,*[13] decided in 1981. The case involved an ordinance that designated most of the utility company's property as open space. The justice rejected the city's argument that invalidating the regulation without payment of monetary compensation is sufficient remedy for a taking. Brennan proposed a different rule:

> In my view, once a court establishes that there was a regulatory "taking," the Con-stitution demands that the government entity pay just compensation for the pe-

riod commencing on the date the regulation first effected the "taking," and ending on the date the government entity chooses to rescind or otherwise amend the regulation.[14]

Justice William Rehnquist voted with the majority on the procedural issue that decided the case, but in his opinion, he implied that he supported Brennan on the substantive issue of compensation, suggesting a possible future majority view on this issue.[15] A dissenting opinion does not, of course, constitute legal precedent. In this instance, however, it did reveal that a majority of the Court might be amenable to stronger protection for property rights should the right case come along.

In the balance of this chapter, I shall consider in greater detail the state of takings law prior to the new course that the Court would adopt in 1987. This chapter covers a time span of 115 years, from 1871 to 1986, and examines decisions which, in my view, were the most influential in shaping takings law as it stood on the cusp of the new era. As in other areas of constitutional law, the course of takings law was not smooth. This is to be expected, considering the many justices that served, the long span of time, and the changes that occurred in philosophical outlook and public opinion, and in the economic and social development of the country.

I. *Pumpelly v. Green Bay Co.*

I begin with an 1871 case, *Pumpelly v. Green Bay Co.*,[16] that was widely heralded as providing strong constitutional protection for property rights. The decision enlarged the meaning of a taking to include a physical invasion of private property by government, or its designee, that destroyed the property's value. Under authority of the State of Wisconsin, Green Bay Company had built a dam across Fox River, raising the level of Lake Winnebago and flooding the property of Pumpelly, who thereafter claimed compensation under the takings clause of the Wisconsin Constitution, which was similar in language to the federal version.[17]

The company conceded that Pumpelly's property had been flooded, but claimed that (1) the dam was authorized by statute and built in conformity with the requirements of existing law; (2) a takings claim was precluded by another law which provided the sole remedy for property flooded by dams; and (3) the damage was not compensable as a taking because it was the remote and consequential result of the government exercising its right to improve a navigable stream.

Furthermore, argued the company, it had not intentionally harmed Pumpelly or acted negligently. Pumpelly's lands were not taken or appropriated. They were only affected by the overflow occasioned by rising water in Lake Winnebago. The state was merely carrying out the will of the people as expressed in its laws. Not everyone will benefit from every law, and some will suffer various levels of loss. Moreover, if losses are to be compensated by the government, should not those who benefit be required to share their windfalls with the government?

The United States Supreme Court was not persuaded. Writing for the Court, Justice Samuel Miller asserted that the defendant raised no valid defense to the claim for compensation under Wisconsin's takings clause:

> It would be a very curious and unsatisfactory result, if in construing a provision of constitutional law, always understood to have been adopted for protection and security to the rights of the individual as against the government, and which has received the commendation of jurists, statesmen and commentators as placing the just principles of the common law on that subject beyond the power of ordinary legislation to change or control them, it shall be held that if the government refrains from the absolute conversion of real property to the uses of the public it can destroy its value entirely, can inflict irreparable and permanent injury to any extent, can, in effect, subject it to total destruction without making any compensation, because, in the narrowest sense of that word, it is not *taken* for the public use. Such a construction would pervert the constitutional provision into a restriction upon the rights of the citizen, as those rights stood at the common law, instead of the government, and make it an authority for invasion of private right under the pretext of the public good, which had no warrant in the laws or practices of our ancestors.[18]

The Court cited *Sinnickson v. Johnson*,[19] an 1839 case in which the state had given a company the right to build a dam across a stream causing water to overflow the plaintiff's land. Although New Jersey had no takings clause, the New Jersey Supreme Court held that the statute authorizing the work was no protection against the action for damages:

> This power to take private property reaches back of all constitutional provisions; and it seems to have been a settled principle of universal law that the right to compensation is an incident to the exercise of that power; that the one is inseparably connected with the other; that they may be said to exist, not as separate and distinct principles, but as parts of one and the same principle.[20]

The New Jersey court held that overflowing land by backing the water on it was a taking within the meaning of the principle. The U.S. Supreme Court also cited Chancellor James Kent's opinion in *Gardner v. Trustees of the Village of Newburgh* (1816), enjoining a city from diverting a stream that provided benefits for the plaintiff's property.[21] The New York Constitution had no takings clause, and the legislative act authorizing the diversion contained no provision for compensation. Even without an explicit takings clause and even though the diversion could be regarded as only a consequential injury, Chancellor Kent held it to be a clear principle of natural equity that the individual whose property is sacrificed must be indemnified.

Conceding that numerous state cases did support the Green Bay Company's position, and that the principle of no redress for "consequential injury to property of the individual arising from the prosecution of improvements of roads, streets, rivers, and other highways, for the public good" is a "sound one in its proper application," Justice Miller in *Pumpelly* criticized those decisions as having "gone to the uttermost limit of sound judicial construction in favor of this principle, and in some cases beyond it."[22]

The Court concluded its opinion with this statement: "[W]here real estate is actually invaded by superinduced additions of water, earth, sand, or other material, or by having any artificial structure placed on it, so as to effectually destroy or impair its usefulness, it is a taking, within the meaning of the Constitution."[23]

The importance of *Pumpelly* is that it broadened the meaning of takings to include a permanent physical invasion, a concept which is now firmly entrenched in takings law. It has been extended in *Loretto* (the 1982 New York City cable TV case) to include an occupation as slight as one and one-half cubic feet.[24] In 1987, the Supreme Court asserted that the physical occupation concept even applied to the imposition of a permanent public easement enabling people to walk along a beach.[25] Subsequent to *Loretto*, the Court in *Lucas v. South Carolina Coastal Council* (1992) reemphasized that a regulation could have the same impact as a physical invasion.[26] As is evident from the *Mugler, Euclid,* and *Schoene* cases, discussed in Sections II, IV, and VI of this chapter, the Supreme Court was not always so interested in protecting property rights.

II. *Mugler v. Kansas*

In 1887, sixteen years after *Pumpelly,* the Supreme Court handed down an opinion giving great deference to government regulation of property. In *Mugler v. Kansas,*[27] the Court considered whether a state law prohibiting the manufacture of alcoholic beverages violated the due process clause of the Fourteenth Amendment when the law was enforced, without compensation, against a business engaged in the forbidden purpose. Mugler had purchased property and erected a brewery in 1877 at a cost of $10,000. In 1879, the Kansas legislature referred to the voters a constitutional amendment to prohibit the manufacture and sale of alcoholic beverages other than for medicinal or scientific purposes. The amendment passed in 1880, by a margin of 52.5 percent to 47.5

percent. Mugler was later convicted for violating an 1881 statute adopted pursuant to the public vote. Although the prohibition law destroyed the value of Mugler's brewery and reduced the value of his entire property from $10,000 to $2,500, the U.S. Supreme Court would hold that no compensation was owed, because the state was merely exercising its police power, that is, its inherent power to protect the public's health, safety, and morals.

Mugler argued that the law was invalid for two reasons. First, it banned the manufacture of alcohol for personal use. "No convention or legislature has the right under our form of government, to prohibit any citizen from manufacturing for his own use, or for export or storage, any article of food or drink not endangering or affecting the rights of others." Second, the law violated the due process clause of the Fourteenth Amendment by taking Mugler's brewery without just compensation.

Citing the Court's decision in *Pumpelly*, Mugler argued that he likewise sustained serious loss as a result of government action. He built the brewery consistent with the laws then in existence. In the absence of any wrongdoing, he argued, the Constitution protected him from the abrogation of his rights by the legislature. His case against the government, he contended, was stronger than Pumpelly's because he was being intentionally deprived of his property; it was not a case of consequential damage (an unintentional injury resulting from a public improvement). Although many may regard alcohol as a noxious or toxic product, it is not inherently of this character; it is not poisonous or dangerous.

Writing for the Court, Justice John Harlan said that in setting the limits of the state's police power, the legislature, not the courts, should decide when the use of property adversely affects the rights of others. "It belongs to that department [the legislature] to exert what are known as the police powers of the state, and to determine, primarily, what measures are appropriate or needful for the protection of the public morals, the public health, or the public safety."[28]

Harlan said that the Court would uphold a regulation as long as there was a "real" or "substantial relation," between it and the public harm, and no "palpable invasion of rights secured by the fundamental law." Applying these tests to Mugler's complaints, Harlan said: "So far from such a regulation having no relation to the general end sought to be accomplished, the entire scheme of prohibition, as embodied in the constitution and laws of Kansas, might fail, if the right of each citizen to manufacture intoxicating liquors for his own use as a beverage were recognized."[29]

On the basis of such reasoning, it is difficult to envision a prohibition measure that might fail such a weak constitutional test, since most tend to be part of "the entire scheme of prohibition." However, this rule has no relevance to the actual deprivation Mugler sustained. Harlan did not consider the linkage between destroying Mugler's brewery and the problems caused by alcohol consumption or whether these problems could be reduced with less restrictive measures than depriving an owner of the use of his property. In later years, such concerns would be considered as factors in determining whether government had sufficient justification for enforcing deprivations upon individual owners.

To uphold the validity of the Kansas legislation, Harlan cited and applied three Supreme Court cases which upheld statutes that prohibited the manufacture and sale of intoxicating liquors.[30] These rulings are the key to understanding the *Mugler* decision. *Mugler* is a product of a period in our history when public and professional opinion viewed the consumption of intoxicating liquors as a serious menace to the health, safety, morals, and welfare of the nation. Although the manufacture or sale of intoxicating liquors did not meet the legal definition of a common-law nuisance, for enlightened opinion of the time, the impact was no less destructive. The traditional, common-law nuisances were physically challenging and highly offensive—loud noises, bad smells, glaring lights, particle emissions—or otherwise noxious and dangerous to health and safety.[31] Even though prohibition laws did not meet nuisance criteria, most judges in that period were reluctant to overturn legislation intended to reduce consumption of liquor. With the exception of the *Wynehamer* case in New York (previously discussed in Chapters 2 and 3), in all other states where the issue was raised, the courts ruled that the police power enabled the legislature to adopt laws for this purpose.[32] This prohibition zealotry is unique to this period in the nation's history, and therefore limits *Mugler*'s applicability as a precedent in land-use cases.

Harlan distinguished the state's use of police power from use of the power of eminent domain, holding that no compensation is owed for a valid application of the police power. He distinguished *Pumpelly* as an extreme exception, where the plaintiff's property was physically invaded and a "practical ouster" resulted. Pumpelly's property was, in effect, required to be devoted to the use of the public. Harlan viewed the facts in *Mugler* differently:

> A prohibition simply upon the use of property for purposes that are declared, by valid legislation, to be injurious to the health, morals, or safety of the community, cannot, in any just sense, be deemed a taking or an appropriation of property for the public benefit. Such legislation does not disturb the owner in the control or use of his property for lawful purposes, nor restrict his right to dispose of it, but is only a declaration by the state that its use by any one, for certain forbidden purposes, is prejudicial to the public interests. Nor can legislation of that character come within the Fourteenth Amendment, in any case, unless it is apparent that its real object is not to protect the community, or to promote the general well-being, but, under the guise of police regulation, to deprive the owner of his liberty and property, without due process of law.[33]

The concept of state police power appears nowhere in the United States Constitution, but was developed many years later from the idea of government sovereignty. The idea is that when the government (state or federal) is exercising police power, it is advancing vital public concerns and, consequently, is not subject to constitutional protections for personal liberty and property. In *Mugler,* the Supreme Court stated that the Fourteenth Amendment's due process clause was not

> designed to interfere with the power of the States, sometimes termed police power, to prescribe regulations to promote the health, peace, morals, education, and good order of the people, and to legislate so as to increase the industries of the State, develop its resources, and add to its wealth and property.[34]

Initially, the United States Supreme Court was hostile to this idea of unlimited popular sovereignty, as revealed in the statement by Justice Joseph Story in 1829 in *Wilkinson v. Leland* (discussed in Chapter 2) that the rights of personal liberty and private property "should be held sacred. At least no court of justice in this country would be warranted in assuming, that the power to violate and disregard them . . . lurked under any general grant of legislative authority, or ought to be implied from any general expressions of the will of the people."[35]

But this concern for liberty faded with the advent of the Court presided over by Chief Justice Roger Taney (1836–1864), which succeeded the Marshall Court (1801–1835). Taney's Court supported the idea of popular sovereignty as embodied in state legislatures and began upholding legislation that the Marshall Court would have struck down.[36] This theory of legislative supremacy also found support in state courts.[37]

At the turn of the nineteenth century, the Supreme Court recognized that great deference to the police power might endanger the exercise of liberties. In 1905, in the famous *Lochner* decision,[38] the Court asserted that there must be a limit to the valid exercise of the police power, for otherwise it "would be a mere pretext—become another and delusive name for the supreme sovereignty of the state to be exercised free from constitutional restraint."[39] The Court enunciated a standard for reviewing the police power in liberty-of-contract cases, one that would in time be applied to protect other liberties:

> It is a question of which of two powers or rights shall prevail,—the power of the state to legislate or the right of the individual to liberty of person and freedom of contract. The mere assertion that the subject relates, though but in a remote degree, to the public health, does not necessarily render the enactment valid. The act must have a more direct relation, as a means to an end, and the end itself must be appropriate and legitimate, before an act can be held to be valid which interferes with the general right of an individual to be free in his person and in his power to contract in relation to his own labor.[40]

To be sure, *Lochner* was not a takings case; that is, it did not involve the property guarantee of the Fourteenth Amendment's due process clause. It was an interpretation of the clause's liberty guarantee. The case concerned a challenge to a New York statute limiting the working hours of bakery employees to ten hours per day and sixty per week. In its jurisprudence, the Supreme Court had distinguished cases involving liberty of contract from cases concerning property. Each area had its own rules. In making this distinction, the Court was, I believe, mistaken: the police power relates to the power of government under the separation of powers of our Constitution, and its meaning should not be conditioned on the activity to which it is applied.

The *Mugler* position on the police power was not followed, or even referred to, in two important property cases, *Buchanan v. Warley* (1917) (discussed here) and *Pennsylvania Coal Co. v. Mahon* (1922) (discussed in the next section). *Buchanan* applied the property protection of the Fourteenth Amendment's due process clause to hold ineffective a Louisville, Kentucky, ordinance forbidding blacks or whites from residing in a city block where most of the houses were occupied by the other race. This case was decided at a time when the Supreme Court still embraced the "separate but equal" interpretation of the equal protection clause that would seem to allow such an ordinance. While acknowledging the validity of "separate but equal" laws segregating the races in public schools and in public conveyances, the Court held that this rule was not applicable to property rights. The ordinance was passed in part to prevent breaches of the peace between the races, a concern under the police power. According to the Court, the ordinance was defective because it annulled the right of an owner to dispose of his property to another person of his choice. "[T]he police power, broad as it is, cannot justify the passage of a law or ordinance which runs counter to the limitations of the Federal Constitution."[41]

The many cases over the years applying the police power can be considered under two categories. First, there are opinions that consider the police power as confined to the inherent power of government to protect people from severe injury. *Lochner* is an example of this perspective. Second, there are opinions which identify the police power with the power of government to advance the public interest, except when it does so in an arbitrary and capricious manner. *Mugler* supports this position. Under the first category the police power is very limited, while under the second it is very broad. The role of judicial review is major in the first category and minor in the second. The first is consistent with the separation of powers concept because it limits the legislature to a role that it must exercise for society to function smoothly—adopting laws protecting the society from severe injury. The second violates separation because it accords the legislature largely unrestricted power, which is proper in a parliamentary system but improper in a government with separation of powers.

The second theory also governed the application of the police power to expression cases for a long period. Thus, in the very important 1925 *Gitlow* decision, the Supreme Court held that the due process clause of the Fourteenth

Amendment incorporated the expression guarantees of the First Amendment and secured them from impairment by the states.[42] Nonetheless, citing *Mugler,* the Court ruled that under the police power a state may penalize utterances advocating the overthrow of government by force, violence, or other unlawful means. The state's determination that such utterances "are inimical to the general welfare and involve danger of substantive evil," the Court held, "must be given great weight. Every presumption is to be indulged in favor of the validity of the statute." In reply to the defendant's plea that his statements were not very dangerous, the Court explained that "a single revolutionary spark may kindle a fire that, smoldering for a time, may burst into a sweeping and destructive conflagration."[43] Both *Mugler* and *Gitlow* seemed to accept legislative omnipotence.

The Supreme Court subsequently adopted the "clear and present danger" test, and the *Gitlow* holding on the police power has been rejected and the opinion reversed. The current standard for utterances which might provoke violence is set forth in *Brandenberg v. Ohio* (1969) (discussed in Chapter 3),[44] the most recent version of the "clear and present danger" test. This case requires the government to prove the existence of a likelihood that serious harm will occur.

This limitation on the police power adopted in the expression cases and the *Lochner*-era liberty-of-contract cases should apply generally. The authority of the legislative branch under our separation-of-powers system should not be dependent on the liberty in controversy, whether it involves speech, contract, or property. To control this legislative authority so that it does not overstep its legitimate bounds and encroach upon liberty (as explained in Chapter 3), our system requires that the judiciary monitor the legislature. Free-speech advocates have noted how bizarre the *Gitlow* decision was, "for it effectively permitted legislatures to legislate themselves out from under the restrictions of the First Amendment. . . . [T]his placed the fox in charge of the chicken coop, and turned the First Amendment on its head."[45] The same should be said when the endangered liberty is the right to property. In any event, the *Mugler* theory of the police power as applied to property regulation was not mentioned in and was effectively disapproved in *Pennsylvania Coal,* as we shall see.

III. *Pennsylvania Coal Co. v. Mahon*[46]

The Kohler Act, adopted by the Pennsylvania legislature in 1921, forbade the mining of anthracite coal in such a manner as to cause the subsidence (sinking below the surface) of any structure used as a human habitation. The Mahons purchased a home situated on land to which Pennsylvania Coal Company retained ownership of the subsurface rights. Their deed included an express provision that the owner of the surface interest waived any future claim against the coal company for personal injury or property damage due to possible subsidence as a result of its underground mining operations.

In large areas of Pennsylvania, both private parties and government agencies purchased surface rights from coal companies over the years subject to the same conditions. The most important reason for this kind of transaction was price. Purchasers were able to acquire the surface interest in a parcel of land for considerably less money than they would have paid for the entire interest. Not only were private parties willing to assume the risk of subsidence, government agencies—which could have acquired an entire interest through eminent domain—also purchased surface rights for public uses. When Pennsylvania Coal notified the Mahons of its intention to mine for coal to a depth where subsidence might result to their property, the Mahons sued to stop the proposed mining on the grounds that the Kohler Act had made such activity illegal.

The Mahons contended that such mining had caused subsidence, destroyed numerous private and public properties, and was consequently a noxious use of the area below the surface. The case was in this respect like *Mugler* and different from *Pumpelly,* because the state regulated the use of property but did not physically invade property. The Kohler Act was a limitation on a use of the subsurface property that would cause subsidence and not an intrusion by the state on the mining company's interest. The property remained in the possession of the owner. The state argued that the restriction on the coal company was not necessarily a permanent one. If mining ceases to be a noxious use, as it might due to future economic or social changes, the restrictions would likely be removed and the owner would again be free to enjoy his property as before.

In its answer to the Mahons' lawsuit, Pennsylvania Coal contended that the Kohler Act had destroyed its mining rights in violation of two constitutional provisions. First, it deprived the company of its contract rights, protected under the U.S. Constitution's obligation-of-contracts provision. Second, the act deprived the company of its property without due process of law. The Pennsylvania Supreme Court upheld the Kohler Act as a valid application of the police power.

On appeal to the U.S. Supreme Court in 1922, Justice Oliver Wendell Holmes, writing for the majority, confined his opinion to the company's second ground of attack. Holmes found strong protection in the Constitution for property rights:

> The protection of private property in the Fifth Amendment presupposes that it is wanted for public use, but provides that it shall not be taken for such use without compensation. A similar assumption is made in the decisions upon the Fourteenth Amendment. [case cited] When this seemingly absolute protection is found to be qualified by the police power, the natural tendency of human nature is to extend the qualification more and more until at last private property disappears. But that

cannot be accomplished in this way under the Constitution of the United States.
. . . In general it is not plain that a man's misfortunes or necessities will justify
his shifting the damages to his neighbor's shoulders. [case cited] We are in danger of forgetting that a strong public desire to improve the public condition is not
enough to warrant achieving the desire by a shorter cut than the constitutional
way of paying for the change.[47]

Contrary to what might be expected from such rhetoric, Holmes did not proceed to invoke a categorical rule on takings, but instead preferred a balancing
approach:

If we were called upon to deal with the plaintiff's [homeowner's] position alone,
we should think it clear that the statute does not disclose a public interest sufficient to warrant so extensive a destruction of the defendant's [coal company's]
constitutionally protected rights.[48]

The general rule at least is, that while property may be regulated to a certain extent, if regulation goes too far it will be recognized as a taking. It may be doubted
how far exceptional cases, like the blowing up of a house to stop a conflagration,
go—and if they go beyond the general rule, whether they do not stand as much
upon tradition as upon principle. . . . As we already have said, this is a question
of degree—and therefore cannot be disposed of by general propositions.[49]

Accordingly, restrictions on use could not be ignored in determining the validity of the regulation, but almost regardless of their severity, this fact was not
decisive to determining whether a taking had occurred. A determination of taking required a balancing of the interests of the state and the owner.

Justice Louis Brandeis, in dissent, presented the police-power position. He
argued that as long as title remained with the owner or the property was not
usurped by government, reduction in the property's value was irrelevant: "Restriction upon use does not become inappropriate as a means, merely because
it deprives an owner of the only use to which his property can be put." However, Brandeis did accept some significant restraints on the police power. He
would invalidate regulations that either did not "protect the public" or were not
an "appropriate means" to a valid public purpose.[50]

Brandeis's position in the case was based on two premises: first, that regulation and taking differ; and second, that a noxious use was involved, which could
be legislatively abated as a public nuisance without compensation. But his theory of regulation would render largely ineffective the constitutional safeguard
for property ownership. It would allow government to reduce through regulation the prerogatives of ownership until the owner's interest was reduced to the
virtual scrap of a naked title. Government could not, however, acquire the remaining scrap without compensating the owner for it. Form would have won

decisively over substance in an area specifically accorded protection by the Constitution. Holmes correctly observed that "[t]o make it commercially impracticable to mine certain coal has very nearly the same effect for constitutional purposes as appropriating or destroying it."[51]

Contrary to Brandeis, Holmes decided that mining coal with the possibility of causing subsidence was not a public nuisance. "This is the case of a single private house. . . . A source of damage to such a house is not a public nuisance even if similar damage is inflicted on others in different places. The damage is not common or public."[52]

In Holmes's view, the police power was not entitled to the great deference which *Mugler* had accorded it:

> Government could hardly go on if to some extent values incident to property could not be diminished without paying for every such change in the general law. As long recognized, some values are enjoyed under an implied limitation and must yield to the police power. But obviously the implied limitation must have its limits or the contracts and due process clauses are gone. So the question depends upon the particular facts. The greatest weight is given to the judgment of the legislature, but it is always open to interested parties to contend the legislature has gone beyond its constitutional power.[53]

Hence, according to Holmes, the legislature's determination is an important consideration, but it is far from virtually decisive as *Mugler* had declared. The police power "must have its limits or the contracts and due process clauses are gone." Holmes was hardly about to acknowledge that the legislative authority under the police powers was nearly conclusive, for he had rejected that very same position in his several opinions supporting the "clear and present danger" test in the freedom-of-expression cases.[54]

Pennsylvania Coal is totally at variance with *Mugler*. Under *Mugler*, the legislature's application of the police power is almost final, while under *Pennsylvania Coal*, the police power is one element in an equation. "The general rule at least is, that while property may be regulated to a certain extent, if regulation goes too far it will be recognized as a taking."[55]

After the *Pennsylvania Coal* decision, *Mugler* has little value as a precedent in takings cases. A product of a period in history that considered alcohol consumption a very serious menace to society—tantamount in impact to that of a public nuisance—*Mugler* had limited relevance to the Mahon situation or any other takings case not involving a highly objectionable use. Most importantly, Holmes's opinion on the police power effectively overrules the interpretation contained in *Mugler*.

Although *Mugler* is not referred to in Holmes's opinion, a letter that he sent to his friend Harold Laski reveals that he considered *Mugler* in writing the

Pennsylvania Coal opinion. He wrote that he had confidence in his own position: "I have always thought old Harlan's decision in *Mugler v. Kansas* was pretty fishy."[56]

IV. *Village of Euclid v. Ambler Realty Company*[57]

The Ambler Realty Company owned a sixty-eight-acre tract of land in the Village of Euclid, a suburb of Cleveland. The tract abutted Euclid Avenue, a major thoroughfare, on one side, and the Nickel Plate Railroad tracks on the other. Under the village's zoning ordinance, development of the land was restricted as to use, height, and area. Apartment, industrial, and commercial uses were prohibited on a portion of the land adjoining and within 620 feet north of Euclid Avenue, but such uses were permitted in the area contiguous to the railroad tracks. The area north of Euclid Avenue was mostly restricted to two-family and single-family dwellings. Ambler Realty alleged that the zoning restrictions permitting houses but not industrial uses reduced the value of the restricted land from $10,000 to $2,500 per acre. Further, if unrestricted, the land along Euclid Avenue would have a value of $150 per front foot, but as restricted its value was only $50 per front foot. The company sued to have the ordinance declared in violation of the Fourteenth Amendment's due process clause.

For United States District Court Judge David Westenhaver, who first heard the case, the issue was not a very difficult one, and he issued a strong decision in favor of Ambler Realty.[58] Clearly, the zoning ordinance, by restricting much of the land to residential uses, meant a loss to Ambler Realty of several hundred thousand dollars. Euclid Avenue was a great business and commercial street in Cleveland and its environs, and this was "its natural, obvious, and ultimate use within and beyond the Village of Euclid." "There can be no conception of property aside from its control and use, and upon its use depends its value."[59]

Judge Westenhaver found that no constitutional basis existed for the imposition of the police power to limit Ambler's use of the land. Therefore, to impose the zoning restraints, Euclid would have to condemn the property under the power of eminent domain and pay for it. "If police power meant what is deemed, all private property is now held subject to temporary and passing phases of public opinion, dominant for a day in legislative or municipal assemblies."[60] Instead of being beneficial, the ordinance would enable the city officials to exercise exclusionary powers to segregate the village, to the detriment of existing and would-be residents:

> The plain truth is that the true object of the ordinance in question is to place all the property in an undeveloped area of 16 square miles in a strait-jacket. The pur-

pose to be accomplished is really to regulate the mode of living of persons who may hereafter inhabit it. In the last analysis, the result to be accomplished is to classify the population and segregate them according to their income or situation in life.[61]

On appeal from the district court decision, the constitutionality of local zoning was upheld by a 6-to-3 majority of the U.S. Supreme Court in *Village of Euclid v. Ambler Realty Company* (1926). The justices declared that a municipality can regulate the use of land by way of a zoning ordinance. Its provisions would be declared unconstitutional only if they were clearly arbitrary and unreasonable, having no substantial relationship to the public health, safety, morals, or general welfare, which is to say, to the police power. The zoning ordinance was to be given a presumption of validity, and whether the test of validity had been met would have to be determined on a case-by-case basis:

> The ordinance now under review, and all similar laws and regulations, must find their justification in some aspect of the police power, asserted for the public welfare. The line which in this field separates the legitimate from the illegitimate assumption of power is not capable of precise delimitation. It varies with circumstances and conditions. A regulatory zoning ordinance, which would be clearly valid as applied to the great cities, might be clearly invalid as applied to rural communities.[62]

However, a judicial inquiry on zoning was not necessarily to be confined solely to the interests of the municipality, as the Court stated in a much discussed sentence of the opinion:

> It is not meant by this, however, to exclude the possibility of cases where the general public interest would so far outweigh the interest of the municipality that the municipality would not be allowed to stand in the way.[63]

Justice George Sutherland, the author of the *Euclid* opinion, did not reply directly to Judge Westenhaver's rulings. Instead of emphasizing property rights, Sutherland's opinion concentrated on the interests of the municipality. The Court's majority seemed to believe that a zoning ordinance did not operate to exclude uses but instead channeled or sorted them within the locality. The majority looked upon zoning as a process for distributing uses within a community, not for barring them, and, therefore, as having little effect exterior to the community's boundaries:

> [The Village of Euclid's] governing authorities, presumably representing a majority of its inhabitants and voicing their will, have determined, not that industrial development shall cease at its boundaries, but that the course of such develop-

ment shall proceed within definitely fixed lines. If it be a proper exercise of the police power to relegate industrial establishments to localities separated from residential sections, it is not easy to find a sufficient reason for denying the power because the effect of its exercise is to divert an industrial flow from the course which it would follow, to the injury of the residential public if left alone, to another course where such injury will be obviated.[64]

When this was not the case, and there were effects of more than a purely local nature—when the "general public interest" was involved—the judicial inquiry should be extended beyond the interests of the municipality in question. Thus, Sutherland felt concern for municipalities and for "the general public interest," but surprisingly, not for the rights of the individual property owners. I say "surprisingly" because this opinion was authored by one of the staunchest advocates of reading freedom of contract into the due process clause, a stance for which he is still maligned as a free-marketeer.

A. The General Public Interest

As interpreted by many lower courts, the *Euclid* decision made zoning largely a matter of local administration with relatively little likelihood of judicial interference. Analogous to the rules courts employ when administrative regulations are challenged, local zoning decisions would stand unless they were clearly irrational. In this area of the law, the judiciary would no longer protect the individual against Leviathan, except in instances of the gravest abuse.

This interpretation of *Euclid,* widely shared by the lower courts, is not supported by subsequent opinions of the *Euclid* Supreme Court itself. There is, however, another reading of *Euclid* that would be more consistent with the generally libertarian tenor of the Court in that era. Within three years after the *Euclid* decision, the Court adjudicated four zoning cases and sustained the property owner's position in two of them, as will be described in Section V of this chapter. In neither of these two cases did the Court accord extensive deference to the municipality.

As previously noted, the Supreme Court's opinion in *Euclid* distinguishes between "the interest of the municipality" and the "general public interest." Matters falling within the latter category will be adjudicated differently than those in the first category. Although Justice Sutherland did not further define or explain this distinction, it is critical to understanding the *Euclid* decision.

The powers of a municipality are confined to regulating local interests. It does not have the power to regulate the interests of nonresidents, inasmuch as they did not elect its lawmakers. Since local politicians have little incentive to consider the interests of outsiders, the latter have no opportunity to exert political pressure on a municipality to enact or change zoning regulations. Under these circumstances, a basic principle of democratic government—that it governs only those who elected it—is violated.

The U.S. Constitution has prohibited this outcome in other contexts. Thus, the commerce clause bars individual states from regulating the commerce of other states.[65] "The Court has often recognized that to the extent . . . the burden of state regulation falls on interests outside the state, it is unlikely to be alleviated by the operation of those political restraints normally exerted when interests within the state are affected."[66] Accordingly, "no state can legislate except with reference to its own jurisdiction."[67] The fact that such legislation might have incidental spillover effects on interstate commerce does not invalidate it.[68]

Relating these concerns to interpreting *Euclid,* the lower courts should have concluded that a zoning ordinance that substantially affects nonresidents should be considered to be in the "general public interest" category and governed by the precedents generally applicable to the regulation of property. Some state courts have accepted this position to some degree, as will be explained subsequently. This rule would have effectively confined the zoning authority of municipalities to local matters, such as those about which Sutherland expressed concern. If the locality is merely sorting out uses to prevent nuisances and eliminating other local health and safety problems, and if the flow of commerce is not otherwise significantly restricted, then the locality is acting within its authorized powers, but it is not doing so when the impact of its rules extends substantially outside of its borders.

For suburbs such as Euclid, much of their zoning ordinances substantially impact residents in other communities. Generally, the boundaries of localities have little relationship to economic markets. Thus, the potential residents of a suburban housing development will come largely from other municipalities. Commercial developments such as shopping centers likewise cater heavily to nonresidents. Industrial plants obtain workers from, and sell to areas outside of, the locality in which they are located. These examples describe commerce in suburbs and, to a lesser extent, large cities. The exceptions are small real-estate developments catering to local residents.

Accordingly, it would seem that under *Euclid* the proper standard for determining constitutionality of much zoning regulation is the one that applies to the "general public interest" category. Under this interpretation, *Euclid* relates only to local zoning matters and was intended to do no more than protect the legitimate local interests of a municipality. It was a limited exception to, and not a change in, the rules of property rights. The opinion made no reference to two cases that the Court had just recently decided, both of which substantially confined the scope of the police powers. These were the 1922 *Pennsylvania Coal* case (previously discussed) and *Adkins v. Children's Hospital,* a 1923 liberty-of-contract decision authored by Justice Sutherland.[69] In 1932, Sutherland would write the *New State Ice*[70] decision, another liberty-of-contract case, in which he limited the reach of the police power. (The *Adkins* and *New State Ice* cases are discussed below.) There is, consequently, much support for the theory that *Euclid* should be considered as a specific and not a general limitation on *Pennsylvania Coal,* confined to protecting legitimate local concerns.

Sutherland's reliance on the police power in *Euclid* conflicts with his opinion in *Adkins,* in which he displayed little deference to this power. Congress had enacted in 1918 a statute for the District of Columbia, establishing a board to fix minimum wages for women and minors in various industries. In his opinion striking down this statute, Sutherland asserted that an employer's legal obligation extended no further than the payment of an agreed wage. The employer was not responsible for otherwise compensating the employee, since he was in no way the cause of the employee's economic status. Sutherland rejected applying the police power to limit constitutionally protected liberties, quoting this passage from *Lochner:*

> Otherwise the Fourteenth Amendment would have no efficacy and the legislatures of the states would have unbounded power, and it would be enough to say that any piece of legislation was enacted to conserve the morals, the health or the safety of the people; such legislation would be valid, no matter how absolutely without foundation the claim might be. The claim of the police power would be a mere pretext—become another and delusive name for the supreme sovereignty of the state, to be exercised free from constitutional restraint.[71]

The justice concluded his opinion with a declaration that appears totally inconsistent with the idea that the police power is vast in scope:

> To sustain the individual freedom of action contemplated by the Constitution, is not to strike down the common good but to exalt it; for surely the good of society as a whole cannot be better served than by the preservation against arbitrary restraint of the liberties of its constituent members.[72]

Sutherland's 1926 *Euclid* opinion should not be considered as necessarily reflecting a change in the position he had taken on the police power in *Adkins* in 1923. Six years after *Euclid,* the justice delivered the Court's opinion in *New State Ice Company v. Liebmann,*[73] a liberty-of-contract case, striking down an Oklahoma statute that made it illegal to manufacture ice for sale and distribution without first obtaining permission from the state corporations commission. In response to the contention that the state had authority under the police power to impose this regulation, Sutherland replied:

> Plainly, a regulation which has the effect of denying or unreasonably curtailing the common right to engage in a lawful business, such as that under review, can-

not be upheld consistent with the Fourteenth Amendment. Under that amendment, nothing is more clearly settled than that it is beyond the power of a state, "under the guise of protecting the public, arbitrarily [to] interfere with private business or prohibit lawful occupations or impose unreasonable and unnecessary restrictions upon them."[74]

This perspective should be quite applicable to zoning regulations because in these cases owners are denied a common use of property that a locality's officials determine to be undesirable. Yet under *Euclid,* courts give great deference to these local decisions.

The police power on which the Court based the *Euclid* decision does not seem to be the same as the one applied in *Adkins* and *New State Ice,* both of which gave priority to Fourteenth Amendment freedoms. In both decisions, Justice Sutherland explained that a substantial deference to the police power threatened or extinguished economic liberties. The only way to discern even the slightest consistency in Sutherland's opinions in these cases, is to adopt the course that I have suggested, and conclude that he intended to limit *Euclid* to legitimate local concerns.

In more-recent cases, some courts have recognized the distinction between zoning regulations that mostly affect residents and those that substantially affect nonresidents: "[U]nlike the situation in the past, most municipalities today are neither isolated nor wholly independent from neighboring municipalities and . . . consequently, unilateral land use decisions by one locality affect the needs and resources of an entire region."[75] In *Associated Home Builders v. City of Livermore* (1976),[76] a California city adopted, by public initiative, an ordinance prohibiting issuance of further building permits until major improvements were made in the quality and quantity of educational, sewage, and water facilities. Builders in the city contended that the ordinance seriously limited development and consequently impaired the rights of people who wanted to live there. The California Supreme Court agreed and found that this ordinance significantly affected the interests of nonresidents who were not represented in the city legislative body and could not vote on the initiative. With respect to ordinances that work to exclude nonresidents, the court modified the highly deferential review it ordinarily applied in zoning matters and replaced it with a heightened scrutiny standard under which the ordinance "must have a real and substantial relation to the public welfare." The initial burden of proof was placed on the challenger to prove that there was no such relationship.

Supreme courts in New Jersey and Pennsylvania, interpreting state statutes, have also entered special rules relating to zoning ordinances that substantially affect nonresidents. In the much-discussed *Mount Laurel* decision, the New Jersey Supreme Court invalidated a zoning ordinance that had the effect of excluding moderate- and low-income housing. Since the ordinance did not classify land for this purpose, people of these socioeconomic levels could not move to the township.[77] The court refused to accord the ordinance the usual high degree of deference on the basis that it had an impact on regional welfare and not merely on local concerns:

> [O]ur opinion is that Mount Laurel's zoning ordinance is presumptively contrary to the general welfare and outside the intended scope of the zoning power in the particulars mentioned. A facial showing of invalidity is thus established, shifting to the municipality the burden of establishing valid superseding reasons for its action and non-action.

On similar grounds, the Pennsylvania Supreme Court, in two separate cases, struck down a four-acre minimum lot requirement for single-family housing, and a zoning ordinance that did not allow apartments.[78]

B. Zoning and Nuisances

Justice George Sutherland is regarded as a strong supporter of property and economic rights. Why would he write an opinion such as *Euclid,* giving local government great power over the use of property within its confines? His three philosophical brethren on the Court—Justices Pierce Butler, James C. McReynolds, and Willis Van Devanter—dissented from the opinion. It is reported that after the oral arguments before the Supreme Court, Sutherland voted to strike down the ordinance. The case was then set for reargument and he subsequently changed his vote. A law clerk for one of the justices explained Sutherland's change of heart as resulting from a newfound conviction that zoning would prevent the existence of nuisances in residential areas and was therefore protective of property rights.[79] Sutherland's much quoted simile in his *Euclid* opinion supports this theory: "A nuisance may be merely a right thing in the wrong place — like a pig in the parlor instead of the barnyard. If the validity of the legislative classification for zoning purposes be fairly debatable, the legislative judgment must be allowed to control."[80]

Yet even this nominal recognition of nuisance doctrine effectively eliminates judicial protection for property rights, since almost all land-use controversies are "fairly debatable." *Euclid* carried the nuisance exception beyond recognition. The ordinance imposed area (four different categories), height (three categories), and use (four categories) restrictions on every square inch of the municipality. There is little relation between such restrictions and the nuisance doctrine. These restrictions constitute prior restraint imposed even before the existence of an offensive use. Sutherland used stereotypes and platitudes, without setting forth any statistical evidence, to argue that the development of apartment buildings in single-family areas threatened the existence of these areas. He omitted any reference to the availability of less-obtrusive alternatives, such as restrictive covenants (which are voluntary deed restrictions that exclude diverse uses) or targeted regulations aimed directly at preserving health and safety.[81] The following declamation from his *Euclid* opinion illustrates that Sutherland did not entertain the possibility of such less-sweeping means:

> These reports [from commissions and experts], which bear every evidence of painstaking consideration, concur in the view that the segregation of residential, business, and industrial buildings will make it easier to provide fire apparatus suitable for the character and intensity of the development in each section; that it will increase the safety and security of home life; greatly tend to prevent street accidents, especially to children, by reducing the traffic and resulting confusion in residential sections; decrease noise and other conditions which produce or intensify nervous disorders; preserve a more favorable environment in which to rear children, etc. With particular reference to apartment houses, it is pointed out that the development of detached house sections is greatly retarded by the coming of apartment houses, which has sometimes resulted in destroying the entire section for private house purposes; that in such sections very often the apartment house is a mere parasite, constructed in order to take advantage of the open spaces and attractive surroundings created by the residential character of the district. Moreover, the coming of one apartment house is followed by others, interfering by their height and bulk with the free circulation of air and monopolizing the rays of the sun which otherwise would fall upon the smaller homes, and bringing, as their necessary accompaniments, the disturbing noises incident to increased traffic and business, and the occupation, by means of moving and parked automobiles, of larger portions of the streets, thus detracting from their safety and depriving children of the privilege of quiet and open spaces for play, enjoyed by those in more favored localities—until, finally, the residential character of the neighborhood and its desirability as a place of detached residences are utterly destroyed. Under these circumstances, apartment houses, which in a different environment would be not only entirely unobjectionable but highly desirable, come very near to being nuisances.[82]

Surely, there were other legal solutions for the alleged problems than controlling the use of every square inch of land in the Village of Euclid.[83]

Sutherland seemed to prefer single-family development over multifamily development. However, this should be a matter for the market and not the judiciary. In the absence of nuisance, judges are not empowered to determine how land should be used. Due to the problems Sutherland said existed in the development of single-family subdivisions, fewer homes and more apartments might have been built in the absence of zoning, but with possibly better consequences for society: less urban sprawl, more open space, less use of land. Of course, no one can be certain about the future. However, Sutherland's generalizations about the negative impact of apartment houses in the absence of zoning are hardly consistent with the development in nonzoned localities of many highly desirable single-family subdivisions over the years. This is due in part to the availability of less-restrictive means than zoning to regulate the use of land.[84]

Sutherland's discussion of single-family dwellings in *Euclid* had little relevance to the Ambler Realty acreage, since this property—located between a railroad and a major thoroughfare and traversed by two other highways—was not particularly suitable for such dwellings. Protecting the exclusivity of single-family districts hardly justified imposing single- and two-family zoning on the property, contrary to the desires of its owner. Nor was there anything in the Court's opinion indicating that Ambler's proposed use of its land for industrial purposes was harmful. Under zoning theory, this serious restraint on property is reasonable because the zoning scheme of which it is part benefits the community and provides reciprocal advantages to the owner. However, from a property-rights perspective, the facts in *Euclid* look very different. Instead of protecting an owner from the community, the justices approved the constitutionality of a system that protected the community from the owner.

Planning the use of land is a highly subjective endeavor. One common position in urban planning is that business and not residential use should be required for land adjoining major thoroughfares. Euclid Avenue was of this character at the time the village's zoning ordinance was adopted. Nevertheless, the portion of the Ambler Realty acreage that adjoined Euclid Avenue was restricted by the zoning ordinance largely to single- and two-family dwellings, forbidding any business or industrial use.

Sutherland's opinion removes the priority of price in determining the use of land. In its place, his opinion accords this status to the political-planning process. Many commentators approve of this, because they contend that the change furthers democracy and popular sovereignty. There are two basic problems with such thinking. First, since any region consists of many separate, autonomous localities, the political power of each must necessarily be limited to its own interests. This issue was discussed previously. Second, price is a much better reflection of regional wants and desires than is a locality's political process.

Under the political-planning system, use of land is determined by the most persuasive and powerful political influences, whether they be the local residents, political contributors, political parties, the media, or a combination of any or all of these. Most politicians want to retain their present office or seek another office. The key to fulfilling either ambition lies with the voters, and that is a highly critical factor in determining how a politician will vote in a land-use matter. To be sure, this may be the democratic way, but democracy is a poor way to make economic decisions. No business would ever use this method to determine production and distribution of its products.

According to the Ambler Realty Company, for industrial uses its property had a market value of about $10,000 per acre, while for residential purposes the market value was not in excess of $2,500 per acre. Purchasers were willing to pay four times as much for the one use as for the other. The price of a commodity is determined by the interaction of supply and demand. This demand is created by the wants and desires of the public as expressed in the market, and it represents considerably more people than those who actually purchase or bid for the property. Price is a mechanism for the communication of information, it reveals how much a particular item is desired. A high price for a commodity reveals that it is much wanted, and a low price reveals the reverse. The price difference between the two uses of Ambler's land was a very persuasive message that it was more advantageous to society for Ambler's land to be used for industrial rather than residential purposes.

C. Is Zoning Necessary?

The *Euclid*-era Court considered other cases involving the constitutionality of economic restraints, but it did so under a less deferential standard. The justices' theory was that legislatures should not enact sweeping restrictions when the same end could be achieved with less onerous rules. Employing this test, the Court struck down measures that imposed unnecessary restraints. Although the Village of Euclid's primary purpose for zoning was to protect single-family exclusivity, the Court gave no consideration to the possibility of other ordinances that could have dealt solely with this problem, while not affecting other matters. One or more ordinances dealing with specific use and development problems—rather than a comprehensive ordinance affecting all property in the village—might have been sufficient to remedy location problems.[85]

A 1926 case, *Weaver v. Palmer Bros.*,[86] is a good example of how the Court employed its "less onerous" test, finding that a sweeping piece of legislation designed to safeguard the consumer—the same objective sought by Euclid's zoning—could be replaced by less restrictive measures. To protect health and prevent fraud, a 1923 Pennsylvania statute prohibited the use of shoddy (secondhand cloth) in mattresses and similar articles. The Supreme Court found that shoddy could be sterilized and that old material could not easily be passed off as new if identifying tags were required to be attached to articles containing it. On the premise that "it is a matter of public concern that the production and sale of things necessary or convenient for use should not be forbidden,"[87] the Court concluded that the legislative ban was not needed to protect the public. The measure needlessly restrained the liberty of the manufacturer.

In a recent study of land-use controls from 1870 to 1926 in New Haven, Connecticut, before the adoption by the city of zoning in 1926, Andrew Cappel, an attorney now practicing in New Haven, writes that the city had adopted an arsenal of rules to prevent undesirable uses. It had enacted specific restrictions relating to the prevention of fire, supervision of building safety, prohibition of private encroachment into public streets and sidewalks, and abatement of public nuisances.[88] Owners were forbidden to build new wooden structures in the downtown area or to add to existing wooden buildings without special city approval. New wooden construction was permitted outside of a designated fire district, and wooden houses could not be built to a height greater than three floors. The construction of multifamily structures had to comply with lot coverage restrictions. The city also enacted ordinances regulating hazardous and noxious uses and adopted remedial actions to abate excessive emissions of smoke and noise. Cappel's conclusions about the sufficiency of these controls undermine a major rationale of the *Euclid* opinion:

> Although the results of a single, small-scale study cannot be considered determinative, this study of New Haven casts doubt upon the prevailing assumption that coherent land use cannot take place without the type of planned public regulation represented by zoning. . . .
>
> In addition, this study suggests that the introduction of zoning into New Haven was not necessitated by actual conditions of local land use, but rather was the work of certain elites, particularly members of the Chamber of Commerce and City Plan Commission, who were influenced by theories developed as part of the national "City Beautiful" movement. Therefore, in contrast to the narrative traditionally advanced by supporters of zoning, the rapid spread of zoning in the 1920s may well have brought zoning to cities like New Haven where it was not really needed.[89]

V. *Zahn, Gorieb, Nectow,* and *Roberge*

From 1926 to 1928, the Supreme Court adjudicated four zoning cases in addition to *Euclid*; in none of these did it consider the "general public interest" distinction referred to in that case. However, in two cases, it applied a standard of scrutiny much higher than the deferential standard set forth in *Euclid*, without expressing any qualification of its earlier holding.

In 1927, the Supreme Court applied its rule of great deference to government and upheld zoning ordinances in Los Angeles and Roanoke, Virginia. The following year, the Court gave far less deference to government and struck down zoning ordinances in Cambridge, Massachusetts, and Seattle, Washington. The opinions in all four cases were unanimous.

The first of the post-*Euclid* cases was *Zahn v. Board of Public Works,*[90] in which a landowner sought to obtain a commercial classification for his property. The land, adjoining Wilshire Boulevard, a major thoroughfare in Los Angeles, was zoned for residential use, as were most surrounding properties. The neighborhood was largely unimproved but was in the path of rapid development. The Supreme Court (per Justice Sutherland), in a one-page opinion, refused to overturn the city's zoning classification. It concluded that the classification was not clearly arbitrary or unreasonable, and was at most an exercise of power that was fairly debatable. The Court did not discuss various interests and concerns relating to the zoning in question, except that the value of the land would be greater if zoned for commercial purposes.

The other 1927 zoning case was *Gorieb v. Fox*,[91] in which a landowner sought to obtain a permit to erect a brick building to contain a store. The structure would have occupied its lot up to the street line. The Roanoke City Council refused this request and instead gave the owner permission to erect the building no closer than thirty-four and two-thirds feet back from the street line. The owner challenged Roanoke's building line as violating the due process and equal protection provisions of the Fourteenth Amendment. Justice Sutherland stated that while the courts were divided on the constitutionality of setback requirements, the Supreme Court in *Euclid* had rejected the basic reasons upon which the opponents of their constitutionality depended, while accepting the arguments of the supporters of constitutionality. Therefore, the Court upheld Roanoke's setback requirement, on the basis of *Euclid*'s deferential standard.

In 1928, in *Nectow v. City of Cambridge*,[92] the Court changed its highly deferential position toward zoning ordinances. Contending that the zoning classification which had been applied to his land violated the Fourteenth Amendment's due process clause, Nectow sued to obtain a mandatory injunction directing the City of Cambridge to issue a building permit on his tract of land, without regard to its having been zoned for residential purposes. He had contracted to sell the bulk of the tract for an industrial use for $63,000, but this land was zoned mostly for residential purposes, for which it was "of comparatively little value." Nectow's land was divided into two zoning classifications. The western portion was zoned to permit dwellings but not business or industry, while the eastern portion was unrestricted. An auto assembly factory was located south of the tract. Properties to the north and west were zoned residential. The city objected to changing the zoning as Nectow had requested, in part because such a change would alter the coherence and symmetry of the zoning plan.

Because adjoining and nearby properties were used or zoned for different purposes, the most appropriate classification for the property was a matter open to a fair amount of debate. Moving the zoning line might dilute the credibility of the city's general plan. According to the Massachusetts Supreme Court, the case was a close one, but the court ruled against Nectow because it found that the city had not acted without foundation in reason.

This would seem an appropriate decision given *Euclid*'s strong presumptions supporting existing zoning. In *Euclid,* the U.S. Supreme Court held that before a zoning ordinance can be declared unconstitutional, "[its] provisions [must be] clearly arbitrary and unreasonable, having no substantial relation to the public health, safety, morals or public welfare." In *Nectow,* however, the U.S. Supreme Court ruled that the zoning at issue violated the Fourteenth Amendment's due process clause. Thus, the *Nectow* decision reduced considerably the level of deference the judiciary must accord to a zoning ordinance, as revealed in this statement in the opinion by Justice Sutherland:

> The governmental power to interfere by zoning regulations with the general rights of the landowner by restricting the character of his use, is not unlimited, and other questions aside, such restriction cannot be imposed if it does not bear a substantial relation to the public health, safety, morals or general welfare.[93]

In other words, instead of *Euclid's* inquiry as to whether the ordinance is "clearly arbitrary and unreasonable," requiring the owner to prove there is no basis for it, *Nectow* requires an inquiry as to whether the ordinance is justified, that is, bears a substantial relation to the public health, etc. The language difference may not be plain, but the result is clear. Sutherland explained that the city had not shown a sufficient reason for the regulation:

> Here, the express finding of the master [an expert appointed by the trial court to advise it on the merits of the controversy], already quoted, confirmed by the court below, is that the health, safety, convenience and general welfare of the inhabitants of the part of the city affected will not be promoted by the disposition made by the ordinance of the locus in question. This finding of the master, after a hearing and an inspection of the entire area affected, supported, as we think it is, by other findings of fact, is determinative of the case. That the invasion of the property of plaintiff in error was serious and highly injurious is clearly established; and, since a necessary basis for the support of that invasion is wanting, the action of the zoning authorities comes within the ban of the Fourteenth Amendment and cannot be sustained.[94]

Also decided in 1928, *Seattle Title Trust Co. v. Roberge*[95] was the next zoning case after *Nectow* and the last to be decided before a forty-year period of abstinence in which the Supreme Court deliberately refused to consider a single zoning case. The lower federal and state courts were left to determine zoning rules affecting the real-estate and construction industries of this vast nation without further guidance from the nation's highest court.

In *Roberge,* the owner of a philanthropic home for the aged poor in Seattle had proposed to demolish the building and replace it with a much bigger one. The new building would be a two-and-one-half story fireproof facility large enough to house thirty people. The existing building had formerly been used as a private residence and only accommodated fourteen people.

Seattle's zoning ordinance prohibited the erection or alteration of a building for any use not specifically authorized. The site in question was in the "first residence district," which permitted a philanthropic home for old people only "when the written consent shall have been obtained of the owners of two-thirds of the property within four hundred (400) feet of the proposed building."[96] The Supreme Court held this consent provision unconstitutional, viewing it as unwarranted delegation of power to some property owners to arbitrarily control the use of another person's property without any standard or rule prescribed by legislative action. Under the provision, the surrounding owners could "withhold consent for selfish reasons or arbitrarily and may subject the trustee [owner] to their will or caprice."[97]

This ruling was supported by earlier rulings of the Court invalidating ordinances that permitted some owners of property to impose restrictions on other nearby owners.[98] There is merit in this delegation argument, for as John Locke argued: "The power of the *Legislative* being derived from the People by a positive voluntary Grant and Institution, can be no other, than what the positive Grant conveyed, which being only to make *Laws,* and not to make *Legislators,* the *Legislative* can have no power to transfer their Authority of making Laws, and place it in other hands."[99]

Without the stricken two-thirds consent provision, there was no authority in the zoning ordinance for the erection of the proposed home. Since the zoning district allowed single-family dwellings, it is likely the local legislature did not want to permit erection of a large multiple-housing facility for the aged poor without consent from the neighbors. However, the Supreme Court rejected this reasoning. In contrast to the deferential level of scrutiny in zoning cases indicated in *Euclid,* the Court asserted that legislators may not "impose restrictions that are unnecessary and unreasonable upon the use of private property or the pursuit of useful activities."[100]

The Court proceeded to explain its position with three major arguments: (1) The evidence disclosed that the exclusion of the new home from the residential district was not indispensable to the general zoning plan. (2) There was no legislative determination that the proposed building and use would be inconsistent with public health, safety, morals, and general welfare. And (3) the two-thirds consent provision plainly implies the contrary, for its enactment shows that the proposed home would be in harmony with the public interest and with the general scope and plan of the zoning ordinance.

Thus, the Supreme Court overruled the local legislature that did not want the erection of a home for old people in a residential area without a two-thirds local consent. Furthermore, the proposed home for the aged poor seems to be the type of multifamily structure that Sutherland in *Euclid* considered to be a harmful use when located near homes. The consent requirement enabled the neighbors to exclude homes for the elderly that were deemed undesirable. Under a *Euclid* standard of review and in the absence of local consent, denial of the permit should not be regarded as arbitrary or unreasonable under the provisions of the zoning ordinance. Nevertheless, the Court ordered the issuance of a building permit.

Roberge confirmed the *Nectow* perspective. After quoting the *Nectow* standard that is set forth above, Justice Pierce Butler, writing for the Court, went on to state the following:

> Legislators may not, under the guise of the police power, impose restrictions that are unnecessary and unreasonable upon the use of private property or the pursuit of useful activities. . . .
>
> The right of the trustee [plaintiff] to devote its land to any legitimate use is property within the protection of the Constitution.[101]

I believe it is fair to conclude that *Nectow* and *Roberge* effectively reversed *Euclid*. Unfortunately, most of the legal community did not recognize this occurrence. The explanation for this probably has to do with the fact that *Euclid* was, in terms of constitutional law, one of the Supreme Court's most important decisions.

Accordingly, the Supreme Court closed its initial excursion into zoning with a pair of decisions casting serious doubt on the continued authority of the rules of judicial review announced in *Euclid*. *Nectow* and *Roberge* substantially protected private ownership, and they reveal the application of a level of judicial scrutiny far higher than that evinced in *Euclid*.

VI. *Miller v. Schoene*

A regulatory takings case from the same era as the zoning cases demonstrates that the Court was uncertain of its constitutional obligation to protect property rights. The Cedar Rust Act of Virginia required the destruction of red cedar trees without compensation to the owners when the trees produced a cedar rust that damaged apple trees. The disease did not damage the red cedar or other plants. *Miller v. Schoene* (1928)[102] was a case brought by owners of red cedar trees who were ordered to cut down their trees. When the case reached the Supreme Court, it upheld a state order requiring the destruction of all red cedar trees suspected of harboring the infection located within two miles of apple orchards, the distance beyond which the infection did not spread. The red cedar owners were allowed to retain possession of the cut lumber.[103]

Thus, cedar rust disease caused a conflict of interest between two industries in Virginia, apple-tree growing and red-cedar-tree growing. However, the two industries differed considerably in their political and economic importance in the state. Apple growing was one of the principal agricultural pursuits in Virginia. Millions of dollars were invested in the orchards, which furnished employment for a large portion of the population, and induced the development of attendant railroad and cold-storage facilities. The red cedar, aside from its ornamental use, had occasional use and value as lumber. It is indigenous to Virginia, not commercially important on any substantial scale, and its value throughout the state was small as compared with that of the apple orchards.

The United States Supreme Court, per Justice Harlan Stone, asserted that when forced to make a choice, the state did not exceed its constitutional powers by deciding upon the destruction of one class of property in order to save another which, in the judgment of the legislature, was of greater value to the public. When the state's public interest is involved, "preferment of that interest over the property interest of the individual, to the extent even of [the latter interest's] destruction, is one of the distinguishing characteristics of every exercise of the police power which affects property."[104] The Court made no inquiry as to whether a nuisance was involved. "For where, as here, the choice is unavoidable, we cannot say that [the police power's] exercise, controlled by considerations of social policy which are not unreasonable, involves any denial of due process."[105]

This decision may be appropriate for a parliamentary government, in which the legislature is supreme, but not for a separation-of-powers government. Under a parliamentary system, in which the legislature is supreme, the legislature may, at its will, take private property from A and give it to B. The separation-of-powers system is intended to limit this power. When a legislature in the United States seeks to take from A to give to B, it must find constitutional justification; otherwise the takings and due process provisions of the Constitution are meaningless. The separation of powers is intended to overcome the failings of the legislature, and a common failing is its subservience to political power, regardless of merit. As a major industry in the state of Virginia, apple growers were a powerful influence in the legislature. At the least, they were much more influential than the cedar-tree growers.

In *Miller v. Schoene,* the United States Supreme Court merely confirmed political reality. It ignored its obligation to determine whether, in this situation, the Constitution shields David from the might of Goliath.

The *Schoene* opinion violates the basic understanding of the separation-of-powers doctrine. One objective of this doctrine is to make certain that the most powerful in society do not always win. To rely on legislatures to determine the public interest is fanciful, since in order to remain in office most legislators must respond to pressure from special interests. While it was stipulated in the

Schoene case that the value of the apple trees saved was far in excess of the value of the cedar trees destroyed, this should not have been conclusive with respect to the rights of property-owners who look for protection to the guarantees of the Constitution.

The cedar rust disease created a problem for both parties, neither of whom was at fault. The cedar owners did not commit harm, and the disease itself would not have been injurious to society if there had been no apple trees in the vicinity. In this sense, only the existence of the apple trees in a nearby area created a problem; rust disease is an affliction of both cedar and apple trees, but only results in monetary loss to the apple-tree growers. Under traditional common-law principles, courts did not find that a nuisance existed when the harm was caused by a natural occurrence.

Under the scrutiny tests used by the Supreme Court of today, the Cedar Rust Act's application to the red-cedar owners would not have passed constitutional muster. These new tests are discussed in Chapter 5 and include two inquiries that the act would have failed. First, did Virginia's purpose in adopting the law constitute a legitimate state interest? The answer is no if Virginia's purpose was to favor one person over another. The state must be impartial in its legislative objectives. In the *Schoene* case, Virginia was seeking to benefit the apple growers at the expense of the red-cedar growers. However, the state might have asserted that its purpose was to preserve the state's economic viability or welfare, either of which purpose the Supreme Court would likely accept as a legitimate state interest. The second inquiry under the current scrutiny tests is whether the legislation substantially achieved either of these legitimate state purposes. It is doubtful that the state would have passed this test. If Virginia had not enacted the Cedar Rust Act, the apple growers would have regarded elimination of the disease as a cost of doing business and would have either purchased the red cedars, made an effort to treat or confine the disease, or located their orchards more than two miles from the cedars. The state might also have passed less arduous legislation, such as legislation prohibiting planting of the cedars within two miles of apple orchards. Or, since the red-cedar growers were not at fault and the cedar rust disease harmed the apple growers (and thereby the state's economy), the state might have compensated the red-cedar growers for being forced to cut their trees down. It is not likely that Virginia's economic viability or well-being would have been seriously compromised in the absence of the Cedar Rust Act.

VII. *Loretto v. Teleprompter Manhattan CATV Corp.*

Sometimes even a tiny intrusion will strike the Court as a taking, an intrusion causing no economic loss whatsoever and nearly no inconvenience. Because this next case—*Loretto v. Teleprompter Manhattan CATV Corp.* (1982)[106]—involved a physical presence on the owner's property, the outcome was far different for the owner than for the hapless red-cedar-tree growers.

A New York statute provided that landlords of rental property must permit cable television companies to install and attach TV cables to their buildings to provide service to their tenants, and that the landlords could not demand payment from the company in excess of the amount determined to be reasonable by a state commission. After purchasing a five-story apartment building in New York City, Loretto discovered that the Teleprompter Company had installed cable facilities occupying one and one-half cubic feet on the exterior of the structure, as well as cables to the tenants' televisions. She then brought a class-action suit for damages and injunctive relief, alleging that the installation of cables and supporting equipment, insofar as the defendant television companies relied on the New York statute, constituted a taking without just compensation. Loretto conceded that owners of other apartment buildings thought that the cable's presence had enhanced the market value of their buildings, and that her own tenants would be upset if the cable connection were removed. The cable installation did not interfere with any use that Loretto intended for the occupied space.

In *Loretto v. Teleprompter,* the United States Supreme Court held that when the character of the governmental action constitutes a permanent physical occupation of real property, there is a taking to the extent of the occupation, without regard to whether the action achieved an important public benefit or had only minimal economic impact on the owner. Inasmuch as the invasion is total over the area involved, its constitutional impact cannot be made to depend on the size of the area permanently occupied. The Court held that this rule applied only to a permanent physical occupation and not to a temporary physical occupation, whose constitutionality would continue to be subject to the customary takings analysis.

The physical occupation in question was infinitesimal compared to the one in *Pumpelly* (the 1871 case that dealt with the flooding of land caused by construction of a dam), which destroyed entirely the value of the owner's property. The installation in Loretto's building involved a physical attachment of plates, boxes, wires, bolts, and screws to the building, completely occupying a small space immediately above and upon the roof and along the building's exterior wall. The television company retained ownership of all this equipment. The statute provided that if the landlord personally occupied the entire building or converted it into commercial property, the owner could require the television company to remove its cables and other equipment. The Court did not find that this limitation made the occupation temporary.

Explaining its decision in light of existing law, the Court, speaking through Justice Thurgood Marshall, observed that while the Court engages in essentially ad hoc, case-by-case inquiries in takings-law cases, the analysis is not totally devoid of standards. The impact of the regulation is of particular significance. A taking may be more readily found when the interference with property can be characterized as a physical intrusion by government than when interference arises from some public program to promote the common good that must adjust the benefits and burdens of economic life. A permanent physical occupation, the Court asserted, is a complete and unqualified deprivation of property. "The government does not simply take a single 'strand' from the 'bundle' of property rights: it chops through the bundle, taking a slice from every strand."[107]

Justice Marshall proceeded to discuss the theory of property rights that supported the ruling, which I shall briefly summarize. Property rights, asserted the justice, have been described as rights to possess, use, and dispose of a material thing. To the extent that government permanently occupies physical property, it effectively destroys each of these rights. First, the owner has no right to possess the occupied space himself and also has no power to exclude the occupier from possession and use of the space. The power to exclude has traditionally been considered one of the most treasured strands in the owner's bundle of property rights. Second, the permanent physical occupation of property forever denies the owner any power to control the use of the property; he not only cannot exclude others, but can make no non-possessory use of the property. Although deprivation of the right to use and obtain a profit from property is not, in every case, independently sufficient to establish a taking, it is clearly relevant. Third, even though the owner may retain the bare legal right to dispose of the occupied space by transfer or sale, the permanent occupation of that space by a stranger will ordinarily empty the right of any value, since any potential purchaser will also be unable to make any use of the property.

This analysis ignores a long-standing trend in takings analysis that says courts should look at the amount of value lost as a result of the deprivation. However, Marshall's opinion has a constitutional basis under the due process interpretation of *Murray's Lessee* (1855) and the many cases and commentaries consistent with it (as discussed in Chapter 2, Section V). Unless it comes about to abate or prevent a nuisance or as a penalty for criminal wrongdoing, a government's permanent occupation of all or a portion of private property is a deprivation of property in violation of the due process clause. This clause would similarly be violated if the government permanently deprived a person of any "portion" of his life or liberty without a due-process proceeding resulting from the wrongdoing of that person.

I shall further consider *Loretto*'s meaning after discussing *United States v. Causby* in the section that follows.

VIII. *United States v. Causby*

In *United States v. Causby* (1946),[108] the U.S. Supreme Court held that the government had taken an easement interest in a portion of Causby's farm by repeatedly flying Army bombers directly above it, emitting loud noises and light which caused him to lose sleep and his chickens to die of shock. His use of the property was partially but not totally destroyed. Acting within its statutory authority, the Civil Aeronautics Authority had approved the glide path followed by the planes. The United States Court of Claims found that there was a diminution in the value of the property and that the frequent low-level flights were the direct and immediate cause. The Supreme Court agreed and found that a servitude (a right to use another's property) had been imposed on the land, entitling Causby to compensation. Government actions had caused diminution, and the fact that the planes never touched the surface was irrelevant.

While upholding the ruling of the Court of Claims that an easement had been taken, the Supreme Court ruled that the judgment entered was defective because the findings of fact contained no precise description as to the easement's nature. The easement was not described in terms of frequency of flight, permissible altitude, or type of airplane, and there was no finding as to whether it was temporary or permanent. Insofar as the taking claim was concerned, it made no difference whether the easement taken was a permanent or a temporary one, but it did of course matter with respect to the amount of compensation to be awarded.

Thus, according to this decision, compensation is required when destruction of property interests has occurred by reason of certain government physical actions, even if there has been no actual or physical invasion of the land or structures involved. There is considerable similarity between this kind of deprivation and one caused by a regulation—more so, at least, than when a permanent physical occupation (such as occurred in *Loretto*) is the cause of the interference with property rights.

IX. Summary of Leading Takings Cases from 1871 to 1987

Judging from the cases discussed in this chapter, the conventional wisdom that the United States Supreme Court had largely abandoned property rights in the century prior to 1987 is not borne out. The best example of this is the 1926 *Euclid* case, which, it is generally assumed, required almost unlimited judicial deference to municipal zoning ordinances. An analysis of the *Euclid* opinion and two other zoning cases decided two years later by the same Court (*Nectow* and *Roberge*) reveals otherwise.

Basic constitutional rules should limit the scope of zoning. The rule that a jurisdiction can only make laws affecting its own residents confines municipal officials to passing zoning ordinances relating exclusively to local matters. Zoning regulations substantially affecting nonresidents are beyond local authority. Unfortunately, the Supreme Court has never ruled on this issue. It has been adjudicated in a small number of state courts, leaving most states with an assumed authority to pass zoning ordinances not limited to regulatory matters of local concern.

Zoning ordinances substantially affecting nonresidents relate to what the *Euclid* opinion identified as the "general public interest" and should be subjected to the usual property-rights examination. *Euclid* was decided in 1926, four years after Justice Holmes's *Pennsylvania Coal* opinion, in which he established the parameters of modern takings analysis by using a balancing test to determine the constitutionality of property-use regulations. This test gave much less deference to government than the test set out in *Euclid*. If examined under this test rather than *Euclid*'s deferential standard, many of our present-day zoning ordinances would fail constitutional muster.

In *Nectow* and *Roberge,* the Supreme Court did not accord great deference to zoning ordinances and instead provided substantial protection for property rights. These decisions portended that owners challenging zoning ordinances would often prevail before the Supreme Court. Unfortunately, the Court would undergo an ideological shift in the late 1930s and would lose interest in zoning cases. Left to their own devices, most state and federal courts would regard the deferential-standard language in *Euclid* as conclusive with respect to zoning challenges.

With *Pumpelly* (1871), the Supreme Court inaugurated inverse condemnation, under which government is liable for a harm to property resulting from carrying out its legitimate functions. *Pumpelly*'s importance was diminished by the 1887 *Mugler* decision (the prohibition case) which many considered to accord vast and almost unlimited power to government to regulate property by way of the police power. *Mugler,* however, can be explained as a response to the public's intense opposition to alcohol consumption. *Mugler*'s position on the police power was rejected in property cases (*Pennsylvania Coal* and *Buchanan*), contract cases (*Lochner, Adkins,* and *New State Ice*) and expression cases ("clear and present danger" decisions). However, *Mugler*'s interpretation of the police power was rejuvenated in *Miller v. Schoene,* a 1928 decision which accorded Virginia the power to destroy diseased red cedar trees in order to save apple trees because the latter were considered more important to the state economy. (Although the decision failed to protect the red cedar owners' property rights, it was made unanimously by a Court containing some strong property-rights proponents and Justice Holmes, author of the *Pennsylvania Coal* decision.) Were *Schoene* to present its issue for the first time today, it would fail the constitutional hurdle of our present scrutiny tests.

That the Supreme Court had not surrendered to government in land-use regulation was made clear by the *Loretto* and *Causby* decisions, both of which were big victories for private ownership. *Loretto* interpreted the takings clause as providing absolute protection for an owner whose property has been subject in whole or in even minuscule part to a permanent physical occupation by or at the behest of government. Although the Court's language was confined to "permanent" physical occupations, *Loretto* did not involve a "forever" occupation but one of defined limitation. Under the statute in that case, government occupation could end if the owner occupied the entire building (instead of renting out apartments) or converted it to commercial use. In *Causby,* the Court found a taking of a portion of a farm by government airplanes, authorized by government regulations, and flying overhead but not actually occupying the land. Both *Loretto* and *Causby* concern physical actions, but it would not be difficult to apply similar reasoning to deprivations by regulation—and this is what in time occurred, as I will explain in the next chapter.

5

Takings Decisions in 1987 and Subsequent Years

In interpreting the Constitution, the United States Supreme Court currently protects liberties under a series of rules that it has enunciated over the past several decades.[1] Each protected liberty is secured under one of three levels of inquiry which the Court applies to determine if the law or regulation at issue violates the Constitution. The difference between the three levels is the intensity of review that is applied. The highest level of scrutiny—referred to as strict scrutiny—is accorded to the freedoms of expression, religion, travel, privacy, and the right to vote. Strict scrutiny provides for only a modest amount of deference to government. At the other end of the spectrum is minimal scrutiny, which is applied to economic liberties (those relating to the production and distribution of goods and services) and accords the government great deference.

Property rights (those relating to ownership and use), in the post-1987 era, are protected under a level of scrutiny that is between strict and minimal, usually referred to as intermediate scrutiny (as noted in Chapter 4, Section II, the Supreme Court has long differentiated between economic rights and property rights). The lines between the three kinds of scrutiny are not certain. In defining the mid-level of scrutiny, one cannot be much more precise than to say that it gives government far more deference than is required under strict scrutiny and much less deference than under minimal scrutiny.

These levels of scrutiny enable the Court to determine whether a challenged regulation is unduly restrictive of constitutionally protected liberties. Application of these standards is one of the ways in which the Court fulfills its duty to secure, as the Constitution's preamble states, "the Blessings of Liberty."[2]

The Court also applies an intermediate level of scrutiny to commercial speech,[3] gender classifications,[4] and, until recently, federal racial preferences.[5] After the zoning cases of the late 1920s and until the 1987 term, property rights in most federal and state courts—except with respect to the issues involved in *Loretto* (the cable case) and *Causby* (the airplane overflight case)—rated somewhat but not considerably more protection than required under minimal scrutiny. As a general matter, property rights joined economic rights in the basement of Constitutional liberties.

In 1987, the U.S. Supreme Court decided three land-use cases that considerably raised the judicial protection of property rights, and three later cases have elevated it even more. In these cases, the Court applied the protective rules that it had adumbrated in 1980 in *Agins v. City of Tiburon,*[6] but now construed them meaningfully as it had not in *Agins*.

Agins involved a facial challenge to a residential zoning ordinance that limited the density of a five-acre tract owned by the plaintiffs to one dwelling unit per acre. The plaintiffs had not submitted a plan for development of their property and, consequently, the only question before the Court was whether the mere enactment of the zoning ordinance constituted a taking. A facial challenge is an attack on the text, as distinguished from a challenge to the law "as applied." The *Euclid* case, discussed in Chapter 4, also involved a facial challenge to a zoning ordinance.

In contrast to the highly deferential standard of *Euclid,* the Court in *Agins* set forth the following test for determining the constitutionality of a zoning ordinance:

> The application of a general zoning law to particular property effects a taking if the ordinance does not substantially advance legitimate state interests, *see Nectow v. Cambridge,* 277 U.S. 183, 188 (1928), or denies an owner economically viable use of his land, *see Penn Central Transportation Co. v. New York City,* 438 U.S. 104, 138, n. 36 (1978).[7]

However, the Court applied a modest level of inquiry in *Agins* and found that the ordinance was valid because it advanced "legitimate governmental goals" such as (1) discouraging the "premature and unnecessary conversion of open space land to urban uses" and (2) protecting the residents of the municipality from the "ill effects of urbanization." The Court's inquiry accorded considerable deference to the locality, and much of the legal community did not recognize that the Court had adopted a new standard for determining constitutionality.

In setting forth the constitutional standard, the Court necessarily evaluated the relevant jurisprudence, and in relying in part on *Nectow* it seemed to fashion a balancing test that reasonably well represented existing law, as explained in Chapter 4. For this Court, *Nectow* was more representative of the law than *Euclid,* although the latter was probably cited much more often in the state and federal courts. *Penn Central* upheld regulations preserving a historical landmark against a takings challenge, and the Court indicated in a footnote (footnote 36, referred to above in the explanation of the standard) that the decision was based on a determination that the operation of the Penn Central Terminal (a historical landmark) was economically viable. The reader should note that *Agins* involved a facial challenge and that both *Nectow* and *Penn Central* were challenges to the law as applied, indicating that the *Agins* Court did not distinguish between these two kinds of proceedings with respect to the constitutional standard it presented.

The Court's citing of *Nectow* in support of its new standard is also relevant in determining the level of scrutiny required under the test it set forth. The *Nectow* decision accorded much less deference to government than is required under the language of *Euclid*. *Nectow* required justification by the locality, whereas the burden for proving the ordinance unconstitutional under *Euclid* rested entirely with the owner, who had to show that the zoning ordinance was "clearly arbitrary and unreasonable." This is not a difficult test for a zoning ordinance to satisfy.

However, as explained in Chapter 4, Section V, the *Nectow* Court altered *Euclid*'s language and held that a zoning restriction "cannot be imposed if it does not bear a substantial relation to the public health, [etc.]."[8] Six months later, in *Roberge,* the Supreme Court cited this language from *Nectow* and went on to state that legislators may not under the police power "impose restrictions that are unnecessary and unreasonable upon the use of private property." The right to devote land to any legitimate use, asserted the Court, "is property within the protection of the Constitution."[9] As the later opinion, *Roberge* was an interpretation of the *Euclid* and *Nectow* decisions.

The *Agins* scrutiny tests presently applied by the Court were developed many decades after the *Euclid-Nectow* period. If, however, one wanted to characterize the level of scrutiny applied in the *Nectow* decision, one might say that it was closest to what we currently identify as intermediate scrutiny.

As a result of the three 1987 land-use decisions (and subsequent decisions), protection of the property right now enjoys very respectable stature at the nation's highest court, which grants it a relatively high level of review—intermediate scrutiny albeit not strict scrutiny protection. Thus, Chief Justice William Rehnquist, writing for the majority in a 1994 land-use case, advised his dissenting brethren that "[we] see no reason why the Takings Clause of the Fifth Amendment, as much a part of the Bill of Rights as the First Amendment or Fourth Amendment, should be relegated to the status of a poor relation."[10]

The seminal 1987 cases are *Keystone Bituminous Coal Association v. DeBenedictus,*[11] *First English Evangelical Lutheran Church of Glendale v. County of Los Angeles,*[12] and *Nollan v. California Coastal Commission.*[13] In 1992, the Court decided *Lucas v. South Carolina Coastal Council;*[14] and, in 1994, it decided *Dolan v. The City of Tigard*[15] and remanded to the California courts *Ehrlich v. Culver City.*[16] I discuss *Keystone, First English, Nollan, Lucas,* and *Dolan* in the following five sections, and I discuss *Ehrlich* in Section I of Chapter 6. After long years of mostly indifference, the United States Supreme Court has, with these cases, set a course in protecting property rights which is consistent with its constitutional mission.

I. *Keystone Bituminous Coal Association v. DeBenedictus*

Keystone upheld by a 5-to-4 vote Pennsylvania's Bituminous Mine Subsidence Act of 1966, which prohibited coal mining that causes subsidence to certain types of structures: public buildings and noncommercial buildings generally used by the public; dwellings used for human habitation; and cemeteries. The Supreme Court held that the act did not violate the takings or obligation-of-contracts (Article I, Section 10) clauses of the Constitution. Pennsylvania's earlier effort at subsidence legislation was the Kohler Act, which had been held unconstitutional in 1922 in *Pennsylvania Coal Co. v. Mahon* (discussed in Chapter 4). In *Keystone,* the plaintiffs owned, leased, or otherwise controlled substantial coal reserves beneath the surface of properties affected by the Subsidence Act. Pursuant to this statute, the Pennsylvania Department of Environmental Resources (DER) applied a formula that required at least 50 percent of the coal beneath protected structures to be kept in place to provide surface support. In addition, the act also authorized the DER to revoke a mining permit if the removal of coal caused damage to a protected structure or area and the operator had not within six months repaired the damage, satisfied any claim arising therefrom, or deposited funds to secure the required repairs.

Keystone was the first of the 1987 takings cases in which the United States Supreme Court exhibited an approach generally more protective of property rights than had long existed in that hallowed tribunal. The opinion applied, to the facts of this case, the rules that *Agins* had held were required to determine if a taking of property had occurred. Regrettably, after setting forth these rules, the *Keystone* majority reverted as if by habit to existing judicial practices in this area of the law, by giving preference in its analysis to government authority over liberty. But this failing would be rectified in subsequent cases.

Citing *Agins,* the majority opinion in *Keystone* held "that land use regulation can effect a taking if it does not substantially advance legitimate state interests, . . . or denies an owner economically viable use of his land." This holding was confirmed in subsequent cases and constitutes three separate rules, each of which must be satisfied before a regulation of property passes constitutional muster: (1) it must have as its purpose "a legitimate state interest"; (2) it must "substantially advance" this interest; and (3) it must not deny the owner "economically viable use of his land."[17] In the balance of this book, I shall refer to these as the "*Agins* Rules" and shall refer by number to each separate rule.

The Court's acceptance of the *Agins* formula is a major event in takings-clause jurisprudence. Previously, anarchy seemed to reign in interpretation, as virtually the only restraints on the government were the undefinable limits of the police power. No matter how a judge ruled, he or she could find solace in Justice Oliver Wendell Holmes's famous and nebulous dictum that "[a]s long recognized, some values are enjoyed under an implied limitation and must yield to the police power."[18] The *Agins* Rules are not a magic formula that imposes principled decision-making in takings-clause jurisprudence, but they are a long step toward this goal.

The kind of inquiry prescribed in *Agins* is similar to the tests used in cases affecting other rights. For both those rights held to a strict-scrutiny test and those examined under intermediate scrutiny share the same apprehension about unchecked power. Both levels of scrutiny are based on the idea that in a democratic society, legislatures are limited in their power to abrogate the people's liberties. Legislatures must show justification for imposing restraints and must not act to bar liberty solely as a matter of preference. Their purpose must be to serve a public and not a private interest, and the laws they adopt must achieve this purpose in varying degrees depending on the right involved.

The tests applied in other areas where intermediate scrutiny is employed do not differ appreciably in language from Rules 1 and 2 of the *Agins* formulation. Thus, gender classifications must (1) serve important governmental objectives and must (2) be substantially related to the achievement of those objectives.[19] Similarly, a restriction on protected commercial speech is constitutional only if it (1) seeks to implement a substantial governmental interest and (2) directly advances that interest.[20] *Agins* Rule 3 relates only to property regulation.

The intensity of the review under intermediate scrutiny is less rigorous than under strict scrutiny, and it is more rigorous than under minimal scrutiny. Under strict scrutiny, a regulation is valid if it is (1) necessary to serve a compelling state interest and (2) narrowly drawn to achieve that interest. Government has a greater burden to meet each of these tests than it has to meet the tests of intermediate scrutiny. The government's burden is least under minimal scrutiny, which requires that the aggrieved party prove that the regulation at issue (1) does not bear a rational relation to a legitimate government purpose or (2) fails to advance such a purpose. As is evident from the language employed in each of the three tests, the government's chances of victory when sued for allegedly violating a fundamental liberty depend very much on the level of scrutiny it must satisfy.

Keystone involved a facial challenge to a statute limiting the use of property. The only question before the Court was whether the mere enactment of the statute constituted a taking, since the plaintiffs chose not to sue in this proceeding for the damages they sustained due to the enforcement of the law. The Court accorded a level of review to government more commensurate with intermediate scrutiny than with minimal scrutiny. The issues were resolved in favor of the government, but the inquiry was much more intensive than *Euclid* required.

The protection of liberties from excessive government restraint is fundamental to English and American law. For Locke, Coke, and Blackstone, government must always justify serious limitations on liberty. Interpreting the
meaning of civil liberty, Blackstone set forth principles that would, in time,
guide the United States Supreme Court in its decisions on the constitutionality
of government regulations:

> [Civil liberty] is no other than natural liberty so far restrained by human laws (and
> no farther) as is necessary and expedient for the general advantage of the public.
> Hence we may collect that the law, which restrains a man from doing mischief to
> his fellow citizens, though it diminishes the natural, increases the civil liberty of
> mankind: but every wanton and causeless restraint of the will of the subject,
> whether practiced by a monarch, a nobility, or a popular assembly, is a degree of
> tyranny. Nay, that even laws themselves, whether made with or without our con-
> sent, if they regulate and constrain our conduct in matters of mere indifference,
> without any good end in view, are laws destructive of liberty. . . . [T]hat consti-
> tution or frame of government, that system of laws, is alone calculated to main-
> tain civil liberty, which leaves the subject entire master of his own conduct, ex-
> cept in those points wherein the public good requires some direction or restraint.[21]

Blackstone provides direction for ascertaining whether a legislative restriction
constitutes a deprivation of a constitutionally protected right. No violation of
the due process or other protective clause can occur in the absence of the deprivation of a secured right.

In constitutional adjudication, Blackstone's exposition takes the form of
tests to determine whether a statute achieves its legislative purposes, whether
the means and ends are legitimate, and, when some restraint is necessary,
whether the one utilized is the least onerous to liberty. Thus, in 1819, Chief Justice John Marshall declared that for legislation to be constitutional, the end has
to be legitimate, and the means appropriate and plainly adapted to that end.[22]

Blackstone's perspective was widely held by early American political leaders such as James Madison. Madison objected to "arbitrary restrictions, ex-
emptions, and monopolies" that deny to part of a nation's citizens free use of
their faculties, and free choice of their occupations.[23] He rejected "commercial
shackles" as generally unjust, oppressive, and unpolitic. If industry and labor
are left to take their own course, Madison asserted, they will generally be directed to those objects which are the most productive.[24]

A. Applying Agins *Rule 1*

The *Keystone* decision applied *Agins* Rules 1 (that a regulatory law's purpose must be a legitimate state interest) and 3 (that it must not deny the owner
economically viable use of his land) to the facts of the case, but it did so in a

remarkably poor way. (The decision did not apply Rule 2.) The majority opinion, authored by Justice John Paul Stevens, distinguished the 1966 Subsidence Act from the 1921 Kohler Act, at issue in *Pennsylvania Coal,* which prohibited mining of anthracite coal in such a way as to cause the subsidence of any dwelling or other designated structure not owned by the coal company. According to Stevens, the 1921 and 1966 acts differed in that the Kohler Act was intended to protect the private interests of those who had purchased surface rights from the coal companies, whereas the new Subsidence Act was intended to serve legitimate public interests in safety, the environment, the economy, and the physical integrity of an area by preventing subsidence of surface areas.

This distinction was also important in order to show that the 1966 Subsidence Act served a legitimate state interest as required under Rule 1 of the *Agins* formula. The Court's majority sought to prove (but, as will be evident, did not succeed in providing convincing arguments) that the Pennsylvania legislature had acted consistent with this rule. Justice Stevens accepted the legislature's declaration of noble public purposes, as this passage from his opinion illustrates: "The District Court and the Court of Appeals were both convinced that the legislative purposes set forth in the statute were genuine, substantial and legitimate, and we have no reason to conclude otherwise."[25] This conclusion may have been warranted by the information contained in the opinion, but it is dubious if all the facts of the controversy are considered. Stevens did not consider the political factors that influenced the Pennsylvania legislature to adopt the statute, an omission that severely weakens his position.

Much similarity existed in the interests that were pressing for the passage of subsidence regulation in 1966 and in 1921. Economic regulations are imposed for one or both of the following reasons: first, to remedy or remove the excesses or limitations of the private market; second, to secure an economic advantage for a person, corporation, or group by the imposition of restraints on the competitive market. Economists refer to the second reason as "rent seeking." In Pennsylvania, supporters of subsidence legislation have always included proponents of each position.

As noted in the previous chapter, because of the extensive coal deposits in some areas of Pennsylvania, coal companies at times sold surface rights to private citizens and government bodies at a price much less than would ordinarily be paid for the entire interest. The purchaser undertook the risk that at a future time the coal company that retained the subsurface rights might mine underneath or close to any structure erected on the land. Both the 1921 Kohler Act and the 1966 Subsidence Act removed this risk, providing many purchasers of the surface rights, both private and public, considerable monetary windfalls.[26]

Justice Holmes in *Pennsylvania Coal* tersely explained the constitutional problem: "If in any case [the government's] representatives have been so short sighted as to acquire only surface rights without the right of support, we see no more authority for supplying the latter without compensation than there was for taking the right of way in the first place and refusing to pay for it because the public wanted it very much."[27] Holmes went on to conclude that so far "as private persons and communities have seen fit to take the risk of aquiring only surface rights, we cannot see that the fact that their risk has become a danger warrants the giving to them of greater rights than they bought."[28]

Since each statute provided considerable monetary benefits for the many owners of surface rights, the pressures on the legislators from this quarter to adopt subsidence legislation were very formidable. The 1966 Subsidence Act also benefited other real-estate interests. It effectively destroyed a system that provided many low- and moderate-income persons an opportunity to purchase surface rights at a low price, thereby removing plots with surface rights from the supply of home sites and enhancing the value of competing lands. When a law greatly enriches many people, the judiciary should at least consider this factor in determining legislative purpose.

Although his opinion does not bear this out, Justice Stevens acknowledged that the Court should not be bound by the stated purposes of the legislature: "*Pennsylvania Coal* instructs courts to examine the operating provisions of a statute, not just its stated purposes, in assessing its true nature."[29] The rule is an obvious one: notwithstanding their real motives, legislators always proclaim their dedication to public welfare, both in their speeches and in their laws. Surely, the legislature's attorneys were aware that for it to survive judicial scrutiny, the 1966 Subsidence Act had to be drafted differently from the Kohler Act, that it had to show a stronger and broader dedication to the public welfare. But reviewing judges should not be misled. As Justice Antonin Scalia would remark in a future case, "the Takings Clause requires Courts to do more than insist upon artful harm-preventing characterizations" since "such a justification can be formulated in practically every case" and "amounts to a test of whether the legislature has a stupid staff."[30]

Nor does Stevens's presentation demonstrate that the legislature was exclusively interested in eliminating subsidence. To show that the legislature which passed the 1921 Kohler Act was not motivated solely by concern over preventing subsidence, Stevens referred to Justice Holmes's observation in the *Pennsylvania Coal* case that the Kohler law "ordinarily does not apply to land when the surface is owned by the owner of the coal."[31] By contrast, Stevens asserts, the 1966 law has no such exception: The current owner may only waive the protection of the act if the Department of Environmental Resources consents. However, Stevens's reasoning is faulty. If the legislature in 1966 was seeking solely to prevent the harms caused by subsidence, why did it apply the

Subsidence Act to certain structures and not all of them? The problems of subsidence also affect commercial and industrial buildings, and roads, and highways; and none of these are protected by the legislation.

In its rights jurisprudence generally, the Supreme Court does not accept all public-oriented purposes as legitimate state interests.[32] It should be equally suspicious when it comes to matters of property. A purpose that imposes restraint on private property use to benefit other sectors of the society is inconsistent with a major tenet of a market economy: that ownership and ordinary uses of property should be protected and encouraged. When the legislature prohibits a use that will cause a nuisance or near-nuisance, it is not taking property, because there is no right to engage in harmful activity; in contrast, when it prohibits a use in order to bestow benefits on others, it is taking from one person and giving to another.[33]

The uses that the 1966 subsidence law restrained would clearly have failed the common-law test of nuisance.[34] Yet Stevens referred to them as "tantamount to public nuisances,"[35] "akin to a public nuisance,"[36] and "similar to public nuisances."[37] Such language camouflages a difference of kind as merely a matter of degree.

The objectives of the 1966 Subsidence Act, as set forth in the statute, included public safety but were not otherwise confined to preventing harm by prohibiting nuisance or near-nuisance uses; instead, they reflected the legislature's concerns to enhance the environment, promote economic development, and maintain and elevate property values to sustain the state's tax base.[38] Abating a serious threat to safety is a legitimate public purpose, but whether this was the overriding purpose in this case is doubtful, in view of Stevens's failure to emphasize or explain it. The safety issue was dismissed by Holmes in *Pennsylvania Coal,* as will be discussed shortly in my consideration of the applicability of *Agins* Rule 2 to *Keystone.*

Unlike the statute in *Mugler,* which only involved prevention of harm (from alcohol consumption), the Subsidence Act was largely intended to confer benefits on the public. Its principal beneficiaries were the public and private surface owners who had previously bargained away all protection against subsidence caused by mining. Few others would sustain significant personal damage. But even if some elements of the public at large did suffer harm, it is difficult to view the 1966 act as anything other than, chiefly, an effort to confer benefits on portions of the public at the expense of the coal companies.[39]

According to Chief Justice Rehnquist, who wrote the dissenting opinion in *Keystone,* accepting this act's objectives as constitutional "would surely allow government much greater authority than we have recognized to impose societal burdens on individual landowners, for nearly every action the government takes is intended to secure for the public an extra measure of 'health, safety, and welfare.' "[40] The nuisance exception to the protections of the takings guarantee, Rehnquist writes, is a narrow one intending only to prevent "a misuse or illegal use" and not "the prevention of legal and essential use."[41]

B. *Applying* Agins *Rule 3*

With respect to *Agins* Rule 3, Stevens found that the Subsidence Act did not deny the plaintiffs economically viable use of their land.[42] He explained that two protections are included within this test, each of which may affect all or a portion of the property: first, the regulation must not make it commercially impracticable to develop the property; and second, there must be no undue interference with an owner's investment-backed expectations.

Stevens denied that the plaintiffs had suffered financially as a result of the subsidence law. The plaintiffs claimed that they had been required to leave a little less than 27 million tons of coal in place to support the required properties. The total coal in the thirteen mines they owned or controlled amounted to over 1.46 billion tons. Thus, concluded Stevens, the law required them to leave less than 2 percent of their coal in place, not significantly affecting their economic interests.

Such inquiry is wrong for two reasons: it makes the wealth of the owner a factor in takings jurisprudence, and it ignores the separable aspect of the coal company's subsurface property. An owner is entitled to constitutional protection for every asset he owns. Surely, if the government seeks to confiscate someone's bank account, it cannot justify this action because the owner has many other accounts at the same bank. The wealth of the owner is not a relevant consideration in legally securing ownership, since the protection of private property is in large measure premised on the societal benefits its private use and development provides. These are the "Blessings of Liberty" which the Constitution secures and the judiciary protects, regardless of whether the person protected is rich or poor, influential or powerless. As Friedrich Hayek put it, government restraint is essential to enable people to freely use their talents to advance society:

> What is important is not what freedom I personally would like to exercise but what freedom some person may need in order to do things beneficial to society. This freedom we can assure to the unknown person only by giving it to all.[43]

Under Pennsylvania law, the support estate, the mineral estate, and the surface estate are three different estates in land which can be individually owned, identified, and separated from each other. The support estate consists of the strata of coal and earth beneath the surface that support the surface estate and prevent subsidence. The owner of each estate can sell it, and therefore each should be considered a different asset. Prior to the 1966 Subsidence Act, there were at least four possible purchasers for a support estate owned by a coal company: the surface rights owner, the mineral rights owner, another coal company, or an investor-speculator. The 1966 law eliminated the value of the support estate by making the mine operator strictly liable for any damages to certain classes of surface structures caused by subsidence. Recognized as a separate asset both in law and the marketplace, the support estate is hardly, as Stevens asserts, "merely a part of the entire bundle of rights possessed by the owner of either the coal or the surface."[44] "It is appropriate," as the dissent contends, "to consider the effect of the regulation on that particular property interest."[45]

Stevens rejected segmentation of the plaintiff companies' coal assets, relying in part on a statement in *Penn Central Transportation Co. v. City of New York,* a 1978 land-use case. *Penn Central* presented the question of whether a city, as part of a comprehensive program to preserve historical landmarks, may place restrictions on individual landmarks without effecting a taking. The Court stated that in determining whether a taking has occurred, the focus should be "both on the character of the action and on the nature of the interference with rights in the parcel as a whole—here the city tax block designated as the 'landmark site.'"[46] However, the block in question contained not only the property in controversy but also other properties owned by the plaintiff. Under this theory, the impact of a regulation on a parcel of property is not determined by the effect on it alone, but in addition by the effect on other properties owned by the same person. Justice Scalia, writing in a later case, would refer to this theory of how to determine diminution in value, as "extreme" and "unsupportable."[47] When ownership of more than the particular site in issue is considered as part of a takings inquiry, the issue becomes one of wealth and not of rights.

Justice Stevens acknowledged that if the subsidence restriction were regarded as a permanent physical occupation, there would be a taking under *Loretto,* regardless of the amount of property involved or the strength of the justification for it. But this rule, he stated, does not apply when a regulatory deprivation is involved.[48] To be sure, physical occupation by or at the behest of government clearly deprives an owner of all interest in the portion occupied. However, as Justice William Brennan had observed in an important dissenting opinion (discussed in the opening section of Chapter 4), total deprivation of beneficial use via regulation is, from the landowner's perspective, the equivalent of a physical occupation. Writing for himself and three other justices, in *San Diego Gas & Electric Co. v. San Diego* (1981), Brennan stated:

> Police power regulations such as zoning ordinances and other land-use restrictions can destroy the use and enjoyment of property in order to promote the public good just as effectively as formal condemnation or physical invasion of property. From the property owner's point of view, it may matter little whether his

land is condemned or flooded, or whether it is restricted by regulation to use in its natural state, if the effect in both cases is to deprive him of all beneficial use of it. From the government's point of view, the benefits flowing to the public from preservation of open space through regulation may be equally great as from creating a wildlife refuge through formal condemnation or increasing electricity production through a dam project that floods private property.[49]

Brennan made a similar distinction in his majority opinion in the aforementioned 1978 *Penn Central Transportation Co.* case, which concerned this issue of regulatory taking among others. There he observed, commenting on the regulatory taking that had disturbed Justice Holmes in *Pennsylvania Coal* (1922), that the Kohler Act "made it commercially impracticable to mine the coal" and consequently "had nearly the same effect as the complete destruction of the rights" that the coal company had reserved.[50] In his *Keystone* dissent, Rehnquist agreed with this perspective: the result should be regarded as the same as a condemnation or physical invasion whenever "the government simply prohibited every use of [a] property."[51] The Court in *Lucas v. South Carolina Coastal Council* (1992) (to be discussed later, in Section IV) eventually agreed with both Brennan's and Rehnquist's position.

Since the coal companies in *Keystone* had suffered only a 2 percent reduction in their coal resources, Stevens wrote in his majority opinion, their investment-backed expectations were not materially affected. But in fact their investment expectations had been adversely affected. The coal companies' sale of surface rights to private and public parties was consistent with the law of Pennsylvania prior to 1966 (when the Subsidence Act was passed), and the companies had good reason to believe that their mining rights, secured by contracts, were valid and binding. The 1966 Subsidence Act was a retroactive measure, effectively denying the companies the opportunity to exploit coal reserves that they had retained under these contracts. It is unlikely that they would have sold the surface rights had they believed that the mineral and support estates they retained would be in jeopardy.

C. The Court Does Not Apply Agins Rule 2

Noticeably absent from Stevens's opinion is any consideration of whether the Subsidence Act fulfills *Agins* Rule 2. No matter how laudable the purpose, if a law does not substantially achieve that purpose, then the restriction it imposes is futile and oppressive. The Court would make this point in *Nollan v. California Coastal Commission,* decided in the same 1987 term (to be discussed in Section III). There, the Court would assume, for the purposes of deciding the case, that the California Coastal Commission's proclaimed objectives in requiring a public easement over an owner's beachfront property were legitimate, but then would conclude that these objectives were not substantially advanced by the easement.

In *Keystone,* the Pennsylvania legislature claimed that it adopted the 1966 Subsidence Act to augment safety and generally preserve and enhance the economy and the environment. In *Pennsylvania Coal* (1922), Justice Holmes asserted that safety is not a concern when the coal companies are required by their contracts to give notice of proposed mining. From Holmes's perspective, it is doubtful that the 1966 Subsidence Act "substantially advanced" safety. Moreover, there is a serious question of whether the state's severe interference with private market forces — including the Subsidence Act's destruction of both the surface ownership system and the value of considerable coal-company assets — would substantially advance the stated objectives. The fit between means and ends is certainly worthy of inquiry when individual rights are extinguished, even though the *Keystone* Court apparently did not agree.

Nonetheless, considering the state of takings law at the time, property owners did obtain some measure of security from the 1987 *Keystone* decision: the Court applied constitutional rules for property rights that were consistent with those that it applied elsewhere for the protection of other rights. Even the *Keystone* opinion itself — when examined closely and despite its immediate effect on the coal companies — advanced the protection of property rights in several respects. It provided an important interpretation of the meaning of *Agins* Rule 1: the requirement that regulatory legislation must be intended to serve a legitimate state interest. *Keystone* understood Holmes's opinion in *Pennsylvania Coal* to mean that an act did not serve a legitimate state interest if it was primarily intended to benefit private interests. Thus, a legislative purpose that benefits a particular group and not the public generally does not serve a legitimate state interest. *Keystone,* in addition, interpreted the "economically viable use" rule (*Agins* Rule 3) to include both destruction of investment-backed expectations and confiscatory diminutions in commercial value, each of which may affect a whole or partial interest in the property. The decision also asserted that in adjudicating regulations that impair property rights, the Court would not be bound by the stated intentions of the legislature. *Keystone* was an important first step in the new takings-clause jurisprudence.

II. *First English Evangelical Lutheran Church of Glendale v. County of Los Angeles*

First English v. County of Los Angeles (1987)[52] is a case that primarily concerns what is referred to as a "temporary taking"—that is, a taking of property that applies for a limited period of time and is not permanent. The First English Evangelical Church was the owner of a twenty-one-acre parcel of land located in a rural

part of Los Angeles County, California, that was subject to a highly restrictive ordinance. The ordinance provided that "[a] person shall not construct, reconstruct,
place or enlarge any building or structure, any portion of which is, or will be, located" in the general area. The county had passed the ordinance as a safety measure to prevent harm due to severe flooding, a recurrent problem in the area.

In 1957, the church had purchased this land for the purpose of operating a
campground, to be known as "Lutherglen," as a retreat and recreational area for
handicapped children. The land is located in a canyon along the banks of a creek
that is the natural drainage channel for a watershed area. In 1978, a flood destroyed all of Lutherglen's buildings. The next year, in response to the flood, Los
Angeles County adopted the ordinance forbidding the construction or reconstruction of any building or structure in a flood-protection area; Lutherglen was
included in this prohibition. Shortly thereafter, the church filed suit in California,
alleging, among other things, that the ordinance denied it all use of its property,
and seeking to recover damages for such loss of use. The trial court dismissed the
suit on the basis of existing California law that barred a landowner from maintaining an inverse-condemnation suit (an action for damages) based on an alleged
regulatory taking. It held that compensation was not required until the challenged
law had been held by a court to be a taking and the government had, nevertheless, decided to continue to enforce it. The California Court of Appeal affirmed
the dismissal and the church sought review by the United States Supreme Court.

The case presented the question of the appropriate relief for an owner who
alleged a taking of property. Is the plaintiff confined to seeking only invalidation of the ordinance, or may he seek compensation for the damages that he sustained as a result of the ordinance? The latter rule would allow compensation
for a temporary taking. If a court found that a taking had occurred, the government could reduce its liability by rescinding the offending ordinance, thereby
precluding a permanent taking of the owner's rights.

In holding that an owner could sue for damages after final passage of the
challenged ordinance, the Supreme Court elevated both substantive and procedural protections for property rights. Under then-existing California law, an aggrieved landowner was limited to suing for invalidation of the offending ordinance. The problem with confining relief to invalidation is that it does not
compensate the landowner for any economic loss suffered during the long
course of litigation. In this case, the ordinance became final in January 1979,
and the merits of the plaintiff's claim had not been decided as of 1987, when
the U.S. Supreme Court considered the matter. Moreover, invalidation of an ordinance does not prevent reenactment of slightly altered regulations by the government, and then the landowner's only recourse would be to instigate litigation yet again.[53] As Justice Brennan observed in the 1981 *San Diego Gas &
Electric Co.* case, the government would be able "to change the regulation in
question, even after trial and judgment, make it more reasonable, more restric-

tive, or whatever, and everybody starts over again."[54] During the lengthy invalidation litigation, the public receives the benefit of continuing the existing land use at relatively little expense, just court costs and attorneys' fees, while the landowner suffers under tremendous burdens.

To decide the issue of appropriate relief, the United States Supreme Court assumed that Los Angeles County had denied the plaintiff *all use* of its property, holding that "invalidation of the ordinance without payment of fair value for the use of the property during this period of time would be a constitutionally insufficient remedy."[55] The Court concluded that the Constitution requires compensation whether the taking is permanent or "temporary" (as alleged in this case). The owner is entitled to just compensation for a temporary taking from the date the offending ordinance is adopted until the date that the ordinance is either rescinded or altered so that it no longer effects a taking of the property. If the government neither rescinds nor modifies the offending ordinance, then the owner becomes entitled to compensation for a permanent taking. "It is the owner's loss, not the taker's gain, which is the measure of the value of the property taken."[56] The holding does not apply to normal delays in obtaining building permits, changes in zoning ordinances, variances, and the like.

Subsequently, the Court in *Lucas v. South Carolina Coastal Council* interpreted *First English* as applying to deprivations of *all economically viable use,* as occurred in *Lucas* when the owner was denied a building permit on his beachfront land. This is a lesser deprivation than the denial of *all use.*[57] Without specifically making the point, the Court assumed that a suit in inverse condemnation is proper whenever the government adopts a land-use regulation that the owner alleges effects a taking of his property. Inverse condemnation had been used, since *Pumpelly* in 1871, by property owners whose land had been incidentally damaged by an act of government, but not for regulatory takings. Thus, *First English* made substantial progress toward shoring up property rights.

Los Angeles County contended that allowing compensation for temporary takings would encourage more landowners to file suit and more courts to find takings, making planning and regulatory decisions more difficult for government. It is worth noting the Supreme Court's qualified agreement:

> [S]uch consequences necessarily flow from any decision upholding a claim of constitutional right; many of the provisions of the Constitution are designed to limit the flexibility and freedom of governmental authorities and the Just Compensation Clause of the Fifth Amendment is one of them. As Justice Holmes aptly noted more than 50 years ago, "a strong public desire to improve the public condition is not enough to warrant achieving the desire by a shorter cut than the constitutional way of paying for the change."[58]

First English supports the principle that people who have been harmed by government should have an opportunity to recover their losses. Accordingly, the decision requires government to provide compensation for the entire period during which a taking is effective. When, after passage of a regulatory ordinance, a court determines that a taking has occurred, the government may exercise various alternative courses of action: amendment of the regulation to eliminate the illegality, withdrawal of the invalidated regulation, or the invocation of eminent domain by maintenance of the regulation. But none of these actions reduce the obligation for payment of compensation for the period from imposition of the ordinance to the determination by a court that it is a taking.

III. *Nollan v. California Coastal Commission*

James and Marilyn Nollan owned a Pacific ocean beachfront lot on which was situated a dilapidated cottage. The lot was located one quarter mile south of Faria County Park, a public beach, and eighteen hundred feet north of the Cove, another public beach. Its ocean-side perimeter was the historic mean high tide, about ten feet seaward from an eight-foot-high concrete sea wall on the property that paralleled the ocean. The Nollans sought permission from the California Coastal Commission to demolish the cottage and replace it with a two-story residence. The Coastal Commission regulates development along and adjoining California's coast (see Section I of Chapter 8 for a fuller discussion). The Commission agreed, subject to a condition: the Nollans were told that they would have to dedicate a public easement across their property between the mean high tide line and the sea wall, or no building permit would be granted.

The Commission explained that the proposed house would increase blockage of the public's view of the ocean, contributing to the development of "a 'wall' of residential structures" that would prevent the public "psychologically . . . from realizing a stretch of coastline exists nearby that they have every right to visit." The new house would also increase private use of the shorefront. These effects of constructing the house, along with other area development, would cumulatively "burden the public's ability to traverse the area along the shorefront."[59] To offset that burden, the Commission required the Nollans to provide additional access to the public beaches in the form of an easement across the entire coastal side of their property.

The Commission had placed similar conditions on forty-three of the sixty coastal development permits it had issued in that general area; and of the seventeen issued without such a condition, fourteen had been approved for building before administrative regulations allowed imposition of the condition. The remaining three permits had not involved shorefront property. The Nollans hence had reason to believe prior to purchase that they would be subjected to the same requirement.

By a 6-to-3 majority, the United States Supreme Court decided that the Commission's ruling was constitutionally defective. Justice Scalia reasoned that if California had imposed an easement across the Nollan beachfront in order to increase public access to the beach, without conditioning a permit on this easement, a taking would have occurred, under *Loretto,* as a "permanent physical occupation." But according to Scalia's opinion, *Loretto* applies to a mandated easement under which individuals are given a permanent and continuous right to pass to and fro. In the *Nollan* case, Scalia held, *Loretto* was inapplicable, because neither the state nor the public had actually occupied the Nollan property. The Nollans' use of the property was subject to a regulatory restraint, the constitutionality of which had to be determined under existing takings law.

Citing and applying *Agins,* Justice Scalia, for the majority, stated that the Commission's regulation did not substantially advance its goals, violating Rule 2 of the *Agins* formula. For purposes of the decision, Scalia assumed that the Commission's objectives to provide the public with physical or visual access to the ocean were legitimate state interests. But the condition imposed on the Nollan land "utterly fail[ed] to further the end advanced as the justification for the [condition]," and, therefore, the relationship between means and ends was devoid of an "essential nexus." In the absence of such a fit, the Commission's condition must be regarded not as a valid regulation of land use but as "an out-and-out plan of extortion."[60]

> It is quite impossible to understand how a requirement that people already on the public beaches be able to walk across the Nollans' property reduces any obstacles to viewing the beach created by the new house. It is also impossible to understand how it lowers any "psychological barrier" to using the public beaches, or how it helps to remedy any additional congestion on them caused by construction of the Nollans' new house.[61]

The fact that the Nollans, prior to purchase, were aware of the Commission's policy on coastal easements did not affect their property rights, Scalia asserted. To require the easement on this basis amounted to a "peculiar proposition that a unilateral claim of entitlement by the government can alter property rights." So long as "the Commission could not have deprived the prior owners of the easement without compensating them, the prior owners must be understood to have transferred their full property rights in conveying the lot."[62] That the Commission sought to achieve its purpose by conditioning the building permit on the dedication of an easement did not alter the Nollans' rights.

The Court also discussed the issue of disproportionate impact raised in the *Nollan* case (though it did not decide the case on this ground).[63] The Commission claimed that allowing the Nollans to build their house without dedicating the easement would result in a row of homes between the ocean and the road that would prevent travelers on the road from being aware of the proximity and accessibility of the ocean. The Court replied that if the Nollans were being singled out to bear the burden of California's attempt to remedy this problem, although they had not contributed to it more than other coastal landowners, then the state's action—even if otherwise valid—might violate the takings clause or the equal protection clause.[64] "The Commission may well be right that [providing coastal access] is a good idea, but that does not establish that the Nollans (and other coastal residents) alone can be compelled to contribute to its realization."[65] There could be no essential nexus between the law's objective and a restraint that could at best only partially (not substantially) advance it.

In his opinion, Scalia applied an intermediate level of scrutiny to the facts of the case, according less deference to the Commission than would be warranted under minimal scrutiny. This position was not acceptable to the dissenting justices. The Court's "exactitude . . . is inconsistent with our standard for reviewing the rationality of a state's exercise of its police power for the welfare of its citizens," protested Justice Brennan.[66] He also attacked the majority's position "as a narrow conception of rationality . . . long . . . discredited as a judicial arrogation of legislative authority."[67] Under a minimal review standard, the regulation would have survived, since the government almost always wins under this standard.[68]

Scalia emphasized that *Agins* Rule 2 required "*substantial* advanc[ing] of a legitimate state interest" and was not of minimal consequence.[69] The *Nollan* majority rejected Brennan's argument that the easement condition was a reasonable "exchange" in return for the "benefit" of the development permit, stating that "the right to build on one's own property—even though its exercise can be subjected to legitimate permitting requirements—cannot remotely be described as a 'governmental benefit.'"[70]

IV. *Lucas v. South Carolina Coastal Council*

Most constitutional disputes about land-use regulations turn on the question of when a regulation becomes a taking. As Justice Holmes observed in *Pennsylvania Coal*: "The general rule, at least, is that while property may be regulated to a certain extent, if regulation goes too far it will be recognized as a taking. . . . [T]his is a question of degree—and therefore cannot be disposed of by general propositions."[71]

In *Lucas,* Justice Antonin Scalia, writing for a 6-to-3 majority, explained that the degree rule does not always apply in takings cases. No matter how worthy the justifications, when government engages in either of two actions, it takes property, requiring payment of compensation: first, when it permanently occupies all or a portion of the property; second, when it denies an owner "all economically beneficial or productive use of land." The first rule was affirmed in the 1982 *Loretto* and 1987 *Nollan* cases (both previously discussed).[72] The second involves a total denial of rights protected in *Agins* Rule 3 and is the basis for Scalia's opinion. He reasoned that the impact on the owner of property is essentially the same in both instances.

The *Lucas* case was a dramatic illustration of the political hazards facing landowners. In 1986, David Lucas paid $975,000 for two residential lots on the waterfront of a South Carolina barrier island, intending to build homes of a kind that already existed on adjacent parcels. At the time of purchase, no law of the state prohibited him from building houses on this land. In 1988, the state legislature passed an act which barred Lucas and other owners of land similarly situated from erecting any permanent habitable structures on their lots.

The South Carolina legislature stated that the regulation was required in order to prevent the erosion and destruction of the state's beach/dune system. This system, said the state, acts as a buffer against high tides, storm surge, and hurricanes. Lives and property might be in danger if properties like Lucas's, which had in the past been flooded and under water, were developed. In addition, the preservation of the beach/dune system promoted tourism, increased public access to beaches, and offered an important habitat for plants and animals.[73]

In a suit subsequently filed by Lucas, the South Carolina trial court found that the state act deprived him of "any reasonable economic use of the lots, . . . eliminated the unrestricted right of use, and render[ed] them valueless." The court found that a taking had occurred and awarded Lucas $1,232,000 as just compensation.

However, notwithstanding the trial court's language, Lucas did not sustain a total deprivation. As Justice Blackmun stated in his dissent, Lucas could still "picnic, swim, camp in a tent, or live on the property in a movable trailer." Furthermore, even with the development ban, he could likely sell the property to one of his neighbors, to other nearby residents, or to an investor-speculator. Nevertheless, Lucas had clearly lost his investment-backed expectation to be able to build a house on each lot. (Interestingly, the U.S. Supreme Court did not reverse the trial court's finding of no value but accepted the case for review because Lucas had shown a constitutional deprivation, under *Agins* Rule 3, of the economically beneficial use of his land.)

The state appealed the trial court's decision to the South Carolina Supreme Court, which reversed the lower court's determination that South Carolina had violated Lucas's rights. The South Carolina Supreme Court accepted the state's assertions regarding the severe harm that Lucas's proposed development would bring. When a land-use regulation is designed "to prevent serious public harm," the state court declared, citing *Mugler,* no compensation is due to an owner, regardless of the regulation's effect on the property's value.[74]

As noted earlier, a harm sufficient to qualify as a nuisance must be of a kind that is clearly damaging to other owners or to the community. Such a serious offense justifies the prohibition of a property use, courts have long held. Nuisance is determined under common law by balancing the "gravity of the harm" suffered by the plaintiff against the "utility of the conduct" of the defendant. It is only when a use is unreasonable, in light of its utility and the harm which results, that it becomes a nuisance.[75] However, as illustrated by *Euclid, Mugler,* and *Keystone,* courts and legislators have applied the concept of harm much more broadly than under traditional common-law analysis to cover a wide range of uses, both to protect the public as well as to benefit it.

Justice Scalia confined his opinion in *Lucas* to regulations that deny an owner all economically beneficial or productive use of property, as in this case. He wrote that when a person buys property, he obtains absolute protection against this kind of government action, subject to the legal restraints such as nuisance or other restrictive-use laws affecting the property at purchase. *Mugler* is not applicable when the state denies an owner all economically viable use of his land. "If it were, departure [from protecting the owner] would virtually always be allowed."[76]

Thus, South Carolina could only impose restraints on Lucas's land that existed at the time of purchase, such as those that "do no more than duplicate the result that could have been achieved in the courts—by adjacent landowners (or other uniquely affected persons) under the State's law of private nuisance, or by the State under its complementary power to abate nuisances that affect the public generally, or otherwise."[77] Included in the "otherwise," Scalia explained, was the power of the state to prevent or forestall grave threats to the lives and property of others.[78] Thus, the Court protected private ownership from both public encroachments (confiscation) and private encroachments (nuisances and near-nuisances). The justices remanded the case to the state for reconsideration on the basis of state nuisance laws and other restrictive laws in effect when Lucas purchased the property.

On remand, the South Carolina Supreme Court found that there was no nuisance-law basis for denying Lucas's proposed use of the land. The state subsequently settled with him for $1.5 million and obtained ownership of the lots. The state thereupon offered the lots for public sale. Although the only uses that the state authorities were willing to allow Lucas were to "picnic, swim, camp in a tent, or live on the property in a movable trailer,"[79] the state, when it became the owner, decided against preserving the lots as either parkland or open space. It sold each lot as a building site for $392,500, rejecting an offer of $315,000 for one lot from a neighbor who promised to keep it vacant to protect his view. For the $77,000 difference, the state could have preserved one of the lots for open space, but chose not to.[80]

The state adopted a regulation in 1990 (after the trial court's initial decision in Lucas's favor) which applied to Lucas and other owners of land similarly situated and required that an owner remove any home that became damaged by floods or, with beach erosion over time, fell seaward of the dunes. The South Carolina Supreme Court did not consider this regulation in its opinion. Had this restriction been applied to Lucas's land instead of the building ban, Lucas would have had much less cause for complaint, since this was not a total prohibition on development.

If the houses that Lucas contemplated erecting posed dangers to life or property, as the state had alleged, then the South Carolina legislature was derelict in not prohibiting such construction when the state became the owner of the property. However, if Lucas's proposed construction did not present such a danger, then the legislature was derelict in depriving Lucas of his rights to develop the lots. Indeed, the final outcome in *Lucas* shows how vital it is in a free society for the judiciary to secure owners against arbitrary and capricious legislation.[81]

Some commentators interpret the *Lucas* decision as applying solely to total (100 percent) denials of land use. After all, it is argued, this was the amount of the deprivation found by the trial court, and Scalia likened the loss to a deprivation caused by physical occupation. However, the facts of the case show that Lucas did not suffer denial of all use or value of his property. His loss was largely confined to the elimination of investment-backed expectations. The Court considered the case on the premise that Lucas had been denied economically viable use of his property. Moreover, a total deprivation means that the owner is denied the rights to occupy, use, exclude, and transfer his property, and all these restraints can only occur when the property is permanently occupied by or at the behest of government.

The comparison to physical occupation does not mean that the *Lucas* decision is applicable solely to a total denial of use. Permanent physical occupations by government, unlike regulatory ones, are always takings, although they may involve only a portion of the property.[82] Even a partial occupation through a permanent public easement, according to *Nollan,* constitutes a taking.[83] As explained in *Keystone,* the "economically viable use" rule comprehends two forms of damage which may affect all or part of the property: elimination of commercial value, and denial of investment-backed expectations.[84] Justice Scalia made the point in a footnote in his *Lucas* opinion:

> Regrettably, the rhetorical force of our "deprivation of all economically feasible use" rule is greater than its precision, since the rule does not make clear the "property interest" against which the loss of value is to be measured. . . . The answer to this difficult question may be in how the owner's reasonable expectations have been shaped by the State's law of property—i.e., whether and to what degree the State's law has accorded legal recognition and protection to the particular interest in land with respect to which the taking claimant alleges a diminution in (or elimination of) value. . . .[85]

It is also evident that "deprivation of all economically feasible or viable use" relates to a taking of a property interest that may be less than the whole, if one compares this wording to the language used by Chief Justice Rehnquist in describing the deprivation in *First English* (the temporary-taking-by-regulation case). The Chief Justice said that the holding in that case concerned an ordinance that "denied appellant all use of its property,"[86] a total wipeout. In *Lucas* the term used for the deprivation is "all economically beneficial or productive use," a lesser imposition.[87] If the *Lucas* rule related only to total wipeouts, it is likely the Court would have employed Rehnquist's language.

In his dissent in *Lucas,* Justice Stevens confirms the point: he worries that under *Lucas* an investor may "purchase the right to build a multi-family home on a specific lot, with the result that a zoning regulation that allows only single-family homes would render the investor's property interest 'valueless.'"[88] In separate opinions, Justices Stevens, Blackmun, and Souter each contended that the trial court's finding of no value was incorrect.[89]

Accordingly, a total deprivation of an investment-backed expectation which relates to a portion of the use, but not all use, of the property constitutes a taking requiring compensation.[90] As with partial physical occupations, the remaining permitted uses are a factor in determining the amount of compensation. The relevancy of investment expectations in determining takings was established prior to *Lucas*,[91] but in the *Lucas* context such expectations take on a much higher level of importance.

The investment-backed expectation concept is not of minor significance in contemporary society. It is not infrequent that an investor purchases land for a specific use and is subsequently frustrated by passage of a zoning regulation denying such use. When residents learn of a proposed development in their neighborhood that they find objectionable, they may demand that the city council change the law to prohibit its construction. Such efforts are often successful in the highly politicized atmosphere of zoning. Thus, in *HFH Ltd. v. Superior Court,* a much-discussed 1975 California case, the plaintiff, a leading supermarket chain, bought land zoned for commercial use in Cerritos, intending to use it for this purpose, but the city later rezoned it for low-density, single-family residential use.[92] Environmental concerns raise similar difficulties. In the famous *Just v. Marinette County* (Wisconsin, 1972), the Justs bought lakefront property to develop for residential housing and proceeded to build houses on it until the county adopted an ordinance prohibiting any further development of the tract.[93] The regulations involved in both *HFH* and *Just* were upheld in their respective state courts. Such decisions raise serious problems for a society. As Justice Kennedy stated: "The Takings Clause . . . protects private expectations to ensure private investment."[94]

The *Lucas* decision does not simply concern takings; it also relates to other important constitutional and economic issues, which I shall now explore.

A. *Applying* Agins *Rules 1 and 2 to the Facts of the* Lucas *Case*

In *Lucas,* Justice Scalia pursued a novel legal theory—that except for nuisances or other uses causing grave public harms, deprivation of all economically viable use was a taking per se. There were, however, already-existing rules that applied to the problem. The validity of the South Carolina law appears doubtful under *Agins* Rules 1 and 2. In adopting the statute, the state's legislature sought both to prevent harm by forbidding activity that allegedly threatened life and property and to confer benefits on the state's tourist industry and beach-loving residents. In *Keystone,* Scalia was part of the minority of four who asserted that prevention of harm is a legitimate state interest (*Agins* Rule 1) while bestowing benefits is not. The *Keystone* minority confined harm to a nuisance or near-nuisance, neither of which was found to exist in *Lucas.*

Even assuming the presence of a legitimate state interest, prohibiting Lucas from building on two of the last four vacant lots in the development would not seem to meet either the "essential nexus" or disproportionate-impact test of *Nollan* (or the "rough proportionality" test of the later-decided *Dolan* case, to be discussed in Section V of this chapter). Given that there was no nuisance or near-nuisance basis for such a prohibition, the fit between banning Lucas's development and substantially achieving the many purposes of the ban is not tight.

Lucas might also fail the *Nollan* test because South Carolina's law operated retroactively. Although a civil law cannot be deemed an ex post facto law under the Constitution (as interpreted in 1798 by the Supreme Court), the judiciary has at times ruled that retroactive laws violate other constitutional protections: due process, equal protection of the law, or obligation of contracts. Consequently, a property law that applies retroactively may not be a constitutionally permissible means for achieving a legitimate state interest. A civil law depriving an owner of a right previously acquired is a retroactive law. The law that was at issue in *Lucas* had this effect by denying Lucas the right to build that he had acquired when he purchased the land.

Because retroactivity increases the burden on a person, such laws would have difficulty surviving strict-scrutiny analysis, the highest level of judicial review, which requires that the means chosen by the state to effectuate its purpose "must be narrowly tailored to the achievement of that goal."[95] While the requirement under intermediate scrutiny is less severe, the legislature is not unrestrained in selecting its means. An owner who is deprived of an existing property interest *retroactively* has a much stronger takings claim than one who seeks to restore a property interest that had been eliminated *prospectively.* As the Court in *Loretto* asserted, the impact of the regulation is of particular significance: "A taking may be more readily found when the interference with property can be characterized as a physical invasion by government, than when interference arises from some public program. . . ."[96] While not as severe as a physical invasion, a retroactive law is a very serious interference with property rights.

In *Board of Trustees of State University of New York v. Fox* (1989), Justice Scalia described the means standard used in intermediate-scrutiny analysis. Although the case dealt with commercial speech, its teaching is relevant here because the same level of scrutiny is utilized:

> What our decision requires is a "fit" . . . that is, not necessarily perfect but reasonable; that represents not necessarily the single best disposition but one whose scope is "in proportion to the interest served" [citation]; that employs not neces-

sarily the least restrictive means but . . . a means narrowly tailored to achieve the desired objective.[97]

Retroactive laws do not comply with this prescription. (I will discuss the evils of these laws at greater length in Section IVB.) While ordinarily valid, retroactive civil laws are infected with the same vice as ex post facto laws, which are retroactive criminal laws. "Instead of packing the actor off to jail, the legislature, with the judiciary's cooperation, more modestly requires the payment of sums of money and reordering of affairs."[98] In the context of the *Agins* Rules, a retroactive law is not a narrowly tailored means to an end; it adds to the deleterious impact on the owner, increasing the severity of the restraint. With respect to the *Lucas* case, it is obvious that Lucas would never have purchased the property if he had known ahead of time that the state would pass a prohibition on building.

Wygant v. Jackson Board of Education (1986),[99] although a civil rights case and one employing strict rather than intermediate scrutiny, does provide a useful lesson on the impact of retroactive laws. An apt analogy can be drawn between that case and the retroactive land-use regulations that were applied to Lucas. In *Wygant,* the Court struck down the means chosen by the Jackson, Michigan, school board to effectuate its civil rights objectives. The board sought a layoff of nonminority teachers with greater seniority in order to retain minority teachers with less seniority. Justice Lewis Powell explained that this requirement was not narrowly tailored because its impact on the nonminority teachers was excessive: "Though hiring goals may burden some innocent individuals," he wrote, "they simply do not impose the same kind of injury that layoffs impose. Denial of a future employment opportunity is not as intrusive as loss of an existing job."[100]

Lucas's loss is comparable. The Jackson school board's adoption of the layoff provision changed its original agreement with the teachers, which had linked layoffs to seniority, and thus was tantamount to a retroactive law with respect to nonminority teachers. The provision deprived these teachers of an important seniority right. South Carolina's law almost totally wiped out Lucas's investment. While Lucas's loss was perhaps not as drastic a personal loss as that suffered by nonminority teachers in *Wygant,* the similarities are sufficient to warrant heightened judicial concern, albeit under an intermediate rather than a strict standard of scrutiny. Thus, South Carolina's law forbidding Lucas from building might well have failed the second *Agins* test.

B. Retroactive Laws Are Unjust and Unwise

As previously noted in Chapter 2, Section I, the holding in *Calder v. Bull* (1798) that the ex post facto clauses apply only to criminal matters and not to retroactive civil laws, has never been reversed, notwithstanding the existence of learned commentary which faults it.[101] Two of the justices in that case premised their decisions in part on the belief that the Fifth Amendment's takings clause provided protection against retroactive legislation, a position never accepted by the Supreme Court. If the Framers considered that the ex post facto clauses extended to property rights, wrote Justice Samuel Chase in his opinion in *Calder v. Bull,* then the takings clause was unnecessary, and they would not have inserted it. In his opinion in the case, Justice James Iredell feared that a broad interpretation of ex post facto clauses would obstruct the government's eminent domain powers; justice can be achieved, he asserted, not by limiting government's condemnation powers but by providing owners with just compensation, as the takings clause provides.[102]

As defined by Justice Joseph Story, "[e]very statute which takes away or impairs vested rights acquired under existing law, or creates a new obligation, imposes a new duty, or attaches a new disability, in respect to transactions or considerations already past, must be deemed retrospective. . . ."[103] Blackstone, among other early commentators, declared that a legislature should not pass retroactive laws: "All laws should be made to commence in futuro, and [those who are affected] should be notified before their commencement."[104]

The basis for this position is both moral and pragmatic. The rule of law is rooted in protected expectations. In the absence of serious error or severe change in conditions, courts observe *stare decisis* (i.e., precedent) to enable people to rely on the law in conducting their lives. "[N]othing seems more basic to the existence of a legal order than the ability to rely upon the actions of others, including the government, with some assurance."[105] Predictability of law protects the individual from arbitrary government rules and rulers. It is unjust for government to penalize a person who has acted in reliance on existing law either by subsequently making the original action illegal or subsequently depriving the person of rights acquired as a result of the action. Sir Edward Coke declared that no act of Parliament should be construed in such a way as to do a man any damage when he is free from wrong.[106]

Nor, as some other commentators insist, should legislators rightfully pass retroactive measures:

> Laws must from necessity and from their nature, be prospective, otherwise they cannot be rules of civil conduct. Laws cannot attach themselves to conduct antecedent to the creation of the rules themselves. This would be a thing impossible, for at the time the particular transaction took place, there being no rule, a law subsequently passed, was not, and from the nature of the case, could not have been an existing rule governing such a transaction.[107]

The United States Supreme Court has placed some limits on retroactive civil laws, distinguishing between such laws and prospective legislation:

> It does not follow . . . that what Congress can legislate prospectively, it can legislate retroactively. The retroactive aspects of legislation, as well as the prospective aspects, must meet the test of due process, and the justifications for the latter may not suffice for the former.[108]

In the case I have just quoted, the Court, despite the foregoing language, applied a minimal level of scrutiny and upheld the law in issue. Economic liberties were involved, and these generally are accorded minimal scrutiny. However, a recently decided case suggests that the Court's position might be flexible in this respect.

BMW of North America v. Gore (1996) was a civil case which concerned the purchase of a new car that had been partially repainted without disclosure of this information to the plaintiff. A jury found the defendant, BMW, guilty of fraud and assessed it $4,000 in compensatory damages and $4 million in punitive damages, later reduced to $2 million by the Alabama Supreme Court.[109]

On appeal to the United States Supreme Court, Justice John Paul Stevens, writing for the majority, found that the due process clause prohibits "grossly excessive" punitive damage awards. The problem in this case was that BMW had no foreknowledge of the consequences of its wrongdoing. The award was excessive in relation to punitive-damages objectives. Stevens asserted that elementary notions of fairness dictate that a person receive fair notice not only of the conduct that will subject him to punishment, but also of the severity of the penalty that a state may impose.[110] The Court's concerns here are applicable to *Lucas,* where the landowner suffered unexpected and severe financial loss as a result of new rules imposed by South Carolina.

In past years, the Supreme Court has invoked due process to strike down retroactive applications of a statute. The common characteristic of these decisions is the element of surprise: "A person who has changed his position, omitted to change it, or made commitments in reliance upon the law in force at the time is suddenly confronted with a change in the law applicable to his prior conduct, resulting in a liability or loss of investment which he had no opportunity to anticipate and avoid."[111]

Although he did not cite these cases, Justice Stevens's reliance on due process in the *BMW of North America* case has origins in decisions that have applied due process to invalidate retroactive civil laws. *Ettor v. City of Tacoma* (1913)[112] involved a Washington State statute according property owners a right to damages against the city for injury resulting from changes in street grade. While this statute was in force, Tacoma changed the grade in front of Ettor's property, leading him to file a suit for damages on the basis of this statute. While this suit was pending, Washington's legislature repealed the original statute. The United States Supreme Court ruled that the application of the second statute operated retroactively to limit Ettor's property rights, violating the Fourteenth Amendment's due process clause.

Ochoa v. Hernandez y Morales (1913)[113] concerned an order of Puerto Rico's military governor regarding the acquisition of legal titles in real estate by those who had previously held the land without title. The military governor's order reduced, from twenty years to six, the period during which real estate must be held by someone before he could obtain title to it. This order permitted a person in possession of land for more than six years to procure a record of ownership in his own name at once and without notice to others alleging an interest in the property. A person who obtained title by using this process could deprive anyone else claiming an interest in the property by selling to a bona fide purchaser. The Supreme Court held that the governor's order, as applied to a person who had an earlier and legitimate title, deprived him of his rights, thereby violating the due process clause of the Fifth Amendment.

In *Forbes Pioneer Boat Line v. Commissioners of Everglades Drainage District* (1921),[114] the plaintiff sought to recover tolls which the state unlawfully collected for passage through the lock of a canal. The legislature subsequently passed an act to validate the collection. The Supreme Court struck down this legislation as violating the Constitution's obligation-of-contracts and due process clauses. Writing for the Court, Justice Holmes stated that "ratification of an act is not good if attempted at a time when the ratifying authority could not lawfully do the act."[115]

Applying due process in tax cases, the Court has indicated that the limit on retroactivity is the date that a specific tax change was in fact proposed in Congress.[116] It has on this basis struck down tobacco,[117] estate,[118] and gift taxes.[119] At the time Lucas bought his property, the South Carolina Coastal Council was not considering a regulation that would prevent him from developing the property. Lucas's position when he purchased the property was analogous to a taxpayer who "has no reason to suppose that any transaction of the sort will be taxed at all."[120] The burden placed on an owner by a retroactive law would seem to be a relevant factor in interpreting *Agins* Rule 2.

In another context, Justice Stevens condemned civil penalties inflicted on people not involved in wrongdoing. He strongly made the point in his dissenting opinion in *Bennis v. Michigan,* a 1996 case. The Court upheld, on the basis of long-existing precedent, the constitutionality of a forfeiture order authorizing the seizure of an automobile owned in part by a wife not involved in the crime and unaware of her husband's intentions. "[W]e have regarded it as axiomatic," wrote Stevens, objecting to the forfeiture of the wife's interest in the car, "that the person cannot be punished when they have done no wrong. . . . I would now hold what we have always assumed: that the principle is required by due process." Two justices joined his dissent.[121] As a practical matter, I would argue that retroactive acts by government have the same element of surprise whether the victim is Mrs. Bennis, BMW of North America, or Mr. Lucas. The principle is the same—retroactive laws offend our basic instincts about justice—and we shouldn't be distracted because one case deals with a forfeiture, another with punitive damages, and the third with a regulatory taking.

Retroactive economic laws are also adverse to the interests of society.[122] The United States is committed to a market economy premised on private ownership and investment. Individual economic welfare depends on the viability of this economy. Western societies have established rules of law without which market economics could not function. Their purpose is to protect the interests of owners and investors. These laws make it reasonably certain that people who acquire property will be able to rely on the legal system if necessary to enforce their rights. Otherwise, there would be fewer investors, and consumers would suffer from the decreased availability, decreased variety, and higher prices of goods and services.

The absence of predictability raises prices. Entrepreneurs invest on the basis of the risks they expect to encounter. The higher the risk, the fewer the number of investors and the greater the expected return must be to elicit them:

> If people generally act like risk averters . . . they will prefer smaller steady incomes to erratic incomes even when these average out to a higher figure. Therefore, economic activities that involve much uncertainty and risk . . . will be forced by comparative entry and exit of risk takers to pay over the long run, a positive profit premium to compensate for aversion to risk. The yield on capital invested in such industries will involve, in addition to pure interest corresponding to safe investments, an extra element corresponding to positive profit.[123]

Takings-clause law prior to *Lucas* offered a moderate amount of protection for investment-backed expectations; these expectations were a factor in determining whether a taking had occurred. Thus, in *Penn Central Transportation Co. v. City of New York* (1978), the Supreme Court enunciated a three-part test for determining whether a taking had occurred: the relevant factors were the character of the governmental action, the economic impact on the claimant, and the extent to which the governmental action had interfered with distinct investment-backed expectations.[124] The courts generally protect an owner who obtains a building permit and in good faith makes substantial expenditures in furtherance of a building project. In these cases, protection against an adverse change in regulations is accorded under theories of estoppel or vested rights[125] — that is, the idea that the government had relinquished its power to prevent building by granting a building permit and that the owner had secured his right to build by spending money in reliance on that permit.

Investment-backed expectations are also important in contract law. Damages based on expectations of a consummated transaction are the usual, and in some situations, the only measure of damages for breach of contract. In imposing expectation damages, a court seeks to place the claimant in the same position he would have been in had the contract been performed by the other party. The objective is not only to award the plaintiff compensation for out-of-pocket costs that have been incurred, but also for the profit which would have been made had the contract been performed.[126] The protection should be no less in the case of a property owner denied his investment-backed expectations when government "breaches" by changing the regulations affecting his land after he has invested heavily in his project.

C. Harms and Benefits of Property Use

The categorical test Justice Scalia applied in *Lucas* met with virtual derision from dissenting Justice Blackmun and disapproval from concurring Justice Kennedy. It is not likely to be praised by many practitioners of cost-benefit analysis applied to the law, who weigh all costs and benefits of a particular action and approve only if the benefits outweigh the costs. These critics believe that government's decisions over property use should never be limited to evaluating anything less than all identifiable factors. In his *Lucas* opinion, Justice Scalia did not refer to cost-benefit analysis. However, he appears to believe that except for enjoining nuisances and grave threats to life and property, government cannot exercise a principled role in protecting the public from harmful uses of property; in other words, it cannot balance harms and benefits. According to him, the distinction between regulation that "prevents harmful use" and that which "confers benefits" is difficult, if not impossible, to discern on an objective, value-free basis. The distinction is too often "in the eye of the beholder":

> One could say that imposing a servitude on Lucas's land is necessary in order to prevent his use of it from "harming" South Carolina's ecological resources; or, instead, in order to achieve the "benefits" of an ecological preserve. . . . Whether Lucas's construction of single-family residences on his parcels should be described as bringing "harm" to South Carolina's adjacent ecological resources depends principally on whether the describer believes that the state's use interest in nurturing those resources is so important than *any* competing adjacent use must yield.[127]

Consequently, chiefly because of the subjectivity of the inquiry, Scalia concludes that "the legislature's recitation of a noxious-use justification cannot be the basis for departing from our categorical rule that total regulatory takings must be compensated."[128]

But, one might ask, if the noxious-use rationale is defective, why should it justify any deprivation of property, even if only partial? It is hardly a tribute to the Bill of Rights to honor its property rights guarantees only when owners are subjected to total or nearly total wipeouts. However, at least within the *Lucas* context, total regulatory takings under *Agins* Rule 3 are now held to include either the denial of investment-backed expectations or the elimination of all commercial value. Each may relate only to a portion of the entire property. To this extent, *Lucas* protects against partial takings. Two years later, in its *Dolan* decision, the Court would apply heightened scrutiny to other partial-deprivation scenarios, as we will see in Section V.

Restraints on a constitutional right can only be justified (to borrow Scalia's language) "on an objective, value-free basis," and this concern is very difficult to satisfy in the regulation of property. Determining whether a use is harmful or beneficial seems to be a matter as much for economists to ponder as for lawyers or politicians. Economics professor Ronald Coase states the problem subtly:

> The traditional approach has tended to obscure the nature of the choice that has to be made. The question is commonly thought of as one in which A inflicts harm on B and what has to be decided is: how should we restrain A? But this is wrong. We are dealing with a problem of a reciprocal nature. To avoid the harm to B would inflict harm on A. The real question that has to be decided is: should A be allowed to harm B or B be allowed to harm A? The problem is to avoid the more serious harm. . . .[129]

> The cost of exercising a right (of using a factor of production) is always the loss which is suffered elsewhere in consequence of the exercise of that right—the inability to cross land, to park a car, to build a house, to enjoy a view, to have peace and quiet or to breathe clean air.[130]

For a Coasian, the decision on whether or not to allow Lucas to build the two houses should rest on which course maximizes the value of production, that is, on cost-benefit analysis. "What has to be decided," Coase asserts, "is whether the gain from preventing the harm is greater than the loss which would be suffered elsewhere as a result of stopping the action which produces the harm."[131] However, the Constitutional position must necessarily be different. In construing the takings clause, the Supreme Court should not conduct a cost-benefit analysis, for such an analysis is utterly devoid of special consideration for the protection of constitutional rights. Cost-benefit analysis may be helpful in determining the existence of a public nuisance—that a certain activity produces minimal benefit at great risk to society. Cost-benefit analysis may also be helpful in deciding whether a regulation is substantially related to its purpose, and thus, it may have a role in the application of *Agins* Rule 2. But it is not a basis for interpreting constitutional mandate. The Supreme Court's *Loretto* opinion—holding that any permanent physical occupation of land is a taking, no matter how tiny—makes little sense from a cost-benefit perspective, i.e., a tiny cost to the owner weighed against a much larger benefit to society. However, it is commendable from a constitutional-rights perspective, since any forced occupation is confiscatory, a total deprivation of the portion affected, and therefore, a taking per se. Similarly, in *Causby,* government airplanes flying over Causby's land effected a taking even though they had not directly invaded the land itself, and they deprived the owner of only a portion of his property. Except when a nuisance is involved, *Loretto* and *Causby* apply, and the government must pay, regardless of the societal benefits achieved from the government action.

Rights are not neutral factors under the Constitution. Our nation adopted a constitution in large part to better secure them. The Constitution trumps economic analysis—cost-benefit analysis—by making the decision in favor of rights. Rights are not up for grabs; they are not to be balanced against other factors, no matter how laudable. The assumption of the Framers was that the exercise of liberty will bring to society many more benefits than harms. The Constitution equates the public interest with freedom.

To be sure, freedom does not include the violation of other people's rights. Property rights have never been interpreted to protect nuisances, that is, the use by A of his property in such an egregious way that it deprives B of his property rights. A nuisance may be private or public, depending on whether it affects one or many people. The nuisance exception eliminates from protection numerous but not all uses that may be regarded as "harmful." As Justice Scalia's opinion in *Lucas* suggests, it is very difficult to get agreement on when a use is harmful, except when it comes to nuisances or grave threats to life or property. Then, most people will agree in principle that such activity constitutes a harm that is not entitled to constitutional protection. The existence of a nuisance is, accordingly, a justifiable reason for restricting property use, because the restriction itself upholds the principle of property rights.[132] What counts as a nuisance? Depending on who replies, the answer may vary from an unsightly fence to a factory emitting loud noises, blinding lights, noxious odors, or heavy smoke. However, before an offensive use can qualify as a legal nuisance, denying an owner constitutional protection, it must be a use that society considers truly unreasonable. Not just any petty annoyance will qualify, or property rights would be at the mercy of every irritable neighbor.

Evaluating public harm is not a constitutional problem unique to nuisance. Certain expressions are also denied constitutional safeguard, such as highly provocative language, libels, obscenities, and false advertising. Ascertaining whether an expression falls within any of these categories requires more than considering harm. The Supreme Court requires that this determination must be based on a weighing of harms and benefits. Thus, under the *Chaplinsky* rule, which applies to libelous or obscene speech or "fighting words," certain "utterances are not considered as an essential part of any exposition of ideas, and are of such slight social value as a step to truth that any benefit that may be derived from them is clearly outweighed by the social interest in order and morality."[133]

To be denied constitutional protection, a provocative utterance must be "directed to inciting or producing imminent lawless action and [must be] likely to incite or produce such action."[134] The Supreme Court has held that because it does not produce this result, the burning of the American flag, while it may be highly repugnant to many, may constitute a constitutionally protected action.[135] For another example, although some may regard a risqué magazine or stage show as highly offensive, to be considered as obscene and, therefore, not constitutionally protected, a work must (1) appeal to the prurient interest; (2) describe sexual conduct in a patently offensive way; and (3) lack serious literary, artistic, political, or scientific value.[136] There is room in these three prongs for a consideration of societal costs and benefits.

The rules are comparable for determining the existence of a private nuisance, which is an unreasonable interference by a property owner with another owner's use and enjoyment of his land.[137] A's activity is unreasonable if it is substantial and is more than B should be required to bear without compensation.[138] Contemporary jurisprudence requires that the utility of defendant A's conduct and the actual harm sustained by plaintiff B should be considered and balanced before a nuisance is found to exist. The inquiry is similar for a public nuisance, where the state acts on behalf of a number of people who individually would find vindication of their rights very difficult.

Some property rights advocates object to the balancing which nuisance law requires because balancing may at times provide legitimacy for a use which on its own might be considered illegitimate. They believe that a nuisance should be found solely when the property use causes more than a *de minimis* (a legally minimal) physical invasion of someone else's property. A contemporary example would be a factory emitting dust particles that settle on neighboring property. These particles invade another person's property, violating that person's property rights. These emissions are consequently an illegitimate use of property.[139] This is a strict rights position with concern over impact limited to the effect on property rights. Under this theory, there is no concern with the value either of the activity or of the total economic impact. A builder of a thousand cars is in the same position as the builder of a single car, and it makes no difference whether the adjoining land is used for homes or farming or is vacant. The strict rights position varies greatly from the position that the extent of harm an activity causes is an important factor in determining whether the activity should be abated. In deciding whether a particular activity should be abated, our legal system is generally favorable to allowing individuals to act as they will unless they inflict great harm on others.

Nuisance rules implement these general societal objectives and I accept them as greatly protective of property rights. Moreover, it would be very difficult to eliminate these rules, which date back to the early common law. Changing the nuisance rules might be a hazardous undertaking, since the result might be new rules that are far worse, considering the influence of preservationists within the legal community. These environmentalists favor the broadening of nuisance to include infliction of environmental harm.

The strict, anti-balancing property rights position on nuisance is questionable, also, because of conceptual and practical problems. Ascertaining the point at which an invasion of a right has occurred is difficult and highly subjective. Consider in this regard the problem created by dust emissions from a plant employing a thousand people that is situated near a development of two hundred houses. Initially, the plant emits small amounts of dust particles, and as its production rises over time, so does the quantity of particles it emits. At what point have the plant's emissions deprived a nearby home-owner of his property rights? Should the line be set at ten, one hundred, or five hundred particles per day that actually land on the home-owner's property? When does the home-owner suffer sufficient damage to warrant bringing a lawsuit and winning it? What if the nearby land was vacant and not improved with houses? From a strict property rights perspective, if an invasion of property has occurred, it makes *no* difference whether the land is vacant or improved. Nor is consideration given to the economic importance of the plant to the community.

Yet these concerns will likely enter into the final judicial decision, regardless of the rules, since judges often try to reach decisions that will be acceptable to the community. Few judges will want to sacrifice the jobs of a thousand people by prohibiting the plant from emitting five hundred dust particles per day, or by assessing a large monetary penalty on the plant. The result would be a balancing of property interests, as is presently the rule in nuisance cases, except that the balancing would be disguised to fit within the strict rules.

The constitutional objective with respect to nuisances and other unprotected activities is to maintain freedom except when to do so clearly injures other people. Justice Holmes's famous observations about the marketplace of ideas are pertinent to the issue of freedom in the marketplace of goods and services:

> [T]he best test of truth is the power of the thought to get itself accepted in the competition of the market, and that truth is the only ground upon which their [i.e., the people's] wishes safely can be carried out. . . . I think that we should be eternally vigilant against attempts to check the expression of opinions that we loathe and believe to be fraught with death, unless they so imminently threaten immediate interference with the lawful and pressing purposes of the law that an immediate check is required to save the country.[140]

Critics of Holmes's free-speech perspective have, over the years, pointed to the serious problems it has imposed on personal reputation, media credibility, and domestic tranquility. Under his test, the public must sustain "harms" that fall short of being clear and present dangers. Nonetheless, the Supreme Court has preserved and enlarged freedom of expression in the belief that society will on the whole greatly benefit from the abundance and exchange of ideas. Free expression is essential to democratic society and its constitutional dimensions are determined on this premise. Economic and property rights are essential to the maintenance of a viable and productive society and, accordingly, warrant similar constitutional consideration.[141]

The theory behind nuisance laws has much in common with this theory of free expression. The early common-law judges were highly pragmatic and, therefore, supportive of economic rights, since the economy depended upon these rights for its viability. The judges were, accordingly, reluctant to abate property uses that were not intentionally harmful and that benefited the society. At the same time, they did not want to protect uses that injured other property owners or the society. Both benefits and harms of a use had to be considered in deciding whether a use should be abated.

Under a cost-benefit analysis, most negative externalities (that is, harms caused to others by a person's conduct of a perfectly legal activity) do not warrant termination of the liberty that is implicated. Both Justice Scalia and Professor Coase explain that the problem of externalities in land use is far less than ordinarily assumed in public discussion. The existence of harm is quite subjective. Consequently, regulatory action to prevent certain uses will often do more harm than good. In the normal growth and development of an economy, it is inevitable that some people will suffer incidental losses that should not be compensable.[142]

Houston, Texas, is the only major city in the United States that has never been zoned. Experience in Houston (to be discussed in Chapter 7) illustrates that the property market itself provides considerable protection for society from incompatible uses. Market forces cause uses to separate themselves.[143] Land developers guarantee home buyers protection from undesirable and incompatible uses by imposing restrictive covenants (legally enforcible restrictions on use and development) on their subdivisions. Owners enter into agreements with each other for the same purpose. Justice Scalia's *Lucas* decision does not limit protection of the public against injury solely to the abatement of nuisances and grave public threats. Consistent with that opinion, government can require an owner to make compensatory provision for costs he imposes on the public attributable to his activity.[144] If the public believed Lucas's proposed development imperiled the beach/dune system, it could have demanded that South Carolina acquire all of his property or certain interests therein through eminent domain. If their interests were greatly threatened, adjoining or nearby home-owners could have sought to purchase from Lucas limitations on the use of his property.

Lucas probably would not have contemplated building the two houses if lenders and insurers were not convinced that they were structurally sound and safe for occupancy.[145] Were this not the case, he or his purchasers would have been unable to obtain either a mortgage or home insurance. A house without either would not be readily saleable.

D. Investment-Backed Expectations

Agins Rule 3—that government may not deprive owners of all economically feasible use of their property—comprehends two guarantees for property rights: first, protection of investment-backed expectations, and second, protection against deprivation of all commercial value. In this subsection, I shall discuss investment-backed expectations, and in the next subsection, I shall turn to deprivation of all commercial value.

Justice Blackmun dismissed the *Lucas* decision as "a missile [launched] to kill a mouse."[146] But denial of liberty is not a mouse; *Lucas* secures a most important liberty—individual choice. A free nation must legally secure the commitments that its citizens voluntarily make with their lives and resources. This is the reason why it is so important for the law to secure investment-backed expectations.[147]

Justice Scalia's categorical solution to the protection of investment-backed expectations applies only to a portion of the problems created by their denial. More often, owners suffer less than total frustration of their use expectations. Suppose, for example, that instead of barring Lucas from building two houses, South Carolina had, by increasing density requirements, barred only one of the houses. If Lucas had ended up with only one site for a purchase price based on two sites, his investment objective would have been partially frustrated. However, a categorical taking rule will not apply when an investment-backed expectation is only partially denied. "Government could hardly go on," Justice Holmes asserted in 1922, "if to some extent values incident to property could not be diminished without paying for every such change in the general law."[148] When the deprivation is less than the whole, the constitutional inquiry should consider the justifications for it, as required under *Agins* Rules 1 and 2.

In support of his categorical takings rule in *Lucas,* Justice Scalia explains the distinction between partial and total deprivations:

> [O]ur "takings jurisprudence" . . . has traditionally been guided by the understandings of our citizens regarding the content of, and the State's power over, the "bundle of rights" that they acquire when they obtain title to property. It seems to us that the property owner necessarily expects the uses of his property to be restricted, from time to time, by various measures newly enacted by the State in legitimate exercise of its police powers. . . . [T]he notion pressed by the Council that title is somehow held subject to the "implied limitation" that the State may subsequently eliminate all economically valuable use is inconsistent with the historical compact recorded in the Takings Clause that has become part of our constitutional culture.[149]

Pursuant to this understanding, an owner should also expect that the Constitution will protect him from the imposition of arbitrary and capricious restrictions on his property. *Agins* Rules 1 and 2—which require regulations to meet the test of substantially advancing legitimate state interests—serve this purpose.

Under contemporary takings law, a finding that an investment-backed expectation has been denied depends on how a court interprets a number of factors. (1) Was the property purchased with a specific purpose in mind? (2) Did the purchaser have prior notice of a possible change in the law? (3) Was the purchaser's evaluation of the legal situation reasonable? (4) Is the purchaser an investor or, rather, a speculator? (I discuss the distinction below.) (5) Must the purchaser have made expenditures based on his expectations for him to have acquired an enforceable right? (6) Has the purchaser's investment objective been rendered worthless by the government's action?[150]

Judicial resolution of these factors creates a substantial hurdle for any owner trying to have his expectation rights vindicated. Yet these factors are not really relevant to the basic issue of guaranteeing property rights. As Justice Kennedy observed, there is "an inherent tendency towards circularity [in protecting these rights,] for if the owner's reasonable expectations are shaped by what courts allow as a proper exercise of governmental authority, property tends to become what the courts say it is."[151]

Given the environmental pressures of the times, one might conclude that Lucas could have anticipated South Carolina's confiscatory action. If the protection of expectations depends on such considerations, the concept will have minimal significance. The possibility of a change in the law should not have the same legal force as the existence of a law. The law could change in myriad ways. Until a law is passed, it is of no force or effect.

Moreover, even the existence of a law is not determinative of the people's rights. Justice Scalia made this point in *Nollan*. Prior to their purchase, the Nollans were aware that the California Coastal Commission required owners of beachfront properties to dedicate pedestrian easements along the ocean. *Nollan* held that the Commission's policies and practices did not limit the owner's rights, which were, of course, constitutionally based. Since government cannot at will enact laws depriving people of their rights, it can hardly be given this power when it merely announces, proposes, or considers such action.

When a person purchases property, he is subject to existing legal restraints on it and acquires all of the rights against government then available to him under the law. Nevertheless, existing investment-expectations law distinguishes between an investor and a speculator. The speculator does not have a distinct use objective when he purchases the property. The courts are much more sympathetic to the distinct expectations of the investor as contrasted with the open-ended profit motive of the speculator. Courts view speculation as akin to gambling. Thus, judges have likened speculators to sweepstakes-ticket holders,[152] a rather shallow assessment of a practice which many economists regard as vital to the smooth functioning of markets.[153] Moreover, in view of the economic and political uncertainties businessmen face, the line between investor and speculator often is not clear. A change in the economy may cause an investor to become a speculator, and vice versa. For example, Lucas presumably would not have wanted to build the two houses if, before he built them, the market for new homes became depressed. But he might have retained the lots for future use or sale in the hope that the market would again become favorable. At what point in time was he an investor, at what point a speculator?

In the words of economist Ludwig von Mises: "One must never forget that every action is embedded in the flux of time and therefore involves speculation. The capitalists, the landowners, and the laborers are by necessity speculators. So is the consumer in providing for anticipated future needs. There's many a slip 'twixt cup and lip."[154]

In a market economy, acquiring an asset is a personal choice, and whether its use or sale is a socially wise or unwise decision will ultimately be determined by the market. Success for an owner depends on the amount of benefit that the market enables him to provide for others. Participants in the marketplace, as economist Israel Kirzner reminds us, are engaged in an incessant race to get or keep ahead of one another—and to be ahead always means "to be offering the most attractive opportunities to other market participants."[155] To achieve success, a speculator, no less than an investor, will seek to do those things (if any) that will sooner or later attract buyers.

Speculators, like others seeking to earn money in private industry, usually serve necessary and useful roles in the economy. For example, speculators in land frequently act as middlemen, preparing the land for sale to builders. They subdivide, rezone, clear title problems, install roads and utilities, each of which can be a lengthy and costly process. They buy large tracts and sell off smaller tracts.

Builders do engage in the same activities, but it requires considerable capital and time seldom available to small and middle-sized concerns. Warehousing and processing land can be costly and burdensome to large builders as well. Consequently, many, perhaps most, builders find it advantageous to pay the middleman's mark-up rather than buy raw land at a lower price.

Land speculators also provide a price floor for developable land. They create much larger markets than would exist if only builders purchased land, allowing farmers and other owners greater opportunities to convert their properties into cash.

In economically depressed times, speculators make up a substantial part of whatever urban land market exists and prevent the bottom from dropping out. By the same token, in better times, their eagerness to unload at a profit serves to hold prices down. Moreover, in readying land for construction purposes, speculators expand the supply of land available for immediate use, reducing the price below what it would otherwise be.

Thus, speculators tend to keep prices from rising too high or falling too low. The higher prices they create at one end of the process are likely to be more than offset by lower ones they cause at the other end. They add stability to the market and reduce price fluctuations, thereby lowering the risks of land ownership.[156]

E. Destroying Commercial Value

Returning the discussion to the *Agins* Rules, the second factor in determining whether all economically viable use has been denied (*Agins* Rule 3) is the extent of the diminution in value caused by the regulations. While serious reduction in value is not per se a taking, it qualifies as such when all commercial value has been destroyed. This rule applies to owners (such as those who inherit property) who have not been denied investment-backed expectations. Both the diminution rule and the expectations rule relate to restraints on use. Both involve serious economic loss to the owner.

When does the elimination of economic viability become a taking? Justice Stevens in *Keystone* (1987) stated that the "economically viable use" rule originated in part in Justice Holmes's holding, in *Pennsylvania Coal* (1922), that the Kohler Act made it "commercially impracticable to mine certain coal" in the areas that were affected.[157] Stevens distinguished the 1966 Subsidence Act on the basis that there was no support in the record for a finding that this statute made it impossible for the coal companies to profitably engage in their business. Consequently, one might conclude that a regulation preventing an owner from profitably engaging in his business will deny an owner economically viable use of his land.

In originally promulgating the *Agins* Rules, the Supreme Court cited a footnote in *Penn Central Transportation Co. v. New York* (1978) as authority for the "economically viable use" rule. The footnote states that the holding in *Penn Central* is based on a concession the City of New York made that was entered into the record. The city conceded that the plaintiff could obtain relief in the future if it could demonstrate at some future time that circumstances had so changed that the terminal ceased to be "economically viable."[158]

The point of both Stevens's and the *Agins* Court's explanations has to do with monetary return. If the property would not produce a reasonable return under any permitted use, then the owner has been denied economically viable use of the property.[159] This principle may be clear, but its implementation is extremely difficult, and it makes judicial redress of a wrong tenuous at best.

A person generally buys property in the belief that it is the best means available to achieve a certain outcome; and when government changes the rules and prevents the anticipated outcome from occurring, the person has sustained an injury. Whether the problem is denial of expectation or destruction of value, the cause is a retroactive law whose adoption should invoke the right to compensation (a matter that will be discussed in greater detail in Chapter 9).

Lucas is not only a takings case: it also constitutes a significant advance for freedom. In a free society, people should be allowed and encouraged to engage in activities of their own choosing, subject to the understanding that in so doing they do not harm others. *Lucas* augments existing protections for property owners. It provides absolute protection against two common and serious legislative deprivations of property rights: destruction of all investment-backed expectations and the elimination of commercial viability. *Lucas* closed the gap between physical and regulatory takings because it is a distinction without a difference from the perspective of the property owner.

V. *Dolan v. The City of Tigard*

This case involves the application to a proposed development of a zoning ordinance enacted by Tigard, Oregon, a city of about 30,000 residents on the southwest edge of Portland. Florence Dolan owned a 71,500 square foot lot in the central business district of Tigard, on which her retail electrical and plumbing supply store stood. In early 1991, she applied for a permit to replace the building with one twice its size. The city refused to grant the permit unless she agreed to dedicate about 7,000 square feet of her property to alleviate the drainage problem and traffic congestion that the city said the new store would create. The city wanted Dolan to dedicate to public ownership two portions of her land: for drainage purposes, one located adjacent to an existing floodplain; and for the relief of traffic, an additional fifteen-foot strip of land, also adjacent to the floodplain, for use as a pedestrian/bicycle pathway. Dolan challenged the city's requirements for dedication of her land as a taking, but she lost her case before the Oregon Land Use Board of Appeals, the Oregon Court of Appeals, and the Oregon Supreme Court. The case finally reached the United States Supreme Court, where Dolan obtained a favorable ruling in 1994.

The problem presented in *Dolan* is a common one under zoning. Municipalities impose regulations and exactions on the use and development of property that are intended to offset the resulting burdens that the public sustains. In all fairness, the owner should only be responsible for remedying those burdens he creates. An excessive restraint or exaction is a confiscation veiled as an exercise of the police power. *Dolan* provides guidance on determining whether a property owner is being required to provide disproportionate payment. It relates to the matter of partial takings left open in *Lucas,* and it fine-tunes the means-ends inquiry required by *Nollan*. A partial taking would be involved if a required dedication or exaction were excessive in relation to the impact caused by the owner's actions.

Implementing its zoning powers, the City of Tigard had enacted and codified a comprehensive land-use plan as part of the Community Development Code (CDC). The plan contained the following provision relevant to Dolan's proposed development:

> Where landfill and/or development is allowed within and adjacent to the 100-year floodplain, the city shall require the dedication of sufficient open land area for greenway adjoining and within the floodplain. This area shall include portions at a suitable elevation for the construction of a pedestrian/bicycle pathway within the floodplain in accordance with the adopted pedestrian/bicycle plan.

Objecting to the application of these requirements to her development, Dolan petitioned the City Planning Commission for a variance (waiver) from them. The planning commission made findings concerning the relationship between the dedication requirement and the projected impact of the Dolan project, concluding that the city's zoning powers provided authority for mandating the land dedications. The commission consequently rejected Dolan's request, and this decision was approved by the Tigard City Council.

Chief Justice Rehnquist, writing for the Supreme Court's 5-to-4 majority, distinguished the *Dolan* case from *Euclid* (the original 1926 Supreme Court decision that had upheld zoning, discussed in Chapter 4), which he described as involving essentially legislative determinations, classifying entire areas of a locality. *Dolan,* stated the Chief Justice, concerned an adjudicative decision relating to an individual parcel and requiring an owner to deed portions of her property to the city; these circumstances made it appropriate for the city to carry the burden of proving that the owner was not being disproportionately assessed.[160] Rehnquist clarified the distinction further in a footnote:

> [I]n evaluating most generally applicable zoning regulations, the burden properly rests on the party challenging the regulation to prove that it constitutes an arbitrary regulation of property rights [citing *Euclid*]. Here, by contrast, the city made an adjudicative decision to condition petitioner's application for a building permit on an individual parcel. In this situation, the burden properly rests on the city [citing *Nollan*].[161]

The adjudicative function is ordinarily not within the authority of a legislature. The principle of separation of powers is the Constitution's safeguard against legislative exercise of the judicial function, which provides many substantive and procedural guarantees absent in the legislative deliberations. Prior to *Dolan,* some state high courts had adopted Rehnquist's position, holding that ordinances laying down general rules are exercises of legislative authority, while a determination on the regulation of a specific parcel is an exercise of judicial authority.[162]

The legal process in *Euclid* concerned a facial challenge to a general ordinance, whereas the legal process in *Dolan* is a challenge to specific provisions of an ordinance as applied to a particular property owner. In *Euclid,* the Court upheld the ordinance as a whole and did not foreclose consideration in the future of suits based on specific provisions. "[T]he ordinance in its general scope and dominant features . . . is a valid exercise of authority, leaving the provisions to be dealt with as cases arise directly involving them." Two years after *Euclid,* the Supreme Court unanimously, in *Nectow v. City of Cambridge,*[163] upheld an order enjoining Cambridge from enforcing a zoning provision prohibiting the plaintiff from using his property for industrial purposes. Subsequently, in *Seattle Title Trust Co. v. Roberge,* the Court unanimously overruled denial of a building permit to construct a home for the aged poor in a residential district.[164] Although the Court cited *Euclid* in its *Nectow* and *Roberge* decisions, it did not employ in either case the same high level of deference to the legislature as required in *Euclid.* Since both cases involved a due process inquiry of a specific restriction on liberty, they, like *Dolan,* dealt with challenges to adjudicative decisions. Rehnquist, accordingly, had support from federal and state decisions for his distinction between the processes in *Euclid* and in *Dolan.*[165]

However, Rehnquist's reasoning with respect to burden of proof does not hold up under the *Agins* Rules. At the time Dolan sought a building permit, *Euclid* was not a controlling precedent in takings jurisprudence. *Agins, Keystone, Nollan,* and *Lucas* applied the rules of *Agins* and not of *Euclid* to determine the constitutionality of the statute in litigation. Indeed, both *Agins,* a zoning case, and *Keystone,* a property regulation case, involved facial challenges to general statutes; that is, each related to a challenge to the text of the law and not to its application. Rehnquist's reference to *Euclid* in his *Dolan* decision has been harmful to takings jurisprudence. It has enabled foes of the *Agins* Rules to obtain victories on the wrongful theory that *Euclid* is still a decisive precedent.

Dolan presented the issue of the required fit between means and ends—an issue that was not decided in *Nollan.* The *Nollan* decision determined that no essential nexus—that is, no reasonable connection—existed between the means and the end in that case, and consequently the Court did not consider the degree of relationship required between the objective of the law and the restraints used to achieve it. Unlike *Nollan,* Rehnquist wrote, an essential nexus was present in *Dolan,* since increasing the size of Mrs. Dolan's structure would also increase drainage and congestion.

The Supreme Court decided that the City of Tigard had not provided evidence justifying either of the dedications it demanded. It had failed to prove a close connection between conveying the property to the public and the reduction of flooding problems. As Rehnquist noted: "The city has never said why a public greenway, as opposed to a private one, was required in the interest of flood control."[166]

> The difference to petitioner, of course, is the loss of her ability to exclude others. . . . It is difficult to see why recreational visitors trampling along petitioner's floodplain easement are sufficiently related to the city's legitimate interest in reducing flooding problems along Fanno Creek. . . .[167]

Similarly, the city had failed to provide sufficient evidence supporting its demand for dedication of land for a pedestrian/bicycle pathway. It had not shown that the additional number of vehicle and bicycle trips generated by the proposed development reasonably related to the city's requirement for this dedication.

Rejecting the proffered explanations as inadequate, the Court held that in such cases the city must initially comply with *Nollan* and show that an "essential nexus" existed between the "legitimate state interest" and the conditions exacted by it. This would amount to proving a reasonable relationship between the two. The city then has the burden to prove that a "rough proportionality"—that is, a close connection—exists between the purpose of the restraint and the means used to achieve it.[168] This test adopts the reasoning (but not the name) of the "reasonable relation" test which had been adopted by a majority of state courts to determine the constitutionality of required restrictions, dedications, and exactions. The "reasonable relation" test is explained in the following quotation from the Nebraska Supreme Court, which Rehnquist included in his opinion:

> The distinction, therefore, which must be made between an appropriate exercise of the police power and an improper exercise of eminent domain is whether the requirement has some reasonable relationship or nexus to the use to which the property is being made or is merely being used as an excuse for taking property simply because at that particular moment the landowner is asking the city for some license or permit.[169]

Accordingly, the Nebraska Supreme Court held that a city may not require a property owner to dedicate property for some future public use as a condition of permit approval when such future use is not "occasioned by the construction sought to be permitted."[170]

In selecting his "rough proportionality" language in *Dolan*, Chief Justice Rehnquist rejected two different positions on determining the constitutionally required connection between means and ends that had been adopted by some state courts: one giving more deference to the legislature ("a necessary connection"), and another giving less deference ("a specific and uniquely attributable connection"). Rehnquist asserted that his was an intermediate position: "No precise mathematical calculation is required, but the city must make some sort of individualized determination that the required dedication is related both in nature and extent to the impact of the proposed development."[171] The city is obligated to "make some effort to quantify its findings in support of the dedication" beyond conclusionary statements related to offsetting some of the burdens created by the project.[172]

The *Dolan* opinion imposes a reasonable burden on government when government demands contributions from an owner seeking to develop his property. The city must show (1) that an "essential nexus" exists, and then (2) "quantify its findings" and make "individualized determinations" with respect to the nature and extent of the connection between the requirement and the problems to be remedied. There is little that is unique about application of these rules under an intermediate standard of review. This level of review is employed in commercial-speech cases, as Justice Kennedy, in an opinion in one such case, explained:

> It is well established that "[t]he party seeking to uphold a restriction on commercial speech carries the burden of justifying it." [citation] This burden is not satisfied by mere speculation or conjecture; rather, a governmental body seeking to sustain a restriction on commercial speech must demonstrate that the harms it recites are real and that its restriction will in fact alleviate them to a material degree. [citations] Without this requirement, a state could with ease restrict commercial speech in the service of other objectives that could not themselves justify a burden on commercial expression.[173]

Nor is the requirement of a tight means-ends fit an unusual doctrine for interpreting a constitutional provision intended to protect the exercise of liberty. As Professor Gerald Gunther, a noted constitutional scholar, has observed, "[t]hat judicial review of legislative means is justified is one of the most pervasive themes articulated in our constitutional jurisprudence."[174] American jurisprudence tends to reject any restraint on rights of free speech, free press, religious choice, privacy, or mobility that is not narrowly tailored to achieve its purpose. The idea is that no person should suffer or sustain loss beyond curing the problem he or she has created. Nevertheless, champions of these rights, such as Justice Stevens, are willing to forgo this requirement when it comes to property rights. In his dissent in *Dolan,* Stevens objects to imposing the burden of proof on the municipality. He contends that the property owner should bear the burden of proving that the government's conditions are not "rational, impartial and conducive to fulfilling the aims of a valid land-use plan."[175]

This position ignores the meaning of ownership in a democratic society: that it must not be limited without just and good cause. "[T]he public good," wrote Blackstone, "is in nothing more essentially interested, than the protection of every individual's private rights."[176] A person should not suffer a penalty except as the result of wrongdoing, and consequently should not have to pay exactions that are not related to his activities or conduct. A majority vote does not justify theft. As I have noted, Justice Holmes warned about such governmental propensities: "[A] strong public desire to improve the public condition is not enough to warrant achieving the desire by a shorter cut than the constitutional way of paying for the change."[177]

Stevens opposes such thinking with respect to the area of property rights. He asserts that government must have decisive power to control the risks of floods, earthquakes, traffic congestion, and environmental harms. But Rehnquist's "rough proportionality" test does not deny government regulatory powers when it can show adequate justification for them. The test does forbid the imposition of restraint in the absence of such justification; ours is, after all, a government based on the separation-of-powers principle, wherein the political branches do not have fiat powers. The American constitutional system rejects legislative finality.[178]

The record is not persuasive that government has special abilities or competence to deal with the "risks" Stevens identifies. Legislators favor particular positions because they believe in them, or cater to voters and financial supporters who do. They often recruit experts to support their views. However, democracy subordinates expertise to the will of citizens. Politicians who ignore the voters' wishes do not remain in office very long. Moreover, in modern society, frequently no single area of expertise is definitive. In many current California land disputes, environmentalists and no-growthers rely on biologists to support their positions, while owners and developers depend on economists to substantiate theirs. Consider the matter of protecting against earthquake damage. Here, one might think, judgments should be left to the experts; yet decisions about the severity of building requirements and the properties to be regulated involve not only issues of safety but also questions of economics and social welfare. The greater the requirements imposed to ensure earthquake resistance, the greater the cost—a consequence which is more adverse to those who are less affluent. Thus, severe earthquake-protection requirements can be very injurious to poor people who rent, own, or seek to own shelter.

Members of city councils and county boards represent various constituencies, a number of which often must be satisfied for a measure to pass. The "perfect" plan is often quite imperfect by the time it emerges from the pressures and compromises of the legislative process, and it might be ravaged still more as it is administered. Consider the comments on regulation by Professor Coase, who was for a long time the editor of the *Journal of Law and Economics*. Over the years, the journal published numerous studies on economic regulation, and Coase concluded that

> [t]he main lesson to be drawn from these studies is clear; they all tend to suggest that the regulation is either ineffective or that, when it has a noticeable impact, on balance the effect is bad, so that consumers obtain a worse product or a higher-priced product or both as a result of the regulation. Indeed, this result is found so

uniformly as to create a puzzle; one would expect to find in all these studies at least some government programs that do more good than harm.[179]

Professor Coase believes that, in theory at least, there is no reason why government regulation cannot improve on market processes. He states, however: "My puzzle is to explain why these occasions seem to be so rare, if not non-existent."[180]

The limitations and infirmities of urban legislative processes necessitate meaningful judicial scrutiny—and not the virtual abstention by the judiciary that Justice Stevens advocates. Restrictions, exactions, and dedications that are excessive in relation to their alleged purposes are not only confiscatory, but also operate to discourage investment and ownership. Only the judiciary is in a position to monitor this problem. The legislature cannot monitor itself—that is the great insight of the Framers, and it is no less true today.

The burden of proof in all takings cases should be borne by government. Our constitutional system guarantees substantial freedom to engage in the material pursuits, and this guarantee is entitled to no less recognition in the courtroom than other constitutional rights. When government proscribes liberties, it has an obligation and a responsibility to justify the restraint. The presumption that the state is correct in curtailing people's liberties can only be accepted in societies where restraint is normal—those which, unlike ours, equate government direction and control with the public interest. Placing the burden of proof on the property owner presumes that the government is right when it curtails liberty. Thus, it is entirely unsuitable for our system.

The preceding observations are taken for granted in our criminal jurisprudence as well as in our fundamental-liberties jurisprudence. Demanding that the aggrieved party assume the burden of proof against the government makes it quite difficult, and usually impossible, for the individual to obtain judicial vindication, as Justice James McReynolds once observed: "If [it was] necessary for appellant to show absence of the asserted conditions, the little grocer was helpless from the beginning—the practical difficulties were too great for the average man."[181] Justice McReynolds worried about the hurdles that such a "little grocer" would face in securing the services of lawyers and other professionals, the testimony of some government officials, and various records, papers, and documents, all of which would be necessary to prove that the government's regulation was invalid. Moreover, requiring that the aggrieved party assume this burden of proof operates to chill the exercise of freedom.[182]

Dolan is an easy case to decide for those who believe in property rights. Without payment of just compensation to the owner, the City of Tigard had no power to acquire any interest in Dolan's land, except that which would directly remedy the drainage and congestion problems created by the proposed construction. Yet two courts and a government agency were willing to defer to

Tigard's demand to acquire some of Dolan's property, without persuasive evidence that it was needed for eliminating these problems.

When I first heard about this case—that the city had only demanded 10 percent of the total land area, consisting of property that was to be left unimproved—I was surprised to learn that Dolan had refused the offer. In my experience in zoning matters, both as an owner and as an attorney, giving government 10 percent of one's land in return for a permit to build is usually considered a bargain, regardless of the merits of one's case. It is not a matter of justice but of expediency; government officials have the power to grant or not grant applications for zoning changes or for building permits, and they often are very cavalier about an owner's property rights.

This assessment is shared by most of the builders and developers I know and have represented. They have no faith that the zoning process will protect their rights. For them, 10 percent is a bargain price to obtain government approval, regardless of the issue. They are usually prepared to settle for a larger amount without much of an argument. Tigard was unfortunate in that it had to deal with a determined Mrs. Dolan, rather than with the typical developer concerned more with the bottom line than with drawing the line against infringement on liberty.

If one assumes that under the United States Constitution, a person who does no wrong should not be penalized, the decisions in *Nollan, Lucas,* and *Dolan* are to be expected. In none of these cases did the owner transgress any law or seek special favor from the government. Building on one's own land is a constitutional right, as the *Nollan* decision recognizes. Under the threat that otherwise the owners' building permits would be denied, government agencies demanded land dedications from Nollan and Dolan that neither had any obligation to surrender. Nollan's house construction would not have significantly changed the accessibility to and view of the California coast, and Dolan's store construction would have caused drainage and congestion increases that could have been be handled without requiring dedication of a considerable portion of her property. In both cases, the government failed to prove that the demanded exactions were needed to alleviate the burdens that construction would place on the community.

Ironically, the lots that Lucas purchased to erect two homes will soon be developed for this purpose, but not by him. After Lucas bought the property, South Carolina sought to ban its development for habitable structures, but the state's environmental and safety justifications proved fanciful. As previously noted, the state acquired these lots in a settlement brought about by a U.S. Supreme Court decision. Instead of retaining them as open space, the state sold these lots to a developer who will build what Lucas wanted to build.

One does not have to be a moral philosopher to conclude that government agencies acted unfairly in their dealings with Nollan, Dolan, and Lucas. Government demanded transfers of resources from private individuals to the public without compensation, acts proscribed by the Constitution.

It does not speak well for the American judicial system that these people had to vindicate their basic rights by the arduous and enormously expensive process of appeal to the United States Supreme Court. These cases did, however, have a very beneficial outcome, for they persuaded the Supreme Court to refine its takings rules to better enable owners to defend themselves against confiscation of their property. Finally, the *Agins* Rules provide the kind of protection that property owners have long sought.

VI. Conclusion

The *Agins* Rules, together with the decisions in *Loretto* and *Causby,* establish a level of protection for liberty highly consistent with constitutional text and meaning. As explained in Chapter 2, the Constitution's greatest protection for property rights is provided by the due process clauses, which unconditionally secure an owner against an uncompensated limitation of his property rights except in two situations: first, when the owner commits wrongdoing causing these rights to be forfeited as a penalty; and, second, when the owner uses the property to create a nuisance or other serious harm to other people. While the current property rules do not fully implement this interpretation, they do secure a high level of protection for this important liberty.

These rules separate into five categories of protection. First, *Loretto* provides absolute protection against any permanent occupation of private property by government. Second, *Lucas* provides absolute protection against total deprivation of an investment-backed expectation or of all commercial viability. Third, *Causby* protects against damages to property caused by physical actions of government that are otherwise valid. Fourth, *Nollan-Dolan* provides close to absolute protection to a property owner against required dedications and exactions not related to activities carried on by the owner. Fifth, *Nollan-Dolan* protects against a deprivation of property rights that does not substantially advance legitimate state interests.

Items two, four, and five are determined under an intermediate standard of scrutiny, which accords much more deference to government than strict scrutiny. I do not favor elevating the level of review accorded property rights to strict scrutiny. In my opinion, strict scrutiny review is not consistent with the separation-of-powers doctrine.

Under the government established by the Constitution, the power of the majority is very great, but it does not possess power to deprive people of their liberties. In a government of such limited powers, the legislature has the burden of proof to show that its measures do not have this adverse impact. This burden of proof should not be unusually stringent inasmuch as the legislature is a co-ordinate branch and not a lesser branch of government; nor should the burden of proof be minimal, since the legislature as a coordinate branch is not entitled to superiority over the other branches. While the lines between the levels of scrutiny are far from precise, it would seem that the intermediate level presently applied to property rights is the most appropriate one for a government whose powers are separated and limited on the premise that excessive government power leads to oppression.

6

Recent Court Decisions Applying *Nollan* and *Dolan*

This chapter is devoted to discussing federal and state decisions interpreting the *Nollan* and *Dolan* opinions. Both opinions involved *Agins* Rules 1 and 2, which state that a land-use regulation can effect a taking if it does not substantially advance legitimate state interests. There are many decisions adjudicating these rules, and the number keeps increasing. I have selected for discussion those from state and federal appeals courts that present important or special issues. I have not considered the aftereffects of *Lucas* because there are few noteworthy cases relying upon it as of this writing.

I. *Ehrlich v. City of Culver City* (1994)[1]

This case involved the imposition by Culver City, California, of two fees as conditions of zoning approval for a $10 million, thirty-unit townhouse development: first, a $280,000 fee to mitigate the impact of a land-use change; and second, a $33,220 fee in lieu of a requirement that art approved by the city be placed in the project.

Ehrlich sought to build the townhouses on land he owned that was previously the site of a defunct private tennis club and recreational facility that he had owned and operated. Although the club's facilities were only available to members, the California Court of Appeal held that the mitigation fee was valid because it compensated the city both for the benefit conferred on the developer by the city's approval of the townhouse project and for the burden on the community resulting from the loss of the private recreational facilities. The mitigation fee was to be used for acquiring additional recreational facilities to replace those formerly contained in the tennis club; the amount of the fee was based on a portion of the city's estimate of the cost of building public recreational facilities. As for the "fee in lieu of art," the Court of Appeal held that there is a legitimate public interest in the expansion of artistic creation, and that the required payment of 1 percent of the total building valuation was reasonably related to the cost of the project. Understandably, in 1994, the United States Supreme Court remanded the case back to the California courts (by a 5-to-4 vote) for reconsideration on the basis of the *Dolan* ruling.[2]

Following remand of *Ehrlich* by the U.S. Supreme Court to the California Court of Appeal, the latter tribunal, in an unpublished opinion, reaffirmed its earlier ruling in favor of the defendant city. On appeal, the California Supreme Court reversed the decision with respect to the mitigation fee and affirmed the arts fee. The California high court decided that the *Nollan-Dolan* tests for determining whether a compensable regulatory taking has occurred—heightened scrutiny, essential nexus, and rough proportionality—apply to the monetary exactions imposed by Culver City as a condition for approving Ehrlich's application for rezoning. In reaching this decision, the California Supreme Court rejected the city's contention that *Nollan* and *Dolan* only applied to cases involving a dedication of property, not money.

Applying the heightened standards from those cases, the California Supreme Court held that the city had not met its burden of connecting the rezoning for townhouses with the monetary exaction that it imposed to mitigate the loss of recreational facilities. But it did find that the city could require certain payments to compensate for the loss of the facilities, as we shall see. With respect to the "fee in lieu of art," the court concluded that it was not a development exaction of the kind subject to the *Nollan-Dolan* takings analyses. It was, instead, a condition of the type long held to be a valid exercise of the city's traditional police power. Such a condition, the court maintained, does not amount to a taking merely because it might incidentally restrict a use, diminish the value, or impose a cost on the property. Exacting a fee for art from a developer is akin to "imposing minimal building setbacks, parking and lighting conditions, landscaping requirements, and other design conditions such as color schemes, building materials and architectural amenities."[3] The requirement of providing art in an area of the project visible to the public is an aesthetic control, the court contended, well within the city's police power.

While rejecting the city's contention that the $280,000 mitigation fee was warranted as partial compensation for the loss of some $800,000 in recreational improvements, the California Supreme Court held that Ehrlich could be required to pay other fees. The city could assess him for its likely administrative costs in replacing the private recreational facilities on his property with comparable private facilities on other privately owned land. This might include expenses incurred in redesignating other property for recreational use, or monetary incentives needed to induce private-health-club development on other land. The city may not "measure magnitude of its loss," the court stated, "by the value of facilities it had no right to appropriate without paying for them."[4]

The court concluded that the heightened standard of scrutiny required by *Nollan-Dolan,* which it applied in this case, is triggered by a relatively narrow class of land-use cases—"those exhibiting circumstances which increase the risk that the local permitting authority will seek to avoid the obligation to pay just compensation." The standard would, thus, be limited to cases in which local government uses its permit power to exact conditions it would otherwise not be entitled to impose.

In this and some other respects, this California decision falls short of implementing the full scope of *Nollan-Dolan.* One of the main purposes of the Fifth Amendment's takings clause is to "bar government from forcing some people alone to bear public burdens."[5] The California Supreme Court was correct in concluding that it should make no difference whether the required exaction consists of money or land; however, the opinion otherwise fails the *Nollan-Dolan* tests by approving exactions not closely linked to Ehrlich's redevelopment of the site for townhouses. Nor is there any language in *Nollan* or *Dolan* confining the reach of either case to a permit exaction. Both cases require the means-ends inquiries of *Agins* Rules 1 and 2.

Ehrlich's health-club facility contained five tennis courts, a heated swimming pool, a Jacuzzi, paddle-tennis courts, an aerobics area, a separate building for lockers, and other related facilities. Unfortunately, it lacked customers. A number of different managers had failed to make the facility operate at a profit. The city refused to purchase the facility because it was unprofitable and, later, when Ehrlich demolished it, decided not to acquire the site for use as a public recreational facility. Under the zoning then in effect, which limited its use to a health facility, the site was not commercially viable. Limiting development of property to a use which is not feasible would be tantamount to confiscation. Dissenting California Supreme Court Justices Kennard and Baxter correctly concluded that if the city refused to rezone the property for any other use, it would deprive the owner of all economically viable use—a violation of *Agins* Rule 3.[6]

A conclusion that a private health club was not an economically viable use of the property would not mean, of course, that the city was required to grant the specific alternative use that Ehrlich requested, a thirty-unit townhouse complex. But the city is required under its zoning regulations to authorize some other appropriate and reasonable use. When Ehrlich first wanted to operate a health club on his property, Culver City had given him a zoning authorization because it decided that this was an appropriate use. The process of rezoning should have been no different after the club failed, when Ehrlich asked the city to rezone the land for townhouses. Zoning theory supports changes in use to accommodate changing conditions; otherwise, land uses would be permanently or excessively fixed. The process involved in rezoning Ehrlich's property to allow construction of townhouses should have been no different than that used in any ordinary rezoning request, and no special fees should have been demanded.

An owner should sustain no penalty for discontinuing a use of property that is not viable. Use changes are in the public interest, because (1) an owner who has done no wrong should not be required to suffer a loss, and (2) the property might be used for a better societal purpose. The city sustained no greater burden from Ehrlich's request than from the typical rezoning petition. Every rezoning eliminates a particular use that was once considered appropriate or desirable. Zoning laws do not grant government ownership rights (a fee interest) or a lien interest in private property. If a city so desired, it could impose fees for expenses relating to the rezoning process itself, but it would be required to treat all applicants the same.

Culver City's "fee in lieu of art" should have raised the court's hackles. The city's arts requirement would place an art object on either an owner's building or his land, thereby mandating a permanent physical occupation of private property, directly contrary to the 1982 *Loretto* decision.[7] The reader will recall that in *Loretto,* mandating the installation of a small cable box on the roof of an apartment building was held to be a taking of that part of the owner's property. That the property owner retains ownership of the art object does not change the fact that government has mandated a physical occupation of private property.

The California Supreme Court's opinion makes no mention of the First Amendment. However, the city's arts fee creates free-speech questions. It forces Ehrlich against his will and at his expense to propagate public art approved by the city council. Art is a form of expression, and the First Amendment requires that expression should not be mandated or controlled by government. As the United States Supreme Court has observed, "it is largely because government officials cannot make principled decisions in this area that the Constitution leaves matters of taste and style so largely to the individual."[8]

In two important First Amendment cases from the 1970s, *Miami Herald Publishing Co. v. Tornillo* (1974)[9] and *Wooley v. Maynard* (1977),[10] the U.S. Supreme Court held that neither an editor nor any other person can be forced by government to publish or disseminate a message contrary to his or her desires. In *Tornillo,* the Court invalidated a Florida statute that compelled newspapers to publish the replies of political candidates whom they attacked. *Wooley* held unconstitutional New Hampshire's requirement that motor vehicles bear a license plate embossed with the state motto, "Live Free or Die." Both decisions reasoned that the power to compel speech does not greatly differ from the power to censor speech. The First Amendment, according to these decisions, protects both the right to speak freely and the right to refrain from speaking at all. The Court has referred to both rights as "components of the broader concept of individual freedom of mind."[11]

Two other cases support the foregoing positions. *West Virginia State Board of Education v. Barnett* (1943)[12] concerned a local school board requirement that students salute the United States flag and recite the pledge of allegiance. The Court rejected the view that we have "a Bill of Rights which guards the individual's right to speak his own mind, [but] left it open to public authorities to compel him to utter what is not in his mind."[13] *Keller v. State Bar of California* (1990)[14] found it a violation of First Amendment rights to require a person to pay dues to fund political and ideological activities as a condition for engaging in an occupation. The Court asserted in *Keller* that it is a bedrock principle of American thought that people should not be compelled to contribute to causes with which they do not agree. In the words of Thomas Jefferson, "to compel a man to furnish contributions of money for the propagation of opinions which he disbelieves, is sinful and tyrannical."[15]

Culver City's art fee is a limitation on the use of private property, and as such should be subject to the *Nollan-Dolan* standards. This is not, as the California Supreme Court contended, a matter of the police power, which is intended to protect the public's health and safety.[16] Merely labeling a regulation as part of the police power does not per se justify a restriction on this basis. In matters of property rights, the *Agins* Rules have replaced the more-deferential police power rules. An aesthetic restriction may have as great an impact on property use and value as, for example, an easement (*Nollan*) or land dedication (*Dolan*), both of which are subject to *Agins*.

The California Supreme Court dismissed Ehrlich's arts-fee objection on the basis that the police power justified the exaction, but it reached its conclusion without adequate consideration of this issue. Justice William Brennan's concurring opinion in *Metromedia, Inc. v. San Diego* (1981), a case involving San Diego's efforts to ban billboards for aesthetic reasons (among others), could have provided a reasoned approach to determining the validity of Culver City's arts fee.[17] The case involved commercial-speech rights, not property rights, but both rights require a tight means-ends fit under an intermediate standard of scrutiny.

It is Brennan's position that "[b]efore deferring to a city's judgment, a court must be concerned that the city is seriously and comprehensively addressing aesthetic concerns with respect to its environment."[18] If billboards alone are banned and no further steps are contemplated or likely, the commitment of a city to improving its physical environment is placed in doubt. According to Brennan, such a restraint by itself would be under-inclusive (that is, it would single out some, but not all, offenders):

By showing a comprehensive commitment to making its physical environment in commercial and industrial areas more attractive, and by allowing only narrowly-tailored exceptions, if any, San Diego would demonstrate that its interest in creating an aesthetically pleasing environment is genuine and substantial. This [i.e., demonstrating such a genuine and substantial interest] is a requirement where, as here, there is an infringement of important constitutional consequence.[19]

The California Supreme Court's *Ehrlich* opinion is devoid of any inquiry along these lines with respect to Culver City's arts requirement.

Among other things, an appropriate inquiry would have to determine whether payment of the arts fee will enhance aesthetics. In imposing the arts fee, the city authorities assume it will be an additional cost for the developer. But a developer may not treat it in this manner. He may reduce his expenditures on the project in order to pay the fee, by installing less-attractive windows, roofing materials, siding, landscaping, etc. Aesthetics or quality may suffer as a result. A municipality has no way to prevent this outcome. Instead of benefiting the community, the arts fee may be harming it.

II. *Manocherian v. Lenox Hill Hospital*

In *Manocherian v. Lenox Hill Hospital* (1994),[20] the New York Court of Appeals (the state's highest court) ruled that the *Agins* standards are applicable in determining the constitutionality of governmental limitations on the acquisition, use, and disposal of private property: "The [Supreme] Court promulgated a principle [in *Nollan*] for all property and land use regulation matters" that requires a heightened scrutiny test of judicial review to determine "if a law 'substantially advances legitimate state interests.'"[21]

The plaintiffs in the case were owners of several New York City apartments subject to the 1983 Omnibus Housing Act (OHA), which exempted from rent-stabilization controls dwelling units "not occupied by the tenant, not including subtenants or occupants, as his or her primary residence." Under OHA, the named leaseholder had to occupy the apartment as a primary residence in order to qualify for a renewal lease. While the subletting of apartments was still permitted, tenants could not sublet units for more than a total of two years out of every four-year period, and only on the establishment of primary residency. For an apartment to remain under rent stabilization, these limitations on subletting had to be observed. This law was harmful to Lenox Hill Hospital, a nonprofit hospital, which was a tenant of the plaintiffs. As a result of the law, the hospital would no longer obtain the benefits of rent stabilization for rental apartments that it sublet to its employees on a long-term basis.

To remedy this problem, the New York legislature adopted in 1984 an amendment to OHA giving special status to not-for-profit hospitals by providing that "[w]here a housing accommodation is rented to a not-for-profit hospital for residential use, affiliated subtenants authorized to use such accommodations by such hospital shall be deemed to be tenants." Under the 1984 enactment, the plaintiffs were required to offer leases to Lenox Hill Hospital for occupancy by some of its employees. The apartment owners sued Lenox to eliminate its claim to the apartments, on the basis that Lenox had no rights under the law since the law was unconstitutional. The trial court (Supreme Court) held the 1984 act to be constitutional in a decision affirmed by the Appellate Division of the Supreme Court. The New York Court of Appeals reversed the Appellate Division, finding that (1) the Lenox Hill Hospital was the principal agent in urging passage of the amendment and its primary and real beneficiary; and (2) the amendment was contrary to the goals of rent stabilization: to provide protection for current occupants while eventually returning the apartment to the open market.

The court rejected the contention of the dissenting justices that the statute was a public-welfare measure falling within the state's police power, because its primary beneficiary was a single industry, not-for-profit hospitals and their employees. Hospitals are an important business in the state, and politically influential. The fact that the state had acted through the "landlord-tenant relationship," the court stated, "does not magically transform general public welfare, which must be supported by the public, into mere economic regulation which can disproportionately burden particular individuals." Since it was not general-welfare legislation, but solely intended to benefit Lenox and other not-for-profit hospitals, the court held that the statute's aim was not a legitimate state interest. The statute thus violated *Agins* Rule 1:

> A proffered state interest, which by definition should serve and protect the general populace on a fairly and uniformly applied basis, should not be countenanced when, as occurs here, the statute instead benefits one special class for an essentially unrelated economic redistribution and societal relationship. . . .[22]

Seeking to invoke the police power, the state claimed that a health-care crisis existed in New York City; but this fact, said the court, does not by itself alter the rights of the parties:

> [S]uch a generalization would precedentially countenance a myriad of favoritism experiments or supplicant demands or preferential entitlements for special classes of entities over the wider, appropriate and constitutionally-authorized and recognized state interests of the general public.[23]

To justify such legislation, "the state must show a legitimate, substantial state interest that is closely, causally related to the action undertaken. The [United

States] Constitution forbids state action by fiat, no matter the economic equation."[24]

III. *Sparks v. Douglas County* (1995)[25]

Herschel and Elizabeth Sparks filed applications with the Douglas County (State of Washington) Planning Office seeking approval to subdivide their vacant land into sixteen separate lots. The planning director determined that the streets bordering the land were deficient in right-of-way width by county standards and thus would not accommodate future construction of street improvements. The subdivision review committee approved the applications conditioned on the Sparkses' dedicating strips of the property to allow the roads to be improved to comply with county standards. After the county board approved the committee's recommendations, the Sparkses filed suit contesting the required dedications as takings.

The required dedication of land along Empire Avenue, one of the abutting roads, was the most contentious part of these proceedings. The county had placed Empire Avenue on its six-year development plan prior to the date that either the planning commission or the county board considered the Sparkses' subdivision application. Had the Sparkses delayed submitting their applications until after the county was able to carry out its roadway improvement plan for Empire Avenue, the county would have had to obtain the necessary frontage by either purchasing the land from them or taking the property by eminent domain and paying "just compensation." In either case, the Sparkses would have obtained payment for their land.

The trial court agreed that all the streets bordering the Sparkses' land were deficient in that they did not meet the county's standards. Further, the court concluded that there was unrefuted evidence showing that when the property was fully developed, an additional 152 to 304 average daily trips (ADTs) would be generated by the sixteen family homes or thirty-two duplexes which the zoning code permitted to be built on the proposed sixteen lots. The court compared the projected ADTs with current traffic counts on the roads in question and found that the proposed development would approximately double the traffic in the area. Based on these findings, the court upheld the county's dedication requirements.

In 1993, the Washington Court of Appeals, citing *Nollan* and other cases, reversed the lower court's decision on the basis that the county's conditions for permit approval were arbitrary and capricious. The Court of Appeals stated that a dedication is required only if it "reasonably prevents or compensates for, in a specific and proportional fashion, adverse public impacts of the proposed development."[26] The court reached these conclusions: (1) The county had no immediate plans for improvements to the roads with the exception of Empire Avenue, which was included in an approved program. The Sparkses' development would not necessitate widening the roads in question. (2) The evidence established that the homes to be constructed in the proposed subdivision would, at most, add only twenty-five vehicles *per hour* to existing traffic. The court determined this figure by dividing 304 ADTs per day by twelve hours, which roughly comes to twenty-five. (3) There was no direct evidence that these already deficient roads would be less safe after the addition of twenty-five cars per hour. "This is not a number of sufficient magnitude to support, by itself, a reasonable inference that the developments will decrease the roads' safety."[27]

In 1995, the Washington Supreme Court reversed the ruling of the Court of Appeals,[28] finding that the county had conducted the inquiry required by *Dolan*, and that the exacting scrutiny of the Court of Appeals was excessive under that standard. The high court interpreted *Dolan* as requiring local government only to "make some effort to quantify its findings to support its permit condition." It stated that the findings made by the county were more than mere conclusory statements of general impact. The report prepared by the Douglas County Planning Office documented deficiencies in the widths of the existing rights of way and in the surfacing of the adjoining streets. The county had determined the likely increase in traffic and the specific need for dedication of rights of way on the basis of the individual and cumulative impact of a series of similar subdivisions.

The state supreme court's majority did not specifically consider the required dedications to broaden Empire Avenue. However, three of the nine justices dissented with respect to this thoroughfare, contending that these dedications were unnecessary.

The high court found the county's permit requirements valid under *Dolan*, for two reasons: first, they were not arbitrary or capricious, because they were reached after due consideration of a matter upon which there is room for differing opinions; second, the required degree of connection between means and ends was established by evidence that the proposed development would generate increased traffic on adjacent roads, which would then be inadequate for safe access under county standards.

In my view, neither reason meets the *Dolan* requirement of "rough proportionality." That the process was not arbitrary or capricious does not relate to the substance of the matter. If the end is illegitimate, no amount of proper process should save the proceedings. Under *Dolan*, local government must demonstrate that the exaction it imposes is "roughly proportional" to the impact of the development. The fact that the adjoining streets were deficient has no relation to the Sparkses' proposed development. The Sparkses have no responsibility for the existence of this condition. The only traffic-related impact of their development is an increase in traffic on the adjacent roads. The burden is on the gov-

ernment to show that this increase justifies the exaction of property that it demanded from the property owners. "No precise mathematical calculation is required," the United States Supreme Court ruled in *Dolan*, "but the city must
make some sort of individualized determination that the required dedication is
related both in nature and extent to the impact of the proposed development."[29]

The Washington Supreme Court's opinion does not confirm that any such
"individualized determination" was made. The court accepted without actual
inquiry the county's findings, calculations, and analyses, and accorded them finality on the issue. This is the kind of minimal review rejected in *Dolan*, which
requires, instead, a serious inquiry under an intermediate standard of scrutiny.

IV. *Schultz v. City of Grants Pass*

Schultz v. City of Grants Pass[30] is a 1994 decision of the Court of Appeals
of Oregon involving the application of *Dolan* to a petition for partition of a
3.85-acre vacant parcel of real estate into two lots. The city rejected the proposed partition because, among other things, not enough land was dedicated for
the widening of adjoining streets. The city demanded that about 20,000 square
feet of land (almost one-half acre) be dedicated for street purposes on the basis
that under the existing zoning, the properties might, in time, be further subdi-
vided into twenty residential lots, producing an amount of traffic that would
greatly burden the adjoining streets. Zoning on the property permitted twenty
residential lots to be situated on it, but the owner was only seeking approval for
two.

The city offered two arguments in support of the validity of its conditions.
First, it contended that because the conditions are based on city ordinances,
they are the "functional equivalent" of legislative decisions, and therefore are
entitled to minimal scrutiny rather than *Dolan*'s intermediate scrutiny. The city
was referring to the legislative/adjudicative distinction that Chief Justice Rehnquist made in his *Dolan* opinion. Second, the city argued that, even if *Dolan*
applied to the case, the conditions the city imposed were valid under it. The city
contended that because it has a legitimate interest in transportation planning, a
sufficient "nexus" exists between this interest and the imposition of the dedication and, thus, the only issue is whether the required degree of connection exists between the dedication condition and the impact of the proposed development. The city maintained that the development against which the dedication
condition ought to be measured is the "potential development of the partitional
tract."

The trial court concluded that there was sufficient evidence under *Dolan* for
a relationship between the conditions the city had imposed and the impact of
the proposed development, and entered judgment for the city. The Oregon

Court of Appeals rejected both arguments advanced by the city and reversed the trial court. The higher court asserted that, pursuant to the *Dolan* opinion, the presumption of validity for legislative decisions attaches only when a petitioner challenges the validity of a zoning ordinance or similar legislative or quasi-legislative enactment that is applied generally to all similarly situated properties (i.e., a facial challenge). Instead, in this case, the challenge was to the city's requirement that the owners of a particular piece of property dedicate portions of it in exchange for approval of their development application, and this requires an adjudicative inquiry.

The difficulty with the second argument, the court asserted, is that *Dolan* requires that the exactions imposed be "related both in nature and extent to the impact of the proposed development." The proposed development in this case was the partitioning of a single lot into two lots and nothing more. The court found nothing in the record to connect the dedication of a substantial portion of the petitioner's land, for the purpose of widening city streets, with the petitioner's limited application. An estimated increase of eight vehicle trips on Beacon Drive and Sarage Street (the adjoining streets) each day "hardly justifies requiring petitioners to part with 20,000 square feet of their land without compensation."[31]

V. *Luxembourg Group v. Snohomish County*

Luxembourg Group v. Snohomish County[32] is a 1995 case decided by Division One of the Court of Appeals of Washington. The Luxembourg Group owned 15.5 acres that adjoined what was referred to as the Lyons property, which had no access to a public road. Originally the two owners had agreed that the Luxembourg Group would acquire some of the Lyons property and provide street access for the balance. On this basis, the Luxembourg Group filed an application for subdivision approval. When Lyons chose not to consummate this arrangement, the Luxembourg Group filed a revised application to provide access to its planned development only and not to the Lyons property.

The Snohomish County's public works department asked the Luxembourg Group to dedicate land to provide road access to the Lyons property, and it refused to do so. The department noted that unless the Luxembourg Group provided this access, the buildable acreage on the Lyons property would be left landlocked. The department relied for support on the state's subdivision statute, one of the purposes of which is to promote "safe and convenient travel by the public on streets and highways [and] to provide for proper ingress and egress." The Luxembourg Group filed an action against the county seeking a decree finding the county's land-dedication requirement to be a taking. The trial court ruled in favor of the county.

The Washington Court of Appeals reversed the trial court's ruling, applying only *Nollan* because it decided that the county had not met the "essential nexus" requirement. (*Dolan* would be applicable only if this requirement were met.) The state must address a problem arising directly from the development under consideration, the court said, and since the Lyons property had never been accessible, it was in no way affected by the Luxembourg Group's development. A county cannot condition the approval of a subdivision on the dedication of property unless a need for the dedication arises from the development under review. A dedication requirement not designed to remedy any problem caused by the subdivision effects a taking of property without compensation, the court concluded.

VI. *Amoco Oil Company v. Village of Schaumburg* (1995)[33]

Amoco Oil Company sought to make substantial improvements to one of its service stations located at the intersection of two heavily traveled roads in the village of Schaumburg, Illinois, and the company applied for a special use permit for this purpose. Because of severe traffic congestion on these roads, the village, together with other governmental bodies, contemplated widening both roads by adding extra lanes of through traffic as well as dual left-turn and right-turn lanes at the intersection adjacent to Amoco's property. The village granted Amoco's petition for a special use permit, but made the permit subject to the company's dedication of twenty-eight feet of additional right-of-way along one road, ten feet of additional right-of-way along the other road, and a forty-foot triangular section immediately contiguous to the intersection. The required dedications involved 20 percent of Amoco's property.

Amoco filed suit against the village, charging that its dedication requirements constituted a taking. Schaumburg relied on two theories: First, "the proportionality [required by *Dolan*] existed because the dedication was directly related to the land sought to be improved, by the special use." Second, *Dolan* did not apply because the village's actions were purely legislative in nature rather than adjudicative, since the Board of Trustees, a legislative body, adopted the special use ordinance.

The evidence showed that Amoco's proposed improvements would have increased traffic approximately four-tenths of 1 percent. However, the trial court held that there was no taking, because the government had not actually invaded the property. Invoking *Dolan*, the Illinois appellate court (First District) reversed the decision, holding that there was indeed a taking. The required dedication had no relationship to the impact of the proposed improvement of the site and was, consequently, not roughly proportional to any burden created by that proposed improvement. The appellate court rejected the argument that the village's action was legislative, reasoning that the matter was adjudicative because it was not a universal but a site-specific one. The fact that the Board of Trustees, a legislative body, adopted the ordinance instead of the Planning Commission, an administrative agency, was not meaningful to the property owner. "Certainly, a municipality should not be able to insulate itself from a takings challenge merely by utilizing a different bureaucratic vehicle when expropriating its citizen's property."[34]

VII. *Parking Association of Georgia, Inc. v. City of Atlanta* (1994)[35]

This case concerned a facial challenge to an Atlanta, Georgia, zoning ordinance imposing restrictions on parking lots with thirty or more spaces in several downtown and midtown zoning districts. The ordinance requires "minimum barrier curbs and landscaping areas equal to at least ten percent of the paved area within a lot, ground cover (shrubs, ivy, pine bark or similar landscape materials) and at least one tree for every eight parking spaces." Its stated purpose is to improve the beauty and aesthetic appeal of the city, promote public safety, and ameliorate air quality and water run-off problems. The lot owners are required to bear the costs of compliance with the ordinance, but no lot owner is required to reduce the number of parking spaces by more than 3 percent. The owners estimate that these requirements will cost $12,500 per parking space and cause a substantial loss of parking and advertising revenue.

The Supreme Court of Georgia, by a 4-to-3 majority, upheld the ordinance against several constitutional challenges, including whether it was valid under the *Agins* tests. The court asserted that the plaintiffs' reliance on *Dolan* was misplaced. First, unlike the city of Tigard (in *Dolan*), Atlanta did make, quoting from *Dolan*, "some sort of individualized determination that the required dedication is related both in nature and extent to the impact of the development." This was a legislative determination, the court held, with regard to many landowners, and it simply limited the use the landowners might make of a small portion of their lands.

Second, the city demonstrated a "rough proportionality" between the requirements and objectives of the ordinance. The Georgia Supreme Court did not specify the reason for this conclusion, relying on its analysis of other constitutional issues that it made elsewhere in the decision. However, this analysis was modeled on the kind of injury required under *Euclid*. Citing *Euclid* and other cases, the court held that the burden "is on the plaintiff to come forward with clear and convincing evidence that the zoning presents a significant detriment to the landowner and is insubstantially related to the public health, safety, morality and welfare."[36] In my opinion, the difficulty with this decision is that the current standard in takings jurisprudence is set forth in the *Agins* decision and not in *Euclid*. Some of my comments about the California Supreme Court's decision in *Ehrlich v. City of Culver City*, discussed in Section I of this chapter, apply to this case as well.

According to the dissent in the *Parking Association* case, *Dolan* "lends support to the proposition that the city should bear the burden of proof." In *Dolan*, said the dissent, the Supreme Court placed the burden on the city because it had singled out a particular parcel to bear the burden of the city's requirements (the dissent referred to these requirements as an "extraction"): "Here, the city has singled out a particular use within the city to bear the extraction. Moreover, the city has retroactively imposed the extraction. These are persuasive reasons to require the city to justify the extraction."[37]

The dissent found fault with the Atlanta ordinance because of its retroactive character. Prior to commencement of a project, the dissenters stated, an owner has the option to determine if the required exactions are too costly. However, in the instance where the property has already been developed, the owner has no choice. The dissent ended with a discussion of aesthetic requirements: "[If] in fact, an extraction would actually promote nothing more than the aesthetics of the community, rather than a more compelling public interest such as the public safety, I would weigh that factor against the local government." According to the dissent, the court's majority was not observing the traditional distinction between a regulation that prevents harm and one that secures a public benefit "at the unfair expense of private owners who are simply convenient targets of opportunity for extracting the benefit."[38]

VIII. *Clark v. City of Albany* (1995)[39]

William F. Clark proposed to locate a fast-food drive-in restaurant in Albany, Oregon, on property zoned "heavy commercial." He submitted a site plan to the city, the review of which is an early stage in that city's zoning application process. When the city imposed conditions on the plan, Clark appealed to the city's land-use board of appeals, which also issued an opinion imposing conditions that he considered to be inconsistent with *Dolan*. Clark petitioned the Oregon Court of Appeals for review of the land-use board's decision. This court stated that *Dolan* requires the city to demonstrate a "rough proportionality" between certain conditions that it "exacts" and the "impacts" of the development that it approves. The principal issue in controversy was this: of the seven conditions imposed by the city, which ought to be considered "exactions," subject to the *Dolan* test?

The Oregon Court of Appeals reached the following conclusions: (1) The conditions requiring that the applicant design and construct street improvements were "exactions." (2) The condition requiring that the applicant designate an on-site area as traffic-free was not an "exaction," because it was essentially a traffic regulation. (3) The condition requiring that the applicant provide a storm-drainage plan to show that he would satisfy the city's storm-drainage requirement was not an "exaction." However, the way in which the city ultimately implements this condition could alter the nature of the condition and affect the relationship to *Dolan*. (4) The condition requiring that the applicant build sidewalks adjacent to the site was an "exaction." "For purposes of takings analysis," the court said, "we see little difference between a requirement that a developer convey title to the part of the property that is to serve a public purpose, and a requirement that the developer himself make improvements on the affected and nearby property and make it available for the same purpose."[40] The matter was returned to the city for reconsideration in accordance with the court's decision and the *Dolan* tests.

IX. *Robert Walz et al. v. Town of Smithtown et al.* (1995)[41]

This case was an appeal by the town of Smithtown, New York, to the United States Court of Appeals for the Second Circuit. The town objected to an award of damages to a home-owner by a New York federal district court. The home-owner had been deprived of water-supply service as a result of the refusal of an official of the town to issue an excavation permit for a public street unless the home-owner dedicated part of his land to the city. The home-owner was told he would not receive water-supply service until he conveyed the front fifteen feet of his property to the town for road-widening purposes. Citing *Dolan,* the Circuit Court stated that property owners have a right not to be compelled to convey some of their land in order to obtain utility service. According to the court, the home-owner, as a resident of the town, was entitled to an excavation permit as a matter of property right. The "absence of nexus between permit conditions and legitimate state interest converts land use regulation into an 'out-and-out plan of extortion.'"[42]

X. *San Mateo County Coastal Landowners' Association v. County of San Mateo* (1995)[43]

Coastal landowners and others challenged the validity of an initiative measure amending San Mateo County's local coastal program (LCP). They contended that certain provisions of the initiative on their face violate *Dolan*. These provisions stated that an applicant for a land division must grant to the county conservation/open space or agricultural easements as a condition of approval. The trial court upheld the measure, and its decision was affirmed by the California Court of Appeal, First District.

The Court of Appeal held that *Dolan* did not apply, because *Dolan* involved an "as applied" challenge to a permit condition imposed by an adjudicatory body, rather than a challenge to a legislatively adopted land-use and zoning scheme, such as the measure here in question. Unlike *Dolan,* there was no immediate requirement that land be deeded to the county. The easement requirements were a general limitation on the use owners might make of their parcels, and would not take effect unless and until a property owner submitted a subdivision application. At that point, an adjudicative decision would be made about the extent and nature of the easements. Once that decision was made, an aggrieved property owner could challenge the ruling as it was applied to his land.

XI. *Santa Monica Beach, Ltd. v. Santa Monica Rent Control Board* (1996)[44]

Santa Monica Beach, Ltd. is a landlord which claimed that it had suffered inverse condemnation because the rent-control law of Santa Monica, California, constitutes a regulatory taking of its property. In April 1979, Santa Monica adopted a rent-control charter amendment and created an elected rent-control board to regulate rentals. The statement of the charter amendment's purpose read, in part:

> A growing shortage of housing units resulting in a low vacancy rate and rapidly rising rents exploiting this shortage constitute a serious housing problem affecting the lives of a substantial portion of those Santa Monica residents who reside in residential housing. In addition, speculation in the purchase and sale of existing residential housing units results in further rent increases. These conditions endanger the public health and welfare of Santa Monica tenants, especially the poor, minorities, students, young families, and senior citizens. The purpose of this Article, therefore, is to alleviate the hardship caused by this serious housing shortage by establishing a Rent Control Board empowered to regulate rents in the City of Santa Monica so that rents will not be increased unreasonably and so that landlords will receive no more than a fair return.

Santa Monica Beach, Ltd. alleged in its complaint that Santa Monica's rent-control law not only failed to achieve its objectives, but to the contrary, made matters worse. The company marshaled statistics to support this claim. Between 1980 and 1990, while the city's rent-control law was continuously in effect, the city's stock of rental-housing units declined by nearly 5 percent and the city experienced a loss of 775 low-income rental units (a 12 percent decline). During the same period, the rental-housing supply and the number of low-income rental units increased in all comparable non-rent-controlled Southern California cities. The city also lost 285 "very low-income" rental units, causing the largest "exodus of economically disadvantaged renters" from any comparable Southern California city.[45]

At the same time, the city experienced a 37 percent increase in the proportion of households with very high incomes (while the proportion of very-high-income households dropped by more than 8 percent in the surrounding county of Los Angeles as a whole). In addition, rental housing in Santa Monica had become increasingly unavailable to young families, with the number of family households with children declining by 1,299, a 6 percent drop, during a period when no comparable non-rent-controlled Southern California city lost young family households.

The California trial court rejected the company's inverse-condemnation claim. On appeal, the California Court of Appeal (Second District) held that if the plaintiff could prove the facts that it had alleged, it would win, even on the highly deferential "rational basis" test that was rejected in *Nollan*. The "rational basis" test is the minimal-scrutiny standard that requires only a loose connection between the purpose of the law and the means used to achieve it. "If, in fact, Santa Monica's rent control law has reduced rather than increased the number of rental units available to those intended to be benefited by the law," the appeals court said, "then the regulation has no relationship (nexus) at all to its stated purpose. Deference to legislative authority cannot salvage a regulation that defeats rather than accomplishes its stated purpose."[46]

The appeals court returned the case to the trial court for adjudication of the inverse-condemnation issue. Although the matter is still pending as I write, I assume that the plaintiff will seek to prove his case with evidence that the law is irrational, or if that fails, that it violates the intermediate-scrutiny test of *Nollan-Dolan*.

XII. The Importance of *Nollan-Dolan*

To be sure, the judiciary is not unanimous in interpreting *Nollan-Dolan*. This is to be expected in the normal course of jurisprudence. All judges do not interpret rules identically. *Nollan-Dolan* essentially concerns the fit between the purpose of the law and the means of achieving it. Much of constitutional law is concerned with this inquiry, and judges and lawyers are accustomed to engaging in such inquiry in matters of speech, press, religion, transit, sexual privacy, and interstate commerce. Based on this long history in other areas of the law, a likely supposition would be that judges could readily apply the same thinking to property rights cases. However, this supposition has already been brought into question.

For a legal community long steeped in *Euclid*—the Supreme Court's first zoning case, generally regarded as highly deferential to government—*Nollan, Dolan,* and *Lucas* represent drastic change. This is particularly true for many judges who, under *Euclid,* virtually regarded themselves as agents of government in the regulation of land use. Nor can we expect law school professors antagonistic to property rights to readily become their defenders. Their students, who become the judges' new law clerks, imbibe their professors' animus toward property rights and, with a few exceptions, do not urge their employers to adopt the rigors of *Nollan-Dolan.* These are powerful reasons why the interpretation of *Nollan-Dolan* is in considerable flux.

As is evident from some of the cases reviewed in this chapter, some courts have diligently applied *Nollan-Dolan.* The New York Court of Appeals accepts the *Agins* tests as controlling in determining the constitutionality of property-use regulation. Appeals courts in Oregon, Washington, and Illinois, and the Second Federal Circuit Court of Appeals, have issued opinions consistent with *Nollan-Dolan.* However, the Georgia Supreme Court observes the distinction set forth in *Dolan* between the legislative and adjudicative processes and has applied a *Euclid* analysis to uphold Atlanta's limitations on the property rights of many parking-lot owners. The California Supreme Court has interpreted *Nollan-Dolan* to allow exactions that are not closely linked to the impact of a development, and has even found that fees for compulsory art are permissible. The Washington Supreme Court, in the name of *Dolan,* applied what amounts to minimal scrutiny to determine the validity of required street dedications, a position in obvious conflict with *Dolan.*

The rulings of the Georgia, California, and Washington high courts relate to regulations that are partial restrictions of property use. These sorts of "partial takings" cases were a matter of ad hoc judicial decision-making in the years prior to the advent of the *Agins* Rules. However, as correctly interpreted by the New York Court of Appeals, the *Agins* Rules have superseded the ad hoc approach and are applicable to both partial and total restrictions on land use.

Prior to the *Dolan* decision, the Federal Circuit Court of Appeals considered the application of *Lucas* to a regulation that did not prohibit all economically beneficial use of a plaintiff's land and caused, at most, a partial destruction of its value.[47] The specific issue was the status in takings law of a partial (but not a total) reduction in the overall market value of the plaintiff's property as a result of a regulatory imposition. Since *Lucas* concerned the elimination of *all* economically beneficial use, it was not directly applicable to this case.[48]

Although Justice Antonin Scalia compared the total regulatory deprivation in *Lucas* with the physical occupation in *Loretto,* takings rules are different when less than the entire property interest is involved. In physical-occupation cases, the owner is entitled to compensation, regardless of the size of the portion of his property affected: even occupation by a small cable box will trigger compensation. Thus, a permanent physical occupation of any part of an owner's property is a taking. However, the physical-occupation rule does not apply to a regulation that affects a portion of one's property.

Seeking to resolve this legal dilemma, Circuit Judge Sheldon Plager, in *Florida Rock Industries, Inc. v. United States* (1994), set forth a test for determining whether a taking has occurred in cases dealing with regulatory restrictions that deprive an owner of the use of part of his property. In addition to finding a loss of economic use to the property owner as a result of the regulation, Plager wrote, the trial court must also consider these additional factors before deciding that a taking has occurred:

> [A]re there direct compensating benefits accruing to the property, and others similarly situated, flowing from the regulatory environment? Or are benefits, if any, general and widely shared through the community and the society, while the costs are focused on a few? Are alternative permitted activities economically realistic in light of the setting and circumstances, and are they realistically available? In short, has the Government acted in a responsible way, limiting the constraints on property ownership to those necessary to achieve the public purpose, and not allocating to some number of individuals, less than all, a burden that should be borne by all?[49]

Plager's test essentially requires the trial court to determine when fairness and justice require that compensation be paid under the accepted doctrine that the takings clause is "designed to bar Government from forcing some people alone to bear public burdens which, in all fairness and justice, should be borne by the public as a whole."[50] Plager's opinion was written prior to *Dolan* but is basically consistent with it. "Rough proportionality" requires a close causal fit between the regulation's impact and the exaction imposed on the owner. An owner's property interest should, otherwise, only be limited in order to prevent a serious harm and not to provide benefits for other people. Thus, with the decision in *Dolan*, closure has occurred at the United States Supreme Court with respect to most regulatory takings controversies. *Lucas* applies to deprivations of all economically viable use of property—denial of investment-backed expectations and elimination of commercial value. *Nollan-Dolan* applies to partial limitations on property use.

7

Zoning: Political Control of Property

Most zoning codes were adopted after the Supreme Court's pivotal zoning case, *Euclid v. Ambler Realty* (1926), when it was generally assumed that the likelihood of judicial interference with a local government's zoning discretion was not very great. That assumption is not realistic in the late 1990s, as a result of the six previously discussed Supreme Court opinions which suggest the contrary— that, when challenged, an application of a zoning regulation will be subjected to a heightened judicial inquiry to determine if it is constitutional. Zoning ordinances as a whole may not be at risk—and Chief Justice William Rehnquist's comment in *Dolan v. City of Tigard* (1994) that a general zoning ordinance was entitled to greater deference than a particular application of it, may be so interpreted.[1] However, owners of individual parcels or tracts of land are now entitled to considerable protection against arbitrary or capricious zoning regulation.

The issues raised by the *Agins* Rules have not been of much concern to the local legislators and planners responsible for making zoning regulations. Zoning is not directed to protecting the freedom of property owners; most regulations are not justified "by some sort of [means-ends] individualized determination" and "rough proportionality."[2] Zoning rules are created by a planning-political process that emphasizes majoritarian values rather than libertarian ones. Before a zoning ordinance or regulation is adopted, it must be prepared by technicians, discussed and considered by the public, and voted upon by the local legislative body (a city council, board of trustees, or county commission). In view of the forces that shape the zoning process, it is doubtful that most regulations in any locality meet *Dolan*'s "rough proportionality" test.

Local legislators make zoning decisions for a variety of reasons. The dominant factors in zoning are public pressure and political influence—the factors

179

that officeholders understand best. Public participation makes it extremely difficult for local legislators to obtain a detached analysis and evaluation of the issues. In zoning hearings, the input from the public may run the gamut from professional analysis to irrational outbursts, with considerable doubt as to which is more effective. Questions involving municipal finances, urban law, and urban economics are much too complex for most laypeople, yet their uninformed opinions on these matters may be critical in deciding a controversy.

For local legislators, the most important factors influencing their judgment in zoning matters appear to be the number and influence of the people who object to a proposal, a new rule, or an amendment to an old one. I reach this conclusion on the basis of my personal experience as a lawyer representing owners and as an owner of property. In the cases in which I participated, probably the most important factor in determining whether or not I succeeded in obtaining a reclassification or variance for my client was the number of people who objected to my client's application. Matters such as efficiency, productivity, competition, and consumer demand were subordinate and often nonexistent considerations for the zoning authorities, unless these factors coincided with the concerns of the objectors.

Another major problem with zoning (previously mentioned in the *Euclid* discussion in Chapter 4) is that the zoning process is often inconsistent with a fundamental democratic principle: that a legislature should represent the people whom its decisions affect. Observing this principle has long been a concern of the courts.[3] Land-use regulations in suburban areas have a substantial impact on members of the population who reside elsewhere. Property owners in outlying areas, would-be residents, and nonresident consumers never had any participation in the selection of the lawmakers who made these zoning decisions. Nonresidents affected by zoning rules are deprived of the opportunity to exert electoral pressures on the zoning regulators to obtain changes in policy. As indicated in Chapter 4, zoning regulations that substantially affect people residing outside of the municipality's boundaries may lack constitutional legitimacy. This issue has never been adjudicated by the United States Supreme Court.[4]

In their dissents in *Lucas* and *Dolan*, Justices Harry Blackmun and John Paul Stevens have expressed confidence in local zoning processes. They worry that the Court's protections of property rights will hamper the work of planners and other government officials regulating land use. Their concern is misdirected. In a system of government premised on the "blessings of liberty," individual rights merit priority. As Justice William Brennan once observed: "After all, a policeman must know the Constitution, then why not a planner?"[5] America's enormous accomplishments in housing, commercial, and industrial development are attributable to the freedom of the market, not the authority of the regulators. There are strong pragmatic reasons for not giving great deference to zoning regulators, as the following discussion will show.

Zoning is one of the most criticized regulatory systems in the United States. Each of the three presidential housing commissions—two appointed by President Johnson and one by President Reagan—has been strongly critical of the zoning process. Law reviews have published articles similarly critical.[6] The term "exclusionary zoning" has become a pejorative part of our language, referring to the exclusion of unwanted people—often minorities—from a locality.

In 1968, the Douglas Commission, appointed by President Johnson, asserted: "In short, although the basic justification for zoning is to protect the overall public good, this often appears to be the last consideration as zoning is now practiced."[7] Johnson's Kaiser Commission concluded that zoning "tends to reduce the supply of new housing and raise prices or rents especially for those least able to pay."[8] Reagan's Commission on Housing urged municipalities not to adopt zoning regulations denying or limiting the development of housing unless their existence is necessary to achieve a vital and pressing governmental interest.[9] The commission concluded that unnecessary zoning and related requirements may often elevate the cost of housing by 25 percent or more.[10]

The most recent national attack on zoning occurred in July 1991, when the Commission on Regulatory Barriers to Affordable Housing, appointed by then Housing and Urban Development Secretary Jack Kemp, concluded that unnecessary zoning and other local government regulation caused substantial increases in housing prices. The commission charged that local regulation was denying many the American dream of home-ownership.[11]

Anthony Downs, a member of the commission and a senior fellow at the Brookings Institute, estimated that "probably well over half of the cost of building new housing in the average United States community is a direct result of local government regulations rather than of any minimum requirements truly necessary for the occupants' health and safety."[12]

I. Zoning Elections

Setting aside the impact of zoning on nonresidents, it is important to note that the existence of zoning in a city, town, or county should not be regarded as always fulfilling the wishes of the people living there. Comprehensive zoning ordinances are adopted by local legislators, usually without a vote of the local residents. Only one major city, Houston, has voted on whether or not to adopt zoning. In 1993, the voters of Houston rejected for the third time in its history the adoption of a zoning ordinance, leaving Houston as the only major city in the nation without zoning. The city had previously voted on the issue in 1948 and 1962. In 1948, only property owners were allowed to vote, and the proposed zoning ordinance was defeated by a vote of 14,142 to 6,555.

The breakdown of the votes on zoning in 1993 and 1962 reveals a stark division based on socioeconomic factors. The 1993 voting pattern was similar to the pattern in 1962, except that in 1993, unlike in the prior vote, the most affluent group voted against zoning. The proposed 1962 zoning ordinance lost by 57 percent to 43 percent,[13] while the 1993 version lost by 52 percent to 47 percent. Breakdowns according to socioeconomic groups, made by the *Houston Post* for each zoning vote, are shown in Tables I and II.

Other, smaller municipalities in the nation have voted on adopting zoning, and, in many instances, the vote has gone against it.[14] The breakdowns on a socioeconomic basis appear similar to Houston's. Interestingly, those in the population most in need of better housing conditions are the strongest opponents of zoning, apparently believing it will not improve their conditions. Whether the absence of zoning in Houston is desirable or not is controversial, of course. The judgment of the people living there—probably as expert as anyone else on the subject—is favorable to the existing free-market system.

Although their properties generally were subject to enforceable restrictive covenants, which prohibited diverse uses within their subdivisions, middle-income property owners in Houston voted to obtain the further protection of zoning.[15] As is evident from their high voting turnout, these owners were largely responsible for the city's efforts to adopt zoning. The view from the low-income areas that were not subject to covenants—which would have afforded them some protection—was entirely different. On each occasion, the voting turnout was relatively low, an event that was not unusual in elections in these areas. Those who did vote feared zoning in large part because it would eliminate some types of housing and some diverse uses that augmented their well-being. They apparently did not believe that use and environmental controls would benefit them. For example, the low-income-housing areas that contained auto-repair shops voted sharply against zoning, which would, in time, have eliminated these shops. Because they usually charge much less than the factory-authorized facilities, install used parts, and are located within walking distance, these local auto-repair shops serve the needs of low-income people. Auto-

TABLE I. 1993 Vote[16]

Group	Turnout	For	Against
Low-income Black	12%	29%	71%
Middle-income Black	23	63	37
Predominantly Hispanic	14	41	59
Low-mid-income White	18	32	68
Middle-income White	29	56	44
Affluent	35	44	56

(A private survey indicates that 75 percent of inner-city precincts voted against zoning in 1993.)[17]

TABLE II. 1962 Vote[18]

Area[19]	Median Value Owner-Occupied Housing[20]	Average Monthly Rental[21]	Turnout	For	Against
Lindale, Melrose	$7,200–9,700	$52–55	43%	16%	84%
Little York, York	8,200–10,600	61–62	49	17	83
Magnolia Park	6,700–6,900	44–47	31	20	80
Heights	7,500–9,000	47–60	42	24	76
Negro	6,600–12,000	42–80	28	28	72
Park Place, Pecan Place	12,300	75	52	38	62
Mason Park, Kensington	7,800–9,000	55–68	51	39	61
Garden Oaks, Oak Forest	11,300–12,300	62–86	56	41	59
Freeway Manor	11,300–12,900	63–95	47	44	56
Golfcrest, South Park	9,900–13,000	79–107	55	51	49
Southland, Hermann Park	9,300–16,500	94–129	51	53	47
Westheimer, Post Oaks	13,800–25,000+	78–132	63	58	42
River Oaks, Tanglewood	25,000+	107–132	61	59	41
Memorial, Spring Branch	11,700–25,000+	85–171	60	61	39
Westbury	18,300–22,600	115–134	65	65	35
Sharpstown	15,600–16,600	123–124	65	68	32

repair shops are not located in middle-income areas that are not restricted by covenants governing property use, because the residents there have no need for them. These people can afford to do business with authorized dealers.

The fact that, in two Houston zoning elections, about 70 percent of low-income voters rejected zoning should impress the judiciary. United States Supreme Court justices have, over the years, shown concern for the disadvantages that poorer people sustain as a result of regulation. An example of this concern, one that is pertinent to the results of Houston's zoning elections, is the Court's 1976 decision in *Virginia State Board of Pharmacy v. Virginia Citizens Consumer Council, Inc.* (discussed in Chapter 3). In that case, the Court accorded First Amendment protection to commercial speech, reversing its previous position that such speech was not constitutionally protected. This reversal was in large measure a reflection of the Court's concern for the welfare of low-income and elderly consumers.[22] The justices found that restrictions on commercial speech by the Virginia Board prevented these consumers from obtaining information on the stores that sold prescription drugs at low prices. The attack on Virginia's law prohibiting the advertising of prescription drugs came from low-income and elderly consumers, not from entrepreneurs. The suit was not brought on behalf of all consumers; rather, it was filed only on behalf of consumers who were most adversely affected by the ban on prescription-drug advertising. The Court identified these people as the poor, the sick, and the aged.

The Houston zoning elections reveal that similar problems exist under zoning. Low-income people voted overwhelmingly against zoning because they regard it as harmful to them. It raises their cost of shelter and creates a homogeneous living environment that they reject. They would prefer to have businesses within walking distance rather than far away. For poor people, these are more than matters of convenience: they are financial necessities. Low-income people also feared that zoning would reduce employment in construction and related industries. In the next chapter, we will see that a similar pattern of voting occurred on the California Coastal Initiative (to control development along the state's extensive coastline) and on two growth-control initiatives in the city of San Diego. Protection for less-affluent people in our society buttresses the argument for heightened scrutiny in judicial review of zoning regulations. Just as the application of intermediate scrutiny in the commercial-speech cases has enabled the Supreme Court to protect the interests of disadvantaged people, so will it operate in zoning cases.

II. The Failure of Land-Use Planning

Zoning, like any other regulation of land use, is supposed to be a tool for planning more efficient and aesthetically pleasing communities. Therefore, we can learn much about the operation of the public planning process from an examination of how zoning works in practice. There is a certain appeal to the notion that we must have more and better urban planning. After all, goes the refrain, if only we had planned our cities better, there would be less congestion, no slums, more beautiful buildings, etc. There is always someone who can describe in exhaustive detail a local horror that could have been avoided by better or stricter planning. Ironically, on investigation, it frequently turns out that the local planning department had approved the particular horror in the first place. But pointing that out rarely quiets enthusiasts for government regulation. Their response typically takes the form of a question: If individuals and corporations carefully plan their activities and outlays, then why shouldn't government be allowed or required to engage in this selfsame activity?

The simple, yet highly profound answer is that public land-use planning in a democratic society is doomed to failure. Public land-use planning implies an orderly, rational process designed to best use the land for the present generation and for future generations. It also implies that there are experts in planning who know how to manage resources to achieve these goals. Although this definition raises many questions, it represents what most people think they are saying when they speak or write about planning. The assumption seems to be that there is something precise, measurable, or quantitative about planning, or its standards—in other words, that planning is comparable to a science.

This assumption is exceedingly difficult to substantiate, and few of even its most ardent proponents make the effort. Is there some precise measurement available to determine the "best" use of some or all of the land, to weigh the merits of growth and anti-growth proposals, or to judge whether the land is better suited for stores, factories, or the housing of people? Should a particular plot of land be developed with two, eight, or twelve housing units to the acre; or is it perhaps better suited for a mobile-home park or a shopping center; or should it be retained as open space? By now, after eighty years of zoning experience in this country, it should be clear that there are respectable, distinguished, and knowledgeable urban planners who would disagree in many if not most instances with respect to any or all of these alternatives. Planning is unquestionably highly subjective, lacking those standards and measurements that are the requisites of a scientific discipline.

The record in many zoning cases supports this conclusion. Typically, one finds testimony from two planners, one supporting the plaintiff (landowner), and the other favoring the defendant (city). At the trial level, many zoning cases have become verbal duels between planners, each promoting a different position. Accordingly, what goes under the name of "scientific" planning is really opinion put forward by those trained to practice the *art* of urban development. The country's zoning experience raises serious doubts that such training and knowledge provide any special insights, either in evaluating the present or in predicting the future.

Planners confront serious problems in fulfilling their responsibilities. Theory and education alone cannot substitute for the actual experience of making practical decisions and suffering their consequences. Few municipal planners have ever been part of the construction or development industry, or responsible for actual decisions in the development of residential, commercial, or industrial projects. Even if they once had been, their information about prices, materials, innovations, trends, consumer desires, and preferences must now come from secondary or more remote sources, not directly from the "firing line." How then can planners possibly be as familiar with the location, development, construction, and operation of shopping centers, housing developments, nursing homes, or mobile-home parks as those who develop, own, and operate them? Owners and their mortgage lenders risk substantial funds on the success of the projects they undertake. Yet, under zoning, planners are expected to regulate land use, an awesome task even for the most knowledgeable. Unfortunately for the community, in lieu of hard information, planners will tend to rely on their own beliefs, experience, and background, and this inevitably creates hardships and problems for those of different perspectives.

But regardless of their knowledge, training, and abilities, the fact is that, in practice, planners do not make a significant impact on the regulation of land use. Decisions and controls affecting land use will be adopted by those elected to public office. These are the local legislators who comprise the city, village, or county councils. They can be expected to respond to a variety of pressures and concerns, a principal one being the interests of those who elect them and keep them in office. Politics, rather than planning, will be the key determinant of land-use policy. In short, zoning and other land-use regulations are and always have been a tool more of politics than of planning.

III. Politics and Pressures

Consider these limitations on the power of the planner. First, he is a paid employee and cannot be expected to espouse, with any degree of consistency, policies contrary to those of his employers. The basic rules are established by those elected to govern or appointed to administer. Confrontations are rare because a planner is not likely to be hired or seek employment if his basic orientation appears to differ substantially from that of his prospective employer. Planners committed to growth could find life quite uncomfortable in the many "no-growth" communities in California, for example. The reverse is equally true. Disagreements will occur and will be tolerated—within limits.

Second, even if a proposed plan appears to be in accord with the general desires of the lawmakers or administrators (and even if its preparation was commissioned by them), there will still have to be public hearings and debates before it can be adopted. Amendments can easily change the meaning and impact of the proposed legislation. In practice, the "perfect" plan stands little chance of remaining intact against the opposition of a group of determined voters or politicians, the pressure exerted by political supporters or contributors, the payment of graft, or perhaps the editorial ridicule of the local newspaper. Accordingly, the "perfect" plan is likely to be quite imperfect by the time it emerges from the legislative process, whether it be on a local or higher governmental level; and it might be ravaged still more as it is administered.

IV. Misusing the Land

The modern world of land development demands a high degree of expertise. Why then are we so willing to allow eminently unqualified people to have a voice in the development of the land? If the experts in this field are the builders and the developers—the people who take the risks—why, paradoxically, does zoning require them to submit their proposals for final decision to the public and its representatives?

The idea is a poor one. If people have reservations about placing their cares and concerns in the hands of general practitioners instead of specialists, then they should be outraged at the prospect of entrusting their futures to those who have little understanding. Some residents in a given community will have specialized knowledge in architecture and design, but experience shows that such people stay away from zoning hearings; or if they do participate, it is to look after their own interests. I have attended zoning hearings where home-owners—whose knowledge of development was, to put it mildly, extremely limited—condemned complex plans prepared by highly skilled specialists for sophisticated developers. Worst of all, local authorities may weigh such comments heavily, because they emanate from sources with a powerful weapon: the ability to vote them out of office.

Invariably, city planners and council members try to upgrade proposed developments. One gets the impression that residents want only Taj Mahals to be built in "their" municipalities. Developers seek to pass-on the cost of upgrading by raising prices or rents. If market conditions do not allow for increases, the projects become economically unfeasible and are not erected. New construction is thereby reduced, and this also causes home prices or rents to rise.

Another possibility is that the developer will compensate for the added expense by reducing the quantity or quality of other amenities. He may attempt to offset the cost of required park dedications, installation of art objects, special architectural treatment, or lower density by, say, lessening the amount or the quality of the windows, doors, plumbing, heating, electrical fixtures, etc.

The developer may proceed in spite of the fact that his horse has been turned into a camel, and the market may not be as favorable for camels. At least one reason for making such a decision might be the "sunk costs" in lawyers', planners', and architects' fees that the developer has already incurred to obtain construction approval. These costs, as well as those invested in holding or optioning the land, would be lost if the project were abandoned.

The foregoing describes zoning in action and highlights the difference between private and public planning processes. The owners of any business have to conduct their operations with maximum efficiency; otherwise their profits will diminish or disappear. They must purchase and produce with minimal waste. Above all, they must create something consumers will buy at a price that includes a profit.

No such limitations confine the public regulators. They make decisions for a large variety of reasons, and consumer preferences and efficiency are not primary ones, for there is little regulators can personally gain from acting efficiently. Even if they wanted to anticipate consumer preferences, how could they in a process that is insulated from the open market? As a result, land-use regulation causes the waste of a great deal of land and resources.

Laws restricting individuals do not necessarily impact all individuals equally. This result stands out prominently in land-use regulation. Those in the best financial position to hire lawyers and experts to negotiate with or battle the regulators will not suffer to the same extent from the regulatory process as those without substantial resources. The more discretion that the law permits to zoning officials, the greater the difference in treatment is likely to be, since the regulators will have greater latitude to respond to pressure. Laws enabling zoning regulators to exercise great powers may be costly to wealthy owners and developers, but may be financially devastating to less-affluent owners. The entry of smaller entrepreneurs into the market (and the value they bring) will be reduced or in time extinguished, if regulation goes far enough.

V. The Failures of Zoning

Because they cannot comprehend market forces as businesspeople do, planners, public officials, and politicians will tend to allow development where it is not feasible and to prohibit it where it is. This will result in the curtailment of much development and will, consequently, be harmful to the vast numbers of people in this country who are dependent on new construction for their earnings, livelihood, and well-being.

The "mistakes" of zoning should not be surprising. The zoning process is limited in its effect on business, since it can only decree what business *cannot do,* not what business *will do.* The fact that zoning allows a business to locate in a certain area is meaningless if economic conditions dictate against it. What the regulations set forth for a particular district is one thing; what actually occurs may be considerably different. Further complicating the problem is the continual change with the passage of time in business methods and consumer preferences. Even if they were appropriate when originally carried out, studies on which planning decisions are based will be less applicable and finally irrelevant in future years, although the zoning ordinance will still be in force.

Supporters defend zoning on the basis of its wide acceptance by almost all American cities. However, while zoning exists in most places, it invariably becomes contentious and much more complicated over time as various forces clamor for changes. Consider the history of zoning. Area-wide land-use controls arrived in this nation in 1916 in the form of the New York City Zoning Resolution, the country's first zoning ordinance. This modest ordinance contained three use districts (residential, commercial, and unrestricted), five classes of height districts, and three classes of area districts.[23] The New York City zoning ordinance in 1996 runs hundreds of pages, and has vastly more zoning districts and a host of other controls never contemplated by the framers of the original ordinance.[24] My home city of San Diego had eight zoning districts in 1952, sixteen in 1962, and over two hundred in 1993.[25] Each zoning district has its own rules on land use and development.

The complexity of zoning laws means more power for regulators. Under most ordinances presently in effect in this nation, the length and cost of the process often gives zoning regulators enormous discretion in determining land plans, building designs, and building materials. These decisions even influence housing prices.[26] Fighting city hall is very expensive, and developers must necessarily limit such activity if they are to stay in business.

The story is now a familiar one. Small, modest zoning ordinances grow into very complex and complicated ones. One reason is, of course, the change in conditions, building techniques, and thinking that occurs over the years and is reflected in our laws. But there are two other explanations for the uncontrolled growth of zoning. The first is that zoning has been a story of unrealized expectations. It usually does not work as represented.[27] Consequently, different zoning strategies have evolved over the years. Each new strategy is touted as a remedy for the failings of the old, but it too will fail to measure up to the expectations of its proponents. The likely result will be another new effort: back to the drawing board, to produce more and increasingly severe rules and regulations that, experience suggests, are not likely to be more successful than the previous round.

Another reason for the proliferation of zoning regulations is that the process is a battlefield for warring interest groups. No matter how well-thought-out a zoning plan might appear, it will help some people and hurt others. Experience shows that soon after passage of an ordinance, the losers will agitate for changes. Landowners will seek to rezone their property to increase its value. Home-owners and environmentalists will lobby to make the rules more stringent and exclusionary—the former to increase their home values, and the latter to "save the earth" from development (although there is considerable overlap between the two groups). Civic groups will urge the adoption of their pet reforms. The courts may also require significant changes. Before long, the original plan may be nearly unrecognizable. And many who relied on it for their protection may, indeed, be very disillusioned.

VI. Zoning and Housing Prices[28]

William Fischel, a professor of economics at Dartmouth College, produced a highly persuasive study demonstrating that strong land-use controls greatly raise the cost of housing. The study is based on California housing prices in the 1970s. After many years of rapid population growth, the median value of owner-occupied housing in California in 1970 was 35 percent higher than that in the nation as a whole. By 1980, after ten years of the slowest rate of population growth in the state's history, this differential in median value of owner-occupied housing had more than doubled, to 79 percent. During the 1970s, California's housing values rose 267 percent, compared to a 176 percent increase for the entire nation. Fischel concluded that democracy in the suburbs accounted for the extraordinary housing price increase in California. Resident voters were able to restrict new development in order to maximize the value of their own homes and maintain neighborhood exclusivity:

> In my opinion, the only remaining explanation for why California's home prices rose so rapidly during the 1970s is that, during that decade, the state was the pioneer in growth controls. By legally removing significant amounts of suburban land from development, by denying those who did have subdividable land essential services like water, and by imposing costly subdivision conditions unrelated to home buyers' demands, growth controls created an artificial scarcity of housing. I submit that politically established and judicially validated scarcity was the newly operative constraint, not physical limitations.[29]

Among the studies that Fischel referred to in support of his position are two that examined price increases resulting from special growth controls that local governments added to their zoning regulations. The first showed a modest housing price increase of about 10 percent in Davis, California, as a result of growth controls there in the 1970s. The other found that housing in growth-controlled communities in the San Francisco Bay area commanded a 17 percent to 38 percent price premium.[30]

Other studies of various California cities over the years show similar results. Economics professors Lloyd Mercer and W. Douglas Morgan conducted a study of Santa Barbara County housing and found that development restrictions accounted for more than 27 percent of the increase in real housing prices from 1972 to 1979.[31] Seymour Schwartz, David Hansen, and Richard Green found that Petaluma's quota on housing permits, adopted in 1972, within a few years raised the city's new home prices by 8 percent above those in nearby Santa Rosa.[32]

Lynn B. Sagalyn and George Sternlieb of Rutgers University's Center for Urban Policy Research studied certain zoning and building requirements in the 1960s in New Jersey. They concluded that reducing three major zoning requirements (lot size, lot frontage, and living area) would lower prices considerably and enlarge the effective housing market. Changing two building-code specifications (thickness of exterior wall sheeting, and size of foundation cinder block) would also lower selling prices, but not to the same degree as altering zoning policies.[33]

To determine the impact of local government regulation on the cost of housing, the Department of Housing and Urban Development initiated a housing cost reduction demonstration project in 1980. Four communities across the country were selected to participate in the project, which used reduced local government regulations as the only variable. In these communities, zoning, building, and subdivision regulations were minimized. In the selected projects subject to the reduced regulations, the prices of new homes were reduced by 21 percent to 33 percent as compared to similar local developments that were subject to traditional regulations. In Shreveport, Louisiana, demonstration housing units had sales prices of $52,850, while homes in a comparable suburban project with conventional regulations and processing sold for $70,000. In Hayward, California, the demonstration units ranged in price from $53,000 to $65,000. Comparable units subject to conventional regulation in the area sold for $79,500 to $97,500. In all instances, the builders sought to obtain a normal profit margin.[34]

In areas of high demand, land-use regulations operate to greatly curb housing production, particularly that which serves less-affluent people. Consider M.I.T. Urban Studies Professor Bernard Frieden's study of three proposals to develop housing projects in northern California. In the first proposal, a developer in 1972 proposed to build 2,200 housing units in the foothills of Oakland, divided about equally between homes and apartments. By 1976, the proposal had been whittled down to the sale of 100 lots for estate homes on a portion of the property and the construction of 150 to 200 single-family homes on the remainder. The second proposal involved acreage on the shoreland of the East Bay across from San Francisco. The plan, originally submitted in 1972, sought permission for the erection of 9,000 moderately priced homes. In 1976, the project was reduced to one-third of its original size. The third proposal involved a site on a mountaintop and adjoining foothills just south of San Francisco. This proposal originally called for 11,000 housing units, but the county supervisors reduced it to 2,200 units, which rendered the project infeasible.

Frieden posed the critical question: developers may be able to make compromises that will get them political approval in these cases, but how much longer can they make these compromises and continue to sell houses to anyone but the very wealthy?[35]

The foregoing are not isolated studies. As Professor Fischel confirms in a 1991 essay, most of the scholarly studies show that growth controls—which are basically strong zoning restrictions—elevate housing prices. According to Fischel, nearly all credible studies find this same outcome (credibility, in this case, is determined by publication in professional journals or books subject to peer review).[36]

These professional studies support the conclusion that the severity of land-use regulations affects the price of housing: in other words, making the restraints more severe drives up the price. It follows as a general proposition that imposing zoning controls in a community where none existed before will increase housing prices. I have reported over the years that rents in zoned Dallas, which is 230 miles from unzoned Houston, are higher than in Houston. In the balance of this section, I shall present evidence showing a differential in housing prices between the areas in which these two cities are located.

Houston is the largest and Dallas the second largest city in Texas. Zoning arrived in Dallas in the early 1930s and is of relatively moderate character. It is far less severe than the zoning regulations in many of the nation's suburbs, including suburbs surrounding Houston and Dallas that have adopted zoning. Other regulations affecting housing costs in the two cities—such as subdivision, building, nuisance, minimum-housing, and traffic regulations—do not differ appreciably.[37] Both have populations that are roughly similar in economic composition and living standards.[38] The analysis that I will present concerns the decade of the 1970s, during which Houston construction costs were higher and site-development costs lower than those in Dallas.[39] But the difference for each was small and not sufficient to significantly affect housing price comparisons between the cities.

According to the United States Bureau of the Census, the population of Texas increased 27 percent between 1970 and 1980, with both the Houston and Dallas areas registering substantial growth. Harris County, in which Houston is located, grew 38 percent, and Dallas County, in which Dallas is located, grew 17 percent. The growth rate for the entire country was 11 percent. During this period, Houston was a major oil industry center, and Dallas a major financial center. Houston's economy suffered greatly when world oil prices fell in the mid-1980s. It has been estimated that real housing prices from 1983 to 1987 (that is, prices adjusted for inflation) plummeted 8 percent annually in the Houston area, while they remained the same in the Dallas area.[40] Accordingly, the decade of the 1980s is not suitable for evaluating housing price differences between the two areas. No such special situation affected the 1970s. Although comparisons between any two localities are always difficult, the 1970s is a suitable period for assessing how housing prices responded to conditions of high demand in a zoned city and in an unzoned city.

I have selected for comparison Harris and Dallas Counties, rather than the cities of Houston and Dallas themselves. The statistics available for the two counties reveal much more useful information on the effects of land-use regulation than do figures for the cities alone. In the 1970s, Harris County did not have zoning in approximately 80 to 90 percent of the areas where residential building occurred.[41] I estimate that the reverse was the case for Dallas County, where zoning obtained in about 80 to 90 percent of the areas where residential construction took place. Some of the following statistics involve the Houston and Dallas Standard Metropolitan Statistical Areas (SMSAs) and the Houston Standard Consolidated Statistical Area (SCSA). SMSAs contain more than one county, and the Houston SCSA contains two SMSAs. SMSAs and SCSAs are geographical-measurement areas designated by the federal government for statistical purposes because they have common economic and social interests. In the 1970s, most of the Houston SMSA was not zoned and most of the Dallas SMSA was zoned.

As I have noted, the populations of both Harris and Dallas Counties increased significantly during the 1970s. All other things being equal, higher demand from population growth will raise prices unless the supply increases to offset it. As the housing price studies discussed earlier in this section indicate, the production of housing is likely to be more responsive to consumer demand in the absence of land-use regulations than in the presence of such regulations. Hence, the price of housing should be less in a nonzoned area than in a zoned one, and statistics from the Houston and Dallas areas support this theory. With respect to both rents and home prices, the following occurred in these areas during the decade of the 1970s.

Rents. The most comprehensive rent comparisons for the Houston and Dallas areas are provided by the Bureau of Labor Statistics, in its annual estimates of living costs at three income levels for both a four-person family and a retired couple. As I will explain, these figures provide very general information about rent relationships between the two cities. The Bureau used the Standard Metropolitan Statistical Area (SMSA) for each city in making its comparisons. For the years 1972 to 1979 (inclusive), these estimates show that Houston SMSA rents were the same or lower than those in the Dallas SMSA in all categories. Totaling all of these figures, Dallas SMSA rents were about 13 percent higher than Houston SMSA rents.[42]

The Bureau's estimates for these years are not based on direct pricing. They are updated annually (by the increase in the residential component of an area's consumer price index) from direct pricing figures obtained in the 1960s. One may reasonably conclude from these estimates that rents in the Houston SMSA were less during this period than those in the Dallas SMSA.

More precise support for the existence of a substantial differential in rents between the two cities comes from the *Eton Journal*'s surveys of 1979, 1980, and 1981 apartment rentals in the nation's sixteen largest real-estate markets. These surveys covered the cities and their suburban areas and controlled for the quality of the units compared. In January 1979, Dallas's rents were 5 percent higher than Houston's rents in both city and suburban sections; and Dallas's rents were 13 percent higher in January 1980. For units located in the cities, Dallas's rents were 14 percent higher than Houston's in December 1980, and 16 percent higher in March 1981. For units identified as "suburban," Dallas's rents were 17 percent higher in December 1980, 25 percent higher in March 1981, and 11 percent higher in May 1981.[43]

Moreover, throughout this period, rental vacancy rates in Houston were much higher than those in Dallas. According to the *Eton Journal*'s figures, Houston averaged the highest vacancy rate (6 to 7 percent) of any city surveyed in both January 1979 and 1980.[44] This finding is not surprising, since Houston frequently has had large vacancy rates due to high productivity. The existence of a high vacancy rate frequently means that the actual rent is lower than the contract rent. For a landlord to lease an apartment when vacancies are high may require giving free rent for several months, a discount not always reflected in statistics.

That a substantial difference in rents existed between Harris County and Dallas County is likewise indicated by the values of multifamily units appearing on building permits for the areas. M/PF Research, a real-estate research firm operating in Dallas since 1960, compiled these values for the period from 1973 to 1980 inclusive. (Harris County did not issue building permits for the county's unincorporated areas before October 1973, although Houston and other local governments did issue them throughout 1973.) During the period from 1973 to 1980 inclusive, the consumer price index (CPI) for the United States increased from 133.1 to 246.8 (1967 = 100), which amounts to an increase of 85 percent. (The CPI measures prices for food and beverages, housing, fuel and other utilities, apparel and other upkeep, transportation, medical care, and entertainment.) The CPI for the Houston SMSA increased from 132.3 to 265.4 (101 percent), and the CPI for the Dallas–Fort Worth SMSA increased from 132.0 to 255.6 (94 percent). In 1973, building permits for multifamily units reveal that the average value per unit in Harris County was $9,775, while the comparable figure for Dallas County was $6,171. The figures in 1980 were $15,138 in Harris County and $21,294 in Dallas County. Thus, values for the units measured rose 55 percent over this period in Harris County and 245 percent in Dallas County, a substantial difference.[45]

The values appearing on the permits are provided by the owner of the property or the builder of the development and, as experience discloses, tend to underestimate the real value. Since the practice in this respect is generally consistent in the industry, it should not significantly affect comparisons between different areas. As a general matter, the value of a unit will relate to the projected rent; higher unit values can be expected to bring higher rents. One may accordingly conclude from the figures set forth that the rise in rents in Dallas County was substantially greater than that in Harris County.

Price of homes. Single-family home values also appear on building permits. M/PF Research surveyed these values on new single-family construction in Harris and Dallas Counties for the period from 1973 to 1980.[46] These figures show that a large gap existed during this period between the two counties in single-family home values, just as a gap existed in rental values.

For 1973, building permits indicate an average value of $22,913 per new home in Dallas County and $31,259 in Harris County. The 1980 figures were $74,651 in Dallas County (an increase of 225 percent) and $50,385 in Harris County (a rise of 61 percent). As previously noted with respect to multifamily building permits, the values shown on building permits are likely to be less than the real values, but the difference should be generally consistent in both areas. Thus, despite the much greater population pressures in Harris County during the 1970s, the price of new homes during this period escalated much more in Dallas County than in Harris County. This survey does not cover existing-home resale prices, which are considered in the surveys to be discussed below.

Inasmuch as Harris County did not issue building permits for the unincorporated areas of the county until October 1973, there is some question as to the accuracy of the figures listed above for Harris County for 1973. If instead of the 1973 figures, the figures for 1974 are applied, the numbers are different but they also show that the increase in housing prices was substantially greater in Dallas County. According to M/PF Research, for 1974, building permits indicate a value of $24,229 per home in Dallas County and $30,252 per home in Harris County. The average value per multifamily unit for 1974 was $7,892 in Dallas County and $12,854 in Harris County. Thus, between 1974 and 1980, values for single-family homes rose 208 percent in Dallas County and 67 percent in Harris County. The values for a multifamily unit during this period rose 170 percent in Dallas County and 18 percent in Harris County.

Another source for determining housing prices is the Federal Home Loan Bank (FHLB), a federal government agency. Its surveys of mortgage loans for the years 1973 to 1980 (inclusive) contain data on the purchase prices of both newly built homes and previously occupied homes in the Houston and Dallas areas. These surveys concern the Houston SCSA and the Dallas SMSA. The Houston SCSA is also referred to as the Houston-Galveston SCSA and consists of both the Houston and Galveston SMSAs. Insofar as the U.S. Census Bureau's figures show that the Houston SMSA constituted 92 percent of the Houston SCSA in 1970, and 93 percent in 1980, comparisons between the Houston SCSA and the Dallas SMSA are appropriate.

The FHLB surveys are based upon conventional, fully amortized, first mortgage loans closed on single-family homes during the first five working days of the month. For new construction, the FHLB data shows that in 1973 the average purchase price for a newly built home in the Dallas SMSA was $40,600, and that the average price in the Houston SCSA was $42,500. In 1980, the Dallas SMSA average purchase price per newly built home was $106,300 (an increase of 162 percent), and the price in the Houston SCSA was $84,100 (an increase of 98 percent). While not as large as the difference between the counties, as indicated by the M/PF Research figures on the values of newly constructed homes (a 225 percent rise in Dallas County, compared to just 61 percent in Harris County), the FHLB figures confirm the existence of a substantial differential in price increases in the two areas, favoring Houston.

The FHLB figures on previously occupied houses show a different trend than the one for newly built housing. According to this information, the purchase price for an existing home in 1973 in the Dallas SMSA was $36,100, and the price in the Houston SCSA was $36,200. In 1980, these prices increased to $76,100 and $90,300, respectively, an increase of 111 percent in the Dallas SMSA and 149 percent in the Houston SCSA, a difference which favors Dallas.[47] Yet while the purchase price increase of existing homes during the period was less in the Dallas SMSA, it still was far short of offsetting the greater increase in the purchase prices of new homes in Dallas than in Houston. Brokers I spoke to advised me that new homes accounted for a greater percentage of the supply of houses for sale during this period than did existing homes. I shall explain the difference in price trends between newly built homes and previously occupied homes later in this section.

The differences between the M/PF and FHLB price-increase figures are attributable in part to the fact that the nonzoned areas—Houston, other smaller cities, and unincorporated parts of Harris County—make up proportionally more of Harris County than of the Houston SCSA. In 1980, the Harris County population was 2,409,544 and that of the Houston SCSA was 3,101,293, the latter being 29 percent greater.

Over the entire decade of the 1970s, the Houston and Dallas areas confronted serious population pressures. As I have noted, Harris County's population increased by about 38 percent, and its builders created enough new structures to house these additional people without significantly increasing the price of housing. This was a remarkable achievement. Dallas County did not do as well; the population increase there was 17 percent and housing prices rose significantly. Other areas of the country were facing similar pressures at the time. Fischel explains that during the same period many restraints on housing development in California caused a substantial rise in housing prices.[48] The impediments to development were less in Dallas County than in California, but were still greater than in Harris County.

In a market economy, entrepreneurs continually seek to obtain profits by producing goods and services to satisfy consumer demand. Thus, if there is an unsatisfied housing demand in Harris County (such as a demand for moderately priced homes or apartments), builders will seek to erect new structures or rehabilitate or remodel existing structures to fill that void. The limit on building in Harris County would be reached when prices and rents fell (or vacancy rates rose) to an extent that would threaten profits. In a largely free market, the amount of a product supplied will be related to its market price. As economists James Gwartney and Richard Stroup put it, "unless the quantity supplied by producers is already precisely equal to the quantity demanded by consumers, there will be a tendency for prices to rise or fall until a balance is reached."[49]

Builders in Dallas County are likewise subject to these economic concerns, but they face an additional impediment that serves as a brake on market efficiency: zoning. Zoning regulations can prevent new development even when the economic outlook for such development is favorable. When this occurs, consumer demand is partially or totally unsatisfied, and prices for housing will escalate. Thus, population expansion will cause a greater increase in price in a regulated market than in an unregulated one.

Supply-and-demand analysis explains another aspect of the data, as well: the steeper rise in price of previously occupied houses compared to newly built houses in the Houston SCSA, as shown in the FHLB data. According to the FHLB, during the period from 1973 to 1980, the price of a newly built house rose, on average, 98 percent, and the price of a previously occupied house rose 149 percent. The explanation for the difference relates to the fact that older houses in established neighborhoods are of a relatively fixed quantity. The huge housing demand in the Houston area included prospective buyers who wanted to buy such housing, and there was little elasticity in the supply. Consequently, the previously occupied houses rose more rapidly in price than the newly built units, which were subject to the competition of other newly built units.

Are housing prices less in Houston because the absence of controls makes it an undesirable place to live? If non-zoning produces objectionable land-use patterns, people might not want to migrate to Houston, and existing residents might be anxious to move away. The statistics on growth in Houston and Dallas during the 1970s do not reveal that people wanted to avoid living in Houston. They indicate the reverse: Houston's population grew by 29 percent during this period, while Dallas's grew by 7 percent. Houston is the largest city in Texas, and the fourth largest in the nation. Cities do not grow if people hate to live in them. Moreover, Houston's zoning elections show that most residents do not want to change the existing land-use system.[50]

The surveys and other statistics discussed in this section confirm that land-use regulation elevates housing prices. This phenomenon is not exclusive to land-use controls. As a general matter, economic regulation causes prices to rise. In my book *Economic Liberties and the Constitution,* I summarized fifty-three studies of government regulation, by more than sixty individual and institutional researchers.[51] These studies appeared in the most prestigious scholarly journals. A common finding is that each sort of regulation studied operated in a way that raised prices: first, by restricting production; and second, by imposing a variety of unnecessary requirements on producers—requirements that were not justified by reasons of health and safety and that increased cost.

More recent academic research confirms these conclusions. Many studies reveal that economic regulation in the United States is very costly. A recent study at the Rochester Institute of Technology estimates that federal regulation may be costing American taxpayers $400–500 billion annually over the visible costs of government revealed in the federal budget. This amounts to an average of $4,000 to $5,000 per household.[52]

To summarize, there are three very persuasive explanations why the absence of zoning results in housing prices that are less than those under zoning. First, the nonzoned housing market functions largely free of land-use regulations that limit production and impose development requirements not related to health, safety, or consumer demand. Second, growth-control regulations are a more severe form of zoning, and virtually all credible studies show that when growth controls are added to the ordinary forms of zoning, housing prices rise. Hence, as the severity of land-use regulation increases, so do housing prices. Third, economic regulation generally causes increases in consumer prices.

VII. The Houston Experience

The absence of zoning has not made the use of land in Houston chaotic or disorderly. If such conditions actually existed, the voters would have demanded zoning, not rejected it. The evidence indicates that various land uses (commercial, residential, etc.) on the whole are about as separated in Houston as they would be under zoning. But even if this is not entirely accurate, any drawbacks of the land-use situation in Houston are more than offset by the economic and social rewards emanating from the absence of unnecessary government restraints over the development of property.[53]

How has this occurred without zoning controls? The answer is that Houston does have land-use controls, but these are primarily economic. Specifically, the use and development of land and property in Houston are controlled in three different ways. First, they are controlled by the normal economic forces of the marketplace; that is, some uses will locate only in certain areas of the city and not in others. Second, they are controlled through legal agreements, principally restrictive covenants that are imposed by developers of subdivisions who restrict the prerogatives of owners who purchase lots. The covenants specify the required use characteristics of each lot, and enable every lot-owner to sue to enforce them in the event of a violation. Third, use and development are controlled through a relatively limited number of land-use ordinances adopted by the city. Houston also controls development through subdivision, building, traffic, nuisance, and housing regulations that do not seem to vary significantly from those of other cities in its region.[54] And it enforces the restrictive covenants that the private sector has imposed on property. But the contrast with zoning is clear: unless a property is subject to an enforceable restrictive covenant, the city exercises minimum control over the uses that will be made of that property.

The Houston experience demonstrates that in the United States, zoning schemes regulating land-use separation and density are not essential to the livability and viability of cities. In the absence of zoning, residential, commercial, and industrial uses will be abundant and will develop separately from each other. Certain uses will locate only in certain places. Gas stations and fast-food franchises, and most other major commercial developments, provide an obvious illustration: regardless of where they are permitted, they will locate only on heavily trafficked streets.[55]

This means that major business and commercial uses generally will be absent from local residential streets, which constitute close to 80 percent of total street mileage within Houston, and probably about the same percentage elsewhere. In areas of Houston no longer subject to restrictive covenants or on which covenants were never executed, these local streets contain relatively few commercial uses, probably no more than 5 percent of structures within a subdivision. The bulk of these are people working out of their homes, and businesses that serve the residents of the area, and therefore are probably compatible with the area.[56]

There is also a great tendency for industrial uses to group and concentrate separately from residential uses. This pattern is generally confirmed by the land-use maps of Texas cities that were not zoned in the 1960s when the maps were drawn: Pasadena, Wichita Falls, Laredo, and Baytown.[57] A comparison of maps showing the location of industrial uses in Houston with comparable maps of Los Angeles or Dallas—long-zoned cities with which Houston is often compared—suggests that the proliferation of industry in the Houston area may be no greater than in these other cities. However, the large territories involved and differing definitions of industry make comparison difficult.

It is generally too costly in terms of land prices and potential hostility for heavy industry to locate near residential subdivisions.[58] The plants and factories in the Houston area which are contiguous to homes and which were erected subsequent to them are usually "light" rather than "heavy" in character. Apartment and condominium development also reflects a pattern of separation from single-family homes. Thus, notwithstanding the absence of location restrictions, the vast bulk of multifamily development in Houston has occurred in the southwest section of the city.

There are substantial areas in and around Houston where there is small demand for multifamily, industrial, or commercial development. These areas provide the land for single-family occupancy. Most single-family developers in Houston (as well as in many other parts of the country before, and even after, the advent of zoning) have traditionally imposed restrictive covenants to permit only the erection of houses of specified characteristics within their subdivisions.[59] Because many of the earlier restrictive covenants in Houston were limited in duration, were legally insufficient, or were not enforced by owners, zoning would probably have kept more areas as single-family.[60]

Studies have shown that market mechanisms operate to reduce the impact of uses that are regarded in zoning theory as adverse to property values.[61] This is evident in Houston, where the price of vacant land depends in part on the actual or potential use of adjoining land. Thus, land on the perimeter of a residential subdivision may sell for much less than that located in the interior if the land adjoining the subdivision is vacant or used for purposes other than similar residential development. In a nonzoned market, economic forces operate to reduce or eliminate adverse economic land development and use.

Most of the covenants in Houston created subsequent to World War II are much more durable than earlier covenants and seem to offer a reasonably practical solution to the conflict between the desire to allow for change and the desire to maintain stability. Most post–World War II covenants contain an automatic extension provision.[62] They provide for an initial duration of twenty-five to thirty years, and an indefinite number of ten-year automatic extension periods. Agreement on the part of 51 percent of the owners (usually one vote per lot or on the basis of frontage) may cancel or amend the covenants before the end of the initial period or before the end of any subsequent ten-year period. Under this provision, a majority of home-owners can control the destiny of their subdivision.

Because enforcement of restrictive covenants can be costly for home-owners in lower-income subdivisions and small subdivisions, Houston adopted an ordinance in 1965 enabling the city to enforce these covenants.[63] Houston has also adopted an off-street parking ordinance for residential development, a limited number of location restrictions (such as prohibiting sexually oriented businesses, junk yards, and helicopter pads in or near residential areas), requirements for minimum lot sizes and building lines, and a relatively small number of other government regulations designed to cure problems of land use not satisfactorily controlled by the private market.[64] As is the case elsewhere in the nation, laws exist to prevent or abate nuisances.

For home-owners, restrictive covenants serve the same purpose of maintaining exclusivity as does zoning. While similar in this respect, the covenants otherwise vary greatly from zoning in both application and operation, and they illustrate the difference between the economic and political marketplaces in determining land use and development. As previously explained, zoning is controlled by the political system and principally achieves those ends which are most important to those who exercise political power or influence. It allows home-owners to influence the zoning of land within their locality, even if that land is far removed from their subdivision.

By contrast, developers and their lenders impose covenants on their subdivisions solely as a means to secure and maximize their investments. They will apply covenants in accordance with what they believe are the desires of their prospective purchasers. Since there is usually no incentive for owners to restrict the use of their land while it is in a raw state, covenants normally affect little more than land already developed or programmed for development, and then largely for homes or townhouses. As a result, probably no more than 25 percent of the land area of Houston is subject to restrictive covenants. Under zoning, every square inch of the city's land would be regulated.

Restrictive covenants are a device of the market to maximize the value of property. Most American home-owners prefer to live in a homogeneous environment, and they should have the freedom to pursue this goal, provided others are not harmed. Restrictive covenants come close to achieving this balance. Under the covenants, home-owners cannot control land that is beyond what they or their neighbors own. However, zoning allows almost unlimited pursuit of exclusionary purposes, often with adverse effects upon nonresidents.

Because Houston imposes little restriction as to size and type of construction, its market for new houses is very flexible. As mortgage rates rise, for example, a developer is able to reduce the size of units to limit prices. In many suburbs of Dallas, on the other hand, where zoning regulates dwelling-unit size and type, it is not possible to construct units below a specified square-footage. A Texas developer testified before the Reagan Housing Commission that, as a result, he had to discontinue building in these suburbs, denying many potential consumers an opportunity to purchase housing.[65]

Critics of Houston's land-use system contend that as a result of the absence of zoning, the city is not very aesthetically pleasing. Since beauty is in the eyes of the beholder, it is not difficult to find others who disagree and consider the city quite attractive.[66] However, the use of land should not be judged by this or any other single factor. If aesthetics were to be the major concern, a tightly zoned, strongly exclusionary suburb might be the ideal. The issue is, instead, to determine what land-use system best serves society, an inquiry that involves a more extensive analysis, of the sort developed in this chapter.

One virtue of the Houston system that I previously discussed is worth reiterating. The absence of regulation in that city affords great opportunity for builders and developers to satisfy consumer demand. Human resourcefulness and inventiveness are able to thrive in Houston because of the absence of their enemy, government regulation. Unfortunately, in zoned cities, these talents are often spent in persuading or outmaneuvering the zoning authorities.

Many commentators have explored the question of whether zoning "works" better than non-zoning. The assumption is that a municipality should adopt the system that is "best." However, the United States Constitution does not give legislators complete discretion in this regard. Whatever system they adopt must conform to constitutional requirements. Dedicated by its preamble to securing the "Blessings of Liberty," the Constitution protects the right of ownership in nearly a dozen provisions. The reasons that caused the Framers of these provisions to adopt them are no less compelling in the 1990s. Experience has shown that economic liberty produces economic welfare. Experience also confirms that economic liberty produces benefits for the poorest members of society that far outstrip the results achieved by highly regulated economic systems.

8

Preserving and Enhancing the Environment

I have attended numerous land-use conferences over the years, and the favorite catchphrases of the environmentalists still ring in my ears. Our "stewardship of the common landscape," says one speaker after another, demands that we preserve and enhance the environment, which means that ever-greater public regulation will be necessary to advance "the larger social and economic good." The nation's land belongs to its citizens, who should mandate that it be preserved and used only for the public good. Planners and politicians, not greedy owners and developers, must control the use of our land.

Experience reveals that following these preachings might lead to a greener and less densely developed landscape, but at great cost to the economic well-being and the home environment of ordinary people. Frequently, the problem is that regulations intended to achieve noble goals will in practice obstruct and deny them. Social and economic good, measured by the welfare of the people, is more likely to be furthered in the absence of land-use laws than in their presence. Freedom—not authority—will provide the most responsible and beneficial stewardship of the planet. It is true that entrepreneurs act largely in their own interest, but probably no more so than officials of government, and the incentives of the private marketplace are much more likely than those of "public service" to advance the general good.

Many laws passed in the name of preserving the environment are prime examples of counterproductive legislation. Numerous zoning laws operate to waste land instead of preserving it. Among the culprits are two kinds of zoning regulations: first, those that reduce density, i.e., the amount of living units, single-family or multifamily, that will be allowed per acre of land; and second, those that prohibit high-rise or low-rise multifamily construction. To require one house on one or two acres of land, without a basis in safety or health requirements, when the potential occupants would be pleased and delighted to have the opportunity to live on a fraction of that amount, is nothing more than a waste of land and of their money.

Similar problems are caused by density limitations on multifamily buildings (apartments, condominiums, and townhouses) or the prohibition entirely of these structures. In effect, each floor of an apartment building adds to the supply of land. Forcing people who prefer to live in apartments to live in homes needlessly consumes the land. Frequently, sites for homes for a given number of families will occupy five or even ten times as much land as would low-rise apartments for the same number of families, and the figure is much greater with respect to high-rises.

Density requirements vary greatly between communities. At public hearings that I attended in the Chicago suburbs, seemingly rational people insisted that a density exceeding twenty apartments per acre would surely lead to slums. At other times, equally concerned residents virtually took oaths that five houses to the acre was the brink of disaster. Zoning is often decided on the basis of such fears. Yet only twenty-five minutes away on Chicago's Gold Coast stood prestigious high-rise apartments in areas zoned for four hundred units per acre. The incidence of crime in these areas was among the lowest and living conditions were among the best in the city. There are innumerable instances throughout the nation of highly successful high-rise buildings catering to families of various income levels. The principal exception, however, is government-sponsored public housing, and it is not limited to high-rise buildings. Many families that occupy such housing are problem-prone, exhibiting the usual pathologies all too familiar in our inner cities. The difficulties arise from these residents, not the housing. Although they may be in the minority, such families can create serious problems for others as well as for the structure. Worst of all, the bad families keep out the good.

One of the most densely populated cities in the world is Hong Kong, and its experience in managing high-rise apartment buildings is instructive for the United States. Former Congresswoman Leonor Sullivan of Missouri was surprised to discover extremely pleasant conditions in high-rises in Hong Kong, although they are jam-packed with poor families. "There is order and control," she concluded. "The places are spotless, the people who live in them are buoyed in spirit and absolutely delighted with the step up the housing ladder to their very own private homes—even a single room for a family." What about those who did not behave? "They were kicked out."[1]

In America, evicting tenants for misbehavior occurs in private rental developments, but is nearly impossible in public housing. The incentives are vastly different. In public housing, what Sullivan suggests is an excessive compassion causes the retention of the problem family. The reaction of public-housing managers, she points out, is "How can we put them out? Where would they go?"

Paradoxically, preventing higher-density projects from being built will only limit competition and supply, ensuring that those most in need of affordable housing will face bleak alternatives: dangerous buildings or, in the worst case, homelessness.

I. Environmentally Sensitive Land

Since the 1970s, considerable attention has focused on imposing state regulation to prevent development in areas considered environmentally sensitive. One major problem is defining environmentally sensitive land. Thus, land within five miles of the California coast has been included in the territory subject to the state's famous 1972 Coastal Zone Conservation Act, adopted by public vote, which established state regulation of coastal development. Probably most voters who supported this measure were not aware that their efforts to save the coast would result in restrictions on land not adjacent to or even visible from the coast. The proposition originally applied only within the area of the coast that was a thousand yards landward from the mean high tide line, but the California legislature subsequently enlarged the protected area to include property within five miles of the coast.

However, regardless of the intent of the supporters of such measures around the country, it is unlikely that legislation can or will prevent development within its target areas. In all probability, what will happen is much more of what already occurs under local zoning. There will be less-intensive development, and thus more land will be used for urban purposes; real-estate prices and rents will increase. Relatively few of the "critical" areas will be preserved in their natural setting.

There are two basic reasons for this. First, there are the takings and due process provisions of federal and state constitutions, which limit the extent to which private property can be regulated. Second, the regulatory process tends to resolve controversies through some compromise formula, an approach reinforced in this situation by the need to placate property owners to some extent in order to avoid constitutional challenges to the regulation.

The history of California's Coastal Zone Conservation Act confirms these generalizations, showing how land-use controls operate in areas designated as environmentally sensitive. In 1973, over 6,200 permit applications were received by the six regional commissions given permit power under this law. Of those applications, about 5,200, or 83 percent, were granted in whole or in part. In 1974, of the approximately 4,700 permit applications received, some 4,400, or 94 percent, were approved in whole or in part. Such figures do not fully reflect the regulation's impact, however.[2]

To obtain a better understanding of what these numbers mean, consider Professor Bruce Johnson's analysis of the operation of the Santa Barbara Coastal

Commission, on which he served. During the first fourteen months in the life of that commission, it approved 95 percent of the applications received for single-family housing developments, but allowed only 60 percent of the single-family units requested on these applications. While 77 percent of the multi-family applications received approval, only 51 percent of the units applied for were accepted.[3]

Thus, if a developer applied for a permit to build a hundred units on his five-acre tract adjoining the Pacific Ocean, he would, after considerable delay, red tape, and possibly political maneuvering, receive approval to build about sixty units.

The five acres in this example would remain in private ownership and would not normally be accessible to the public. A public easement from a public street to the beach might be required in some cases, but because the area containing the development is private this would have more theoretical than practical value. It is questionable whether better views would be provided for the public, since the regulators would impose their own aesthetic preferences.

The question that never gets asked is: What happens to the forty units (out of a hundred) that were disallowed? One possible answer is that these, along with other disallowed units, represent unsatisfied demand for coastal housing and would, in time, cause greater or more rapid development of the coast, something entirely inconsistent with the aims of the legislation. It is, of course, possible that the forty units will never be built. Then society will lose the advantages of considerable private expenditures that would have benefited business, employment, tax revenues, and housing supply, and there will be less housing in desirable areas and at higher prices. Some people will be denied the pleasures of living in coastal housing.

Possibly, these forty units may find their way into existing vacant land within a developed city. But this would then reduce the amount of land available there for other projects. Another alternative is that the disallowed units will increase demand for building houses in rural, undeveloped areas at the expense of land used for agriculture, grazing, and mining. The result would be more sprawl, exactly the horror from which regulation is supposed to protect us. But this consequence is not an unusual one these days. Slow-growth and controlled-growth policies have caused development to leapfrog restricted areas and spread into outlying areas that could be used for other purposes. Instead of preserving greenbelts around cities, as the environmentalists proclaimed, their restrictive policies would produce more-distant suburbs, further commuting distances, and more highways.

An article in the *Texas Monthly* describes the situation succinctly. Although commenting on the policies pursued by Austin's City Council in the 1970s, the point applies with no less force two decades later:

The irony is that the most anti-growth council in Austin history may have done more to bring about urban sprawl than did any of the pro-developer councils that preceded it. Over 75 percent of the homes built in the Austin metropolitan area last year were outside the city's extraterritorial jurisdiction.[4]

These experiences reveal just how disastrous no-growth policies can be: when development in "environmentally sensitive areas" is severely restricted, other unanticipated social harms are created. This lesson, which should have been learned in the 1970s, has still not been absorbed by environmental enthusiasts and their legislative supporters. Development takes place in these areas anyway, but with less intensity of use, and whatever additional open space is salvaged remains privately owned and not normally accessible to nonresidents. State controls in California accomplished more of what their proponents said they wanted to prevent: instead of preserving a natural resource (land), they ensured that more of it needed to be developed to accommodate the same number of people.

Developers quickly caught on to the regulatory dynamics. An article in the *San Diego BCA Builder* advised its readers in the mid-1970s on how to cope with public proceedings: "It is generally advisable to be prepared to give something up. Don't go into the public hearing with a bare minimum proposal. Be ready to barter something away."[5]

Over the years, many developers learned how to beat the system by asking for more than they really wanted. The entire process became a game, accomplishing little more than wasting the public's time and money, increasing development costs, and further undermining the government's credibility.

Regulation of use and development of California's eleven hundred miles of shoreline was imposed by the California Coastal Zone Conservation Initiative (Proposition 20) adopted by a 56 to 44 percent vote in 1972. Final authority under the initiative was entrusted to an appointed regulatory commission of twelve members whose power is subject only to judicial review. The governor, assembly speaker, and senate president each appoint four members. Given the subjectivity of the responsibility, administering the Coastal Zone Conservation Act has been difficult and far from the routine ministerial endeavor its proponents claimed it would be. Philosophical and political considerations have always been major factors in the commission's operation. In early 1996, the Republican assembly speaker appointed four members who were promptly fired when a Democrat assumed the office of speaker after the November 1996 election, in which the Democrats regained control of the state assembly. In the summer of that year, the Republican members of the commission sought to dismiss the commission's executive director because of his tendency to favor positions advanced by environmentalists. Democrats on the commission accused the Republicans of attempting to ram through the director's ouster at the behest of the governor and the state assembly speaker. As is evident from the commission's experience, regulating development of an ocean coast comes down to implementing philosophical and political preferences. California Democrats are generally in favor of preservation while the Republicans prefer development. The winning party, during its tenure in office, will control the commission. To those familiar with the fate of sweeping regulatory schemes, this ought not be surprising.

A breakdown of the 1972 vote on the Coastal Zone Conservation Initiative in the city of San Diego reveals much about its supporters and opponents. The initiative won 54 percent of San Diego's vote, while receiving only 49 percent in the balance of San Diego County. Overall, it won in the entire county by 52 to 48 percent. Contrary to a widely held assumption, most opponents were members of the lower income brackets, those in whose name the coastal preservation effort was initiated. The most fervent supporters were students and wealthy people.[6] The breakdown of voters is set forth in Table I below.

TABLE I. **Breakdown of Vote Results on California Coastal Zone Conservation Initiative and Two Subsequent Local Initiatives in San Diego**[7]

Selected Areas*	1970 Median Income	Yes on Prop 20 (1972)	Yes on Prop A (1985)	No on Prop C (1994)
San Diego City	$10,166	54%	56%	54%
Student Areas				
Ocean Beach #23500	NA	81	74	64
Ocean Beach #23691	NA	84	74	68
Mission Bay #23000	NA	77	NA	NA
Mission Bay #23021	NA	79	72	64
UCSD #12000	NA	93	89	58
UCSD #12004	NA	94	63	61
San Diego State #28150	NA	89	NA	NA
San Diego State #28171	NA	84	NA	NA
High Income				
La Jolla	19,249	57–81	54–77	57–73
Mission Hills	15,328	58–59	60–71	58–60
University City	14,979	57–63	63–68	56–61
White, Blue-Collar				
Encanto	8,370	49	51	44
Normal Heights	7,568	46	54	49
Paradise Hills	9,204	46–48	41–52	46–49
Nestor	8,710	42–46	39–49	46–51
South Park	9,244	42–44	NA	NA

TABLE I. Breakdown of Vote Results on California Coastal Zone Conservation Initiative and Two Subsequent Local Initiatives in San Diego (*Continued*)

Selected Areas*	1970 Median Income	Yes on Prop 20 (1972)	Yes on Prop A (1985)	No on Prop C (1994)
Mexican-American				
Barrio Logan #35150	6,495	39	37	38
Barrio Logan #35500	6,255	39	49	36
Barrio Logan #35521	6,859	46	40	39
Barrio Logan #35570	5,859	38	40	34
Otay Mesa #39020	7,367	48	50	36
San Ysidro #39530	NA	46	55	38
San Ysidro #39500	7,367	48	NA	NA
Centre City #34200	7,150	49	49	37
SE San Diego E #35130	6,720	42	NA	NA
SE San Diego W #35500	6,073	39	NA	36
SE San Diego W #35510	7,029	50+	NA	NA
SE San Diego W #35520	7,029	46	NA	NA
Golden Hill #34630	5,679	43	36	45
African-American				
SE San Diego E #35060	5,965	36	44	28
SE San Diego W #35560	6,311	31	NA	NA
SE San Diego W #35650	6,311	34	NA	NA
Chollas Park #37180	10,127	42	NA	NA
Chollas Park #37060	6,627	36	47	40
Chollas Park #37300	6,627	36	NA	NA
Chollas Park #37320	6,627	35	43	39
West Encanto #36500	9,530	37	33	42
West Encanto #36530	9,530	38	NA	NA
West Encanto #36590	10,149	42	32	55
East Encanto #36070	9,625	46	44	35
East Encanto #36080	10,366	43	36	47
Logan Heights #35030	5,965	NA	33–44	41

*Numbers after area names are precinct numbers.

Strongest support for the initiative came from young voters living on college campuses and in residences on or near the coast. Precincts which were mostly made up of these people voted anywhere from 77 percent to 94 percent in favor. This return is quite understandable. Young people are the most frequent users of beaches and tend to support environmental measures.

Running close behind youth-dominated areas in support were the affluent communities of La Jolla, Mission Hills, and University City. La Jolla is an exclusive community adjoining the ocean and the latter two areas are within five miles of the coast. These wealthy communities gave support to the initiative ranging from 57 to 81 percent (depending on the specific precinct).

The less well-off people, who could not afford to live close to the coast, opposed the Coastal Zone Conservation Initiative. Largely white, blue-collar precincts voted against it, with only 42 to 49 percent in favor. These voters lived in Encanto, Normal Heights, Paradise Hills, and Nestor. Mexican Americans also usually voted against, with only 38 to 50 percent favoring it. The strongest opposition of a large, identifiable group came from African-American voters, who ranged from only 31 to 46 percent favorable. Interestingly, Democratic registration among African Americans is over 90 percent; for Mexican Americans, it is over 80 percent; and in blue-collar white precincts, it is about 55 percent. Yet most Democratic Party leaders usually support measures that the major environmental organizations favor.

Table I is a breakdown showing median household income and votes on Proposition 20 (the Coastal Zone Conservation Initiative) and on two subsequent local propositions (A and C) for key precincts in the previously mentioned areas of San Diego. Propositions A and C related to San Diego City's growth, and will be discussed subsequently.

People enjoy the California coast in different ways. For some, the natural setting provides physical, visual, and psychological enjoyment. Others benefit from residential and commercial development. They may live in houses or high-rises or stay at hotels or motels on or near the coast. Some will also benefit financially, in jobs, wages, and profits. Regulation of the coast is usually intended to benefit the first group—those who seek to enjoy the natural setting—but this result is doubtful since, as I have explained, controls (by greatly limiting density) may cause greater private development of the shoreline.

Why was there so much opposition to the Coastal Zone Conservation Initiative from the less-affluent people living away from the coast? Many do not go to the beach or walk along the shore very often. They probably had little concern about the coast's availability or appearance. However, preventing development might deprive them or their relatives or friends of an opportunity to live on the coast. It would also raise the price of housing, which would have a detrimental impact on the less affluent and their children. Moreover, less-affluent people would benefit economically by obtaining construction and maintenance jobs at new housing or commercial developments. The strong anti-Proposition 20 vote by African Americans may have been attributable in part to opposition to any exclusionary regulations.

Another view of these election returns was that they did not have much to do with California's coast: the more important issue may have been limiting growth. Subsequent to the vote on the coastal initiative, San Diego voters considered two local growth measures, and a breakdown of the results of these votes does not appear to differ appreciably from the breakdown in the vote on the coastal initiative. On November 5, 1985, San Diego voters considered Proposition A, a measure that barred land-use changes in the city's northern tier unless specifically approved by voters in an election. Nearly a decade later, the city council placed Proposition C on the June 7, 1994, ballot; Proposition C amended Proposition A to allow development of lower-density housing and commercial centers in the northern tier without the necessity of voter approval. Anti-growth forces supported Proposition A and opposed Proposition C. Voters approved Proposition A by a 56 percent to 44 percent margin and rejected Proposition C by 54 percent to 46 percent. In both instances, the student and higher-income areas strongly voted in favor of no-growth, and racial minorities substantially opposed it. White blue-collar voters apparently split their vote on the two propositions, voting by small margins to approve Proposition A (anti-growth) but approving with a greater margin Proposition C (pro-growth). Because of the similarities in voting on these three propositions in the San Diego area, one might conclude that the issue of growth was the predominant factor in the 1972 vote on the Coastal Zone Conservation Initiative.

These elections indicate that the San Diego population is almost equally split on the regulation of growth and development. Except with respect to the outcome, the pattern of voting in all three elections corresponds to what occurred in Houston's zoning elections, socioeconomic breakdowns of which appeared in Chapter 7. That is, significant correlation exists in both the San Diego and the Houston voting patterns between one's wealth and one's position on land-use controls. As one descends the economic ladder, one is most likely to oppose growth controls. Students are an exception to the pattern, since they usually have very little income. However, many come from the wealthy classes that support land-use regulation, and although penurious as students, they expect to rejoin the affluent classes. As previously noted, students tend to favor environmental controls. The greatest opposition to zoning in Houston was found among low-income blacks, and the same held true with respect to the three development-control propositions voted on in San Diego.

The voting pattern shown in Table I above is confirmed by a San Diego General Market Survey conducted in 1991 for the San Diego Association of Governments. Most respondents were in the middle on growth—opposed to the government either actively limiting or promoting growth. However, responses to two of the four questions on growth show significant differences between ethnic minorities and whites, and between wealthy groups and poor ones. The percentage of people from various racial groups who wanted to "actively limit growth" was as follows: Hispanic, 15 percent; black, 20 percent; white, 31 percent. The breakdown by annual income was: under $25,000, 19 percent in favor of limiting growth; $25,000 to $49,999, 28 percent; over $50,000, 34 percent. The percentages of those who wanted to "actively promote growth" were:

Hispanics, 16 percent; blacks, 14 percent; whites, 7 percent. The breakdown on an income basis was: under $25,000, 15 percent in favor of promoting growth; $25,000 to $49,999, 8 percent; over $50,000, 8 percent.[8]

The survey shows that whites are the least likely to believe that growth always has positive effects. Less than one in ten whites strongly agree with this statement, as opposed to one in four blacks and Hispanics. The opposing notion—that controls on growth hurt the economy—is strongly agreed to by 28 percent of Hispanics and 17 percent of whites. According to the survey, groups that are most likely to believe that growth is good, and that growth control is bad, are also likely to consider local growth controls to have been effective. While 31 percent of Hispanics strongly agree that local controls have been effective, a mere 7 percent of whites do.[9]

II. Environmental Controls Limit Housing Production

The apprehensions of people who vote against no-growth measures are well founded. Prohibiting or limiting development will injure the portion of the environment that is unquestionably the most important: that which houses the people and supplies their material needs. For most people, the home is where the major part of life is spent. Its characteristics greatly influence the quality of one's life. Similarly, a comfortable neighborhood, and convenient access to work and shopping are requisites for a good and pleasurable life.

It is not a question of whether the land should be used for development or open space. Sufficient land exists to accommodate both. The overwhelming portion of land in the United States is neither urbanized nor developed. Statistics compiled by the Economics and Statistics Administration of the United States Census Bureau indicate that as of 1992 less than 6 percent of the total surface area of the nation was developed.[10] This is my estimate based on two separate figures. The bureau's census figures reveal only the amount of nonfederal developed land (about 4.8 percent of the total surface area of the country), and I have added to it my rough estimate of the amount of federal land that is developed (5 percent). This information should not be a surprise to air travelers who, on a trip of almost any length, will fly most of the time over undeveloped areas. The great bulk of the land is not suitable for housing; comparatively few people are willing to live in remote areas that are not served by roads or utilities. Also, much of the country's terrain is unsuitable for urban development. Given the relatively small amount of land presently in use, it is in the realm of science fiction to contemplate a time when urban development might extinguish most open space within relatively short distances of our cities and towns.

Concern for the protection of endangered species must also take into consideration the vast amount of territory available for wildlife. Urban development may destroy some of nature's creatures, but that is only part of the story. Development will also elevate the living standards of other valuable creatures who often are neglected in the panegyrics of no-growth environmentalists: namely, human beings.

A letter to the editor in my local newspaper caught my eye, for it captured a key motivation of no-growth voters. The writer complained about a developer who was grading a tract of land near the writer's home in preparation for the construction of homes. He was upset that he would no longer be able to walk among and observe the plants and animals in this tract. I find it very hard to sympathize with this attitude. The letter writer had enjoyed free use of someone else's land. He had a free lunch and wanted to continue consuming it indefinitely. The developer had not graded the land in order to destroy this person's pleasures but to provide housing for human beings. In San Diego within fifteen to twenty minutes by car of one's home, wherever one lives, one can walk among hundreds of acres of vacant land containing innumerable species of wildlife. This indignant fellow completely failed to grasp the irony of his own position: his own home, from which he enjoyed nature walks, existed only because a builder had destroyed plant and animal life.

One direct consequence of antidevelopment policies will be to deny those who would occupy the excluded housing an opportunity to better their environment. Another consequence is that the many people dependent on construction and related industries for their livelihoods will see their living standards decline as a result of declining production.

The indirect effects of antidevelopment policies will be considerably more pervasive. Living conditions for many people in the affected housing market will also decline. These policies will (1) slow the "filtering" process by which young adults and the less affluent enter the market by purchasing the homes of those who "trade up" to newer and bigger homes, (2) raise the cost of shelter, (3) cause many residents of apartments to become stuck in inferior dwellings, and (4) cause greater spreading and scattering of housing accommodations, popularly condemned as "urban sprawl." The environment that human beings inhabit will be significantly degraded.

"Filtering" is a powerful engine for social improvement. As new homes and apartments are constructed, families move into them, vacating their former residences. Others, in turn, vacate still older units, and the process continues in a chain reaction. A study of this process in seventeen metropolitan areas, conducted in the late 1960s by the Survey Research Center at the University of Michigan, shows that, on average, the construction of one new unit triggers 3.5 moves by families seeking better housing accommodations. Thus, new construction benefits more people indirectly than it does directly—2.5 moves to existing housing generated by one move to a new house.[11]

For every 1,000 new housing units built, there are approximately 3,500 relocations. Of these 3,500, an average of 333 moves are by families defined as poor, and another 933 are by moderate-income families. Thus, more than one-third of all those who move are likely to be in the lower-income and moderate-income categories. While most construction occurs in the outer portions of metropolitan areas, many of the resulting moves extend to older areas near the center of a city. The nation's worst environmental conditions for human beings exist in these inner-city areas, and conditions will further deteriorate if "filtering" is reduced. Housing subsidy programs provided by government have not done much to alleviate the problem of poor housing in the inner cities: improvement depends upon a healthy and vigorous private housing market.

While those who benefit from the "filtering" process do not obtain newly built housing, the housing that they do acquire is usually better than what they vacated. In the University of Michigan's survey of 2,050 families who moved into pre-owned housing, 75 percent said that they liked their new home better than their former one, 16 percent liked the new home about the same, and 9 percent did not like the new home as much as their old one.[12]

The "filtering" process that results from new construction is the best means available for improving housing conditions. Building new housing for lower-income people is very expensive and, on a large scale, beyond the financial capability of government. Consider the expenditures required in 1996 to build 1,000 new apartments. The cost of construction of an 850 square foot moderately equipped apartment in San Diego, of the kind that is built in subsidized housing projects, is about $65,000. Construction of 1,000 new units would cost about $65 million, plus another $10 to $20 million for land (priced at $10,000 to $20,000 per unit in low-income and moderate-income areas), for a total cost of $75 to $85 million.

Some localities have sought to provide more low-cost housing by requiring developers to set aside 10 to 20 percent of the units in their up-scale developments for this purpose. Among other things, such requirements raise the costs of other units and erode development feasibility, thereby limiting production of housing.[13]

Those of slightly higher income who are ineligible for subsidized housing and who cannot afford new housing are dependent for better housing on the "filtering" process induced by new construction. The University of Michigan survey makes it clear that prohibiting new construction, or so heavily regulating it that cost makes it unfeasible, seriously harms the income groups that are most in need of better housing.

When government curtails construction in a housing market, competition will decrease and prices will increase. In the case of apartments, vacancies will decrease. Rents will be raised either directly, through the amount actually charged, or indirectly, through reduction in services, repairs, maintenance, and improvements—or probably, in many instances, through a combination of all or most of these factors. Higher rents will cause more doubling-up, thereby increasing population density. These conditions will be intensified as the "filtering" process is reduced or halted. The end result will be much poorer housing conditions for a great many people, and further deterioration for marginal, older buildings and communities. Buildings that otherwise would be torn down and replaced by new construction will remain in service. More people will be paying more for the same or lesser quality housing.

Although antidevelopment zealotry will curtail much construction, it cannot stop it all. Demand for new housing will remain undiminished, and that demand will be met in places where the least resistance is offered. The underpopulated rural areas will be the likely targets, areas that otherwise would not be in demand. The result will be a greater scattering of housing, and all of the problems and detriments that come with "urban sprawl." These include the cost of installing new sewer and water facilities or extending existing ones, and building new or wider roads and highways. More telephone poles, utility lines, and generating stations will have to be installed. The cost of school bus transportation will increase. More people will be spending greater amounts of time driving to and from work and shopping. The extra driving will disgorge more pollution. Open space and green and wooded areas will be disturbed or destroyed by this intrusion of housing and related facilities. Land that should be used for crops, pastures, and forests will be converted into suburban developments.

Similarly, density restrictions will cause housing to spread out, also necessitating the installation of more streets and other facilities, and creating greater burdens and inconveniences for more people. Obviously, if a town mandates a two-acre minimum lot size, then homes consume more land and require the installation of more linear feet of road than a one-acre or smaller minimum. An apartment or townhouse project would provide accommodations for many more residents at only a fraction of the land and pavement needed for a single-family development.

A study of infrastructure costs in 1980 in Westchester County, New York, showed that as housing density decreases, infrastructure costs dramatically increase: this includes the costs of streets, curbs, lighting, sidewalks, sewers, and water lines. At that time, the infrastructure cost at one-half acre density was $18,075 per dwelling unit, while at one acre density the cost was $30,125 per unit.[14] These costs have only escalated over the intervening years.

III. Preserving the Physical Environment

Journalists often contend that the United States has not adequately preserved the environment. But how much preservation is "enough"? Contrary to the critics' claims, the record indicates that the U.S. has in fact done extremely well.

As previously noted, a relatively small portion of this nation's land, probably no more than 6 percent, is developed for urban purposes. The federal government owns about 29 percent of the total land mass of the United States,[15] most of which is protected from or unsuitable for development. According to the World Resources Institute's *1993 Environmental Almanac,* the United States pioneered the idea of national parks and wilderness reserves; the *Almanac* reports that in 1993 the United States had protected areas totaling over 10 percent of the country's land area.[16] In 1996, the federal government owned 369 national parks, 192 million acres of national forests, 508 wildlife refuges, and 267 million acres of western heritage lands administered by the Bureau of Land Management. There are 104 million acres of designated wilderness in forty-four states.[17] National and state parks contain 87 million acres.[18] In the following pages we will see how our nation preserved and enhanced its physical environment while remaining within the confines of a general system of free enterprise in land development.

We begin with the National Wilderness Preservation System, covering the most environmentally secured areas. As of 1996, 104 million acres of public lands were restricted to or managed for "wilderness" use.[19] That is an area larger than the combined total area of Maine, New Hampshire, Vermont, New York, New Jersey, Maryland, Delaware, and West Virginia. In wilderness areas, federal law prohibits the use of automobiles or other mechanical transport, the installation of roads, or the construction of any structures. Millions of acres of productive forest land are included under this program, but timber cannot be harvested on this land. With the exception of sections at the perimeters, the bulk of these enormously scenic territories can be enjoyed only by those physically able to walk, hike, or ride mules for very long distances, and some areas are accessible only to mountain climbers.

In late 1995, the federal Fish and Wildlife Service acquired 92 million acres for the National Wildlife Refuge System. This land is used for the conservation of fish and wildlife and to provide wildlife-oriented public displays for educational and recreational purposes. This system includes national wildlife refuges, national fish hatcheries, and research facilities.[20] Some areas within the system have been set aside for wilderness preservation.

A 1968 federal statute protects about 10,000 miles of rivers in the National Wild and Scenic Rivers System. These are free-flowing rivers that have "outstandingly remarkable" natural, cultural, scenic, and recreational features. Little or no development or human activity, other than controlled recreation, is allowed in these areas. Other specially protected areas include National Marine Sanctuaries, comprising over 4 million acres, and National Estuarine Research Reserves of close to 400,000 acres. In the 1970s, the Federal Bureau of Land Management closed 800,000 acres of California's desert land to any use by recreational vehicles and placed another 10 million acres under strict regulation.

As of 1993, 36 million acres were included in the Conservation Reserve Program. This program encourages farmers, through ten-to-fifteen-year contracts with the Department of Agriculture, to stop growing crops on land subject to excessive erosion or on land that contributes to a significant water quality problem. Farmers must, instead, plant a protective cover of grass or trees.[21]

Federal protection of wetlands and endangered species limits private ownership in suburban, rural, farming, and undeveloped areas of the country. The nation's wetlands are protected as an important environmental resource under section 404 of the Clean Water Act of 1972. Both the U.S. Army Corps of Engineers and the U.S. Environmental Protection Agency administer the act. Wetlands are defined as lands having three characteristics: (1) the predominance of wetland indicator plants; (2) hydric soils; and (3) land that is "wet." To be defined as wetlands under current federal regulations, the soil need only be saturated some of the time. Under this definition, land that is totally dry nearly all of the time can be declared wetland, and its use for development denied. It is estimated that there are 95 to 97 million acres of wetlands in the continental United States, of which nearly 75 percent are on privately owned land.[22]

The Endangered Species Act of 1973 (ESA) contains a variety of protections designed to save from extinction species on private or public lands that the Secretary of the Interior designates as endangered or threatened. It is unlawful under the act to harass, harm, pursue, hunt, shoot, wound, kill, trap, capture, or collect a protected species. Interior Department regulations define harm to include "significant habitat modification or degradation where it actually kills or injures wildlife by significantly impairing essential behavioral patterns, including breeding, feeding, sheltering." The ESA makes no distinction between high-risk and low-risk endangerment—requiring the Interior Department to protect every species that it determines to be endangered "without reference to possible economic or other impacts." California and other states have enacted endangered species acts of their own.

When the federal endangered-species legislation was enacted, most supporters assumed that it would mostly preserve the more revered animals—the grizzly bears and bald eagles—but its impact has been far wider. As of the end of 1994, 895 species were protected, of which 424 were animals and 471 plants. Over 70 percent of the protected species are vertebrates—animals with a backbone—and the rest are invertebrates. Invertebrates include insects, clams, mussels, snails, spiders, crabs, and crayfish. In August 1994, there were 3,941 additional candidates for the endangered and threatened list, 70 percent of which were invertebrates. As a result of the act, a large amount of land, some in every state, is not available for private development, because it is the habitat of one or more of these creatures on the endangered list.

Consider some examples of land-use restrictions that have been imposed under federal or state endangered species acts, as set forth in the report of the Advisory Commission on Regulatory Barriers to Affordable Housing (published in 1991 by the Kemp Commission):

1. A study on the golden-cheeked warbler was used as a basis for an emergency order by the federal Fish and Wildlife Service listing this bird as endangered. This listing severely restricted development in thousands of acres of Travis County, Texas, with localities around Austin especially affected. The methodology of the study was subsequently criticized by an acknowledged authority on the bird.

2. The October 1988 listing of the Stevens Kangaroo Rat as an endangered species has led to a thirty-square-mile system of rat preserves in the western part of Riverside County, California.

3. New York State law bars development within a hundred-foot radius around a breeding pond of the endangered tiger salamander.

4. The California gnatcatcher, a rare bird found in Orange County and other nearby counties, was a candidate for the endangered list, an addition that would affect proposed tollways and many housing developments.[23]

The National Environmental Policy Act (NEPA) of 1969 establishes a formal regulatory process to review the environmental effects of federal actions; and state environmental protection acts (SEPAs) establish comparable regulatory processes at the state level. Owners and developers must often comply with both NEPA and SEPA regulations. Depending on their size, housing projects are subject either to an environmental assessment statement (EAS) or an environmental impact statement (EIS). An EAS is a qualitative analysis by the Department of Housing and Urban Development (HUD) of possible environmental effects. No public notice and comment are required. An EIS is a formal analysis conducted by HUD and subject to public comment.

According to the Advisory Commission on Regulatory Barriers, environmental-protection regulations often act as barriers to the development of affordable housing by significantly reducing the supply of land for this purpose. This occurs in three ways. First, these regulations impose requirements that are costly. Second, they frequently interject delays into the building-permit review process. Third, federal, state, and local agencies charged with environmental protection overlap each other, adding additional delays.[24]

At the local level, the vast majority of cities and counties have adopted zoning ordinances that control land use. All contain provisions limiting density, and many preserve open space and natural resources. Some states have also enacted land-use regulations that control use and development within designated coastal zones.

Accordingly, our nation has preserved or controlled immense amounts of natural terrain and has set aside enormous amounts of land for recreation. The private sector has also participated mightily in preserving and enhancing the nation's physical environment. Private enterprise created the Disneylands, Sea Worlds, Safaris, Busch Gardens, and a variety of recreational projects catering to millions. Users may pay an entry fee, but the public parks do not come free either. We are taxed to acquire and maintain them, and they do not pay taxes.

Residential developments frequently install recreational facilities, and it is quite common for new apartment, townhouse, and condominium developments to contain swimming pools, tennis courts, and club houses. This also occurs in single-family subdivisions. Throughout the country, lush "country club" developments surrounded by golf courses are available to middle-class home, condominium, and apartment dwellers. Resorts, hotels, and motels provide abundant recreational facilities, with many acres devoted to golf, swimming, and tennis.

Although large areas of the eastern United States were deforested in the eighteenth and nineteenth centuries, the trend dramatically reversed beginning in the early 1950s. As of 1992, annual timber growth in the United States has exceeded harvest every year since 1952, according to the U.S. Forest Service. By the mid-1990s, the number of wooded acres in the nation was three times what it was in 1920. The results in two northeastern states, New Hampshire and Vermont, are dramatic. New Hampshire is now about 86 percent forested, compared to 50 percent in 1850. In Vermont, the area covered by forest is about 76 percent, up from 35 percent one hundred years ago.[25] Accordingly, "[b]y most measures, the condition of forests in the United States is improving, not deteriorating."[26]

Economist Stephen Moore notes that no current or future shortage of trees is evidenced by the price data on forestry products. Writing in 1992, he stated that over the past decade, the real prices of paper and lumber fell by 10 and 30 percent respectively. Indexed to wages, 1992 lumber prices were one-third of those in 1950, one-sixth of those in 1900, and roughly one-tenth of prices in 1800.[27] Human resourcefulness—improved forestry technologies and other innovations—has in large measure been responsible for the increase in wood inventory that accounts for the improved affordability of paper and lumber over time.

Private owners and conservation groups across the country have preserved thousands of pristine acres and their natural resources. Collette Ridgeway of the Institute for Humane Studies, George Mason University, has described some of these preserves in a recent article. Her list includes the North Maine Woods (3 million acres of working forest), Maine Coast Heritage Trust (thousands of acres of unspoiled islands and coastal properties), Pennsylvania's Hawk Mountain Sanctuary (a 2,000-acre bird reserve), South Dakota's Iram Wild House Sanctuary (11,000 acres), and Oregon's Yamsi Ranch (250,000 trees).[28] The most prominent organization that acquires land and maintains it in its natural state, free from development, is the Nature Conservancy, which had a budget of $275 million in 1992. Over the years, it has purchased or been given over six million acres.

Nevertheless, despite the enormous quantity of undeveloped land, demands are continually made that more beaches and waterfronts be preserved. But developments in these areas do not sacrifice environmental values, if the welfare of human beings is considered as an environmental concern, as I think it should be. Coastal developments have been extremely beneficial to the environment of a great many Americans. Consider the case of Miami Beach. Like many other beach resorts, Miami Beach's hotels, apartments, and condominiums have served millions well. Tourists have had an opportunity to live next to the ocean for short periods, eat in restaurants overlooking it, and swim, play, and lounge in well-maintained beach areas. Off-season and special group rates have allowed people of modest means to live in luxurious accommodations.

That is only part of the story. Thousands of people work in the Miami area and are employed in the construction of buildings and facilities. People and businesses have prospered. Federal, state, and local governments collect huge amounts of tax revenue from these facilities. A community has developed in the area to cater to people of all income levels. Had present environmental pressures prevailed in earlier years, Miami Beach might still be in a natural, uninhabited condition, benefiting wildlife but hardly any humans. Once a playground of the affluent, Miami Beach in recent years has been a haven of middle-income and lower-income tourists. Many of the old estates have been broken up, and homes, condominiums, and apartments for the middle class have taken their place.

The term "environmentally sensitive" is, of course, applied to much land that does not front on water, such as mountains. Controversy over development in mountainous areas appears to be no less intense than controversy over development in coastal regions, as illustrated by a dispute in central California that triggered a public hearing that I attended.

Not even standing room was available in the City Council Chamber of San Luis Obispo, California, the night of July 21, 1975. Seventy residents spoke. No one in that small community of 30,000 could remember any local controversy that had attracted as much attention or elicited such impassioned oratory.

At issue was a 1,300-foot mountain just outside the city limits. It was privately owned, and the owner, a prominent businessman in the area, was in the process of cutting a road leading to the mountaintop. Development had not otherwise touched the mountain. The owner wanted eventually to erect a chalet-restaurant at the peak. Thirty-seven of the seventy speakers supported his efforts, while the rest opposed creation of the road or any development of the mountain. One councilman had introduced three resolutions intended to prevent development, and the debate concerned those proposals.

One opponent after another voiced the same refrain: that this was "our mountain," a rare and beautiful resource, an inseparable part of the community. Some described the pleasures of climbing it; some displayed reverence for this "irreplaceable and majestic natural occurrence" and felt that it had been scarred by the road. According to some environmentalists, such places belong to all of the people and must remain in a natural state. Environmentalist literature refers to private owners as "tenants" and "caretakers" serving at the pleasure of the people, and these citizens of San Luis Obispo echoed such sentiments.

But these claims are based on a totally unwarranted assumption. Private ownership and development does not destroy or remove land from the reach of the people. On the contrary, it is the best means to bring land to the public. In San Luis Obispo, it is more likely to be "our mountain" if developed than if left untouched. Private owners are caretakers, but only in the sense that, if left free to do so, they tend to utilize the land to its highest and best advantage and enable the maximum number of people to benefit from it.

A mountain provides beauty from two perspectives: at its foot and at its peak. The view from the peak is usually more impressive than the one from the valley. If a mountain remains undeveloped, only climbers or hikers will have the opportunity to enjoy its magnificent vistas. A chalet-restaurant would enable many more people to enjoy the beauty of nature. Moreover, as a private development it will also provide a host of economic benefits.

For the many dedicated environmentalists, anything man-made on that mountain would desecrate it. Their feelings on this issue border on the religious: a special reverence for nature. Yet government has no more obligation to support this faith than any other, for there must be separation of religion and state under our Constitution. As the foregoing discussion reveals, however, the environmentalists' faith is already amply served in this nation.

Few things are more subjective than the perception of beauty. The mountain in dispute, one of a chain leading to the ocean, is not particularly distinguished and would scarcely elicit special attention, except from local residents who wished to preserve their mountain scenery. The new road threading its way to the top was like so many other access roads on mountains everywhere, barely noticeable to anyone except those with a special interest.

Many who came to the hearing to condemn development on the mountain would not have been residents of San Luis Obispo but for past development. The human condition has been greatly enhanced as nature has succumbed to the designs of builders. In many areas, man's efforts created wondrous and beautiful sights. Marshes were drained and trees and foliage planted. Houses, buildings, stores, and factories were erected to satisfy human needs. All became "ours" upon completion.

IV. Modern Soothsayers

Environmentalists rarely justify their positions on the ground of personal pleasure. They most often frame their complaints in the name of concern about the future of planet earth. They urge the adoption of highly restrictive laws over human conduct because they fear the future and predict doom. Two aspects of their dire forecasts are particularly suspect: first, the advocacy of extreme environmental and conservation measures because that is what "generations yet unborn" would want; and second, the claim that future generations will suffer as a result of depleted natural resources.

In the absence of special occult powers, how can one possibly know the wants and desires of "generations yet unborn"? How many parents can accurately predict the course even of their own children's lives?

But environmentalists make these forecasts regularly, in speech after eloquent speech urging the adoption of ever more severe regulations. Not surprisingly, the world that these speakers envision the unborn desiring is no different from the one they seek for themselves. Of course, our children's children should inherit the best of all possible worlds, a world that includes clean air and water, beaches, parks, open space, and scenic areas. But it should also be a world in good economic condition: with plentiful jobs, desirable housing conditions, and fewer slums, among other things.

Tomorrow's children will be stronger in body and mind if the economic prospects of their parents and grandparents are constantly expanding. The world of the future will be infinitely superior if it is freer: without government coercion stifling its citizens' aspirations. In actuality, disputes about the future are really about the present, about the needs and priorities of our society.

Environmentalists are similarly off-target when they predict a future of depleted natural resources—they simply project their own limited imaginations onto future generations. Since environmentalists are typically hostile to technology and materialism, they tend to ignore the consequences of limiting mankind's adaptability through overzealous regulation.

In contemplating the future, one must always be cognizant of the incredible creativity of the human mind. The reputations of forecasters who forgot this have suffered humiliating reversals. The story of Reverend Thomas Malthus needs frequent retelling. Malthus was a prominent British political economist who predicted, in his 1798 *Essay on the Principle of Population,* that the food supply could not keep pace with population growth. Consequently, the world was doomed to widespread starvation, disease, and warfare to keep population in check, for Malthus doubted that mankind had sufficient moral restraint to avoid these perils of overpopulation.

Although his analysis seemed plausible to many intelligent people in light of the information then available, his fundamental error was in making a prediction that ignored the human capacity to innovate and create. No matter how clever Malthus might have been, he could not have envisioned that about a century and a half after he wrote, many governments would pay farmers billions of dollars *not* to grow crops. Humans became *too* resourceful. Perhaps the resourcefulness of the mind matters more than even the natural resources of the earth in securing a prosperous life for future generations? Apparently, we are better "doers" than soothsayers.

The outcome of a famous bet on future commodity prices between biologist Paul Ehrlich and economist Julian Simon shows that scarcity predictions are no less risky in the twentieth century than they were in the eighteenth. In 1980, these distinguished gentlemen bet on future prices for five resources. Ehrlich selected the resources, and he chose copper, chrome, nickel, tin, and tungsten. Consistent with his notion that increasing population and industrial activity would create shortages in natural resources, Ehrlich bet that at the end of the 1980s these five metals would command higher prices. He lost the bet because all five declined in price.

Human experience reveals the fallibility of Ehrlich's position. Even if there will, in time, be less tonnage of each of these resources, human ingenuity will provide substitutes to satisfy needs and the market will efficiently allocate the scarce resources. Every day, in places all over the world, people are seeking to create substitute products that will be cheaper and more useful than each of these metals. Others are discovering less expensive ways to bring these resources to market. These processes have been ongoing since the beginning of civilization, and they have been much more successful since the Industrial Revolution that began in the eighteenth century. The major impediment to ingenuity is government regulation which clamps artificial impediments on the human mind.

We enjoy vastly more material comforts than our ancestors did because of human skill, ingenuity, and creativity. The basic resources of the earth may have dwindled since prehistoric times, but knowledge and understanding of how to obtain, amplify, and substitute for them has multiplied exponentially. As long as incentives exist and government does not interfere, man's wisdom will operate to improve the old and create the new.

Historical experience demonstrates that substitutes or new products normally replace essential materials and resources as those materials and resources become scarcer, and that when necessary, man adjusts reasonably well to a reduction in the supply of a particular resource. To insist that we live a life of self-sacrifice based on a faulty premise of a resource-depleted earth is an abuse of a precious resource: human beings. Not very long ago, no one would have conceived of many of the innovations we enjoy today: antibiotics, space travel, atomic energy, synthetic fabrics, plastics, television, computers, lasers, jet propulsion. Who now knows what amazing inventions the human mind of the future will bring forth?

Accommodating our modern neo-Malthusians requires considerable inconvenience and hardship, especially on the part of the less affluent, who depend for a better life on productivity and growth. Soothsayers preaching such human sacrifice should lose their licenses.

V. The Benefits of Growth

Since the nineteenth century, there has been a remarkable improvement in the living conditions of the average citizen of the U.S. Those in the lower and middle classes have earned steadily rising incomes and have enjoyed an increasing standard of living. Goods that once were so expensive that only the very rich could afford them are now priced for sale to people of moderate income. These gains are attributable to the growth in the nation's production of goods and services. Growth, consequently, must not be discouraged by any level of government if this trend is to continue.

Greater production leads to better living conditions for two reasons. First, it results in the employment of larger numbers of people, and that, of course, means larger incomes for more people. Wages and salaries rise as the percentage of employed people increases. Second, the more goods that are produced, the greater the probability that everyone, from top to bottom in the income scale, will own more goods. If, over a period of time, twenty million homes are built, it is much more likely that someone of average or less income will own one than it would be if half that number had been built. The more houses that are built, the lower will be the cost of each, and in time existing homes will filter down from rich to middle class to poor.

There is little disagreement among economists about the role of growth in raising living standards. In his book *The Affluent Society,* published in 1958, liberal economist John Kenneth Galbraith states: "It is the increase in output in recent decades, not the redistribution of income, which has brought the great material increase, the well-being of the average man."[29] He notes that increasing aggregate output has the practical effect of reducing inequality between income groups, and thereby eliminating the more acute tensions associated with inequality. He says that increased production "has been the great solvent of the tensions caused by inequality."[30]

Growth in the capitalist countries has enabled people to prosper and has allowed their conveniences of life to multiply. In 1983, a few years prior to the collapse of communism, there was one car for every 1.8 Americans, 4.4 Japanese, 2.5 Germans, and 2.8 Italians, but one for every 14.2 Soviets, 5.8 Czechs, and 10.8 Poles.[31] In the United States, growth has meant that "the masses" now enjoy amenities that were once reserved exclusively for the wealthy. Consider some obvious examples. In 1969, of those households with annual incomes below $3,000, 77 percent owned television sets and 75 percent owned refrigerators or freezers. For those with incomes between $3,000 and $4,000, 85 percent owned televisions and 76 percent owned refrigerators or freezers.[32] In 1993, of those with family incomes under $25,000, over 95 percent owned a color TV and 99.7 percent owned refrigerators. Of those with incomes from $25,000 to $34,999, over 99 percent owned color TVs and refrigerators.[33]

Governmental economic controls invariably reduce growth. Economist Jeffrey Sachs of Harvard University presents figures showing that after the fall of communism in Poland in 1989, people benefited very quickly from economic freedom. In just the first three years, Poles bought consumer goods that were out of their reach under communism. VCR ownership among employees rose from 1.9 per hundred households at the end of 1988, to 41 per hundred households at the end of 1991. Automobile ownership went from 30 to 38 per hundred households during the same period; ownership of stereo radios rose from 22 to 38 per hundred households, and ownership of color televisions rose from 41 to 82.[34]

Growth is not without its problems, however, and no-growth advocates are always eager to point them out. It is said that great material accomplishments have not made people more happy and contented.

This may be true for the wealthy. For those who already own five cars and six homes, the opportunity to purchase another is hardly inspirational. That is clearly not the situation of those without either, who have to rely on growth to obtain them. Surely, the people who buy automobiles, TVs, and household appliances must believe that they will be better off with them than without them. Can anyone seriously suggest that recession makes people happy and contented? The history of recessions in this nation clearly shows that we have much to fear from pursuing no-growth policies.

No-growthers contend that growth causes pollution and wastes the world's resources. But what they neglect to tell us is that no-growth does not provide solutions to these problems. Consider two examples. First, as I mentioned, density restrictions on land use favored by preservationists tie up excessive amounts of land for housing and cause urban sprawl. Second, nuclear power— the primary target of the no-growthers' anti-technology animus—is the least polluting of our energy sources. Yet environmentalists oppose its use. In general, no-growthers exhibit a greatly exaggerated fear of modern living. If life were as perilous as they claim, I doubt that life expectancy would have risen so dramatically over this century. In the United States in 1900, life expectancy at birth was 47.3 years; by 1990, it had risen to 75.4 years, and it has continued to gradually increase. Some of this gain may be attributable to a reduction in pollution, but not a reduction of the sort mentioned by no-growthers: it may be attributable, for instance, to the replacement of horses by cars on our city streets and the resulting improvements in public sanitation. But most of the gain results from advances in technology that have reduced disease, accidents, and other health hazards, and improved diet and living conditions.

To be sure, some modest limits to growth are sometimes necessary, but only when growth causes serious harm. The right of property does not include the right to use property for harmful purposes. No one has the right to create a nuisance or to pose serious perils to the lives and property of others.

Many environmentalists stretch this principle beyond all reasonable bounds because they regard normal growth as harmful. Everyone wants clean air and water, but most of us do not take this wish to the extreme of damaging our economic system. Although automobiles annually take thousands of lives, few demand their elimination. To be sure, harmful uses of property are not entitled to protection, but broadening the meaning of harm beyond all reasonable bounds will create the greater harm of undermining ownership and investment.

VI. The Huge Cost of Regulation

It is often asserted that a strict interpretation of the Fifth Amendment's takings clause will require the government to spend more than it does now for open space, parks, and recreational sites, or to do without them. The conclusion of this argument is that modern needs mandate that regulation of land use not be considered a taking, and thus that such regulation should not require payment of compensation to owners. For example, it would cost enormous amounts of money to purchase some or most of the waterfronts, mountainous areas, canyons, and other lands that environmentalists consider "ecologically sensitive." Were the takings clause not in the way, states might regulate the use of these lands to achieve conservation goals, and would not have to compensate the owners. More development could be prohibited and more land kept in a natural state. The public, it is said, would be saved from incurring considerable expenses.

My judgment is to the contrary. For the reasons discussed in this chapter, ignoring the takings clause would be an extremely costly mistake, for the prime casualty would be the country's private-enterprise system. Regulating property rights to a nullity would increase substantially the risk and uncertainties of ownership and would, consequently, inhibit investment, raise prices, and limit competition. Employment and commerce would likewise suffer. Total tax receipts would fall. In view of the adverse consequences to the nation's economic system, it is far less expensive in the long run for government to pay compensation for the rights it negates by regulation.

If there is no takings restraint on government's ability to acquire land or curb its use, government will arbitrarily restrict large quantities of land for passing political advantage and at the expense of more socially and economically desirable uses. This is bad public policy, as the high court of New York explained in a 1976 case:

> The ultimate evil of a deprivation of property . . . is that it forces the owner to assume the cost of providing a benefit to the public without recoupment. . . . [T]he ultimate economic cost of providing the benefit is hidden from those who in a democratic society are given the power of deciding whether or not they wish to obtain the benefit despite the ultimate economic cost, however initially distributed [citation]. In other words, the removal from productive use of private property has an ultimate social cost more easily concealed by imposing the cost on the owner alone. When successfully concealed, the public is not likely to have any objection to the "cost-free" benefit.[35]

In this chapter, we have seen how preserving and enhancing the environment is achieved through the normal functioning of our free-enterprise system. While government intervention is necessary in its proper sphere—preventing harms that property owners might inflict on others, or purchasing land for preservation or parkland—overzealous regulation in pursuit of ill-advised environmentalist goals is both counterproductive and unnecessary. Stifling initiative and creativity by undermining property rights can never be a prescription for human betterment, nor can it save the earth for generations yet unborn.

9

Conclusions and Recommendations

The Framers of the original Constitution, Bill of Rights, and Section 1 of the Fourteenth Amendment had a common goal: to create and maintain a free, viable, and abundant nation. To achieve these objectives, they separated and limited the powers of government, believing that freedom would maximize the people's creative, productive, and intellectual abilities. A major concern was to secure economic liberties, including property rights.[1]

In the more than two hundred years since the framing of the Constitution, world experience has proven the wisdom of our Framers. Nations that have embraced a free economy have prospered, while those that have opted for collectivism have suffered egregiously. Clearly, a strong correlation exists between economic freedom and economic well-being.

To maintain a successful economy, private owners and investors must be protected in their endeavors. People will not own property or invest their resources if they risk the loss of all or part of their property or resources through confiscation or regulation. Those willing to assume such risks will demand higher prices to compensate for higher risks. Thus, by substantially securing property rights in recent years, the United States Supreme Court has considerably advanced the welfare of the American people.

I have referred in this book to the new standards employed by the Court as the *Agins* Rules. Consistent with the separation of powers, these rules provide protection for property rights under an intermediate level of judicial review. Unlike strict scrutiny, this mid-level test does not subject the legislature to the maximum burden of justification, but it imposes a lesser yet still substantial burden on this branch to justify its regulation.

The Supreme Court also applies the intermediate level of scrutiny to gender-discrimination and commercial-speech cases. Its experience in these cases is relevant to the protection of property rights. Since the intermediate scrutiny test is based on similar considerations wherever it is applied, the inquiry for each liberty should not be limited to the precedents affecting it alone, but should benefit from decisions concerning others in the group. Or to put it another way, owners should not be deprived of their liberty on the basis of interpretations that would be found oppressive with respect to these other liberties.

In adopting the *Agins* Rules, the United States Supreme Court has placed property rights among the liberties to which it accords heightened scrutiny as a protection against arbitrary and capricious legislation. This jurisprudence is based on the idea that under the separation of powers, the powers of the majority do not include the power to deny or deprive people of their rights. Under intermediate scrutiny, no legislature has the power to limit a liberty unless it can prove that its purpose in doing so is constitutionally legitimate and that its law will substantially achieve this purpose. As Blackstone observed, legislators should not pass laws that cause "wanton and causeless restraint of the will of the subject." Laws are "destructive of liberty," he asserted, "if they regulate and constrain our conduct in matters of mere indifference, without any good end in view."[2] A nation governed by a Constitution dedicated in its preamble to the "Blessings of Liberty" can demand no less from its officials.

Accordingly, the *Agins* Rules state that a land-use regulation "effects a taking if the ordinance does not substantially advance legitimate state interests . . . or denies an owner economically viable use of his land."[3] These rules govern land-use regulation and supersede a long period in property jurisprudence, dating back to the late 1920s, dominated mostly by deference to government regulation. Under the *Agins* Rules, the Supreme Court invalidated land-use regulations imposed by the California Coastal Commission, the State of South Carolina, and the City of Tigard, Oregon. It is likely that, under the legal doctrines previously in effect, government would have prevailed in each instance. With a handful of notable exceptions, it had long been assumed by most state and federal courts that government regulation enjoyed the presumption of validity, and that property owners carried a heavy and usually insurmountable burden to prove invalidity.

The new rules first appeared in *Agins v. City of Tiburon,* a 1980 case that most of the land-use bar failed to recognize as setting a precedent for providing greater security for property rights. The Court applied these rules more meaningfully in *Keystone Bituminous Coal Association v. DeBenedictus* (1987), while still according considerable deference to the state. The case that affixed the *Agins* Rules to the legal map was *Nollan v. California Coastal Commission* (1987), which applied them effectively and established the intermediate standard of review as the appropriate test. *Nollan, Lucas v. South Carolina Coastal Council* (1992), and *Dolan v. City of Tigard* (1994) are now generally accepted by both federal and state courts as controlling in most or all land-use cases. In the balance of the chapter, I shall summarize the holdings of these cases and present my views on them.

I. Determining a Legitimate State Interest

According to *Agins* Rule 1, a legitimate state interest must (a) serve a public and not a private interest and (b) prevent harm and not confer benefits. *Keystone* provides recent authority for part (a). In his opinion for the majority in *Keystone,* Justice John Paul Stevens characterized the Kohler Act—declared unconstitutional in the leading case from the 1920s, *Pennsylvania Coal Co. v. Mahon*—as a private-benefits statute enacted to advantage the owners of surface land rights. He distinguished the 1921 Kohler Act from the 1966 Subsidence Act at issue in *Keystone,* arguing that the latter served legitimate public interests in safety, protecting the environment, etc. As Stevens understood this distinction, the Kohler Act violated a long-held principle of American law as articulated by Justice Samuel Chase in 1798: "[I]t is against all reason and justice, for a people to entrust a legislature" with the power to pass a law "that takes property from A. and gives it to B."[4] The principle applies to favors and preferences accorded by a legislature to individuals or identifiable groups (such as the surface owners in *Pennsylvania Coal*). This principle is not confined to property cases, as Stevens stated in a different context: "[E]lements of legitimacy and neutrality [must] characterize the performance of the sovereign's duty to govern impartially."[5] Curiously, Stevens saw no such problem of taking from A to give to B with the 1966 Subsidence Act, despite its abundant parallels with the earlier legislation.

With respect to part (b) of *Agins* Rule 1, *Keystone*'s language supports the conclusion that the concept of a legitimate state interest embraces only the abatement of harm. Stevens refers to the actions prohibited by Pennsylvania's 1966 Subsidence Act as "tantamount to," "akin to," or "similar to" a public nuisance and cites *Mugler* (the 1887 brewery case) and *Schoene* (the 1928 cedar rust disease case) as constitutional authority for sustaining regulations forbidding a harmful use of property. But Stevens failed to realistically apply the harm/benefit distinction in *Keystone*. Thus, *Keystone* badly misfired, and it hardly qualifies as precedent for the harm/benefit distinction, since the subsidence law which it upheld bestowed substantial benefits that were not related to the abatement of injury on some members of the public at the expense of others. The Pennsylvania legislature's stated purpose was to serve the public interest in safety, the environment, and the fiscal viability of the area by minimizing damage to surface areas. The safety issue had been asserted in *Pennsylvania Coal* as well, and Justice Oliver Wendell Holmes rejected it.

Since the deed restriction affecting the Mahons' surface interest required the coal company to notify them before the commencement of mining operations, Holmes found the legislature's safety justification unconvincing. By preventing coal mining, the Kohler Act benefited the surface owners, who had a strong financial interest in eliminating the coal company's mining rights. Following Holmes's reasoning and the harm/benefit distinction, it is difficult to reconcile Stevens's divergent conclusion in *Keystone*.

In contrast to Stevens's handling of the harm/benefit distinction, Chief Justice William Rehnquist's dissent in *Keystone* clearly supports the principle that only the abatement of nuisances or other grave threats to life and property justifies a limitation on property use. Because the infliction of harm on others is not a legitimate use of one's property, it is not entitled to protection. Hence, the government secures and does not take property when it abates or forbids a nuisance. In contrast, when government restricts A's property in order to provide benefits for B, it not only takes from A and gives to B, it also forces A to "bear public burdens which, in all fairness and justice, should be borne by the public as a whole" (*Armstrong v. United States* [1960]).[6] Consistent with these principles, Rehnquist would later hold in *Dolan* that requiring Mrs. Dolan to eliminate drainage and congestion problems attributable to her new construction were legitimate state interests, but forcing her to bear general public burdens from flooding by providing a greenway on her property was not.

Applying the "legitimate state interest" test will be a meaningless exercise, unless the Court makes a searching inquiry into the purpose that the legislature proffers when it enacts a restriction on property use. If an owner challenges the restriction as a regulatory taking, the Court should pierce the veil of legislative intent. This does not require the Court to do anything unusual or unfamiliar. In fact, such inquiries are routine under both intermediate and strict scrutiny in other areas of fundamental rights analysis. Similarly, in deciding commerce-clause controversies, the Court engages in such a searching analysis to see whether a state's declared purpose is a subterfuge for protectionism or, instead, a legitimate local concern.[7]

The Court's experience in deciding commercial-speech cases—another area of the law in which the Court applies an intermediate scrutiny test—is instructive in discerning a legislature's true motivation. Although Justices William Brennan, Harry Blackmun, and John Paul Stevens have been willing to give great deference to local legislators in property issues, they have had almost the reverse position with respect to restraints on commercial speech. The Court defines commercial speech as speech which does no more than propose a commercial transaction. Because free speech is a hallowed First Amendment right, these liberal justices applied heightened scrutiny, examining both a legislature's purpose and its chosen means.

Consider the concurring opinions of Justices Brennan and Blackmun in *Metromedia, Inc. v. San Diego,* a 1981 case in which San Diego's ban on billboards was at issue.[8] The city justified its ordinance prohibiting most billboards in part on the grounds that such a prohibition would advance the city's aesthetics, which the Court's majority accepted as a "substantial governmental interest." Brennan and Blackmun contended that by not demonstrating a comprehensive commitment to making its physical environment in commercial and industrial areas more attractive, the city had failed to prove that its interest in creating an aesthetically pleasing environment was genuine and substantial.

In *Posadas de Puerto Rico Associates v. Tourism Co. of Puerto Rico* (1986), another commercial-speech case, Justices Brennan and Blackmun (along with Justice Marshall) disputed Puerto Rico's argument that the purpose of its law was to discourage gambling, because the law only restricted advertising for casino gambling and not advertising for other kinds of gambling (horse racing, dog racing, cock fighting, and the territory's lottery).[9] In *Cincinnati v. Discovery Network* (1993), Justice Stevens, writing for the majority, refused to accept the city's assertion of an aesthetic purpose in banning only commercial newsracks because they "are no greater an eyesore than the [noncommercial] newsracks permitted to remain on Cincinnati's sidewalks."[10] In these cases, these justices carefully examined the legislature's stated purposes to determine if they were credible. If heightened scrutiny is to be meaningful, the Court should not accept a lesser inquiry when land-use issues are at stake.

Under an intermediate scrutiny test, zoning should be particularly vulnerable to a legislative-purpose inquiry because special-interest pressures often influence zoning decisions. Planners and city and county councils are continually under pressure from constituents seeking to benefit themselves by having regulations imposed on vacant property. These local legislators have often responded by forbidding development that local voters consider objectionable. The most widely adopted exclusionary device throughout the country is large-lot zoning, by which a jurisdiction limits development in substantial portions of its territory to single-family residences on very large lots. This practice is often referred to as "snob zoning." Similar pressures sometimes explain the exclusion of multifamily dwellings and mobile homes and the requirement that only houses or apartments having stated minimum interior space may be erected in certain areas. While there may be occasions when the prevention of harm warrants these restraints, many are intended to benefit existing residents by excluding unwanted people. Some state courts have stricken zoning regulations with such a purpose. The New Jersey Supreme Court explained why it found such an exclusionary purpose unacceptable:

> We have no hesitancy in now saying, and do so emphatically, that, considering the basic importance of the opportunity for appropriate housing for all classes of our citizenry, no municipality may exclude or limit categories of housing for that reason or purpose [i.e., for the purpose of reducing the burden of local taxes by excluding low-income housing]. While we fully recognize the increasingly heavy

burden of local taxes for municipal governmental and school costs for home-
owners, relief from the consequences of this tax system will have to be furnished
by other branches of government. It cannot legitimately be accomplished by restricting types of housing through the zoning process in developing municipalities.[11]

II. Substantially Advancing a Legitimate State Interest

It is a long-established principle of Anglo-Saxon jurisprudence that a law
which does not substantially achieve the objective that the legislature declared
in enacting it is futile and oppressive. A 1996 commercial-speech case, *44
Liquormart, Inc. v. Rhode Island,*[12] provides strong evidence of just how well-
accepted this principle is by the nine justices of the Supreme Court. The case
concerned a Rhode Island law banning the advertisement of retail liquor prices
except at the place of sale. All the justices agreed that the stated purpose of the
law—to reduce alcohol consumption—was a valid constitutional purpose.
However, all nine also agreed that Rhode Island had failed to establish a reasonable fit between the regulation and the goal of promoting temperance. They
unanimously struck down the law, largely on this basis. While acknowledging
that the law would have some effect in reducing alcohol consumption, they concluded that the state had presented no evidence to suggest that the ban would
produce a significant reduction. The justices were, in effect, asserting that the
Rhode Island law accomplished little more than oppressing the sellers of liquor.
In other words, the Court reasoned that the state had adopted a *means* that was
unlikely to achieve the *end*.

In property rights cases, no less than in commercial-speech cases, insisting
that means fit ends is now a constitutional requirement, thanks to the new takings jurisprudence. Thus, *Agins* Rule 2, which requires a substantial linkage between a law's means and ends, is an important guarantee of liberty. To obtain
judicial approval under Rule 2, the government must prove a tight means-ends
fit as required by (a) the essential-nexus test of *Nollan,* coupled with the rough-
proportionality requirement of *Dolan,* and (b) the disproportionate-impact principle, as explained by Justice Antonin Scalia in *Nollan.*[13] The latter condition
ferrets out governmental restrictions on land use that hit one or a small number
of owners while ignoring the greater number of owners who contributed to a
problem. The fit between a general problem and a restraint imposed on only a
few of the owners who may contribute to it would ordinarily not be a tight one.[14]

In addition to the specific *Agins* Rules, the Court has raised the level of
scrutiny required in land-use cases. This is crucial, since the outcome of a case
often depends on the level of scrutiny applied. If the Supreme Court had applied to *Nollan, Lucas,* or *Dolan* the minimal level of scrutiny utilized in *Eu-*

clid (1926), the opposite result would have been reached in each case — government vindication. Instead, the Court raised the level of scrutiny considerably above the level applied in *Euclid,* to a level equivalent to that applied in gender-discrimination and commercial-speech cases: intermediate scrutiny.

Another important issue that the Court has addressed is the burden of proof. Who bears this burden in land-use cases, as in other areas of the law, is very important to the outcome. In First Amendment cases, for example, the government, not the person who challenges the legislation, bears the burden. That burden is a heavy one, and the government often loses. Traditionally, in land-use cases, landowners shouldered the burden of proof, and landowners mostly lost.

Agins has changed this outcome. Referring to the *Agins* Rules, Justice Scalia asserted in *Nollan* that this standard required the California Coastal Commission to justify its access requirement:

> We view the Fifth Amendment's Property Clause to be more than a pleading exercise in cleverness and imagination. As indicated earlier, our cases describe the condition for abridgment of property rights through the police power as a "substantial advanc[ing] of a legitimate state interest."[15]

Subsequently, Chief Justice Rehnquist likewise placed the burden of proof in the *Dolan* case on the government, but had a different explanation for doing so. He made a distinction in land-use cases between legislative proceedings (as in *Euclid*) and adjudicative proceedings (as in *Nollan*). The Chief Justice stated that when a landowner contests a "generally applicable zoning regulation" — that is, makes a facial challenge to the ordinance — the burden rests with him, but when he contests a specific application to his property, the government must bear the burden.

Rehnquist's distinction has created some confusion because it suggests that *Euclid* is still a binding precedent relevant to general zoning ordinances. However, as explained in Chapter 5, the 1980 *Agins* case involved a facial challenge to a zoning ordinance and the Court in that case applied the standard now referred to as the *Agins* Rules. The portion of the *Agins* Rules pertinent to the substance of the *Agins* case was based on *Nectow* and not on *Euclid*. *Nectow*, together with *Roberge,* effectively reversed *Euclid*. Since most judicial challenges to land-use regulations are in the "as applied" category, Rehnquist's error is not a very serious one. Moreover, an unfavorable judicial opinion in a facial challenge does not foreclose a subsequent "as applied" challenge. However, judicial errors are costly and otherwise harmful to society, and they should be corrected.

Not only is the distinction between facial and "as applied" challenges technically incorrect, it is also flawed conceptually. Justice Clarence Thomas made this point recently. The U.S. Supreme Court denied the parking-lot owners a writ of certiorari in the case of *Parking Association of Georgia, Inc. v. City of Atlanta* (discussed in Chapter 6, Section VII). Granting of the writ would have enabled the Supreme Court to adjudicate the matter, and denying it leaves the state court's opinion as final. In the *Parking Association* case, the Supreme Court of Georgia ruled against the owners on the basis that the ordinance at issue was a general zoning ordinance that (per *Euclid*) did not require more than a minimal-scrutiny inquiry. Justice Thomas, joined by Justice Sandra Day O'Connor, dissented to the denial of certiorari, stating that "the general applicability of the ordinance should not be relevant in takings analysis." A taking is harmful regardless of the source. "The distinction between sweeping legislative takings and particularized administrative takings," asserted Justice Thomas, "appears to be a distinction without a constitutional difference."[16] (The refusal of the Supreme Court to consider the decision in the Atlanta case does not indicate that it has taken any position on the issues involved.)

III. Expanding *Lucas* to Include Retroactive Laws

Agins Rule 3, as interpreted in *Lucas,* protects an owner from being denied all economically viable use of his land by forbidding the passage of retroactive laws having this effect. Included within this prohibition are laws eliminating "commercial viability" and laws denying an owner his "investment-backed expectations." Intended to secure and enhance ownership and investment, these concepts have not always been interpreted from this perspective. A virtual labyrinth of legal verbiage presently surrounds each phrase, encouraging extensive and costly litigation and effectively denying justice to many aggrieved landowners.

Courts that have invalidated regulatory ordinances for economic reasons may couch their decisions in terms of economic deprivation, but the basic wrong they usually remedy is the adoption of a retroactive law. Most purchases of property are made in reliance on the uses legally permitted for the property at the time. Thus, an ordinance eliminating an owner's rights to use his property as authorized when he bought it ought to be considered wrong because it is a retroactive law. Every purchaser should be able to pursue his or her economic purpose on the basis of existing law. As Edward Coke remarked centuries ago: "[F]or what is the land, but the profits thereof[?]"[17]

Protecting expectations is vital to securing property rights, and yet it does not receive the recognition accorded to other sticks in the bundle of property rights. *Loretto,* the 1982 cable TV case that protected owners against any permanent physical occupation by government no matter how minuscule, was premised in part on "an owner's expectation that he will be relatively undisturbed at least in the possession of his property."[18] *Nollan* extended this rule to apply to a permanent public easement. Likewise, *Causby,* the 1946 airplane overflight case, secures an owner from a loss that a physical action of government short of an occupation inflicts on his property.[19] Denying an owner a permitted use results in as complete a loss as if the government had permanently occupied a portion of the land, imposed a public easement on it, or damaged it.

Retroactive laws raise issues of governmental unfairness and coercion.[20] As the Supreme Court explained in 1886 in an equal-protection case that concerned the discretionary powers of a board administering a laundry licensing law, "the very idea that one may be compelled to hold his life, or the means of living, or any material right essential to the enjoyment of life, at the mere will of another has been thought intolerable in any country where freedom prevails, as being the essence of slavery itself."[21]

One hundred ten years later, the Supreme Court, in the voice of Justice Stevens, made the identical point in another case: "Elementary notions of fairness enshrined in our constitutional jurisprudence dictate that a person receive fair notice not only of the conduct that will subject him to punishment but also the severity of the penalty that a State may impose."[22] This case, *BMW of North America, Inc. v. Gore,* concerned the imposition of punitive damages on a corporation found to have committed a tort by touching up the paint on cars scratched in transport and then selling them as new. The Court found the $2 million punitive damage award "grossly excessive," in part because the company had no adequate notice that its action might trigger such a large sanction.

There is sufficient precedent in case law, I believe, to warrant extending *Lucas* to include retroactive laws that forbid exercise of a land use permitted at the time of acquisition.[23] Notwithstanding the holding in *Calder v. Bull* (restricting the Constitution's ex post facto clauses to criminal law), the Supreme Court has over the years struck down civil retroactive laws basically on the grounds that they were oppressive.[24] The holding in that case might have been different had two of the justices not believed (wrongly) that the takings clause required compensation for a loss caused by a retroactive property law.[25] The rule that I would favor on retroactivity would provide additional protection against a wipeout of investment-backed expectations or commercial viability.

As used in takings cases, the term "investment-backed expectations" refers to (a) expectations that one will be able to exercise existing rights to which one had previously been entitled, as well as (b) expectations that one will be able to acquire and exercise such rights in the future. *Lucas, HFH Ltd. v. Superior Court* (1975), and *Just v. Marinette County* (1972) (the latter two were discussed in Chapter 5, Section IV) are examples of cases where the owner sought to exercise rights that were available to him at the time of purchase. Laws depriving property owners of the rights that they purchased are retroactive laws, and governments that impose them should have to compensate the owners for what they have taken.[26]

My proposal to expand *Lucas* would only apply to changes in use; that is, I would protect an owner against a retroactive change to a less valuable use—say, mutifamily zoning to single-family zoning, or industrial or commercial zoning to single-family or mutifamily zoning, or single-family to open-space zoning.

Thus, in the *Lucas* situation, I would award compensation upon proof that when Lucas bought the property it could be used for the construction of single-family homes, the use to which he subsequently sought to put the property. The governmental inquiry should go no further than ascertaining whether the use presently proposed was authorized at the date of purchase.

Thus, the proposed rule on retroactivity would apply to the kind of zoning change made in *HFH* and *Just,* where the owners purchased the property for a particular purpose and the zoning was subsequently changed, forbidding this use. However, the government would not violate the rule by adopting a general regulation that indirectly limited the scope of the authorized use, such as increasing the required area or density, or imposing height limitations. *Agins* Rules 1 and 2 relate to these regulations, and retroactivity should be a factor in applying Rule 2, as previously explained in Chapter 5, Section IVA.

To be more specific, consider a 2,500-acre section of land that is zoned to permit the erection of multifamily units at a density of thirty units to the acre with a height limitation of four stories. Suppose an ordinance is proposed to change the zoning in the section to allow single-family dwellings at a density of five units to the acre. Under my proposal, a person who purchased land in this section under the multifamily zoning classification as described would be protected against the land being rezoned to single-family use. The owner would not be secured by the retroactivity protection against a change in density to ten per acre or in the height limitation to two stories. He might, however, challenge the density and height limitations as violations of *Agins* Rule 1 (purpose) and *Agins* Rule 2 (means-ends).

The principal change my proposal makes to the law in many jurisdictions is to move the initial event for determining retroactivity from the date of application for a building permit to the date of acquisition of the property. At present, for example, San Diego County ordinance provides that "[a]ny application for a permit or other approval regulated in any manner by the provisions of this zoning ordinance shall only be required to meet the provisions of this ordinance that were in effect on the date the application is filed."[27] The California Court of Appeal held that the ordinance confers "the vested right to have a building permit application reviewed and considered in light of the regulations existing on the date of application." It also held that such a right may be impaired by zoning changes reasonably necessary to protect the health and safety of the public, but may not be impaired by later-enacted provisions not so related—for instance, "ordinances or regulations down-zoning from one use to another, limiting subdivision densities or imposing height requirements."[28]

A market economy is premised in large part on the idea that legislatures are ill-suited to make economic rules. With respect to many issues legislatures decide, those in the minority have not been as influential, persuasive, clever, ruthless, or fortunate as those in the majority in convincing the lawmakers. Society should, consequently, make certain that laws do not needlessly or wantonly diminish or wipe out people's acquisitions and investments. Suffering that kind of loss is an unconscionable penalty to pay for one's failure to persuade politicians.

IV. Implementing the Judicial Responsibility to Protect Property Rights

In my view, the *Agins* Rules are generally consistent with the guarantees provided for property rights in the U.S. Constitution. It is also my position that the intentions of our various Framers should be fully observed when to do so would be advantageous and not harmful to modern society. Preservation of constitutional government requires at least this kind of commitment. In the absence of overriding necessity, I see no reason to depart from the protections for property rights given in our fundamental documents: the Constitution, the Bill of Rights, and the Fourteenth Amendment.

The *Agins* Rules are a significant limitation on the powers of government over property. While earlier in this century government intervention in the economy was thought to be essential to success, time has shown the error of that position. The great lesson of our times is that the forces of production, conservation, and creativity rely principally on the marketplace and not on government. World leaders, including those who head the many nations that were once part of the Soviet bloc, have come to embrace this truth. Even China's still nominally communist leaders have abandoned the system that brought them only misery. Because of the free-market system's success in elevating living standards wherever it has been permitted to function, that system is likely to continue to proliferate and to be of even greater importance in the future.

Some may still argue that free markets are too simplistic an answer for an advanced economy like that of the United States. However, it is my belief that protecting freedom in the land-use market is essential to the future of our nation. Especially for those concerned about expanding opportunities for the least well off and for minorities, the lesson of this book is that free markets offer the disadvantaged the greatest prospect for success. We should recall the experience of nonzoned Houston. A majority of its voters have, on two occasions, rejected the imposition of zoning. The greatest opposition to zoning came from people at the lower end of the economic spectrum, who voted against it by substantial majorities. They obviously understood that heavily regulating property restricts opportunity rather than enhancing it.

We have seen that zoning and other land-use regulations raise housing prices, just as prices rise as a result of other economic regulation. Poor people seem to intuitively grasp this point, at least when they are allowed to vote directly on land-use issues that affect them. The less affluent voted against the California Coastal Zone Conservation Initiative and, on two occasions, voted against growth controls in San Diego. Thus, judges should understand that when they are asked to strike down land-use regulations, they will be acting not only in the cause of a particular (possibly wealthy) plaintiff, but in accordance with the desires of the less affluent members of the community. This, of course, should not be the reason for their decisions, but this understanding is important because it reveals that property rights are not only, or even primarily, the concern of the affluent owners and developers who usually file the lawsuits.

As we saw in our examination of voting records, less affluent people do not support the exclusionary, no-growth positions of most environmental groups. Instead, they view the environment in human terms, desiring better and more housing and jobs—all concerns that are seriously threatened by regulations that limit growth and development. After all, for those of limited income, the most important environmental concerns are better housing and employment opportunities. The environmentalists' emphasis on preserving nature and not developing land are alien and most harmful to those who are of limited means.

But, as I have argued, an emphasis on property rights is not harmful to the physical environment. This country provides generously for nature; only about 6 percent of the country's total land is developed, and that leaves about 94 percent that is not occupied for urban purposes. Nor does our Constitution protect nuisances or near-nuisances in the developed areas. Accordingly, in protecting property rights by striking down, under the *Agins* Rules, arbitrary and capricious regulations, the United States Supreme Court fulfills its constitutional responsibility in a manner consistent with contemporary societal aspirations.

I have titled this book *Property and Freedom,* but it is essentially about the pursuit of happiness. World experience shows that a high correlation exists between economic freedom and material abundance. To be sure, material abundance does not necessarily produce happiness, but its absence clearly impedes it. The Framers of our Constitution and Bill of Rights understood this correlation—even without the many economic studies and the communist debacle evidencing it—and designed a government to enable its constituents to pursue happiness. The separation of powers, limitation of powers, and guarantees of individual rights are the Constitution's safeguards for freedom and, accordingly, for happiness. When judges enforce these provisions, they are fulfilling their legal responsibilities as well as securing our happiness.

Notes

Introduction

1. Village of Euclid v. Ambler Realty Co., 272 U.S. 365 (1926).
2. *Id.* at 395.
3. *Id.* at 390.
4. THE REPORT OF THE PRESIDENT'S COMMISSION ON HOUSING (Government Printing Office, 1982).

Chapter 1. Why Property Rights Are Important

1. ZBIGNIEW BRZEZINSKI, THE GRAND FAILURE: THE BIRTH AND DEATH OF COMMUNISM IN THE TWENTIETH CENTURY 165–66 (1989).
2. THE CZECH REPUBLIC, COUNTRY ECONOMIC REPORT (1996).
3. NATIONAL CHAMBER FOUNDATION REPORT OF THE BULGARIAN ECONOMIC GROWTH AND TRANSITION PROJECT (1990); *Bulgarians Go on Rampage to Force Socialists' Ouster,* SAN DIEGO UNION-TRIBUNE, Jan. 11, 1997, at A14; *Bulgaria's Premier Likely to Keep Job Despite Mess,* N.Y. TIMES, Dec. 24, 1996; *Bulgaria, Once a Showcase, Is Now a Health Care Wasteland,* N.Y. TIMES, Dec. 25, 1996, at A13.
4. *See* ROGER W. FONTAINE, RED PHOENIX RISING? (Cato Institute 1996). *See also* comparative economic statistics in POLISH AGENCY FOR FOREIGN INVESTMENT IN POLAND, FUNDAMENTAL FACTS, FIGURES, AND REGULATIONS (1996), and discussions in THE POLITICAL ECONOMY OF POLICY REFORM (John Williamson ed., 1994).

   Harvard economics professor Jeffrey Sachs, an advisor to the Polish government, has written about the increase in private businesses and employment in these businesses soon after the end of communist rule in Poland. The elimination of regulatory restraints in that nation led to thousands of new private businesses and job opportunities. From 1989 to mid-1992, the number of individual proprietorships increased by close to 710,000, and the number of partnerships, limited-liability companies, and joint-stock companies rose by nearly 40,000. Sachs writes that the increase in the number of small business owners represented about 4 percent of the working population and that employment in these businesses for this period rose from 1,475,000 to 2,800,400, an increase of more than 7 percent of the labor force. *See* Jeffrey Sachs, POLAND'S JUMP TO THE MARKET ECONOMY 62–63 (1993).

5. Gerald W. Scully, *The Institutional Framework and Economic Development,* 96 JOURN. POL. ECON. 952 (1989).
6. JAMES GWARTNEY, ROBERT LAWSON, AND WALTER BLOCK, ECONOMIC FREEDOM OF THE WORLD: 1975–1995 (1996). *See* James Gwartney, *Toward a Measure of Economic Freedom,* APEE NEWSLETTER 1 (Winter 1996).
7. BRYAN T. JOHNSON AND THOMAS P. SHEEHY, 1996 INDEX OF ECONOMIC FREEDOM.
8. CATO INSTITUTE, THE TEN FREEST ECONOMIES IN 1995 (1996).
9. CATHERINE DRINKER BOWEN, MIRACLE AT PHILADELPHIA 71 (1966).
10. FELIX FRANKFURTER, MR. JUSTICE HOLMES AND THE SUPREME COURT 74 (1961).
11. FEDERALIST NO. 45, at 292–93 (J. Madison). (All citations of THE FEDERALIST PAPERS herein refer to the Clinton Rossiter edition of 1961.)

Professor William Grampp observes that the economic controls which the Constitution expressly authorizes are modest when compared with those that France and England exercised or tried to exercise during their mercantilist period (from the sixteenth century through the mid-eighteenth century). Their governments, for instance, regulated the quality of goods, licensed labor, granted monopolies and other exclusive rights, protected domestic industries, and controlled foreign trade and finance. Grampp writes:

> Not even proposed [at the Philadelphia Convention] were the powers to control prices, wages, interest rates, the quality of goods, the conditions of their sale, and the allocation of labor. All of these powers were cherished by the practitioners (although not the theorists) of mercantilism, and could they have been asked for an opinion of the Constitution, they would have said it provided a feeble economic policy indeed.

1 W. GRAMPP, ECONOMIC LIBERALISM 109 (1965).
12. FEDERALIST NO. 44, at 282–83 (J. Madison).
13. FEDERALIST NO. 84, at 513 (A. Hamilton).
14. 3 DEBATES ON THE ADOPTION OF THE FEDERAL CONSTITUTION 424 (I. Elliott ed., 1888).
15. THE LIFE AND SELECTED WRITINGS OF THOMAS JEFFERSON 299 (Adrienne Koch and William Peden eds., 1993).
16. An example of the first limitation is the prohibition against nuisances; an example of the second is a requirement that a builder create facilities or pay compensation to alleviate drainage problems that his new structure has caused.

Chapter 2. The Constitution Secures Property Rights

1. *See generally* BERNARD H. SIEGAN, ECONOMIC LIBERTIES AND THE CONSTITU-
   TION (1981). *See Resolution of General Assembly of Virginia,* Jan. 21, 1786, and
   Proceedings of Commissioners to Remedy Defects of Federal Government, Sept.
   11, 1786, in THE MAKING OF THE AMERICAN REPUBLIC (Charles Callan Tansill
   ed., 1972).
2. SIEGAN, *supra* note 1.
3. THE COMPLETE MADISON at 45 (Saul K. Padover ed., 1953), letter to James Monroe, Oct. 15, 1786.
4. FEDERALIST NO. 48, at 309 (J. Madison). (All citations of THE FEDERALIST PA-
   PERS herein refer to the Clinton Rossiter edition of 1961.)
5. 1 THE RECORDS OF THE FEDERAL CONVENTION OF 1787, at 450 (Max Farrand ed.,
   1911).
6. Padover, *supra* note 3, at 267–68, remarks published in NATIONAL GAZETTE, Mar.
   29, 1792.
7. *Id.* at 268–69.
8. William M. Treanor, *The Origins and Original Significance of the Just Compensation Clause of the Fifth Amendment,* 94 YALE L.J. 694, 710 (1985).
9. 1 ANNALS of CONGRESS 431–32 (J. Gales ed., 1834). This is one of a series of
   amendments Madison proposed that later became the Bill of Rights. He drafted the
   changes in the form of amendments to specific sections of the Constitution. Congress changed the form into a Bill of Rights, omitting Madison's introductory language.
10. 1 Farrand, *supra* note 5, at 533–34.
11. 2 U.S. (2 Dall.) 304, 310 (1795).
12. 1 Farrand, *supra* note 5, at 533–34; 541–42; 469–76; 528; 542; 2 *id.* at 202.
13. ROBERT A. HENDRICKSON, THE RISE AND FALL OF ALEXANDER HAMILTON 214
    (1985).
14. 1 Farrand, *supra* note 5, at 605.
15. Stanley N. Katz, *Thomas Jefferson and the Right to Property in Revolutionary
    America,* 19 J. L. & Econ. 467, 469–70 (1976).
16. FEDERALIST NO. 79, at 472 (A. Hamilton).
17. D. BOORSTIN, THE MYSTERIOUS SCIENCE OF THE LAW at 3 (1941) (quoting C.
    WARREN, HISTORY OF THE AMERICAN BAR at 187 [1911]).
18. DAVID LOCKMILLER, SIR WILLIAM BLACKSTONE 174 (1938).
19. Robert E. Riggs, *Substantive Due Process in 1791,* 1990 WISC. L. REV. 941, 992.
20. W. J. Brockelbank, *The Role of Due Process in American Constitutional Law,* 39
    CORNELL L.Q. 561, 562 (1954).
21. *See* GORDON S. WOOD, THE CREATION OF THE AMERICAN REPUBLIC 1776–1787,
    283, 601 (1969).
22. John Locke, *Second Treatise* § 124, *in* LOCKE, TWO TREATISES OF GOVERNMENT
    (Peter Laslett ed., Cambridge University Press 1960).
23. *Id.* at § 137.
24. *Id.* at § 138. Locke did not require actual consent of the owner and accepted in-

stead tacit consent (*id.* at § 119), a position which is inconsistent with the idea of a limited government. *See* RICHARD EPSTEIN, TAKINGS, 14 (1985) and Note, *Richard Epstein on the Foundations of Takings Jurisprudence,* 99 HARVARD L. REV. 791, 805–7 (1986).

25. Locke, *Second Treatise* § 222.
26. Dr. Bonham's Case, 77 Eng. Rep. 646 (K.B. 1610); 2 EDWARD COKE, INSTITUTES OF THE LAWS OF ENGLAND 46, 47, 50 (1797).
27. 1 WILLIAM BLACKSTONE, COMMENTARIES 134 (1765–69).
28. *Id.* at 135.
29. *Id.* at 134–35.
30. *Id.* at 135.
31. *Id.*
32. 4 BLACKSTONE, COMMENTARIES 167–68; 3 BLACKSTONE, COMMENTARIES 5–6.
33. 1 BLACKSTONE, COMMENTARIES 140.
34. 3 U.S. 386 (1798).
35. *See* SIEGAN, *supra* note 1, at 67–82.
36. Fletcher v. Peck, 10 U.S. 87, 138 (1810).
37. *See* Philip A. Hamburger, *Trivial Rights,* 70 NOTRE DAME L. REV. 7 (1994).
38. 3 Farrand, *supra* note 5, at 435.
39. FEDERALIST NO. 84, at 513 (A. Hamilton).
40. *See* Bernard H. Siegan, *Separation of Powers and Economic Liberties,* 70 NOTRE DAME L. REV. 436–44 (1995).
41. Amendments II, III, IV, V (2 provisions), VII, VIII.
42. *See* Chicago B. & Q. R. Co. v. Chicago, 166 U.S. 226 (1897).
43. FEDERALIST NO. 84, at 515 (A. Hamilton).
44. 1 ANNALS OF CONG. 451–52 (J. Gales ed., 1834).
45. Translations of the Latin original differ. Justice Bradley translated the chapter as follows: "No freeman shall be taken or imprisoned, or be disseised of his freehold or liberties or free customs, or be outlawed or exiled or any otherwise destroyed; nor will we pass upon him or condemn him but by lawful judgment of his peers or by the law of the land." Slaughter-House Cases, 83 U.S. (16 Wall.) 36, 111 (1872) (Bradley, J., dissenting).
46. GEORGE MACAULAY TREVELYAN, A SHORTENED HISTORY OF ENGLAND 132 (1944). *See* RODNEY L. MOTT, DUE PROCESS OF LAW: A HISTORICAL AND ANALYTICAL TREATISE OF THE PRINCIPLES AND METHODS FOLLOWED BY THE COURTS IN THE APPLICATION OF THE CONCEPT OF THE "LAW OF THE LAND" (1926); ERWIN N. GRISWOLD, THE FIFTH AMENDMENT TODAY (1955); Robert E. Riggs, *Substantive Due Process in 1791,* 1990 WISC. L. REV. 941; WILLIAM MCKECHNIE, MAGNA CARTA (2d ed. 1914); J. HOLT, MAGNA CARTA (1965); Powicke, *Per Iudicium Parium Vel Per Legem Terrae,* in MAGNA CARTA COMMEMORATION ESSAYS (H. Malden ed., 1917).
47. Wynehamer v. People, 13 N.Y. 378, 433 (1856) (per Selden, J.). This is a famous and important property case, discussed in Section V *infra.*
48. 28 Edw. III, C.3 (1354). The change also imposed a judicial role in enforcing the guarantee.
49. 4 BLACKSTONE, COMMENTARIES 417.
50. *Id.*

51. 1 BLACKSTONE, COMMENTARIES 119–41. Absolute rights could not be limited except in accordance with the law of the land.
52. *Id.* at 140.
53. *Id.* at 122.
54. *Id.*
55. *Id.* at 140.
56. 2 EDWARD COKE, INSTITUTES OF THE LAWS OF ENGLAND 45–47, 50 (1628–44).
57. *Id.*
58. *Id.* Technically speaking, the case disallowed the king's grant of a "Letters patent," an exclusive right to make, use, and sell one's creation or invention.
59. *Id.* at 47.
60. *Id.* at 50.
61. Dr. Bonham's Case, 77 Eng. Rep. 646 (K.B. 1610).
62. Chaplinsky v. State of New Hampshire, 315 U.S. 568 (1942).
63. THE BILL OF RIGHTS AND THE STATES 362 (P. T. Conley and J. P. Kaminski eds., 1992). According to Dumbauld, "of the twenty-two amendments, which were supported by four or more states, fourteen were incorporated by Madison." E. DUMBAULD, THE BILL OF RIGHTS AND WHAT IT MEANS TODAY 33 (1957).
64. Tansill, *supra* note 1, at 1027–33.
65. *Id.* at 1052–59.
66. *Id.* at 1034–44.
67. 4 THE PAPERS OF ALEXANDER HAMILTON 35 (H. Syrett and J. Cooke eds., 1962); emphasis is in the original. By "process and proceedings" Hamilton meant judicial actions, as is apparent from the text accompanying notes 68–70 *infra.*
68. *See* Douglas Laycock, *Due Process and the Separation of Powers: The Effort to Make the Due Process Clause Nonjusticiable,* 64 TEX. L. REV. 875, 891 (1982). *See* Riggs, *supra* note 46, at 989–90.
69. Syrett and Cooke, *supra* note 67, at 35.
70. Conley and Kaminski, *supra* note 63, at 362.
71. Calder v. Bull, 3 U.S. 386, 400 (1798).
72. 1 ANNALS OF CONG. 431–32 (J. Gales ed., 1834).
73. Tansill, *supra* note 1, at 47–54.
74. 1 ANNALS OF CONG. 431–32 (J. Gales ed., 1834).
75. Armstrong v. United States, 364 U.S. 40, 49 (1960).
76. Calder v. Bull, 3 U.S. 386 (1798).
77. 10 U.S. (6 Cr.) 87 (1810).
78. *Id.* at 139.
79. *Id.* at 135–36.
80. 10 U.S. at 143 (Johnson, J., concurring).
81. 13 U.S. (9 Cranch) 43 (1815).
82. *Id.* at 50–51.
83. 27 U.S. 627 (1829).
84. *Id.* at 657.
85. Bank of Columbia v. Okely, 17 U.S. (4 Wheat.) 235, 244 (1819).
86. 59 U.S. 272 (1856).
87. *Id.* at 276.
88. *Id.*

89. *Id.* at 280. The citations omitted in the text are: 2 COKE, INSTITUTES 47, 50; Hoke v. Henderson, 4 Dev. N.C. Rep. 15 (N.C. 1833); Taylor v. Porter, 4 Hill 146 (N.Y. 1843); Vanzant v. Waddel, 2 Yerger 260 (Tenn. 1829); State Bank v. Cooper, 2 Yerger 599 (Tenn. 1831); Jones' Heirs v. Perry, 10 Yerger 59 (Tenn. 1836); Greene v. Briggs, 1 Curtis 311 (Fed. Cir. Ct. RI 1852).

90. *See* notes 67–70 *supra* and accompanying text.

91. 59 U.S. at 280.

92. 10 F.Cas. 1135 (Cir.Ct.D. Rhode Island 1852).

93. *Id.* at 1140, citing Hoke v. Henderson, 15 N.C. Reports 1 (1833); Taylor v. Porter, 4 Hill (N.Y.) 140 (1843); 3 JOSEPH STORY, COMMENTARIES ON THE CONSTITUTION OF THE UNITED STATES 661 (1833); and 2 JAMES KENT, COMMENTARIES ON AMERICAN LAW 13n. (1826).

94. 1 S.C.L. (1 Bay) 252 (1792).

95. *Id.* at 254.

96. Zylstra v. Corporation of Charleston, 1 S.C.L. (1 Bay) 382 (1794), and Lindsay v. Commissioners, 2 S.C.L. (2 Bay) 38 (1796).

97. 10 Va. (6 Call) 113 (1804). The statutory provision that was challenged in this case was not overturned, because the court was evenly divided on that question.

98. Trustee of the University of North Carolina v. Foy and Bishop, 5 N.C. (1 Mur.) 58 (1805).

99. *Id.* at 89.

100. 2 Johns. Ch. 162 (N.Y. 1816).

101. *Id.* at 164.

102. *Id.*

103. 15 N.C. Reports 1 (1833).

104. *Id.* at 13–14.

105. 4 Hill (N.Y.) 140, 145 (1843).

106. 13 N.Y. 378 (1856). This decision was not followed in other states, probably for the most part because of the sensitivity of the liquor issue. For a survey of pre–Fourteenth Amendment cases involving due process or law of the land provisions, *see* SIEGAN, *supra* note 1, at 24–46.

107. 13 N.Y. at 393 (per Comstock, J.). "[B]oth courts and commentators in this country have held that these clauses [law of the land and due process], in either form, secure to every citizen a judicial trial, before he can be deprived of life, liberty or property [citation of decisions]. . . . It follows that a law which should provide in regard to any article in which the right of property is recognized, that it should neither be sold or used, nor kept in any place whatsoever within this state, would fall directly within the letter of the constitutional inhibition; as it would in the most effectual manner possible deprive the owner of his property, without the interposition of any court or the use of any process whatever." *Id.* at 433–34.

108. EDWARD CORWIN, LIBERTY AGAINST GOVERNMENT 114–15 (1948).

109. 2 JAMES KENT, COMMENTARIES ON AMERICAN LAW 340–47 (1826).

110. *Id.* at 256–57.

111. *Id.* at 13.

112. Gardner v. Trustees of the Village of Newburgh, 2 Johns. Ch. 162 (N.Y. 1816).

113. 2 KENT, COMMENTARIES 340–47.

114. CONG. GLOBE, 35th Cong., 2d Sess. 983 (1859).

115. *Id.* at 985.
116. Adamson v. California, 332 U.S. 46, 74 (1947) (Black, J., dissenting).
117. CONG. GLOBE, 35th Cong., 2d Sess. 983, 985 (1859); CONG. GLOBE, 34th Cong., 3d Sess. App. 140 (1857).
118. CONG. GLOBE, 39th Cong., 1st Sess. 1094 (1866).
119. *See* notes 67–70 *supra* and accompanying text.
120. For a summary (from different perspectives) of the congressional debates relating to Section 1, *see* Charles Fairman, *Does the Fourteenth Amendment Incorporate the Bill of Rights?* 2 STANFORD L. REV. 5 (1949), and William W. Crosskey, *Charles Fairman, "Legislative History," and the Constitutional Limitations of State Authority,* 22 U. CHICAGO L. REV. 1 (1954).
121. *See* Section VIII *infra.*
122. CONG. GLOBE, 39th Cong., 1st Sess. 1294 (1866).
123. CONG. GLOBE, 39th Cong., 1st Sess. 1152 (1866).
124. *Id.* App. at 256.
125. *Id.* at 2961, 2510.
126. *Id.* at 1063.
127. JACOBUS TENBROEK, EQUAL UNDER LAW 119–22 (1969); Alfred H. Kelly, *The Fourteenth Amendment Reconsidered,* 54 MICH. L. REV. 1053–55 (1956).
128. HOWARD JAY GRAHAM, EVERYMAN'S CONSTITUTION 250 (1968).
129. TenBroek, *supra* note 127, at 121. "In comparison with the concept of equal protection of the law, the due process clause was of secondary importance to the abolitionists. It did, however, reach a full development, and by virtue of its emphasis in the party platforms, a widespread usage and popular understanding." *Id.* at 119–20.
130. *Id.* at 139. The Liberty Party was formed in 1840 and dedicated to antislavery. In 1844, its presidential candidate received 60,000 votes. It continued to be strong in local elections in 1846, but united in 1848 with the antislavery Whigs and Democrats to form the Free Soil Party. COLUMBIA ENCYCLOPEDIA 1212 (1963).
131. TenBroek, *supra* note 127, at 140–41, nn. 3 and 4. The Free Soil Party came into existence during 1847–48 and polled 300,000 votes. Its 1852 candidate for president received over 150,000 votes. It was absorbed into the new Republican Party in 1854. COLUMBIA ENCYCLOPEDIA, *supra* note 130, at 767.
132. TenBroek, *supra* note 127, at 141, nn. 5 and 6.
133. Graham, *supra* note 128, at 80.
134. Dred Scott v. Sandford, 60 U.S. 393 (1857).
135. *Id.* at 450.
136. Bloomer v. McQuewan, 55 U.S. 539 (1853).
137. Baltimore v. Pittsburgh & C.R. Co., 2 F. Cas. 570 (C.C.W.D. Pa., 1865) (No. 827).
138. 75 U.S. 603 (1870). Justice Grier was no longer a member of the Court when this decision was handed down, but he had been when the case was decided in conference on November 27, 1869, at which time he concurred with the majority.
139. *Id.* at 624.
140. 79 U.S. 457 (1871).
141. *Id.* at 570.
142. 83 U.S. 36 (1872). (In *Knox,* Bradley filed a concurring opinion, arguing that Congress had full power to enact the disputed legislation. He did not discuss due

process directly. Presumably, Swayne agreed, although he did not file a separate opinion in either *Knox* or *Hepburn*.)

143. CONG. GLOBE, 39th Cong., 1st Sess. 1089 (1866).
144. Vanzant v. Waddel, 2 Yerger 260 (1829).
145. Wally v. Kennedy, 2 Yerger 554 (1831).
146. 83 U.S. 36 (1872). Clint Bolick and Bill Mellor of the Institute for Justice, Washington, D.C., have aptly referred to the decision as the *Plessy v. Ferguson* of economic liberties law.
147. 83 U.S. at 53.
148. 6 F. Cas. 546 (C.C.E.D. Pa, 1823) (No. 3,230).
149. *Id*. at 551–52.
150. 83 U.S. at 78.
151. *Id*. at 80–81. Justice Miller's assertions that the restraints imposed on the butchers of New Orleans were not deprivations of property within the meaning of a due process clause should not be construed as indicating that his position was not favorable to the constitutional protection of property. That Miller was inclined to support such protection is revealed by his decision in a case that was submitted in briefs at the time that *Slaughter-House* was argued but that was not decided until the following year: Bartemeyer v. Iowa, 85 U.S. 129 (1873). In this case, Iowa's statewide prohibition law, which had been enacted in 1851, came under attack as a violation of due process. Miller wrote that a statute prohibiting the sale of property would raise "very grave questions" under the Fourteenth Amendment's due process clause. However, according to Miller, the Iowa case did not present this issue, for it was "absurd to suppose that the plaintiff, an ordinary retailer of drinks, could have proved [in 1870] . . . that he had owned that particular glass of whisky prior to the prohibitor liquor law of 1851." *Id*. at 135. Miller again acknowledged the substantive aspects of the clause in an 1877 decision in which he asserted:

> It seems to us that a statute which declares in terms, and without more, that the full and exclusive title of a described piece of land, which is now in A., shall be and is hereby vested in B., would, if effectual, deprive A of his property without due process of law, within the meaning of the constitutional provision. Davidson v. New Orleans, 96 U.S. 97 (1877).

In *Pumpelly v. Green Bay Co.*, Miller wrote the opinion supporting an inverse condemnation claim based on an overflow of water on plantiff's property caused by a legislatively authorized construction of a state dam. (This case is discussed in Chapter 4.) He interpreted the takings provision of the Wisconsin Constitution, which was similar to the one in the federal constitution, as applicable to the overflow and rejected the position that the injury sustained was merely consequential and remote. *See* Pumpelly v. Green Bay Co., 80 U.S. 166 (1871). At the time of this decision, most cases in the country on this point were decided contrary to Miller's position.
152. 83 U.S. at 81.
153. *Id*. at 101 (Field, J., dissenting).
154. *Id*. at 122 (Bradley, J., dissenting).

155. *Id.* at 128 (Swayne, J., dissenting).
156. *Id.* at 116, 122 (Bradley, J., dissenting).
157. FEDERALIST NO. 44, at 283 (J. Madison).

Chapter 3. The Judicial Obligation to Protect Liberty

1. Robert Girard, *Constitutional Takings Clauses and the Regulation of Private Land Use,* LAND USE LAW 4 (Nov. 1982).
2. Thomas v. Collins, 323 U.S. 516, 530 (1945).
3. R. H. Coase, *The Market for Goods and the Market for Ideas,* 64 AMER. ECON. REV. 384 (1974).
4. Lucas v. South Carolina Coastal Council, 112 S.Ct. 2886 (1992), discussed in Chapter 5 *infra.*
5. R. S. Radford, *Land Use Regulation and Legal Rhetoric: Broadening the Terms of the Debate,* 21 FORDHAM L.J. 413 (1994). Radford is an attorney employed by the Pacific Legal Foundation, Sacramento, California.
6. Janet McClafferty Dunlap, *This Land Is My Land: The Clash Between Private Property and the Public Interest in Lucas v. South Carolina Coastal Council,* 33 B.C. L. REV. 797, 389 (1992). The comments contained in the text accompanying this note and notes 7–9 are quoted in Radford, *supra* note 5.
7. John M. Payne, *Takings and Environmental Regulations,* 21 REAL EST. L.J. 312, 320 n. 35 (1993).
8. Richard J. Lazarus, *Putting the Correct "Spin" on Lucas,* 45 STAN. L. REV. 1411, 1422 (1993).
9. Judith M. LaBelle, *Takings Law in Light of Lucas v. South Carolina Coastal Council,* 10 PACE ENVTL. L. REV. 73, 83 (1992).
10. FEDERALIST NO. 48, at 309 (J. Madison). (All citations of THE FEDERALIST PAPERS herein refer to the Clinton Rossiter edition of 1961.)
11. *See* introductory discussion in Chapter 2.
12. FEDERALIST NO. 9, at 72–73 (A. Hamilton).
13. GORDON S. WOOD, THE CREATION OF THE AMERICAN REPUBLIC, 1776–1787, at 151 (1969).
14. Quoted by JAMES BRADLEY THAYER, OLIVER WENDELL HOLMES AND FELIX FRANKFURTER ON JOHN MARSHALL 85 (Phoenix ed., Univ. of Chicago Press 1967).
15. Bernard H. Siegan, *Majorities May Limit the People's Liberties Only When Authorized to Do So by the Constitution,* 27 SAN DIEGO L. REV. 309, 334–35 (1990).
16. Slaughter-House Cases, 83 U.S. (16 Wall.) 36, 115 (1873) (Bradley, J., dissenting). "In England, a simple majority of Parliament is capable, with the assent of the Crown, of carrying out any constitutional change, however revolutionary; and the House of Commons, in practice, has absorbed to itself all the main power in the Constitution. . . . The Royal veto has become wholly obsolete. The Royal power under all normal circumstances is being exercised at the dictation of a ministry which owes its being to the majority of the House of Commons. . . . The House of Lords has, it is true, greater power, and can still, by a suspensive veto,

delay great changes until they are directly sanctioned by the constituencies at an election." 1 WILLIAM EDWARD HARTPOLE LECKY, DEMOCRACY AND LIBERTY 56 (1896). "But from 1869 onwards no King, not even George III in his youth, ever attempted to govern without Parliament, or contrary to the votes of the House of Commons." GEORGE MACAULAY TREVELYAN, A SHORTENED HISTORY OF ENGLAND 335 (1942).

17. BERNARD BAILYN, THE IDEOLOGICAL ORIGINS OF THE AMERICAN REVOLUTION (1967).

18. *See* Wood, *supra* note 13, at 9–13, and Gary J. Schmitt and Robert H. Webking, *Revolutionaries, Antifederalists, and Federalists: Comments on Gordon Wood's Understanding of the American Founding,* 9 THE POLITICAL SCIENCE REVIEWER 195 (1979).

19. FEDERALIST NOS. 47, 48, 49, 50, and 51 (J. Madison).

20. FEDERALIST NO. 47, at 301 (J. Madison).

21. *Id.*

22. *Id.*

23. FEDERALIST NO. 51, at 320 (J. Madison).

24. *Id.* at 321–22.

25. *See* note 10 *supra* and accompanying text.

26. FEDERALIST NO. 51, at 322 (J. Madison).

27. 2 THE RECORDS OF THE FEDERAL CONVENTION OF 1787, at 74 (Max Farrand ed., rev. ed. 1937).

28. THE FORGING OF AMERICAN FEDERALISM: SELECTED WRITINGS OF JAMES MADISON 45 (Saul K. Padover ed., 1965).

29. Letter from Madison to Jefferson (Oct. 17, 1788), reprinted in 1 BERNARD SCHWARTZ, THE BILL OF RIGHTS: A DOCUMENTARY HISTORY 616 (1971).

30. FEDERALIST NO. 10, at 79 (J. Madison).

31. SOL BLOOM, THE STORY OF THE CONSTITUTION 141 (1937).

32. INS v. Chada, 462 U.S. 919, 959 (1983).

33. John Locke, *Second Treatise* § 222, *in* LOCKE, TWO TREATISES OF GOVERNMENT (Peter Laslett ed., Cambridge University Press 1960).

34. *See* ADAM SMITH, AN INQUIRY INTO THE NATURE AND CAUSES OF THE WEALTH OF NATIONS (The Modern Library 1937). Originally published in 1776, this work considerably influenced thinking during the American revolutionary and constitutional periods.

35. FEDERALIST NO. 10, at 81 (J. Madison).

36. Padover, *supra* note 28, at 267–68. (National Gazette, March 29, 1792.)

37. *Id.* at 268.

38. *Id.* at 269. Stated in First Congress, April 9, 1789.

39. *See generally* discussions about Blackstone and Coke in Chapter 2 *supra.*

40. 1 PHILIP B. KURLAND AND RALPH LERNER, THE FRAMERS' CONSTITUTION 323 (Univ. of Chicago Press 1987).

41. FEDERALIST NO. 6, at 56–57 (A. Hamilton).

42. FEDERALIST NO. 78, at 466 (A. Hamilton).

43. CHARLES GROVE HAINES, THE AMERICAN DOCTRINE OF JUDICIAL SUPREMACY 209–10 (1959).

44. FEDERALIST NO. 78, at 469–70 (A. Hamilton).
45. *See* discussion on Blackstone and Coke in Chapter 2 *supra*.
46. 3 THE DEBATES IN THE SEVERAL STATE CONVENTIONS ON THE ADOPTION OF THE FEDERAL CONSTITUTION 348 (Jonathan Elliot ed., 2d ed. 1901).
47. 1 PAPERS OF ALEXANDER HAMILTON 122 (H. Syrett and J. Cooke eds., 1961).
48. BENJAMIN WRIGHT, THE CONTRACT CLAUSE OF THE CONSTITUTION 22 (1938). The quote is from an opinion written by Hamilton relating to the matter subsequently litigated in Fletcher v. Peck, 10 U.S. (6 Cranch) 87 (1810).
49. FEDERALIST NO. 44, at 286 (J. Madison).
50. *Id.* at 282. The clauses were inserted, according to Madison, because our "own experience has taught us . . . that additional fences against these dangers ought not to be omitted." *Id.*
51. 2 Farrand, *supra* note 27, at 376.
52. *Id.*
53. D. CRUMP, E. GRESSMAN, AND S. REISS, CASES AND MATERIALS ON CONSTITUTIONAL LAW 519–20 (1989).
54. 1 ANNALS of CONGRESS 456 (J. Gales and Seaton eds., 1834) (Speech of J. Madison). This passage follows the ones quoted in the text accompanying the next two footnotes, in which Madison refers to protecting unspecified rights, warranting the conclusion that he looked to the judiciary to protect rights, whether or not they were enumerated.
55. *Id.*
56. *Id.* at 435.
57. U.S. Constitution, Amendment IX.
58. FRIEDRICH A. HAYEK, THE CONSTITUTION OF LIBERTY 187 (1960).
59. Marbury v. Madison, 5 U.S. 137, 178 (1803).
60. Dred Scott v. Sandford, 60 U.S. 393 (1857).
61. CONGRESSIONAL GLOBE, 39th Cong., 1st Sess. 2765 (1866).
62. "Dicta" is a judicial assertion that is not binding as a matter of precedent.
63. CONG. GLOBE, 39th Cong., 1st Sess. at 2542.
64. In speeches he presented before Congress in 1857 and 1859, Bingham articulated his views on the issues with which the three major guarantees of Section 1 are concerned. *See* CONG. GLOBE, 34th Cong., 3d Sess. App. 135 (1857), and CONG. GLOBE, 35th Cong., 2d Sess. 981 (1859).
65. *See* Chapter 2, note 149 *supra* and accompanying text.
66. CONG. GLOBE, 39th Cong., 1st Sess. 2765–66 (1866).
67. *Id.* at 2459.
68. *See* BERNARD H. SIEGAN, THE SUPREME COURT'S CONSTITUTION 41–93 (1987).
69. 3 Farrand, *supra* note 27, at 435.
70. Wood, *supra* note 13, at 538.
71. 3 Elliott, *supra* note 46, at 620.
72. FEDERALIST NO. 84, at 513 (A. Hamilton).
73. *Id.* at 515.
74. *Id.* at 513–14.
75. PENNSYLVANIA AND THE FEDERAL CONSTITUTION 1787–1788, at 308–9 (J. McMaster and F. Stone eds., 1988).

76. FEDERALIST NO. 78, at 470 (A. Hamilton).

77. Wood, *supra* note 13, at 10.

78. *See* SYLVIA SNOWISS, JUDICIAL REVIEW AND THE LAW OF THE CONSTITUTION 13–44 (1990); Haines, *supra* note 43, at 89–112; 2 WILLIAM CROSSKEY, POLITICS AND THE CONSTITUTION 938–75 (1953).

79. Calder v. Bull, 3 U.S. (3 Dall.) 386, 387–89 (1798).

80. *Id.* at 388.

81. *See* LAURENCE H. TRIBE, AMERICAN CONSTITUTIONAL LAW 428–29 (1978).

82. *See* Griswold v. Connecticut, 381 U.S. 479 (1965) (majority opinion of Douglas, J., and dissenting opinion of Black, J.).

83. 6 F. Cas. 546 (C.C.E.D. Pa. 1823) (No. 3,230).

84. *Id.* at 551.

85. *Id.*

86. Dash v. Van Kleeck, 7 Johns. 477, 505 (N.Y. 1811).

87. *See* PAUL BREST AND SANFORD LEVINSON, PROCESSES OF CONSTITUTIONAL DECISIONMAKING 116 (2d ed. 1983).

88. Edward Corwin, *The Basic Doctrine of American Constitutional Law,* 12 MICH. L. REV. 247 (1914).

89. J. A. C. Grant, *The Natural Law Background of Due Process,* 31 COLUM. L. REV. 56 (1931).

90. Separation of powers restricts the judiciary solely to negative powers over legislation and regulation; the judiciary has no authority to impose affirmative mandates: "[O]ur cases have recognized that the Due Process Clauses generally confer no affirmative right to governmental aid, even where such aid may be necessary to secure life, liberty, or property interests of which the government itself may not deprive the individual." DeShaney v. Winnebago County Dep't of Social Servs., 489 U.S. 189, 196 (1989). "Although the liberty protected by the Due Process Clauses affords protection against unwarranted government interference . . . it does not confer an entitlement to such [governmental aid] as may be necessary to realize all the advantages of that freedom." Harris v. McRae, 448 U.S. 297, 317–18 (1980); *see* Maher v. Roe, 432 U.S. 464 (1977); BERNARD H. SIEGAN, ECONOMIC LIBERTIES AND THE CONSTITUTION 304–17 (1981). *Contra:* Plyler v. Doe, 457 U.S. 202 (1982); Shapiro v. Thompson, 394 U.S. 618 (1969).

91. Marbury v. Madison, 5 U.S. (1 Cranch) 137 (1803).

92. Calder v. Bull, 3 U.S. (3 Dall.) 386, 388–89 (1798).

93. Patterson v. Colorado, 205 U.S. 454 (1907).

94. 4 WILLIAM BLACKSTONE, COMMENTARIES 151–52 (1765–69).

95. Schenck v. United States, 249 U.S. 47 (1919). *See* Robert Bork, *Neutral Principles and Some First Amendment Problems,* 47 IND. L.J. 1 (1971), for discussion of the relation between the Framers' views and those of Justice Louis Brandeis on free expression.

96. New York Times Co. v. Sullivan, 376 U.S. 254 (1964).

97. *See* New York Times Co. v. United States, 403 U.S. 713 (1971). This is the Pentagon Papers case, in which the executive department sought to obtain an injunction from the judicial department. Congress had not enacted any legislation relating to the matter.

98. Brandenberg v. Ohio, 395 U.S. 444, 447 (1969).

99. Texas v. Johnson, 491 U.S. 397 (1989).

100. 425 U.S. 748 (1976).

101. *Id.* at 756.

102. *Id.* at 763–64.

103. *Id.* at 765, 763, 769, 770.

104. 116 S.Ct. 1495 (1996).

105. *Id.* at 1508.

106. *Id.*

107. Roe v. Wade, 410 U.S. 113 (1973). *But see* Planned Parenthood of Southeastern Pennsylvania v. Casey, 112 S.Ct. 2791 (1992).

108. Shapiro v. Thompson, 394 U.S. 618, 630 (1969).

109. 404 U.S. 71 (1971).

110. Craig v. Boren, 429 U.S. 190, 197 (1976).

111. 381 U.S. 479 (1965).

112. *Id.* at 484.

113. *Id.*

114. *Id.* at 485.

115. *Id.*

116. 1 BLACKSTONE, COMMENTARIES, at 91.

117. *Id.* at 121–22.

118. 381 U.S. at 610 (Black, J., dissenting).

119. However, Justice Black himself at times argued for a broad defense of rights without much basis in constitutional text or history. For example, nowhere in the Constitution does it state that freedom of expression is absolute and subject at most only to minor limitations. As previously explained, this was not the meaning of free expression at the time the First Amendment was framed. Yet this was the position long taken by Justice Black. The justice also concluded that the First Amendment establishes a wall of separation between church and state, a view that is clearly not evident from the language or history of the amendment's establishment clause. I suggest that the position that an excessive or seriously overinclusive law is invalid under the constitution is entitled to more support than either one of Black's interpretations. *See* JUSTICE HUGO BLACK AND THE FIRST AMENDMENT (Dennis, Gillmor, and Grey eds., 1978), and Justice William Rehnquist's dissenting opinion in Wallace v. Jaffree, 472 U.S. 38 (1985).

120. ROBERT BORK, SLOUCHING TOWARDS GOMORRAH 117 (1996).

Chapter 4. Major Takings Cases Prior to 1987

1. A position endorsed by the Presidential Commission on Housing, on which I served. REPORT OF THE PRESIDENT'S COMMISSION ON HOUSING 201–2 (1982).

2. 272 U.S. 365 (1926).

3. 123 U.S. 623 (1887).

4. 123 U.S. at 665.

5. 276 U.S. 272, 280 (1928).

6. 272 U.S. at 388.
7. 447 U.S. 255 (1980).
8. 328 U.S. 256 (1946).
9. 328 U.S. at 260.
10. 328 U.S. at 261.
11. 458 U.S. 419 (1982).
12. 458 U.S. at 434–35, citing Penn Central Transp. Co. v. City of New York, 438 U.S. 104, 124 (1978).
13. 450 U.S. 621 (1981).
14. 450 U.S. at 653.
15. 450 U.S. at 633.
16. 80 U.S. 166 (1871).
17. The U.S. Supreme Court did not adjudicate this case under the due process clause of the Fourteenth Amendment. Acknowledging that the case only related to the takings provision of the Wisconsin Constitution, the opinion said that the Wisconsin provision is "almost identical in language" to the Fifth Amendment's takings provision:

> Indeed this limitation on the exercise of the right of eminent domain is so essentially a part of American constitutional law that it is believed that no State is now without it, and the only question that we are to consider is whether the injury to plaintiff's property, as set forth in his declaration, is within its protection. (80 U.S. at 177)

However, the Green Bay Company asserted a federal connection. It claimed that under federal legislation the river bordering the Pumpelly land was to be forever preserved as a navigable stream and adjoining land burdened with an easement in favor of maintaining the river in this condition. The U.S. Supreme Court rejected this claim.
18. 80 U.S. at 177–78.
19. 17 N.J.L. 129 (1839).
20. *Id.* at 145.
21. Gardner v. Trustees of the Village of Newburgh, 2 Johns. Ch. 162 (N.Y. 1816). See discussion of this decision in Chapter 2 *supra.*
22. 80 U.S. at 180–81.
23. 80 U.S. at 181.
24. Loretto v. Teleprompter Manhattan CATV Corp., 458 U.S. 419 (1982).
25. Nollan v. California Coastal Commission, 483 U.S. 825 (1987).
26. Lucas v. South Carolina Coastal Council, 505 U.S. 1003 (1992).
27. 123 U.S. 623 (1887).
28. *Id.* at 661.
29. *Id.* at 661–62.
30. Bartemeyer v. Iowa, 85 U.S. 129 (1873); Boston Beer Co. v. Massachusetts, 97 U.S. 25 (1877); Foster v. Kansas, 112 U.S. 201 (1884).
31. *See* definition and discussion of common-law nuisances in Chapter 5, Section IVC *infra.*

32. EDWARD S. CORWIN, LIBERTY AGAINST GOVERNMENT 107 (1948). Indiana courts initially held a prohibition statute void but later reversed this decision. *Id.*

33. 123 U.S. at 668–69.

34. *Id.* at 663. Citing Barbier v. Connolly, 113 U.S. 27, 31 (1884).

35. Wilkinson v. Leland, 27 U.S. 627, 657 (1829).

36. License cases, 46 U.S. 504 (1847).

37. *See* Commonwealth v. Algers, 7 Cush. 53 at 85 (1851).

38. Lochner v. New York, 198 U.S. 45 (1905).

39. 198 U.S. at 56. Quoted approvingly by Justice Sutherland writing for the majority in Adkins v. Children's Hospital, 261 U.S. 525 (1923). The justice made no reference to it in *Euclid. See* Section IV *infra.*

40. 198 U.S. at 57–58. While the *Lochner* decision has been reversed, this kind of test is applied currently in property cases, as explained in Chapter 5. My book ECONOMIC LIBERTIES AND THE CONSTITUTION (1981) contains a discussion of the Supreme Court's liberty-of-contract jurisprudence.

41. 245 U.S. 60, 74 (1917).

42. Gitlow v. New York, 268 U.S. 652 (1925).

43. 268 U.S. at 668, 669.

44. 395 U.S. 444 (1969).

45. 1 RODNEY A. SMOLLA, SMOLLA AND NIMMER ON FREEDOM OF SPEECH, § 10:11 at 10–15 (3d ed. 1996).

46. 260 U.S. 393 (1922).

47. 260 U.S. at 415–16.

48. 260 U.S. at 414.

49. 260 U.S. at 415–416.

50. 260 U.S. at 417–18.

51. 260 U.S. at 414.

52. 260 U.S. at 413.

53. 260 U.S. at 413.

54. *See* Holmes's dissents in Abrams v. United States, 260 U.S. 616, 624 (1919), and Gitlow v. New York, 268 U.S. 652, 672 (1925).

55. 260 U.S. at 415.

56. 1 HOLMES-LASKI LETTERS 473 (Howe ed., 1953).

57. 272 U.S. 365 (1926).

58. Ambler Realty Co. v. Village of Euclid, 297 F. 307 (1924).

59. 297 F. at 309, 313.

60. 297 F. at 314.

61. 297 F. at 316.

62. 272 U.S. at 387.

63. 272 U.S. at 390.

64. 272 U.S. at 389–90.

65. Southern Pacific Co. v. Arizona, 325 U.S. 761 (1945); South Carolina State Highway Department v. Barnwell Bros., 303 U.S. 177 (1938).

66. 325 U.S. at 767–68 n. 2.

67. Bonaparte v. Tax Court, 104 U.S. 592, 596 (1881).

68. *See* Raymond Motor Transportation, Inc. v. Rice, 434 U.S. 429 (1978); Hunt v.

Washington State Apple Advertising Commission, 432 U.S. 333 (1977); Hughes v. Oklahoma, 441 U.S. 322 (1979); Carbone v. Clarkstown, 114 S.Ct. 1677 (1994).

69. Adkins v. Children's Hospital, 261 U.S. 525 (1923). This case was reversed in Morehead v. New York *ex rel.* Tipaldo, 298 U.S. 587 (1936).
70. New State Ice Company v. Liebmann, 285 U.S. 262 (1932).
71. 261 U.S. at 548–49.
72. 261 U.S. at 561.
73. 285 U.S. 262 (1932).
74. 285 U.S. at 278, citing two cases.
75. Construction Industry Ass'n v. City of Petaluma, 522 F.2d 897 (9th Cir. 1975), *cert. denied,* 424 U.S. 934 (1976). The federal court that asserted this view made no ruling with respect to the rights of nonresidents, although it held that the rights of builders and landowners were not violated, that their remedy would have to come from the state legislature.
76. 18 Cal.3d 582 (1976).
77. Southern Burlington County NAACP v. Township of Mount Laurel, 67 N.J. 151 (1975), 336 A. 2d 713, 730 (1975).
78. National Land and Investment Co. v. Kohn, 419 Pa. 504 (1965); Appeal of Kit-Mar Builders, 439 Pa. 466 (1970); Appeal of Girsh, 437 Pa. 237 (1970).
79. See D. R. MANDELKER, R. A. CUNNINGHAM, AND J. M. PAYNE, PLANNING AND CONTROL OF LAND DEVELOPMENT 89 (4th ed. 1995).
80. 272 U.S. at 388.
81. *See* notes 87, 88, and 89 *infra* and related text.
82. 272 U.S. at 394–95.
83. The passage quoted above is the kind of "archaic and overbroad generalization" that the Court in later years asserted was responsible for discriminatory gender legislation, and the Court would reject it as being part of the "baggage of sexual stereotypes." Judges should be bound by facts, not broad generalizations. See Califano v. Westcott, 443 U.S. 76 (1979); Mississippi v. Hogan, 458 U.S. 718 (1982).
84. *See* discussion of Houston in Chapter 7, Section VII *infra.*
85. *See* discussion of Houston's system of non-zoning in Chapter 7, Section VII *infra.*
86. 270 U.S. 402 (1926).
87. 270 U.S. at 412.
88. Andrew Cappel, *A Walk Along Willow: Patterns of Land Use Coordination in Pre-Zoning New Haven (1870–1926), in* PERSPECTIVES ON PROPERTY LAW 439 (Bruce A. Ackerman et al. eds., 1995).
89. *Id.* at 453.
90. 274 U.S. 71 (1927).
91. 274 U.S. 603 (1927).
92. 277 U.S. 183 (1928).
93. 277 U.S. at 188.
94. 277 U.S. at 188–89.
95. 278 U.S. 116 (1928).
96. 278 U.S. at 117.
97. 278 U.S. at 122.

98. Eubank v. City of Richmond, 226 U.S. 137 (1912); Cusack v. City of Chicago, 242 U.S. 526 (1917).
99. John Locke, *Second Treatise* § 141, in LOCKE, TWO TREATISES OF GOVERNMENT (Peter Laslett ed., Cambridge University Press 1960).
100. 278 U.S. at 121.
101. *Id.* Justice Sutherland filed no opinion in the case.
102. 276 U.S. 272 (1928).
103. Justice Holmes, the author of *Pennsylvania Coal,* was a member of the Court that decided *Schoene,* but did not file an opinion.
104. 276 U.S. at 280.
105. 276 U.S. at 280.
106. 458 U.S. 419 (1982).
107. 458 U.S. at 435.
108. 328 U.S. 256 (1946).

Chapter 5. Takings Decisions in 1987 and Subsequent Years

1. *See* Bernard H. Siegan, *The Supreme Court: The Final Arbiter, in* BEYOND THE STATUS QUO (David Boaz and Edward H. Crane eds., 1985).
2. *Preamble,* U.S. CONSTITUTION. One problem with these rules is that they employ a predetermined hierarchy of values to decide the level of protection accorded to various human actions. *See* Siegan, supra note 1.
3. City of Cincinnati v. Discovery Network, Inc., 113 S.Ct. 1505 (1993).
4. Craig v. Boren, 429 U.S. 190 (1976).
5. Adarand Constructors, Inc. v. Pena, 115 S.Ct. 2097 (1995), overruling Metro Broadcasting, Inc. v. F.C.C., 497 U.S. 547 (1990). Since *Adarand,* the level of scrutiny for federal racial preferences has been raised to strict scrutiny (as with state racial preferences). This issue of the level of scrutiny has been highly contentious since the Court heard its first affirmative action case in 1978: Regents of the University of California v. Bakke, 438 U.S. 265 (1978).
6. 447 U.S. 255 (1980). *See* note 7 in Chapter 4 *supra* and relevant text.
7. 447 U.S. at 260.
8. 277 U.S. 183, 188 (1928).
9. 278 U.S. 116, 121 (1928).
10. Dolan v. The City of Tigard, 114 S.Ct. 2309, 2320 (1994).
11. 480 U.S. 470 (1987).
12. 482 U.S. 304 (1987).
13. 483 U.S. 825 (1987).
14. 112 S.Ct. 2886 (1992).
15. 114 S.Ct. 2309 (1994).
16. 114 S.Ct. 2731 (1994).
17. 480 U.S. at 485, citing Agins v. City of Tiburon, 447 U.S. 255, 260 (1980).
18. Pennsylvania Coal Co. v. Mahon, 260 U.S. 393, 413 (1922).
19. Craig v. Boren, 429 U.S. 190 (1976).

20. Cincinnati v. Discovery Network, 113 S.Ct. 1505 (1993). *See* Central Hudson Gas and Electric Corp. v. Public Service Commission of N.Y., 447 U.S. 557 (1980); and Board of Trustees of State University of New York v. Fox, 492 U.S. 469 (1989). The recent case of Florida Bar v. Went For It, 63 USLW 4644 (1995) added a third prong: the regulation must be narrowly drawn. However, Justice Antonin Scalia, writing for the majority in the *Fox* case, considered this test to be included as part of the second prong.

21. 1 WILLIAM BLACKSTONE, COMMENTARIES 121–22 (1765–69).

22. McCulloch v. Maryland, 17 U.S. 316, 421 (1819).

23. FORGING OF AMERICAN FEDERALISM: SELECTED WRITINGS OF JAMES MADISON 268 (Saul K. Padover ed., 1965) (National Gazette, March 29, 1792).

24. *Id.* at 269 (First Congress, April 9, 1789).

25. 480 U.S. at 488–89.

26. The dissenting opinion in *Keystone* concluded that both acts rested on similar public purposes.

27. Pennsylvania Coal Co. v. Mahon, 260 U.S. 393, 415 (1922).

28. 260 U.S. at 416.

29. 480 U.S. at 489, n. 16. Determining legislative purpose does not require the Court to evaluate each legislator's mind at the time he or she voted on a measure. Many factors may explain a legislative decision. An important way to ascertain purpose is by the impact and operation of a statute. *See* Washington v. Davis, 426 U.S. 229 (1976).

30. Lucas v. South Carolina Coastal Council, 112 S.Ct. 2886, 2892, n. 12 (1992). In Maine v. Taylor, 477 U.S. 131 (1986), Justice Stevens quoted from a prior case to the same effect: "[T]hat the ordinance is valid simply because it professes to be a health measure, would mean that the commerce clause itself imposes no restraints . . . save for the rare instances where the state artlessly discloses an avowed purpose to discriminate against interstate goods. Dean Milk v. Madison, 340 U.S. 349, 354 (1951)."

31. 480 U.S. at 489.

32. *See* Regents of the University of California v. Bakke, 438 U.S. 265 (1978).

33. *See* Armstrong v. United States, 364 U.S. 40, 49 (1960). This issue will be discussed in Section IV of this chapter.

34. *See* WILLIAM L. PROSSER, CASES AND MATERIALS ON TORTS 596 (8th ed. 1988) and discussion in Section IV *infra*.

35. 480 U.S. at 492.

36. 480 U.S. at 490.

37. 480 U.S. at 493.

38. 480 U.S. at 488, citing Pennsylvania Statutes Annotated, Tit. 52 § 1406.2 (Purdon Supp. 1986). Under their contracts of sale, the coal companies agreed to provide the surface owners notice at a reasonable time prior to mining, thereby minimizing the threat to personal safety.

39. For a discussion of the distinction between regulations preventing harm and those conferring benefits, *see* analysis of *Lucas* decision, Section IVC *infra*.

40. 480 U.S. at 513.

41. *Id.,* citing Curtin v. Benson, 222 U.S. 78, 86 (1911).

42. The *Keystone* decision concerned only a facial challenge to the Subsidence Act: whether its mere enactment constitutes a taking. The plaintiffs presented no evidence about the actual effects the law had or would have on them. The decision left open for future disposition challenges to the law as applied.

43. FRIEDRICH A. HAYEK, THE CONSTITUTION OF LIBERTY 32 (1978).

44. 480 U.S. at 498.

45. 480 U.S. at 520.

46. Penn Central Transportation Co. v. City of New York, 438 U.S. 104, 130–31 (1978).

47. Lucas v. South Carolina Coastal Council, 112 S.Ct. at 2894, n. 7. This case is discussed in Section IV *infra*.

48. 480 U.S. at 488, n. 18.

49. San Diego Gas & Electric Co. v. City of San Diego, 450 U.S. 621, 652 (1981) (Brennan, J., dissenting).

50. 438 U.S. 104, 129 (1978).

51. 480 U.S. at 517 (Rehnquist, C.J., dissenting).

52. 482 U.S. 304 (1987).

53. *See* San Diego Gas & Electric Co. v. City of San Diego, 450 U.S. 621, 655 (1981) (Brennan, J., dissenting).

54. *Id.* at 655, n. 22.

55. 482 U.S. at 322.

56. 482 U.S. at 319, citing United States v. Causby, 328 U.S. 256, 261 (1946).

57. 112 S.Ct. at 2891.

58. 482 U.S. at 321.

59. Nollan v. California Coastal Commission, 483 U.S. 825, 828–29 (1987).

60. 483 U.S. at 837, citing J.E.D. Associates, Inc. v. Atkinson, 121 N.H. 581, 584 (1981).

61. 483 U.S. at 838.

62. 483 U.S. at 833, n. 2.

63. 483 U.S. at 835, n. 4.

64. *Id.*

65. 483 U.S. at 841.

66. 483 U.S. at 842–43 (Brennan, J., dissenting).

67. 483 U.S. at 846.

68. 483 U.S. at 835, n. 3.

69. "[T]here is no reason to believe (and the language of our cases gives some reasons to disbelieve) that so long as the regulation of property is at issue the standard for takings challenges, due process challenges, and equal protection challenges are identical . . ." (483 U.S. at 834, n. 3).

70. 483 U.S. at 833–34, n. 2.

71. 260 U.S. at 416.

72. Loretto v. Teleprompter Manhattan CATV Corp., 458 U.S. 419 (1982), discussed in Chapter 4.

73. South Carolina Code Annotated § 48-39-250 (Law. Co-op. Supp. 1992).

74. Lucas v. South Carolina Coastal Council, 304 S.C. 376, 383 (1991).

75. *See* RESTATEMENT (SECOND) OF TORTS §§ 826–28.

76. Lucas v. South Carolina Coastal Council, 112 S.Ct. 2886, 2899 (1992).
77. 112 S.Ct. at 2900.
78. 112 S.Ct. at 2900, n. 16. In the balance of this book, I refer to such grave threats as constituting "near-nuisances" because no balancing of interests is required.
79. 112 S.Ct. at 2908 (Blackmun, J., dissenting).
80. Gideon Kanner, *Not with a Bang, but a Giggle: The Settlement of the Lucas Case,* *in* TAKINGS, LAND-DEVELOPMENT CONDITIONS, AND REGULATORY TAKINGS AFTER DOLAN AND LUCAS (David L. Callies ed., 1995).
81. In the words of Justice Stephen Breyer, in an opinion in a 1996 case: "This constitutional concern, itself harkening back to the Magna Carta, arises out of the basic unfairness of depriving citizens of life, liberty, or property, through the application, not of law and legal processes, but of arbitrary concern." BMW of North America, Inc. v. Gore, 116 S.Ct. 1589, 1605 (1996) (Breyer, J., concurring).
82. Loretto v. Teleprompter Manhattan CATV Corp., 458 U.S. 419 (1982).
83. 483 U.S. at 831–32. The easement in *Nollan* was not established on the land by the California Coastal Commission, and therefore was not subject to *Loretto*.
84. 480 U.S. at 485.
85. 112 S.Ct. at 2894, n. 7.
86. 482 U.S. at 322. "Here we must assume the Los Angeles County Ordinance has denied appellant of all use of its property. . . ." *Id.*
87. 112 S.Ct. at 2893. Justice Scalia also refers to the concept as "deprivation of all economically feasible use." *Id.* at 2894, n. 7.
88. 112 S.Ct. at 2919–20 (Stevens, J., dissenting).
89. 112 S.Ct. at 2919, n. 3 (Stevens, J., dissenting), at 2908 (Blackmun, J., dissenting), and at 2925 (statement of Souter, J.).
90. The *Lucas* rule has been interpreted as relevant to partial deprivations. *See* Florida Rock Industries, Inc. v. United States, 18 F.3d 1560 (Fed. Cir. 1994). *See* discussion in Chapter 6, Section XII.
91. *See* Penn Central Transportation Co. v. City of New York, 438 U.S. 104, 127 (1978); *see also* note 124 *infra* and accompanying text.
92. HFH Ltd. v. Superior Court, 15 Cal.3d 508 (1975).

      In 1966, Von's Grocery Co., a supermarket chain in California, and another investor, HFH, agreed to buy 5.8 acres at a major intersection in Cerritos, provided that the property was rezoned for commercial use to permit the development of a shopping center. (It had been zoned for agricultural purposes.) The city reclassified the property as requested and Von's and HFH purchased the property for $388,000. In 1971, the city began to change its position about this zoning. Although the other three corners of the intersection were either classified or used for commercial purposes, Cerritos in 1972 rezoned the property owned by Von and HFH to low density, single-family residential. In their suit, the owners claimed that the value of the property had been reduced to $75,000 and that their development plans were entirely frustrated.
93. 201 N.W.2d 761 (1972). Ronald and Kathryn Just were wage earners of modest means. In April 1961, the Justs purchased thirty-six acres of land in Marinette County, Wisconsin, of which 1,266 feet fronted on Lake Noquebay. They planned to sell most of the land and build a house for themselves on the balance. By 1967, they had made five sales, leaving them a tract fronting about 367 feet on the lake. They wanted to sell

another portion and build a house on the remainder. In 1967, Marinette County adopted an ordinance controlling the use of privately owned shorelands, which forbade the Justs from using their land to construct any residential buildings. The Justs lost their case in the Wisconsin Supreme Court, in an opinion which held that "it is not an unreasonable exercise of [police] power to prevent harm to public rights by limiting the use of private property to its natural uses." 201 N.W.2d at 768.

94. 112 S.Ct. at 2903, concurring in *Lucas.*
95. Wygant v. Jackson Board of Education, 476 U.S. 267, 274 (1986) (race); Simon and Schuster, Inc. v. New York Crime Victims Board, 112 S.Ct. 501, 509 (1991) (expression).
96. 458 U.S. at 426.
97. 492 U.S. 469, 480 (1989). To determine if a sufficient fit exists in commercial-speech cases requires inquiry into whether the government can employ a less-intrusive means. Rubin v. Coors Brewing Co., 115 S.Ct. 1585, 1593–94 (1995).
98. Ralis v. RFE/RL, Inc., 770 F.2d 1121, 1127 (D.C. Cir., 1985).
99. 476 U.S. 267 (1986).
100. 476 U.S. at 282–83.
101. See discussion in BERNARD H. SIEGAN, ECONOMIC LIBERTIES AND THE CONSTITUTION 67–81 (1981).
102. 3 U.S. 386, 400 (1798).
103. Society for the Propagation of the Gospel v. Wheeler, 22 F.Cas. 756, 767 (C.C.D.N.M. 1814) (No. 13,156).
104. 1 BLACKSTONE, COMMENTARIES 46.
105. W. David Slawson, *Constitutional and Legislative Considerations in Retroactive Lawmaking,* 48 CALIFORNIA L. REV. 216, 225 (1960).
106. E. M. Smead, *The Rule against Retroactive Legislation: A Basic Principle of Jurisprudence,* 20 MINN. L. REV. 775, 777 (1936).
107. FORTUNAS DWARRIS, A GENERAL TREATISE ON STATUTES 162 (1885), cited in Bryant Smith, *Retroactive Laws and Vested Rights,* 5 TEXAS L. REV. 231 (1927).
108. Usery v. Turner Elkhorn Mining Co. et al., 428 U.S. 1, 16–17 (1976).
109. BMW of North America, Inc. v. Gore, 116 S.Ct. 1589 (1996).
110. *Id.* at 1598.
111. Edward S. Stimson, *Retroactive Application of Law—A Problem in Constitutional Law,* 30 MICHIGAN L. REV. 30 (1939).
112. 228 U.S. 148 (1913).
113. 228 U.S. 139 (1913).
114. 258 U.S. 338 (1921).
115. *Id.* at 339.
116. United States v. Darusmont, 449 U.S. 292 (1981).
117. Burgess v. Salmon, 97 U.S. 381 (1878).
118. Nichols v. Coolidge, 274 U.S. 531 (1927).
119. Untemeyer v. Anderson, 276 U.S. 440 (1928).
120. Cohan v. Commissioner, 39 F.2d 540 (2d. Cir. Ct. App. 1930).
121. Bennis v. Michigan, 64 U.S.L.W. 4124 (1996) (Stevens, J., dissenting).
122. *See* Siegan, *supra* note 101, at 67–81 (discussions of Framers on meaning of *ex post facto* laws).

123. PAUL A. SAMUELSON, ECONOMICS, AN INTRODUCTORY ANALYSIS 604 (7th ed. 1967).
124. Penn Central Transportation Co. v. City of New York, 438 U.S. 104, 127 (1978).
125. *See* ROBERT C. ELLICKSON AND A. DAN TARLOCK, LAND-USE CONTROLS 203–12 (1981).
126. *See* Lon L. Fuller and William R. Perdue, Jr., *The Reliance Interest in Contract Damages (Parts 1 and 2),* 46 YALE L.J. 52 (1936–37); Michael B. Kelley, *The Phantom Reliance Interest in Contract Damages,* 1992 WISCONSIN L. REV. 1755 (1992); Richard Epstein, *Lucas v. South Carolina Coastal Council: A Tangled Web of Expectations,* 45 STAN. L. REV. 1369, 1379–82 (1993).
127. 112 S.Ct. at 2898.
128. 112 S.Ct. at 2899.
129. Ronald Coase, *The Problem of Social Cost,* 3 J. L. AND ECON. 2 (1960).
130. *Id.* at 44.
131. *Id.* at 27.
132. The common-law definition of nuisance is a form of cost-benefit analysis predicated on the probable existence of an offensive use. *See* notes 137 and 138 *infra* and accompanying text.
133. *See* Chaplinsky v. New Hampshire, 315 U.S. 568 (1942).
134. Brandenburg v. Ohio, 395 U.S. 444 (1969).
135. Texas v. Johnson, 491 U.S. 397 (1989).
136. Miller v. California, 413 U.S. 15 (1973).
137. Restatement (Second) of Torts § 826 (1979).
138. *Id.* at 827.
139. "[W]hen the activity prohibited is a rights violating activity, no compensation is required, for the activity is illegitimate to begin with. . . . [W]hen the activity is legitimate, the state has no right to prohibit it." Roger Pilon, *Property Rights and a Free Society, in* RESOLVING THE HOUSING CRISIS 369, 385–86 (M. Bruce Johnson ed., Ballinger Pub. Co. 1982).
140. Abrams v. United States, 250 U.S. 616 (1919) (Holmes, J., dissenting).
141. As stated in the introduction, the original Constitution, Bill of Rights, and protections of Section 1 of the Fourteenth Amendment are based on this understanding. Six recent recipients of Nobel prizes in economics share this position. They are Friedrich Hayek, Milton Friedman, George Stigler, James Buchanan, Ronald Coase, and Gary Becker. All believe that substantial limitations on government regulatory powers will encourage and enhance economic well-being.
142. Consider the comment of the U.S. Supreme Court with respect to a right of shelter. "We do not denigrate the importance of decent, safe, and sanitary housing. But the Constitution does not provide judicial remedies for every social and economic ill. We are unable to perceive in that document any constitutional guarantee of access to dwellings of a particular quality or any recognition of the right of a tenant to occupy the real property of his landlord beyond the terms of his lease." Lindsey v. Normet, 405 U.S. 56 (1972).
143. *See generally* BERNARD H. SIEGAN, LAND USE WITHOUT ZONING (1972) and Chapter 7 *infra.*

144. *See* discussion of *Dolan* in Section V *infra*.
145. *See* BERNARD H. SIEGAN, OTHER PEOPLE'S PROPERTY 27–29 (1976).
146. 112 S.Ct. at 2904.
147. Pursuant to the doctrine of vested rights, early American state courts protected the right of a person who had legally acquired title to tangible property to continue exercising control over it. Although police-power regulation was permissible, destruction of the interest without compensation was not. Siegan, *supra* note 101, at 42.
148. Pennsylvania Coal Co. v. Mahon, 260 U.S. 393 (1922).
149. 112 S.Ct. at 2899–2900.
150. *See* Frank Michelman, *Property, Utility, and Fairness: Comments on the Ethical Foundations of "Just Compensation" Law,* 80 HARVARD L. REV. 1165, 1229–34 (1967).
151. 112 S.Ct. at 2903.
152. *See* Michelman, *supra* note 150.
153. Samuelson, *supra* note 123, at 422–28.
154. LUDWIG VON MISES, HUMAN ACTION 253 (3d ed., Henry Regnery Company 1966).
155. ISRAEL M. KIRZNER, COMPETITION AND ENTREPRENEURSHIP 20 (1973).
156. *See* Bernard H. Siegan, *Land Speculators,* THE FREEMAN 183 (March 1975). Contemporary world experience reveals that a nation that discourages market processes does so at its economic peril. *See* Bernard H. Siegan, *Promote Free and Not Command Constitutions,* THE FREEMAN 191 (April 1994).
157. 260 U.S. at 414–15.
158. Penn Central Transportation Co. v. City of New York, 438 U.S. 104, 138 n. 36 (1978).
159. *See* De St. Aubin v. Flecke, 68 N.Y.2d 66, 77 (1986); Penn Central Transportation Co. v. City of New York, 42 N.Y.2d 324, 329–31 (1977), affirmed 438 U.S. 104 (1978).
160. Dolan v. The City of Tigard, 114 S.Ct. 2309, 2316–17 (1994).
161. 114 S.Ct. at 2320, n. 8.
162. *See* DANIEL R. MANDELKER, ROGER A. CUNNINGHAM, AND JOHN M. PAYNE, PLANNING AND CONTROL OF LAND DEVELOPMENT 495–507 (4th ed. 1995).
163. 277 U.S. 183 (1928).
164. 278 U.S. 210 (1928). *See* discussion of this case and *Nectow* in Chapter 4.
165. It is difficult to succeed in a facial challenge in a takings case, as the Court has explained in another case:

> Because appellees' taking claim arose in the context of a facial challenge, it presented no concrete controversy concerning either application of the Act to particular surface mining operations or its effect on specific parcels of land. Thus, the only issue properly before . . . this Court, is whether the "mere enactment" of the Surface Mining Act constitutes a taking. (Hodel v. Virginia Surface Mining and Reclamation Association, 452 U.S. 264, 295 [1981])

166. 114 S.Ct. at 2320.
167. *Id.*
168. 114 S.Ct. at 2319.
169. *Id.*
170. *Id.*
171. 114 S.Ct. at 2319–20.
172. 114 S.Ct. at 2322.
173. Edenfield v. Fane, 113 S.Ct. 1792, 1800 (1993).
174. Gerald Gunther, *Foreword: In Search of Evolving Doctrine on a Changing Court: A Model for a Newer Equal Protection,* 86 HARVARD L. REV. 1, 43 (1972).
175. 114 S.Ct. at 2329 (Stevens, J., dissenting).
176. 1 BLACKSTONE, COMMENTARIES 139.
177. Pennsylvania Coal Co. v. Mahon, 260 U.S. 393, 416 (1922).
178. *See* B. H. Siegan, *Separation of Powers and Economic Liberties,* 70 NOTRE DAME L. REV. 415 (1995). As Gerald Gunther has observed:

> A common defense of extreme judicial abdication is that the state has con-sidered the contending considerations. Too often the only assurance that the state has thought about the issues is the judicial presumption that it has. Means scrutiny would provide greater safeguards that the presumed process corresponds to reality—and would thereby give greater content to the un-derlying premise for deferring to the state's resolution of the competing is-sues. (Gunther, *supra* note 174, at 44)

179. Ronald Coase, *Economists and Public Policy, in* LARGE CORPORATIONS IN A CHANGING SOCIETY 184 (J. Fred Weston ed., 1974).
180. *Id.* The desire to control economic activity extensively is an application of the mas-ter-plan mentality, now completely discredited in its crucible, the former commu-nist nations. Government planning was a major factor in the economic collapse of these countries.

   I was in Ukraine in October 1992, and heard many instructive reminiscences about that nation's planning experience under communism. Before it achieved in-dependence, Ukraine's economy was controlled by planners located in Moscow. All firms in Ukraine were government-owned, and Moscow planners directed the exercise of major economic decisions in each. A firm's managers were supposed to do little more than follow these instructions.

   My Ukrainian hosts told of the inherent irrationality of the system. In the ab-sence of the material incentives that fuel capitalist societies, the base incentives of greed, avarice, and stupidity ran rampant. There was little incentive for the plan-ners to change or improve a firm's products. Moreover, innovation in one factory might require changes in production elsewhere, dislocating operations in other parts of the system. Consequently, companies continued to make essentially the same products year after year, while producers in the capitalist nations were con-tinually creating new or improved products.
181. Nebbia v. New York, 291 U.S. 502, 548 (1939) (McReynolds, J., dissenting).
182. *See* Speiser v. Randall, 357 U.S. 513 (1958).

Chapter 6. Recent Court Decisions Applying Nollan *and* Dolan

1. Ehrlıch v. City of Culver City, 114 S.Ct. 2731 (1994).
2. *Id.* The U.S. Supreme Court subsequently vacated another decision of a state court on the basis of *Dolan*: Altimus v. Oregon Dept. of Transportation, 115 S.Ct. 44 (1994).
3. Ehrlich v. City of Culver City, 12 Cal. 4th 854, 886 (1996).
4. 12 Cal. 4th at 882–83.
5. Penn Central Transportation Co. v. City of New York, 438 U.S. 104, 123 (1978), quoting Armstrong v. United States, 364 U.S. 40, 49 (1960).
6. 12 Cal. 4th at 910.
7. Loretto v. Teleprompter Manhattan CATV Corp., 458 U.S. 419 (1982), discussed in Chapter 4.
8. Cohen v. California, 403 U.S. 15 (1971).
9. 418 U.S. 241 (1974).
10. 430 U.S. 705 (1977).
11. *Id.* at 714.
12. 319 U.S. 624 (1943).
13. 319 U.S. at 634.
14. 496 U.S. 1 (1990).
15. 496 U.S. at 11, quoting *Abood v. Detroit Board of Education,* 431 U.S. 209, 234–35 n. 31 (1977) (quoting IRVING BRANT, JAMES MADISON: THE NATIONAL-IST 354 [1948]).

    Aesthetics are highly subjective, and acceptance by the city council of an art object is no more than the opinion of an elected body, whose members are hardly experts in the matter. Art critic Leo Steinberg provides a series of dramatic examples showing how even established painters have responded to new art in ways that were later deemed inappropriate. Thus, Henri Matisse's first exhibition in 1906 of *The Joy of Life,* subsequently hailed as one of the century's breakthrough paintings, was greeted with derision and anger. Paul Signac, a leading modern painter and vice president of the Paris salon displaying the work, said he would have rejected the picture. He fumed, "Matisse seems to have gone to the dogs." Only a year later, it was Matisse's turn for anger and scorn. *Les Demoiselles d'Avignon* is Picasso's landmark introduction to cubism, now a classic housed in the Museum of Modern Art. But Matisse viewed it, writes Steinberg, as "an outrage, an attempt to ridicule the whole modern art movement. He swore that he would 'sink Picasso' and make him regret his hoax." Steinberg, *Contemporary Art and the Plight of Its Public, in* THE NEW ART: A CRITICAL ANTHOLOGY 27–28 (Gregory Battcock ed., rev. ed. 1973).
16. In the famous words of law professor Ernst Freund, "the state takes property by eminent domain, because it is useful to the public, and under the police power, because it is harmful." E. FREUND, THE POLICE POWER: PUBLIC POLICY AND CONSTITUTIONAL RIGHTS 546–47 (1976).
17. Metromedia, Inc. v. San Diego, 453 U.S. 490, 521 (1981) (Brennan, J., concurring).
18. *Id.* at 530.
19. *Id.* at 532–33.

20. 618 N.Y.S.2d 857 (Ct.App. 1994).
21. *Id.* at 860.
22. *Id.* at 862–63.
23. *Id.* at 863.
24. *Id.* at 864.
25. 127 Wash.2d 901 (1995).
26. 72 Wash.App. 55 (1993).
27. 72 Wash.App. at 58.
28. 127 Wash.2d 901 (1995).
29. The quote is from Dolan v. The City of Tigard, 114 S.Ct. 2309, 2319–20 (1994).
30. 131 Ore.App. 220 (1994).
31. *Id.* at 228.
32. 76 Wash.App. 502 (1995).
33. 661 N.E.2d 380 (Ill. 1995).
34. *Id.* at 390.
35. 450 S.E.2d 200 (1994).
36. *Id.* at 201.
37. *Id.* at 204, n. 5 (Sears, J., dissenting).
38. *Id.*
39. 137 Ore.App. 293 (1995).
40. *Id.* at 300.
41. 46 F.3d 162 (Fed. 2d Cir. 1995).
42. *Id.* at 169.
43. 45 Cal.Rptr.2d 117 (1995).
44. 50 Cal.Rptr.2d 784 (1996).
45. *Id.* at 729.
46. *Id.* at 735.
47. Florida Rock Industries, Inc. v. United States, 18 F.3d 1560 (Fed. Cir. 1994).
48. *See* Chapter 5, Section IV.
49. 18 F.3d at 1571.
50. Armstrong v. United States, 364 U.S. 40 (1960).

Chapter 7. Zoning: Political Control of Property

1. Dolan v. The City of Tigard, 114 S.Ct. 2309, 2316 (1994).
2. Constitutional requirements set forth in Dolan v. The City of Tigard, 114 S.Ct. 2309 (1994), previously discussed in Chapters 5 and 6.
3. Edwards v. California, 314 U.S. 160, 174 (1941); South Carolina Highway Dept. v. Barnwell Bros., 303 U.S. 177, 185, n. 2 (1938).
4. In Warth v. Seldon, 95 S.Ct. 2197 (1975), the U.S. Supreme Court ruled by a 5-to-4 margin that nonresidents were not entitled to sue for relief from zoning ordinances of the town of Penfield, New York. The Court held that the plaintiffs lacked "standing" to sue (legal authority to institute litigation); it did not consider the merits of the claim.
   In 1974, a California federal district court ruled that the growth-control ordi-

nance of Petaluma violated the constitutional right to travel. Under this right, the U.S. Supreme Court has protected the freedom of citizens to travel unimpeded from one state to another. The California court decided that by limiting the number of people who could live in Petaluma, the city had interfered with the right of citizens to migrate and settle in places of their own choosing. Construction Industry Ass'n of Sonoma County v. City of Petaluma, 375 F.Supp. 574 (N.D. Cal. 1974). This decision was reversed on other grounds by a three-judge panel of the U.S. Ninth Circuit Court of Appeals, 522 F.2d 897 (9th Cir. 1975), *cert. denied,* 424 U.S. 934 (1976).

5. San Diego Gas & Electric v. City of San Diego, 450 U.S. 621 (1981) (Brennan, J., dissenting).

6. Norman Karlin, *Back to the Future, From Nollan to Lochner,* 17 SOUTHWESTERN U. L. REV. 627 (1988); David J. Mandel, *Zoning Laws: The Case for Repeal,* ARCHITECTURAL FORUM 58 (December 1971); Note, *The Constitutionality of Local Zoning,* 79 YALE L.J. 896 (1970); Note, *Land Use Control in Metropolitan Areas: The Failure of Zoning and a Proposed Alternative,* 45 CAL. L. REV. 335 (1972); Lawrence Gene Sager, *Tight Little Islands: Exclusionary Zoning, Equal Protection, and the Indigent,* 21 STANFORD L. REV. 767 (1969); Robert Ellickson, *Suburban Growth Controls: An Economic and Legal Analysis,* 86 YALE L.J. 385 (1977); Douglas Kmiec, *Deregulating Land Use: An Alternative Free Enterprise Development System,* 130 U. PA. L. REV. 28 (1981); Sheldon J. Plager, *The XYZ's of Zoning,* PLANNING 271 (1967); Mark Pulliam, *Brandeis's Brief for Decontrol of Land Use: A Plea for Constitutional Reform,* 13 SOUTHWESTERN U. L. REV. 435 (1983); Norman Williams, *Planning Law and Democratic Living,* 20 LAW & CONTEMP. PROBS. 317 (1955); Jan Krasnowiecki, *Abolish Zoning,* 31 SYRACUSE L. REV. 719 (1980); Robert Ellickson, *Alternatives to Zoning: Covenants, Nuisance Rules, and Fines as Land Use Controls,* 40 U. CHI. L. REV. 681 (1973).

7. NATIONAL COMMISSION ON URBAN PROBLEMS, BUILDING THE AMERICAN CITY 20 (1968).

8. PRESIDENT'S COMMITTEE ON URBAN HOUSING, A DECENT HOME 143 (1969).

9. REPORT OF THE PRESIDENT'S COMMISSION ON HOUSING, section IV (1982).

10. *Id.* at 180.

11. THE ADVISORY COMMISSION ON REGULATORY BARRIERS TO AFFORDABLE HOUSING, "NOT IN MY BACK YARD"—REMOVING BARRIERS TO AFFORDABLE HOUSING (1991).

12. Anthony Downs, *The Advisory Commission on Regulatory Barriers to Affordable Housing: Its Behavior and Accomplishments,* 2 HOUSING POLICY DEBATE 1095, 1109 (1991).

13. *See* HOUSTON POST, November 7, 1962, and BERNARD H. SIEGAN, LAND USE WITHOUT ZONING 25–29 (1972).

14. *See* BERNARD H. SIEGAN, OTHER PEOPLE'S PROPERTY 52–54 (1976).

15. The covenants were enforceable both by owners subject to them and by the city. See W. A. Olson, *City Participation in the Enforcement of Private Deed Restrictions,* PLANNING 266 (1967); Thomas M. Susman, *Municipal Enforcement of Private Restrictive Covenants: An Innovation of Land Use Control,* 44 TEX. L. REV. 741 (1966); Comment, *Houston's Invention of Necessity—An Unconstitutional*

Substitute in Zoning?, 21 BAYLOR L. REV. 307 (1969); Comment, *The Municipal Enforcement of Deed Restrictions: An Alternative to Zoning,* 9 HOUS. L. REV. 816 (1972).

16. Source: *Zoning Goes Down for 3rd Time,* HOUSTON POST, Nov. 3, 1993, at A-18.

17. Letter to author from James H. Meredith, Jr., a retired real-estate appraiser, Houston, Texas, on file with author.

18. Source: HOUSTON POST, Nov. 7, 1962 (report of results of election of November 6, 1962).

19. These are the area designations given in the HOUSTON POST, Nov. 7, 1962. The "Negro" area is scattered among numerous voting precincts on the east side of Houston; concentrations of this group occur just east of the Central Business District and in both the northeast and the southeast quarters.

20. "Median value" is the census tract term used to identify the value of owner-occupied housing units for each census tract area. Where more than one value is shown, more than one (often several) separate census tract areas are represented. Only the high and low medians are indicated in this table. *See* HOUSTON POST, Nov. 7, 1962, for further information.

21. Average monthly rentals are, again, based on census tract area figures, with a range indicating high and low rentals for the designated voting area. *See* HOUSTON POST, Nov. 7, 1962, for further information.

22. Virginia State Board of Pharmacy v. Virginia Citizens Consumer Council, Inc., 425 U.S. 748, 763–64 (1976).

23. SEYMOUR I. TOLL, ZONED AMERICAN 172–87 (1969). Area districts control the proportion of the land that a structure may occupy.

24. Zoning Resolution, City of New York (1984) (adopted Dec. 15, 1960, as amended through May 24, 1984).

25. Letter from Joseph T. Flynn, Deputy Director, Neighborhood Code Compliance Department, to author (June 21, 1993), on file with author.

26. By having the power to delay something which may be very costly to a developer obligated to pay loans and taxes, the zoning authorities can extract substantial concessions. They also have the option to interpret the regulations strictly or loosely. A developer may seek legal redress, but this is also expensive.

27. *See* Toll, *supra* note 23, at 181.

28. I have revised some of the figures in this section from those appearing in two articles I have previously written: Siegan, *Conserving and Developing the Land,* 27 SAN DIEGO L. REV. 279 (1990), and Siegan, *Commentary on Redistribution of Income through Regulation in Housing,* 32 EMORY L.J. 720 (1983).

29. William A. Fischel, *Comment on Anthony Downs's "The Advisory Commission on Regulatory Barriers to Affordable Housing: Its Behavior and Accomplishments,"* 2 HOUSING POLICY DEBATE 1139, 1154 (1991).

30. *Id.* at 1145. The Davis study appears in Seymour I. Schwartz, Peter M. Zorn, and David E. Hansen, *Research and Design Issues and Pitfalls in Growth Control Studies,* 62 Land Economics 223 (1986). The San Francisco study is in Lawrence Katz and Kenneth Rosen, *The Interjurisdictional Effects of Growth Controls on Housing Prices,* 30 J. L. & ECON. 149 (1987).

31. Lloyd Mercer and W. Douglas Morgan, *An Estimate of Residential Growth Con-*

trols' Impact on Housing Prices, in RESOLVING THE HOUSING CRISIS: GOVERN-MENT POLICY, DECONTROL, AND THE PUBLIC INTEREST 189 (B. Johnson ed., 1982).

32. Seymour I. Schwartz, David E. Hansen, and Richard Green, *Suburban Growth Controls and the Price of New Housing,* 8 J. ENVTL. ECON. & MGMT. 303 (1981).

33. LYNN B. SAGALYN and GEORGE STERNLIEB, ZONING AND HOUSING COSTS: THE IMPACT OF LAND USE CONTROLS ON HOUSING PRICES (1972).

34. D. Bjornseth, *No-Code Comfort,* REASON, July 1983, at 44.

35. BERNARD FRIEDEN, THE ENVIRONMENTAL PROTECTION HUSTLE (1979).

36. Fischel, *supra* note 29, at 1141.

37. During the 1970s, much of the building in the Houston area occurred in the unin-corporated sections of Harris County, which had few building regulations. The cities of Houston and Dallas had building regulations during that period. The ab-sence of building codes would operate to reduce costs of construction. Accord-ingly, the comparisons between the two areas are subject to possible modification, depending on how much new construction in the 1970s occurred in areas without building codes. Houston's building costs are apparently higher than those in Dal-las. *See* note 39 *infra.* Due to Houston's favorable attitude toward development, the percentage difference between building costs in the city and those in Harris County are probably in the low, single-digit area.

38. Generally similar figures for economic composition and living standards appear in the 1980 census figures. *See* U.S. DEPARTMENT OF COMMERCE, 1980 CENSUS OF HOUSING (GENERAL SOCIAL AND ECONOMIC CHARACTERISTICS—TEXAS) 45–21. One difference is that the median income in 1979 was about 10 percent higher in the Houston SMSA than in the Dallas–Fort Worth SMSA. This difference does not significantly affect any Houston-Dallas comparisons contained in this chapter. For information on living standards, *see* U.S. DEPARTMENT OF LABOR, BUREAU OF LABOR STATISTICS, THREE BUDGETS FOR A FOUR-PERSON FAMILY AND FOR AN URBAN RETIRED COUPLE (1970–1980 editions).

39. Boeckh building cost figures show that for the sample years of 1970, 1976, and 1980, Houston construction costs were a little higher than those in Dallas; *see* BOECKH DIVISION, AMERICAN APPRAISAL COMPANY, BOECKH BUILDING COST INDEX NUMBERS (Jan.–Feb. 1982). As of 1980, Houston used the 1970 Uniform Building Code, and Dallas used the 1979 Uniform Building Code, with each city imposing its own modifications. For information on site-development costs in both cities, *see* Richard B. Peiser, *Land Development Regulations: A Case Study of Dallas and Houston, Texas,* 9 AMERICAN REAL ESTATE & URBAN ECONOM-ICS ASSN. (AREUEA) JOURNAL 397 (1981). Peiser concluded that in 1981 a home lot in the areas compared was $1,000 to $2,000 cheaper in Houston than in Dallas, after accounting for user charges, taxes, and differences in development standards.

40. Jesse M. Abraham and Patric H. Hendershott, *Bubbles in Metropolitan Housing Markets,* 7 J. HOUSING RESEARCH 192 (1996).

41. The unincorporated area of Harris County has never been zoned. In the 1970s, the county also contained two moderate-sized nonzoned cities, Pasadena and Bay-town, and some smaller nonzoned local governments.

42. *See* U.S. DEPARTMENT OF LABOR, BUREAU OF LABOR STATISTICS, THREE BUD-

GETS FOR A FOUR-PERSON FAMILY AND FOR AN URBAN RETIRED COUPLE (1972–79 editions).

43. 2 ETON J. 6 (1981); 1 ETON J. 9 (1980). Dallas suburban figures relate to North Dallas and other north and northwest suburbs, all zoned; and Houston suburban figures relate to areas largely within city limits.

44. The 1980 Census lists the rental vacancy rates for the Houston and Dallas–Fort Worth SMSAs as 15 percent and 10 percent respectively. This figure is broken down into urban and rural. For the urban areas, the figures were 14 percent and 11 percent, and for the rural areas, 22 percent and 8 percent, respectively. U.S. DE-PARTMENT OF COMMERCE, 1980 CENSUS OF HOUSING (GENERAL HOUSING CHARACTERISTICS — TEXAS) 45-9 to 45-10. These figures differ from the *Eton Journal* figure (6 to 7 percent for Houston) given in the text. The *Eton Journal* figure is for the city and suburbs.

45. M/PF RESEARCH, INC., DALLAS, TEXAS, CONSTRUCTION RESEARCH SUMMARY FOR HARRIS COUNTY, TEXAS, AND DALLAS COUNTY, TEXAS (1973–1980). The percentage figures in the text are mine, based on M/PF Research's information. Since Harris County did not issue building permits until October 1973, the 1973 figures do not include structures erected in the county's unincorporated areas prior to that time. The 1973 figure in the text is based on permits issued in Houston and by other local governments in the county in 1973, and permits issued in the unincorporated areas after October 1, 1973.

46. *Id.* The figures that follow do not reflect the values of structures built in the areas of Harris County that did not issue permits prior to October 1973 (as explained in the note above).

47. FEDERAL HOME LOAN BANK BOARD, MORTGAGE INTEREST RATE SURVEYS IN THE HOUSTON SCSA AND DALLAS SMSA (1973–1980). The above percentage figures are mine, based on FHLB's information.

48. *See* Fischel, *supra* note 29 and accompanying text. *See also* Kenneth T. Rosen and Lawrence F. Katz, *Growth Management and Land Use Controls: The San Francisco Bay Area Experience,* 9 AREUEA JOURNAL 321 (1981).

49. JAMES D. GWARTNEY AND RICHARD L. STROUP, ECONOMICS, PRIVATE AND PUBLIC CHOICE 59 (5th ed. 1990).

50. *See* discussion in Section I *supra. See also* references in footnote 56 *infra* that find Houston to have a pleasing appearance and to be a very livable city. Population figures are from the U.S. Census Bureau.

51. BERNARD H. SIEGAN, ECONOMIC LIBERTIES AND THE CONSTITUTION (1980).

52. THOMAS A. HOPKINS, COST OF REGULATION (A Rochester Institute of Technology Working Paper, Rochester, NY, Dec. 1991). *See* Robert W. Hahn and John A. Hird, *The Costs and Benefits of Regulation: Review and Synthesis,* 8 YALE JOURN. ON REGULATION 233 (1991); ROBERT E. LITAN AND WILLIAM D. NORDHAUS, RE-FORMING FEDERAL REGULATION (1983); MURRAY L. WEIDENBAUM, THE COSTS OF GOVERNMENT REGULATION OF BUSINESS (A Study for the Joint Economic Committee, Congress of the United States, April 10, 1978).

53. *See generally* Siegan, *supra* note 13; R. Jones, *Houston City Planning without Zoning, in* ZONING: ITS COSTS AND RELEVANCE FOR THE 1980s (Michael Goldberg & Peter Horwood eds., 1980).

54. Most cities in the region use either the Southern Standard Building Code or the Uniform Building Code, with modifications. Both codes were drafted by private industry organizations. However, Texas law prevents most counties from adopting and enforcing building codes, and city governments' extraterritorial jurisdiction does not include any power to enforce building codes beyond their city limits. Bjornseth, *supra* note 34, at 43, 44.

55. On the rare occasion when this does not occur, the life of the enterprise will be very short.

56. These conclusions are based on surveys made in December 1969 of three substantial areas of Houston never restricted or no longer restricted at the time: Denver Harbor (which contained about 950 structures), Montrose (about 450 structures), and Riverside (about 240 structures). Denver Harbor was never subject to restrictive covenants; most covenants in Montrose expired in 1936; and one-half of Riverside's covenants terminated in 1950. *See* Siegan, *Non-Zoning in Houston,* 13 J. L. & ECON. 71, 83–86, 91 n. 42 (1970).

   Houston's appearance has long been a subject of considerable controversy. For a favorable view of this aspect of the city, see Ada Louise Hustable, *Houston is the Future . . .,* HOUSTON CHRON., Feb. 22, 1976, § 4, at 7, col. 1. Hustable was then the architecture critic of the *New York Times,* and a Pulitzer Prize winner. *See also* Hustable, *Houston Will Never Be New York,* HOUSTON CHRON., Feb. 22, 1976, § 4, at 7, col. 1. According to Hustable, "Houston is all process and no plan . . . and yet, as a 20th century city, it works remarkably well." In 1990, the Population Crisis Center rated Houston as the seventh most livable city in the world. *Study Names World's Best, Worst Cities,* SAN DIEGO UNION, Nov. 20, 1990, at A2, col. 2.

   Distinguished architects Robert Venturi and Denise Scott Brown have written commentaries favorable to a non-government-controlled urban environment and critical of the "garden city" and other conventional planning approaches. *See* Robert Venturi and Denise Scott Brown, *A Significance for A&P Parking Lots or Learning from Las Vegas,* ARCHITECTURAL FORUM 37 (March 1968); Venturi, *A Bill-Ding-Board Involving Movies, Relics, and Space,* ARCHITECTURAL FORUM 75 (April 1968); Brown, *Mapping the City, Symbols and Systems,* LANDSCAPE 22 (Spring 1968); Brown, *The Meaningful City,* AIA JOURNAL 27 (January 1965). *See also* John B. Jackson, *Other Directed Houses,* LANDSCAPE 29 (Winter 1956–1957); and J. M. Richards, *Lessons from the Japanese Jungle,* THE LISTENER 339 (March 13, 1969). For a commentary on the approach taken by these authors, *see* VINCENT SCULLY, AMERICAN ARCHITECTURE AND URBANISM 240–43 (Frederick A. Praeger 1969).

57. BERNARD JOHNSON ENGINEERS, INC., SUMMARY REPORT OF THE COMPREHENSIVE CITY PLAN FOR BAYTOWN, TEXAS 32, pt. 7 (1964); MARMON, MOK & GREEN, INC., DEVELOPMENT PLAN FOR PASADENA, TEXAS 77 (1967); TEXAS HIGHWAY DEPARTMENT, LAREDO URBAN TRANSPORTATION STUDY, fig. 9 (1964); WICHITA FALLS, TEXAS, URBAN TRANSPORTATION PLAN 1964–1985, at fig. 9 (1964).

58. Siegan, *supra* note 13, at 62–65.

59. In recent decades, regardless of whether zoning exists in a community, develop-

ers of planned-unit developments—both detached and attached housing—usually impose restrictive covenants as a sales device to accommodate the needs and desires of future residents.

60. Siegan, *supra* note 13, at 33.
61. John P. Crecine, Otto A. Davis, and John A. Jackson, *Urban Property Markets: Some Empirical Results and Their Implications for Municipal Zoning,* 10 J. L. & ECON. 79 (1967); Steven M. Maser, William Riker, and Richard Rosett, *The Effects of Zoning and Externalities on the Price of Land: An Empirical Analysis of Monroe County, New York,* 20 J. L. & ECON. 111 (1977); Frederick H. Reuter, *Externalities in Urban Property Markets: An Empirical Test of the Zoning Ordinance of Pittsburgh,* 16 J. L. & ECON. 313 (1973); William J. Stull, *Community Environment, Zoning, and the Market Value of Single-Family Homes,* 18 J. L. & ECON. 535 (1975).
62. Siegan, *supra* note 13, at 34–35.
63. *See* note 15 *supra.*
64. Ordinances as of 1972 are set forth in Siegan, *supra* note 13, at 26–31. More recent land-use ordinances are reported in *Houston's Council Tries to Control City Growth,* N.Y. TIMES, June 23, 1982, at A12, col. 1.
65. REPORT, *supra* note 9, at 204.
66. *See* note 56 *supra.*

Chapter 8. Preserving and Enhancing the Environment

1. CONGRESSIONAL RECORD (Oct. 21, 1971), at E11122.
2. M. Bruce Johnson, *Piracy on the California Coast,* REASON 18 (July 1974).
3. *Id.* For an interesting socioeconomic analysis of growth controls, see Construction Indus. Ass'n v. City of Petaluma, 375 F.Supp. 574 (N.D. Cal. 1974), *rev'd on other grounds,* 522 F.2d 897 (9th Cir. 1975), *cert. denied,* 424 U.S. 934 (1976). In this case, a federal judge found that Petaluma, California's growth controls would lead to a smaller housing supply and increased prices in its region.
4. Paul Burka, *Liberal Education,* TEXAS MONTHLY 109 (March 1977). According to economist William Fischel, zoning contributes to low-density development and, therefore, causes cities to spread out. WILLIAM FISCHEL, THE ECONOMICS OF ZONING LAWS: A PROPERTY RIGHTS APPROACH TO AMERICAN LAND USE CONTROLS (1985).
5. Harrison Waite, *How to Preserve an Endangered Species,* SAN DIEGO BCA BUILDER 10 (October 1975).
6. Nonetheless, supporters of the coastal initiative give the impression that it was enacted in response to the wishes of the less affluent: "Remember that the Coastal Act and the Coastal Commission are the direct result of a public mandate. One of the primary driving issues was the public's desire to be able to access the beach. The beach below the mean high-tide and the ocean belong to the public—not just to the people who are lucky enough to have money to buy property along the coast." Coastal Commissioner SARA WAN, TPR, THE PLANNING REPORT (Sept. 1996).
7. These statistics were compiled by James Sills, Jr. (of James Sills Consulting) who has been a staff member and consultant to elected officials in San Diego city and

county government. "Ironically," says Sills, "the principal allies of high-income, heavily Republican neighborhoods on these issues are the enclaves of heavily liberal and Democratic college students. With equal irony, the principal allies of minority voters are the mainly white, working-class neighborhoods of San Diego."

In putting together the statistics in Table I, Sills did not follow Registrar of Voters designations in voting areas when they did not disclose the desired information. For example, University of California, San Diego (UCSD) campus precincts are in a much larger community called "North University," which includes many condo dwellers. Reporting the entire North University vote as the vote for UCSD students would produce a flawed impression, so Sills chose precincts that were actually on campus. Similarly, instead of using all of Ocean Beach, Sills chose solely those precincts closest to the ocean, where young people and college students usually live. He also separated precincts in Southeast San Diego, which includes both Mexican-American and African-American communities.

Election results for some precincts are not available (indicated by "NA"). Adjacent precincts are sometimes consolidated, and their results reported as one unit.

8. NuStats, Inc., San Diego General Market Survey 1991, at 22.

9. *Id.* at 25–26.

10. U.S. Department of Commerce, United States Statistical Abstract: 1996, at 229. This figure excludes Alaska and the District of Columbia and includes urban and built-up areas in units of ten acres or greater, as well as rural transportation (roads, highways, railroads). Based on these statistics, the following figures explain my estimate that about 6 percent of the land is developed for urban purposes:

Total surface area	1,940,011 (thousands of acres)
Amount of developed nonfederal land	92,352
Total amount of federal land	407,969
Five percent of federal land	20,398
(My estimate of amount developed)	
Approximate total developed land	112,750
Percent of developed land	5.81%

(Alaska contains 385,482,000 acres of total surface area and the District of Columbia contains 39,000 acres. Including the amount of development in these two areas would lower the percentage of total developed land.)

See also U.S. Department of Agriculture, The Farm Index 9 (Dec. 1973). This study shows that in 1969, cities, highways, and airports occupied about 2.5 percent of the nation's land area. A more recent estimate states that urban areas use about 60 million acres, or 3.1 percent of the over 1.9 billion acres of land in the continental U.S. (not including Alaska and Hawaii). Steven Hayward, Job Nelson, and Sam Thernstrom, *Leading Environmental Indicators* 34 (Pacific Research Institute for Public Policy, 1993). Thomas Frey indicates that in 1974, urbanized areas and urban places, rural roads, railroads, airports, and military and nuclear installations occupied 4.4 percent of the area of the forty-eight contiguous states. Thomas Frey, Major Uses of Land in the United States: 1974 (U.S. Department of Agriculture, Economics, Statistics, and Cooperative Service, 1979).

11. John Lansing, Charles Clifton, and James Morgan, New Homes and Poor People: A Study of the Chain of Moves (1969).

12. *Id.* at 130. The interviews were conducted by the Institute for Social Research, University of Michigan.
13. Robert Ellickson, *The Irony of "Inclusionary" Zoning, in* RESOLVING THE HOUSING CRISIS: GOVERNMENT POLICY, DECONTROL, AND THE PUBLIC INTEREST 135 (M. Bruce Johnson ed., 1982).
14. THE EFFECTS OF ENVIRONMENTAL REGULATIONS ON HOUSING COSTS 71 (Cambridge, MA: Urban Systems Research and Engineering, Inc., 1982).
15. U.S. DEPARTMENT OF COMMERCE, UNITED STATES STATISTICAL ABSTRACT: 1996, at 228. (As of 1993.)
16. WORLD RESOURCES INSTITUTE, THE 1993 ENVIRONMENTAL ALMANAC, at 602–3.
17. Ed Dentry, *Every American Owns Millions of Prime National Real Estate Acres,* ROCKY MOUNTAIN NEWS 16c (June 19, 1966).
18. U.S. DEPARTMENT OF COMMERCE, UNITED STATES STATISTICAL ABSTRACT: 1994, at 249 and 251. I believe part of this land is included in the acreage designated as wilderness, but I am uncertain as to the amount.
19. Dentry, *supra* note 17, at 16c.
20. National Fish and Wildlife Service, Division of Realty, per e-mail communication from Ronald Fowler.
21. U.S. DEPARTMENT OF AGRICULTURE, CONSERVATION RESERVE PROGRAM (Oct. 1993).
22. Hayward, Nelson, and Thernstrom, *supra* note 10, at 36.
23. REPORT OF ADVISORY COMMISSION ON REGULATORY BARRIERS TO AFFORDABLE HOUSING, chap. 4 (1991).
24. *Id.* at 4-1.
25. JOSEPH BAST, PETER HILL, AND RICHARD RUE, ECO-SANITY 22–24 (1994). Hayward, Nelson, and Thernstrom, *supra* note 10, at 33.
26. Bast, Hill, and Rue, *supra* note 25, at 24.
27. Stephen Moore, *So Much for "Scarce Resources,"* THE PUBLIC INTEREST 97, 103 (Winter 1992). Moore points out that the most objective method of resolving the question of whether resources are becoming more or less scarce is by examining their price trends. "Price is the most objective way that economists have of measuring the relative scarcity of a good or service." *Id.* at 100. He concludes that, following a decade of declining prices, "[t]oday most natural resources are cheaper in the U.S. than at any time in the last 200 years." *Id.* at 107.
28. COLLETTE RIDGEWAY, PRIVATELY PROTECTED PLACES 1 (Cato Policy Report, March/April 1996).
29. JOHN KENNETH GALBRAITH, THE AFFLUENT SOCIETY 80 (4th ed. 1984).
30. *Id.*
31. ZBIGNIEW BRZEZINSKI, THE GREAT FAILURE: THE BIRTH AND DEATH OF COMMUNISM IN THE TWENTIETH CENTURY 238 (1989).
32. HENRY HAZLITT, THE CONQUEST OF POVERTY (1973).
33. U.S. DEPARTMENT OF COMMERCE, STATISTICAL ABSTRACT OF THE UNITED STATES: 1996, at 723.
34. Jeffrey Sachs, *Life in the Economic Emergency Room, in* THE POLITICAL ECONOMY OF POLICY REFORM 509 (J. Williamson ed., 1994).

35. Fred S. French Investment Co., Inc. v. City of New York, 385 N.Y.S. 2d 5, 11 (Ct. App. 1976).

Chapter 9. Conclusions and Recommendations

1. BERNARD SIEGAN, THE SUPREME COURT'S CONSTITUTION 41–88 (1987). "The prosperity of commerce," Hamilton stated in *Federalist No. 12,* "is now perceived and acknowledged by all enlightened statesmen to be the most useful as well as the most productive source of national wealth, and has accordingly become the primary object of their political cares." FEDERALIST NO. 12, at 91 (A. Hamilton). (All citations of THE FEDERALIST PAPERS herein refer to the Clinton Rossiter edition of 1961.)
2. 1 WILLIAM BLACKSTONE, COMMENTARIES 122 (1765–69).
3. Agins v. City of Tiburon, 447 U.S. 255, 260 (1980).
4. Calder v. Bull, 3 U.S. 386 (1798).
5. Cleburne v. Cleburne Living Center, Inc., 473 U.S. 432, 452 (1985) (Stevens, J., concurring) (footnote omitted). With respect to property, the fairest remedy for a constitutional violation is compensation. "When one person is asked to assume more than a fair share of the public burden, the payment of just compensation operates to redistribute that economic cost from the individual to the public at large." San Diego Gas & Electric v. San Diego, 450 U.S. 621, 656 (1981) (Brennan, J., dissenting).
6. Armstrong v. United States, 364 U.S. 40, 49 (1960). The purpose of the takings clause is to "prevent the public from loading upon one individual more than his share of the burdens of government." Monongahela Navigation Co. v. United States, 148 U.S. 312, 325 (1893).
7. *See* Hughes v. Oklahoma, 441 U.S. 322 (1979).
8. Metromedia, Inc. v. San Diego, 453 U.S. 490 (1981) (Brennan, J., concurring). The Court struck down San Diego's ordinance on grounds other than those stated in the text, and Brennan and Blackmun concurred that the ordinance was invalid.
9. 478 U.S. 328, 348 (1986) (Brennan, J., dissenting).
10. 113 S.Ct. 1505, 1514 (1993). Justice Blackmun, who filed a concurring opinion, long sought to restrain legislative powers over commercial speech. He wrote opinions upholding this right against assertions that it would destroy professionalism among pharmacists and lawyers. *See* Virginia State Board of Pharmacy v. Virginia Citizens Consumer Council, 425 U.S. 748 (1976); and Bates v. State Bar of Arizona, 433 U.S. 350 (1977). The state authorities had insisted that the regulations struck down were essential to protect these professions from subservience to profitmaking. Admittedly, there are differences between property rights and commercial-speech rights, but these differences are hardly sufficient to warrant according legislators almost fiat powers over property rights, as Blackmun proposes. Further evidencing his apprehensions about legislators, Blackmun urged the court to "hold that truthful, noncoercive commercial speech concerning lawful activities is entitled to full First Amendment protection." Cincinnati v. Discovery Network, 113

S.Ct. 1505 (1993) (Blackmun, J., concurring). Blackmun's desires to remove leg-islators' power over abortion are, of course, widely known.

11. Southern Burlington County NAACP v. Township of Mount Laurel, 67 N.J. 151, 186 (1975). According to the Pennsylvania Supreme Court, "[a] zoning ordinance whose primary purpose is to prevent the entrance of newcomers in order to pre-vent future burdens, economic and otherwise, upon the administration of public services and facilities cannot be held valid." National Land and Investment Co. v. Kohn, 419 Pa. 504 (1965).

12. 116 S.Ct. 1495 (1996).

13. 483 U.S. 825, 835, n. 4 (1987), quoting Armstrong v. United States, 364 U.S. 40, 49 (1960). *See* Chapter 5, notes 63, 64, and 65, and the relevant text.

14. Common examples are ordinances that limit or tax new development because of alleged inadequacies of existing facilities. Thus, congested roads may become more congested with the arrival of newcomers, but the problem is not solely at-tributable to the new arrivals; rather, it is due to the growth of the entire locality.

    For a discussion of how the disproportionate-impact rule affects wetlands reg-ulation, *see* MARK L. POLLOT, GRAND THEFT AND PETIT LARCENY 176–82 (1993). "If wetlands protection advocates are correct when they assert that wet-lands preservation is now so important because of the vast losses caused by past activity, is it not disproportionate for the government to ask present wetlands own-ers to pay the cost for wetlands destruction that not only occurred in the past but also occurred because the government encouraged destruction of wetlands through its own program?" *Id.* at 179–80.

15. 483 U.S. at 841.

16. Parking Association of Georgia, Inc. v. City of Atlanta, 115 S.Ct. 2268 (1995).

17. 1 EDWARD COKE, INSTITUTES OF THE LAWS OF ENGLAND, ch. 1, § 1 (1628–44).

18. Loretto v. Teleprompter Manhattan CATV Corp., 458 U.S. 419, 436 (1982).

19. United States v. Causby, 328 U.S. 256 (1946).

20. *See* Richard O. Zerbe, Jr., Fairness and Efficiency in Development of Institutions in the California Gold Fields: Right Makes Might (unpublished paper).

21. Yick Wo v. Hopkins, 118 U.S. 356, 363 (1886).

22. BMW of North America, Inc. v. Gore, 116 S.Ct. 1589, 1598 (1996).

23. *See* Chapter 5, Section IVB.

24. *Id.*

25. *Id.*

26. But owners who contend that they are entitled to protection of "investment-backed expectations" based on proposed land-use plans, approval of local officials, or laws that are not ripe for adjudication do not present issues of retroactivity. A com-plaint about the existence of a law requires, of course, the existence of a valid law. A land-use plan or verbal or written approval of a development proposal by city officials does not constitute a law. Under current takings law, a plaintiff must demonstrate that a final law has been passed by the locality with respect to a pro-posed development. *See* Suitum v. Tahoe Regional Planning Agency, 117 S.Ct. 1659 (1997).

27. San Diego County Zoning Ordinance, Section 1019(a).

28. Davidson v. County of San Diego, 49 Cal.App.4th 639, 648 (1996).

Index

Pennsylvania Coal Company, 84–85
Pentagon Papers, 252 n. 97
Picasso, Pablo, 265 n. 15
Pinkney, Charles, 15
Plager, Sheldon (Judge), 177
Planners, 188, 203, 233; background of, 185–86
Planning, 154, 264 n. 180; land-use, 96, 184–86, 198–99. *See also* Land-use regulation; Zoning
Poland, 7, 225, 241–42 n. 4
Poland, Luke P., 38
Police power, 86–87, 89–90, 92–93, 103, 108, 115, 121, 128, 152, 160, 163, 165, 263 n. 147, 265 n. 16; limits of, 80–84, 88, 102
Politicians, 96, 154, 186, 188, 203, 233
Politics, 200; and the environment, 207–8; and planning, 186
Pollution, 142–43, 215
Poor, the, 182–84, 191, 201, 208, 210, 214, 239–40
Population, 222–23; density of, 215; growth of, 193, 196–97
Powell, Lewis (Justice), 134
Power, delegation of, 101. *See also* Separation of powers. *See also under* Government; Legislatures
Precedent, 135
Predictability, 135, 138
Predictions, of environmentalists, 222–24
Prescription drugs, 68–69, 183–84
Prices, 96–97, 138, 219, 274 n. 27; of housing, 187, 189–98, 210, 214–15, 240; of land, 147–48
Privacy, 70, 175; marital, 71–72
Private ownership, 6–7, 29, 137, 221. *See also* Property; Property rights
Privatization, 6–7
Privileges and immunities, 37, 42–46, 60–61
Productivity, 224
Prohibition, 79–80. *See also* Alcohol, control of
Promiscuity, 72
Property, 36; invasion of, 76–79, 104–7, 109, 133; occupation of, 121, 127–28, 131, 140–41, 157, 162, 176–77, 236–37. *See also* Private ownership
Property rights, 1–3, 7, 106; defended by Constitution, 13–46 *passim;* and the environment, 226–27, 240; and freedom, 9–12; and

harms and benefits, 139–45; importance of, 47–49, 54, 226–27; protection of, 73–77, 82, 84, 90, 111–14, 145, 149, 157–58, 176–77, 229–30, 239–40, 246 n. 107; strict view of, 142–43; and the Supreme Court, 1–2, 50, 107–9, 177, 180, 229–30, 239–40. *See also* Private ownership
Proportionality, 152, 154, 160, 165, 167, 170–72, 177, 179. *See also* Disproportionate impact
Proposition 20, vote on, 208–12
Protectionism, 232
Public good (Public interest), 6, 83, 89–94, 103, 108, 141, 155, 165, 203; and rights, 153–54. *See also* Welfare, public
Public health, 113, 172, 238
Pufendorf, Samuel, 18
Punishment, 19
Punitive damages, 136, 138, 237

Radford, R. S., 48–49, 249 n. 5
Reagan, Ronald, 2, 181
Reasonable relation, 152
Recessions, 225
Reconstruction, the, 35, 37
Recreation, 218–19
Regulation, 2, 36, 73; costs of, 226–27; economic, 6, 117, 123, 154–55, 197–98, 225, 240; environmental, 217–18; of property, 47–49, 76, 79–80, 86, 102, 109. *See also* Land-use regulation; Zoning
Regulators, 188–89
Regulatory takings, 122, 125, 140, 149, 160, 177; Holmes on, 86–87, 108, 117–18, 128; Rehnquist on, 131, 150–53, 235; Scalia on, 121, 127, 130, 131
Rehnquist, William (Justice), 122, 168, 179; and *Dolan,* 150–53; and the harm/benefit distinction, 232; on regulatory takings, 131, 150–53, 235; and rough proportionality, 152–53, 154; on the Subsidence Act, 119–20; on takings, 77, 113
Rent control, 164–65, 174–75
Rents, 193–94, 187, 214–15
Rent-seeking, 117
Republican Party, 39, 247 n. 131
Resources, natural, 222–23, 274 n. 27
Retroactive laws, 11, 19, 27, 42, 46, 55, 57, 65–66, 122, 133–39, 149, 236–39
Revolution, American, 51, 63

Index of Cases

287

About the Author

Bernard H. Siegan is Distinguished Professor of Law at the University of San Diego School of Law, where he has taught since 1975. He received his J.D. degree from the University of Chicago Law School in 1949. He is the author of *The Supreme Court's Constitution: An Inquiry into Judicial Review and Its Impact on Society* (1987), *Economic Liberties and the Constitution* (1980), *Land Use without Zoning* (1972), and *Drafting a Constitution for a Nation or Republic Emerging into Freedom* (1992).